DONALD ATWELL ZOLL

Reason and Rebellion

an informal history of political ideas

PRENTICE-HALL, INC.
Englewood Cliffs, N.J. 1963

PRENTICE-HALL INTERNATIONAL, INC., *London*
PRENTICE-HALL OF AUSTRALIA, PTY., LTD., *Sydney*
PRENTICE-HALL OF CANADA, LTD., *Toronto*
PRENTICE-HALL FRANCE, S.A.R.L., *Paris*
PRENTICE-HALL OF JAPAN, INC., *Tokyo*
PRENTICE-HALL DE MEXICO, S.A., *Mexico City*

Library of Congress Catalog Card No.: 63-12013

PRINTED IN THE UNITED STATES OF AMERICA
C

This book
is respectfully dedicated to a revered
philosophic colleague,

ELISEO VIVAS

Tout est perdu, fors l'honneur

PREFACE

This book is at once a departure from and a reiteration of tradition. It is a departure in that it elects to choose a somewhat unconventional mood for the discussion of the history of political ideas. It is traditional in that it endeavors to present political philosophy in historical perspective, and in so doing it covers once again the well-ploughed fields of traditional scholarship. It adheres to this familiar schema because the author feels that such an orientation is reputable—and, indeed, inevitable. A history of ideas is a history of ideas. This patent tautology may be initially either nonsensical or superfluous, but the fact remains that some would have us believe that the thinkers of the past are antiquated curiosities or pleasant characters in some slightly effete romance. The author rejects the view that historical political theory is sentimental attitudinizing, especially since it affects the intellectual respectability of students.

At the same time the author is aware—as he must be—that historical accounts of the growth of political thought are already available and that included in these works are many of distinguished merit. To stride confidently in their wake requires a certain bravado. But the author's purpose is not to superannuate these commendable accomplishments; it is only to build upon them and to undertake an understandable division of labor. To this end, *Reason and Rebellion* was hopefully conceived as an articulate and assimilable introduction for those to whom historical political thought is a new experience. The style is overtly conversational, and the objectives must of necessity be somewhat limited. It is a basic premise of the author that it is important to "feel" as well as to "know" and that political ideas are fraught with drama, poignancy, and wit—as well as substance.

Some concrete explanations are indicated. The book is designed for either of two uses: (1) as a one-semester text used alone or (2) as the basis of a full-year course supplemented by additional readings of the instructor's choice. It is urged that instructors take advantage of the availability of a wide range of paperback editions; the book is designed with this in mind. The bibliographic sections at the conclusion of each chapter contain as many references in paperback form as possible. It is hoped that this will encourage students to purchase these books as the basis for private libraries of their own.

Chapter 1 contains no quotations from the Platonic dialogues. This omission is the result of two convictions: (1) that the nature of the dialectical form of argument employed by Plato is such that truncated quotation is virtually meaningless and that if the main segments of argument were to be reproduced, the resulting length would be prohibitive and (2) that the student, regardless of the length of the course, should be expected to read portions of the *Republic*.

Chapter 18, dealing with contemporary ideas, is necessarily far more subjective in judgment than the remainder of the book and thus more argumentative. The author feels that the very contemporaneity of the chapter makes this inevitable. The instructor not sharing the author's views at this point should feel free either not to assign it or to offer the chapter as the basis for his own rebuttal.

D.A.Z.

Hinsdale, Illinois
May, 1962

TABLE OF
CONTENTS

16 **DARK EMPIRES**   312

17 **DEMOCRACY AT THE BAR OF REASON— AND UNREASON**   329

18 **UNDER THE MUSHROOM CLOUD**   349

1

THE WORLD OF MEN
AND THE WORLD
OF IDEAS

Most areas of our modern life seem to have some origin in Greece. This thought usually occasions one of two reactions—skepticism or the notion that Hellas was peopled by a race of supermen. The truth lies somewhere in between. Greece was neither the product of an historical press agent nor an earthly paradise. The Greeks had their ups and downs like everyone else and suffered from as many vices and miscalculations. But it does seem that every history of political ideas begins with the Greeks. Hadn't anyone ever thought about political problems before the age of Athens? How about the Egyptians or the Persians, for example? The operation of any empire as vast and complex as the Egyptian or the Persian required by the nature of the case considerable attention to politics. One could go even further and say that any primitive tribe also had its political problems wanting solution. It is a common practice to begin with the Greeks not because they were the first people to pay attention to politics, but because they were the first people to *study* politics, quite as one would study astronomy or geometry, and because the inhabitants of Hellas had the ability to take this view of politics "abstracted," if you will, from the day-to-day routine of political life.

This ability to view things in an abstract way was a characteristic of the Greek mind. Originally these Greeks were like most other Mediterranean peoples, almost exclusively concerned with the more elemental problems of war, conquest, love, and avarice. Homer, the greatest of the Greek poets, captured this early era in his epic tales of the Greek heroes. Sometimes termed the "Heroic Age," it was a time of military feats, strong passions, and life on the grand scale—men and gods intermingled. As Greece grew up, men of more contemplative nature appeared and began to speculate about the character of the world. Such speculation was really a luxury—most of the earlier civilizations couldn't afford such effete indulgences, as they never managed to be secure enough to provide themselves a breathing period. But the Greek victories over the rapacious Persian Empire gave them a security that permitted relatively impractical pursuits. Isocrates, Anaximander, and Pythagoras, among others, began to let their curiosities have free rein. They wondered about the origin of the earth, the basic nature of matter, the destiny of man, and all the other nagging questions that still persist. This was the beginning of a tradition that we have conveniently labeled *philosophy*—literally, "love of wisdom."

Moreover, the Greeks were quite evidently a sensitive people with a strong fondness for the beautiful. This did not set them apart from many other civilizations even in their own time, but it does help to explain why reflective thought had considerable appeal. Further, the Greeks were a passionate people. The word "passionate" can be interpreted in a number of ways—and the Greeks were all of them. When you add up the characteristics of curiosity and reflection, sensitivity and passion, and couple them with the fortunate circumstances of culture and geography (such as a common religion, language, and tradition plus relative geographic isolation), you can better understand why the Greeks were the first to think about politics in a philosophical fashion.

The full flowering of Greek culture took place in Athens. Indeed, much of what we casually call "Greek" might more accurately be termed "Athenian." Athens became the "school of Hellas," and its political and social institutions were widely copied, first in the rest of Greece and later elsewhere. Though the Greek city-state came in various sizes and shapes, ranging from the military oligarchy of Sparta to the merchant cities of the coast, we tend to use Athens as a model because it was the most culturally active and politically experimental.

Over the history of Athens falls a shadow cast by a native son of that city-state who arose to represent all that was lofty in Greek thought and who was eventually denied by his own people. This great Athenian was Socrates, who looms as both a commanding and obscure figure—commanding because of his influence, obscure because we possess little documented knowledge about this stonecutter-philosopher. That he lived we know only by references to him in Plato, Xenophon, and Aristophanes. The most detailed source is that of his brilliant pupil, Plato, and from this quarter we learn that a man called Socrates was born in 469 B.C. and that in 406 he was condemned to death for corrupting the morals of the Athenian youth. Plato gives us a full account of Socrates' unique behavior, which included wandering about the streets of Athens, participating in street corner conversations about love and justice and virtue, and arguing against the expedient morality of the Sophists, a group of professional rhetoric teachers.

It is likely that this unassuming philosopher shook Athens to its foundations. Indeed, it found it necessary to kill him to put a stop to him. What did Socrates agitate for that was so threatening to the communal security of Athens? Once more, what we know we know from the dialogues of Plato, where Socrates appears as a major character, and one can justifiably raise the question as to whether the personality portrayed is actually that of Socrates or whether Plato uses him as a mouthpiece for his own ideas, a not uncommon device among writers.

Socrates did not directly agitate for anything. As a matter of fact, he made few pronouncements. Instead, he asked questions—always a dangerous game. They were disturbing questions because they were very basic questions and involved fundamental definitions. He was ruthless—as Plato depicts him anyway—in his demands for precise and logical definitions. He was certainly a master of oral argument. This interrogation proved embarrassing to many. What is justice, he asked, for example? What is the nature of love? What is civic virtue? In short, he stirred the conscience of Athens and was condemned for it. Plato, in one of the sublime literary accomplishments of the ancient world, describes his trial and eventual death, Socrates tranquilly drinking the famous cup of hemlock. These moving passages can be found in Plato's dialogues: *Apology, Crito,* and *Phaedo.*

But besides rousing the minds of Athens—particularly young Athens—Socrates made one other momentous contribution. He made an indelible impression on the mind of a youthful Athenian aristocrat named *Plato* (427-347 B.C.). However "obscure" or shadowy is Socrates as a historical figure, the legacy of Plato has come down to us in virtual completeness. In truth, Plato appears as the most majestic figure of the ancient world and perhaps the most influential thinker in the history of Western society. Happily, most of Plato's work remains for us to examine, and it is here that Socrates comes alive.

In the beginning there was nothing very unusual about Plato, except, perhaps, for the fact that as a youth he once wrestled in the Olympiad and that he was inordinately fond of making verses. He was fortunate enough to be born into the comfortable upper levels of Athenian society, even though the political fortunes of Athens were in considerable flux. Plato's uncles were involved in politics to their misfortune, and were banished by a popular reaction against aristocratic control. The view, however, held by some scholars that this family reverse caused Plato to be suspicious of democracy seems far-fetched. More plausible is Plato's disquiet over the popular excesses that followed. Perhaps the two influences that caused the young Plato to digress from the conventional ways of his contemporaries were the teaching of Socrates and his own fascination with mathematics.

At base, Socrates was a moralist. This is not to say that he was a curbstone evangelist or an anti-vice crusader. Unfortunately, the label "moralist" takes on dour connotations in our culture. As a matter of fact, Socrates was possibly a sturdy hand with the wine goblet, if we are to take Plato literally in the *Symposium,* where, after a night of carousal—both intellectual and libational—only Socrates remained sober at dawn. Socrates was a moralist in that his investigations were aimed largely at questions relating to the Good, to the nature of virtuous conduct. Moralists of this sort are frequently appealing to youth, and Plato had a superb teacher in that this moral concern was coupled in Socrates with a mind given to rigorous logical examination. Indeed, Plato appears to have inherited a questioning skepticism from his mentor—so often the soundest road to the sort of belief ultimately possessed by both Socrates and Plato. Like Socrates, Plato, however analytical his mental processes became, remained essentially a moralist in spirit.

Plato's mind was similarly stirred by mathematics, an infant discipline

among the Greeks, but gaining sophistication at the hands of geome-
tricians like Pythagoras. One senses an almost aesthetic feeling in
Plato about the essentially geometric character of this ancient mathematics; the purity, symmetry, and tranquil harmony of Pythagoras'
theorems suggested the existence of an order at once beautiful and
comprehensible. Plato responded to this with almost sensual ardor—
with the spirit of "eros," the Greek conception of earthly and cerebral
love. Throughout his life, Plato would be dominated by the inner discipline suggested by his study of mathematics. The framework of his
thought is best understood in the light of his belief that human
affairs, like the natural world, could be ordered by the principles of
mathematics. This sounds like a very modern view. Political and social
philosophers have suggested that the principles of science can be
applied with success to the realm of human affairs. But Plato was not
in any real sense a scientist—unless the speculative mathematician can
be so described. Plato was not much concerned with what we call
"scientific method," based as it is upon observation and general statements drawn from the scrutiny of experience. Plato's propositions were
"analytic" as contrasted with "synthetic"—that is, his propositions, like
geometric ones, assumed an internal proof not requiring the existence
of external evidence. Plato assumed that in human affairs—as in mathematics—one starts with certain "givens." Philosophers were later to
call these "givens" a priori statements. Truth for Plato, was to be found
in the area of logic, in abstract propositions not requiring recourse to
observation of the real world.

But let us not get ahead of ourselves. What sort of world did the
youthful Plato contemplate? The glories of Athens were passing. The
political and military fortunes of the city-state were at an ebb; the
easy life of the Athenians had introduced some decay in their vigor
and inventiveness. Athens had been engaged in a long and costly
series of wars with her archrival Sparta and had generally come out
the loser. Her influence over much of Greece had been seriously reduced by Spartan military success. Nonetheless, Athens remained an
important center of culture and learning. The Peloponnesian Wars,
though harmful to Athenian interests, had not obliterated the customary
regard for richness and variety in living. There remained both a love
of the beautiful and a love of the citizen for his city-state—something
akin to what we call patriotism.

But political conditions were unsettled. The so-called "Golden

Age" had passed. The high water mark of Athens had been realized under Pericles and was never to be equalled. Perhaps it is during this time of the early wars with Sparta that it is simplest to view the character of Athens, the Athens of Plato. In the first place, Athens was a bustling and successful commercial city. There were actually more foreign residents there than Athenian citizens due to the mercantile nature of the city's life. Politics, however, were reserved to the citizens who took an active role in public matters. Something similar to popular democracy was the generally prevailing political arrangement, and it involved popular elections, civil rights, and even a form of representative government. So anxious were the Athenians over the threat of the return of the Tyrants that, even when menaced by the armies of Persia, the commanding general of the Athenian army was elected to command for but one day at a time. This libertarian political life was viewed as the crowning glory of the city-state, and the citizens were zealous in their love of city and their belief in civic duty. The city-state of Athens became something more than a governmental arrangement; it was a totality of the political, social, and even religious community. The Greek word *polis* (from which we draw the word "polity"), although almost impossible to translate accurately, gives hint of the inclusive meaning of the city-state to the citizen. This sense of popular identification, of the total meaning of the political and social composition of a state, has never again been realized in the West since the passing of the Greek *polis*.

An Athenian's view of his city is perhaps best captured in Pericles' moving oration on the dead of the first war with Sparta. This remarkable speech comes down to us from Thucydides, the historian, and, considering his penchant for personal judgments and extrapolations, it may be that this oration as reported is partially the product of Thucydides' imagination. Regardless of whose words they are, portions of the Periclean oration constitute a veritable apologia for the Athenian way of life. Let's look at a few samples:

> Our form of government does not enter into rivalry with the institutions of others. We do not copy our neighbors, but are an example to them. It is true that we are called a democracy, for the administration is in the hands of the many and not of the few. But while the law secures equal justice to all alike in their private disputes, the claim of excellence is also recognized; and when a citizen is in any way distinguished, he is preferred to the public service, not as a matter of privilege, but as the reward of merit. Neither is poverty a bar, but a man may benefit his country whatever be the obscurity of his position. There is no exclusiveness in our public life, and in our private inter-

course we are not suspicious of one another, nor angry with our neighbor if he does what he likes; we do not put on sour looks at him which, though harmless, are not pleasant. While we are thus unconstrained in our private intercourse, a spirit of reverence pervades our public acts; we are prevented from doing wrong by respect for authority and for the laws, having an especial regard to those which are ordained for the protection of the injured as well as those unwritten laws which bring upon the transgressor of them the reprobation of the general sentiment.

And we have not forgotten to provide for our weary spirits many relaxations from toil; we have regular games and sacrifices throughout the year; at home our style of life is refined; and the delight which we daily feel in all these things helps to banish melancholy. Because of the greatness of our city the fruits of the whole world flow in upon us; so that we enjoy the goods of other countries as freely as of our own.

Then, again, our military training is in many respects superior to that of our adversaries. . . . Our enemies have never yet felt our united strength; the care of a navy divides our attention, and on land we are obliged to send our citizens everywhere. But they, if they meet and defeat a part of our army, are as proud as if they had routed us all, and when defeated they pretend to have been vanquished by us all.

If then we prefer to meet danger with a light heart but without laborious training, and with a courage which is gained by habit and not enforced by law, are we not greatly the gainers? [1]

Unfortunately for the citizens of Athens, the Spartan army, a product of "laborious training," had proved superior, and the confident sentiments of Pericles rang hollow. The liberality, the assurance of the Athenians in the superiority of the amateur in war and politics, the cosmopolitan urbanity, the belief in creative improvisation had all been put to the test and found in some particulars wanting. Athens was confused, even frightened. She turned to violent political experimentation that ranged from rule by aristocratic juntas to radical democracy that bordered on anarchy and often featured vindictive mob rule. The sense of proportion, the moderate approach, the equilibrium that marked Athenian political experience began to vanish.

Plato remained in Athens, even though disturbed by the political instability around him. After sitting at the feet of Socrates, in 388 he founded a school—the great Academy—with which he was associated until his death. His travels were few, the most noteworthy being two trips to Syracuse (367 and 351) at the request of a friend, Dion, adviser to the young king Dionysius II. His purpose in journeying halfway across the Mediterranean was to aid in the political instruction of the

---

[1] Thucydides, *History of the Peloponnesian War*, Book II, Chapter 6.

ruler, and it is thought by some Plato scholars that he was much involved emotionally in the success of the project, hoping that he could have the opportunity, through the person of Dionysius, of putting his theories into practice. Since the instruction of the Syracusan ruler came to naught, it is sometimes further concluded that this led to a growing pessimism in Plato's outlook.

Whether or not this is true must remain an historical conjecture. But Plato was indeed troubled by the decadence of Athens, and he bore a marked suspicion of the optimistic philosophy of the Periclean Age—the praise of "happy versatility." Some would have us believe that this concern over political flux in Athens caused Plato to spurn democracy and become the first totalitarian thinker.[2] It is fair to say that Plato—like his own distinguished pupil Aristotle—had deep reservations about popular rule, but it is likely that these views stemmed more from his assumptions about the nature of the ethical than from his reactions to Athenian political turbulence. Plato's alarm over the growing decadence of Athens does not differ much from the reactions of many men of wisdom who were by accident thrust into times of flux and irrationality. Essentially, Plato's concern arose from the most basic assumption in his philosophy—he would have us believe that he learned it from Socrates—and that is that virtuous conduct and knowledge are inseparable. In this assertion, Plato combines his moralistic spirit with his mathematical orientation—but the proposition goes considerably deeper than that.

In order to understand this pivotal assumption it is necessary to grasp Plato's general view of the world—the Germans have a handy word for this: *Weltanschauung*, or "world-view." Sometimes Plato's *Weltanschauung* is described as his doctrine of Ideas, since Ideas are the main element in his conceptual picture of the world or worlds. In the first place, the world as we know it is not the only realm of existence. In fact, it is an imperfect form of reality, just as a triangle drawn on the blackboard is an imperfect copy of the Idea: Triangle. There is another realm, Plato tells us, of pure ideas enjoying perfection and existence. It is a world apart from ours, having an independent existence but informing our world by its utter perfection. Thus it is inconceivable to think of a horse without conceptualizing as to the

---

[2] For an example of this view, see Karl Popper, *The Open Society and Its Enemies*, Book I, "The Spell of Plato." Other critics of Plato include such diverse persons as Thomas Jefferson and Bertrand Russell.

possibility of an ideal horse. For each phenomenon in our world of material things Plato asserts that there is an ideal form existing in the world of Ideas. It is true, then, that if a horse implies an ideal horse, so a polity implies an ideal polity. To know what is just depends upon knowing what is justice.

If, then, ideal forms exist, how do they inform our world? First, the imperfect copies of things in the material world are actually products of the world of Ideas. Here presented by Plato is one side of the age-old philosophic quarrel: Does substance (matter) produce intelligence or does intelligence produce substance? Plato assumes that a higher intelligence, a "demiurge," exists above the world of mere substance and that such a substantial world depends for its existence upon higher orders of reality. It is not too important to press this line of reasoning much further for our purposes; the vital notion to retain is that the world of Ideas is at least partially discoverable. If it were a complete mystery—as some pre-Platonic Greeks believed—then serious philosophic speculation would obviously be impossible. But Plato contended that the world of Ideas, like the structure of mathematics, is rational and orderly and that it can be understood on rational terms, even if this means only a glimpse of the total framework of an ideal form. Perfection might be impossible of actual realization, but it is not impossible of conceptualization. Moreover, once certain principles are understood it is possible to deduce an entire sequence of inferences from the understood or "given" principle, once more like geometry. Now the basic idea of deduction is simple, and in his dialogues Plato provides some flashingly spectacular examples of it. Deduction is the process whereby from a general given premise a series of inferences or consequence is drawn. You are doubtless familiar with such reasoning; it is the tool of the mathematician or the detective story writer.

But let's get back to our original question regarding the statement that virtuous conduct and knowledge are inseparable. What is the "Good"? Whatever it is, Plato would argue, it exists and it has ideal form in the world of Ideas. Consequently, if I am to practice goodness, I must be familiar with the Idea of the Good. This involves what we might call an intellectual operation—the process of discovering the nature of the Good. I cannot find out what it is by looking around me; I must find it somewhere else and by a purely mental procedure, by the use of speculative reason. The Good—like a triangle—is conceivable in terms of logical laws, and a structure of reasoning about the Good can be constructed quite in the same manner as with a triangle.

Therefore, to go one step further, the act of being Good depends upon the knowledge of the Good. Knowledge, then, can be equated in this sense with Virtue. Virtue is impossible without knowledge; but the converse is also true, Plato would argue. But what about a question that is even more perplexing: Is it possible to know and yet to act without virtue? Plato would answer "no," giving as his reason that the knowledge of anything increases the capacity of the individual to pursue the Good. If a potter knows more about the nature of pottery, he is therefore bound to produce better pottery. (Would he, with this knowledge, produce poorer pottery?) Merely on the basis of self-interest—to use a modern and singularly un-Greek term—this would seem to be true. Similarly, if a poet comes to increase his knowledge of the Beautiful, this is causative of the increase in beauty in the work of the poet.[3] It would be difficult to imagine him doing otherwise, deliberately creating that which is ugly. If a man knows the Good, then, is it likely or even conceivable that he would consciously seek to do evil? Evil must be a lack of knowledge as to the nature of the Good.

This is in essence the Platonic argument. The theme of the moral life built upon rational knowledge persists throughout the Platonic dialogues, whether they deal specifically with politics, aesthetics, or ethics. Very frequently this argument is developed by means of a dialogue in which Socrates is portrayed as arguing against the morality of expediency in one guise or another. In places, this expediency takes the shape of "might is right" or "success is the only criterion" or "enjoyment is more to be prized than virtue"; whether Socrates is arguing against Thrasymachus, Callicles, or Gorgias, the debate is essentially the same.

Such a discussion is found in the opening skirmish in Plato's famous dialogue the *Republic,* his first and most widely read treatise on politics. It is nearly impossible to classify the *Republic.* Is it a political tract? Is it a romance? Is it an intricate allegory? A fable? A treatise on philosophy? It contains elements of all of these. One thing it certainly is, and that is a great literary accomplishment. Like all the dialogues, the *Republic* is the work of a polished literary craftsman,

---

[3] In general, Plato was suspicious of poets and held them in rather low esteem. But bad poets, says Plato, are poets without knowledge, guided only by the lower animal proclivities. When they operate on this basis, Plato argues, they are detrimental even to the health of the society. In his dialogue *Ion* he discusses poets in general. In another dialogue, the *Laws,* Plato even goes so far as to regulate poets and turn their services into the composition of patriotic odes.

subtle, urbane, witty, ironic, frequently profound, and always provocative. If Plato were remembered for nothing else, he would be remembered as a brilliant stylist. Even in translation he is a consummate
artist. The dialogue form of exposition is challenging in that there is
an obvious temptation to be excessively rhetorical and pompous. This
pitfall Plato escapes. The result is that the *Republic* is one of the
major works of the Western world and, perhaps, Plato's crowning
achievement.

Plato would doubtless not object to the thought that his dialogue
on politics would rank as his major work, for he viewed the study of
politics as the highest human calling. He even refers to politics as the
"royal science." This phrase is meaningful, as both the words "royal"
and "science" give a clue to Plato's cast of mind. First, the term "royal"
suggests, rather vaguely, Plato's fundamentally aristocratic outlook,
while the word "science" suggests that he believed that the political
affairs of men could eventually be treated in the orderly manner of
scientific principle—not forgetting that Plato's understanding of "science" is considerably more limited in meaning than ours.

Plato himself described the *Republic* as a dialogue concerning
justice. And it is interesting to note here that it is a treatise on justice
that contains no mention of law. But this is only one of the many
singular features of this work. In looking at the *Republic* over-all, one
is tempted to speculate that Plato began it with more limited objectives than he ultimately embraced. The dialogue widens in scope as it
moves along. But considered as a whole, the *Republic* is a brilliant,
though perhaps futile, attempt to depict the ideal state, to capture
from the world of ideal forms for men to see the outline of the ideal
polity, unattainable and conceptual, but an eternal measuring-rod
against which the real states of men could be judged. The common
complaint that the *Republic* is visionary, impracticable, and even
ridiculous is itself a foolish charge, because it does not take into
account the totality of Plato's thought or appreciate the fact that the
Republic was not constructed as a blueprint for political action nor
even as a recommendation for existing states, but as a speculative
embodiment of the moral principles that *ought* to guide men in the
realm of political decision. The machinery of Plato's ideal state is of
relatively small importance. Quite obviously its social divisions, for
example, do not take into account the effects of the industrial revolution or even the technology of weapons, but this is beside the point.
The essential doctrine of the division of labor in society may be as
valid today as it was in fourth-century Greece, even though we may

not choose to classify our social structure in terms of philosopher-rulers, guardians, and farmer-artisans. The *Republic* is a constant jab to the intellectual flexibility and social sensitivity of our times, as it has been to the generations that fall between Plato's era and our own.

There is no subsitute for reading Plato—any more than there is a substitute for reading Horace, Shakespeare, Kant, or T. S. Eliot. The *Republic* cannot be crushed into an abbreviated summary; it must be digested entire and, probably, more than once. Our discussion, then, is not a replacement for the original, only a means of under- scoring some of its more important features.

Essentially, the *Republic* contains four major subdivisions, dealing with, in turn: (1) a discussion of the nature of justice, (2) the divi- sions of society, (3) education, and (4) Platonic "communism." While at first glance these might appear to be unconnected considerations, they are in fact closely allied in Plato's view of the ideal polity. The first section of the *Republic*—and there is some doubt among scholars as to the proper order of the books of the *Republic*—contains a brisk trial of logic between Socrates and two formidable opponents: Thrasymachus and Glaucon. Each of Socrates' adversaries has his own concept of justice to advance, but Socrates accepts none of the arguments and demolishes each of them in turn.

Of these arguments, those of Thrasymachus are the most striking and, at the same time, the most familiar to the modern reader. In essence, Thrasymachus presses Socrates with three propositions: first, that those who rule do so for their own advantage; second, that power justifies itself; and third, that injustice is to be preferred to justice. Most contemporary readers, when perusing the first two books of the *Republic,* are startled by the "modernity" of Thrasymachus' contentions. These are well-known themes, and the world has grown accustomed to the "might makes right" argument. In our own time, the rationaliza- tions of dictators and the cynicism of those convinced of the futility of combating entrenched power ("you can't lick city hall") are at once wearily commonplace and trace their long ancestry back to Thrasymachus.

How does Socrates answer these imposing charges? He does so by attacking the assumption behind Thrasymachus' position that politics and ethics are separate fields of action. On the contrary, Socrates main- tains, the principles that should govern the conduct of individual men prevail when men are associated together in a society or in a state. Civic ethics are individual ethics "writ large." The base of politics, then, is ethics, and ethics consists of the knowledge of the Good, the same existing for individuals and polities. The art of politics consists in facilitating human associations in such a fashion as to promote virtue. Justice (or "righteousness," as it may also be translated in this context) is the art of moral enlightenment, the dispensation of the opportunity for moral fulfillment. A selfish ruler is doomed to failure for the quite simple reason that his selfishness is rooted in ignorance. Sheer power or coercion can never provide the effective political cohesion, because it operates without understanding the ethical imperatives that underlie both the nature of individual men and of polities. Wisdom must be the prerequisite of political authority, and that wisdom is clearly indistinguishable from virtue. The just man, then, is quite obviously the stronger. Thrasymachus' view of justice as the will of the stronger contains a damning circularity; it is also a prescription for dissension and political collapse. In Book I, Socrates summarizes his argument:

> For that reason neither money nor honour will make the good men consent to be rulers. They are unwilling to be called hirelings for openly exacting wages for their office, or to get themselves the name of thieves by fraudulently enriching themselves from it. Nor will honour move them, for they are not ambitious. Therefore if they are to consent to rule the compulsion of a penalty must be laid upon them (this may be why to take office without compulsion is considered disgraceful); and the greatest penalty is to be ruled by an inferior if you will not take rule yourself. When virtuous men take office I think they are prompted by this fear; and they approach it not as a blessing or with any prospect of good fortune: they face it as a compulsory task because they find none superior or equal to themselves to whom they might entrust it. Were there a city of good men, it is probable that men would contend to escape office as they now contend to gain it, and it would then be clearly shown that a true ruler is in reality one who seeks not his own advantage but the advantage of the subject, so that every man of understanding would prefer to be benefited by another rather than labour for another's benefit. Therefore I in no way agree with the statement of Thrasymachus that justice is the advantage of the stronger.[4]

Replying to the second of Thrasymachus' charges, Socrates exacts the admission that while to Thrasymachus injustice is both more profitable and more powerful, it is also a vice, and that justice is a virtue. Thrasymachus appears to attach little importance to this concession and does so only to expedite the discussion. However, it is this admission that allows Socrates to dispose of Thrasymachus' argument. He

---

[4] The *Republic*, Book I, trans. A. D. Lindsay. (New York: E. P. Dutton & Co., n.d.), p. 30.

accomplishes this by subtly leading his opponent into the trap of acquiescing that "a man is good in respect that he is wise." From this point, Socrates develops his argument that the wise man is the just man, but that the unjust man is ignorant and ignorance can hardly be a profitable or powerful condition. Later, he further demonstrates that happiness must also be predicated upon wisdom and hence upon just action.

The argument presented by Glaucon on the nature of justice is not as strenuous or as radical as that of Thrasymachus. It, too, bears resemblance to familiar themes. Glaucon argues that justice is, after all, a matter of convention, based upon custom and not upon immaterial principles. He further develops the notion of a "social contract" upon which men founded the state and defends an "individualist" view of social participation. (We will encounter the social contract more full-blown some centuries later.)

Plato, through his articulate spokesman Socrates, endeavors to refute Glaucon upon very fundamental grounds. He asserts that justice is eternal because it rests upon the nature of the human soul and that the just fulfillment of individual good, the spiritual aspiration of a human being, is paralleled by the state in the just pursuit of the collective moral good. It is perhaps curious that Plato attempts no psychological account of human nature—as Aristotle later does—in developing this argument, accepting human spirituality *prima facie*.

Having introduced the subject of justice in rather abstract terms, Plato offers an account of justice by constructing a hypothetical just polity. If we accept the idea of the just man, he reflects, why can we not conceive of the just state? Plato responds to his own question with a description of his ideal state.

There appear to be three major considerations in the discussion of the ideal state. The first of these is the *division of society*. Plato quite arbitrarily divides the population of the *Republic* into three distinct classes (which he poetically labels the "gold," the "silver," and the "brass"). These classes might simply be described as the philosopher-rulers, the guardians, and the farmer-artisans. The first class is entrusted with political rule that is complete and in no way subject to interference from the other two. It consists quite candidly of complete autocrats. Obedience to the philosopher-rulers (sometimes misleadingly referred to as "philosopher-kings") is an unquestioned obligation. These are very evidently powerful figures indeed. Is this not a prescription for sweeping dictatorship? What about Lord Acton's famous quip: "If power tends to corrupt, absolute power corrupts absolutely"?

The philosopher-rulers, as their name suggests, are philosophers first and rulers second. The word "philosophy" in Plato's usage implies that the philosopher as a lover of wisdom is clearly a lover of virtue, and, beyond merely loving it, the rulers are best equipped to know what it is, since the good is that which is the province of those who are wise. And, further, if individual virtue and political virtue are essentially one and the same, the only moral or just rule is rule by the wise. Wisdom is legitimacy. The alternative is worse than folly; it is wickedness.

It can be concluded, if we accept Plato's premises, that the philosopher-rulers are motivated by the highest ideals of service and govern with no thought of personal reward. As a matter of fact, Plato devises a most severe and almost monastic life for the *Republic*'s rulers. Devoid of luxury or pomp, the philosopher class lives in bare quarters, detached from the common joys, almost like a college of Buddhist priests.

Who are the philosopher-rulers? Since wisdom is the prerogative for political authority, the philosopher-rulers are the product of intensive education, much of which is designed solely for ruler-designates. (A bit further on we shall examine Plato's educational ideas in some detail.) Since it is one of the duties of the rulers to decide who shall belong to the "gold," the "silver," and the "brass" (hereditary rights are not considered by Plato, although his recommendations on eugenics cause him to believe that it will be likely that "gold" will reproduce "gold"), the rulers select their own successors to receive the rigorous education for leadership. The other classes, "silver" and "brass," receive different types of education, planned to equip them for their civic responsibilities.

The class of guardians is charged with preserving the security of the state. They are fundamentally soldiers, the most dutiful ever conceived. Plato was apparently conscious of the problem of military ambition and the possibility of the soldiery endangering the civil government, for he subjects the guardians to a careful indoctrination with emphasis upon their role of service, circumspection, and obedience to authority.

The farmer-artisans produce the material fibre of the state. In some ways, this is the most unrestricted class in the *Republic*. Its members are not subject to the ascetic confines of the rulers or to the strenuous duty code of the guardians. They are exempt in large measure from the controls over marriage and the family directed at the other classes. They live as family units rather than in barracks or cells and can even reside beyond the walls of the city. Their role is primarily economic.

This hasty description of the division of society in the *Republic* raises many questions. These are best answered, perhaps, by considering four implications of this social system: (1) moral development, (2) the division of labor, (3) harmony and the absence of coercion and (4) the absence of law.

Plato's division of society is intelligible only when the aim of *moral fulfillment* is kept in mind. The Book of Matthew echoes the *Republic* when it advises: "What is a man profited if he shall gain the whole world and lose his own soul?" The objective is omnipresently the virtuous life, both individual and social. The lack of what we of the twentieth century might call "freedom of opportunity" or "individual rights" would seem to Plato to be an illogical complaint against the *Republic*. The opportunity or "right" to behave according to the dictates of one's own will is not a good in itself. Is it just, Plato would ask, to be able to choose ignorance over wisdom, wickedness over virtue? Man must and does seek virtue as his end, but this is not a simple quest. There are pitfalls along the way. There are the gross and vulgar passions, the bestial urges that, unchecked, corrupt men and societies. Self-mastery is imperative. Not all men are capable of this; few, if any, are capable of it without education. Consequently, Plato would conclude that it is an indispensable principle in the ideal state that direction and education should prevail over licentious freedom. That fools—and, by definition, the nonvirtuous—should enjoy an equal voice with the wise and the good is clearly unthinkable.

And it is not, for Plato, merely a question of the preservation of the state. Individual welfare is involved as well. How is a fool to be made wise? By allowing him to persevere in his foolishness? Clearly not. He must be taught wisdom. Rulers, then, are unmistakably cast in the role of teacher or, perhaps, of parents supervising the moral growth of children. Plato himself was fond of the analogy between a ruler and a physician prescribing to a patient or a shepherd caring for his flock.[5]

Next, there is the principle of the *division of labor*. Plato reasons that a society is a complex of reciprocal services. How should social roles be assigned? It is not only just but practical that each man should do that for which his nature fits him. Within the *Republic*, some men [6]

---

[5] This is not an infrequent Greek metaphor—early absorbed into Christian literature.

[6] Perhaps it would be more exact to say "men and women," because in the *Republic* Plato advocated an "emancipation" of women that was most radical for his day. The role of women will be commented on later in the chapter.

are best suited to govern, others to grow grain, and yet others to bear a shield. This is not only the most efficient division of chores from the standpoint of the state, but it provides the maximum degree of personal contentment. Is a shoemaker apt to be happy serving as a professional in an infantry phalanx? Would a farmer be satisfied spending his hours at the desk of a scribe? Adequate self-knowledge would permit a man to know what his true calling, his social role, was. But the Socratic injunction, "Know thyself!" is a difficult assignment. Plato was dubious about the possibilities of such general self-knowledge and in the *Republic* felt that the deprivation of private choice was a lesser evil than wholesale social maladjustment and unrest. As we have commented earlier, Plato yearned for a "science of politics" embracing the graceful exactitudes of geometry. Such convictions were irreconcilable with the disorder suggested by a division of labor based upon individual whim.

The indispensable ingredient in the *Republic* is *harmony*. At no time does Plato suggest the advisability of coercion. The guardians are not political police; philosopher-rulers do not remain in power with the help of ranks of spears. Plato does not directly consider the problem of insurrection, civil disorder, or wholesale opposition to authority in the *Republic*. Was this because Plato was insulated against these unpleasantnesses in an intellectual ivory tower? Hardly. He had seen Athens in riot, and in the later dialogue, the *Laws*, he dealt directly and firmly with these matters. In the ideal state, however, these are superfluous considerations. Unrest and rebellion are the result of the absence of justice. A truly just state—like a just man—is tranquil. The just polity need not be concerned with threats, nor does it need to enforce its will by naked power. Harmony exists because each man is receiving justice and is presumably content because he is doing what his nature decrees.

Whether or not this is as simply disposed of in fact is certainly questionable. But Plato does not advance this point of view as an expedient procedure for existing societies. The *Republic* is not a blueprint for an earthly commonwealth; it is a graphic means of exposing the principles upon which the wise and just state ought to be founded.

No mention is made in the *Republic* of *law*. This usually strikes the first-time reader of the dialogue as amazing. By virtue of our cultural orientations, we Anglo-Americans are legalists at heart. Law is not only precious, but indispensable. Plato's reason for the avoidance of law in his ideal state is not as bizarre as one might at first think. Plato reasons this way: Laws are for imperfect states and for imperfect states are most necessary. Why are states imperfect? They are imperfect because they are imperfectly governed. They are imperfectly governed because those who govern are not at all times wise and virtuous. Law, then, is a means of attaining a relatively high degree of justice by imposing reasonable limitations upon rulers and those who are ruled. If, however, the rulers are all-wise and all-virtuous, to limit these rulers by imposing law is manifestly illogical. To a man who fully knows the Good, law is not only an unnecessary guide, but conceivably an inhibition that might interfere with the full operation of his wisdom translated into political decision-making. In the *Republic,* consequently, the philosopher-rulers are not bound by law, because they are in possession of ideal reason. Full play is given to the imaginative wisdom in the *Republic;* it is a poetic expression of the highest arts of government. Law remains, for Plato, a compromise, a second-best means of attaining justice.

In outline, we have examined the Platonic concept of the division of society. This must be complemented by the principles of *education.*[7] In a way, Plato's perfect state is a large-sized schoolroom. Successful government rests upon education. It would be easy to make a simplistic comparison between this notion and the American vision of universal education coupled with the almost unquestioning faith in education as a solution for social ills that seems common in our time. The similarity is very superficial. In the first place, Plato's view of education is not that of "training." Education is neither preparation for life, vocational instruction, nor what we would call "citizenship training." Platonic education contains both the positive character of rigorous intellectual discipline and the negative component of self-mastery and -control. Further, a distinction can be made between the education of the individual and the education of society. They are similar in purpose, for Plato, but different in technique.

The education of the individual in the *Republic* is directed at the human soul and the problem of harmonizing that soul with the environment. Thus Plato thought that he could strike at the root of human evil itself by providing an entirely new concept of living. In this sense, all the social prescriptions of the dialogue are subordinated to the educational process. Education must precede social action.

It has been pointed out that Plato's educational ideas in the

---

[7] For a detailed examination of Plato's theories of education, see R. L. Nettleship, *The Theory of Education in Plato's Republic.*

Republic are a fusion of the existing Athenian view of education for the "whole man" and the Spartan code of education in service of the state. This is not entirely accurate, because no such bifurcation is implied in Platonic ethics. Further, the problem of education rests upon the assumption that the human soul, the object of Platonic education, can be dealt with through the solitary category of reason. More specifically, education in the *Republic* consists of two general phases. The first phase, constructed around feelings and imagination, is designed to accommodate the preoccupations of the young, those under the age of eighteen. The major emphasis of this phase is self-mastery and the use of the imaginative faculties to free the individual from the confines of the lower instincts.

After a two-year period of military service, a more rationalistic phase is entered. Stressed now is the role of reason. This stage, for Plato, can end only with the termination of the individual's life; education is a continuing pursuit. It is during this second phase that education becomes less uniform and more personalized to the varying talents of individuals.

On the purely pedagogical side, the basic curriculum is mathematics and music. The use of the latter term is somewhat misleading. The "music" referred to in the *Republic* includes both literature and the plastic arts, as well as strictly musical exercises. Furthermore, the common element in all these arts is believed to be rhythm, and stress is laid upon the abstract formal character of art. One interesting implication can perhaps be detected in this concern for rhythm, recalling the Platonic convictions about self-discipline and obedience to the state. Underscored is the evil of individual variation. In Plato's thought, the arts are turned away from any notion of "art for art's sake," and art is integrated into the welfare of the polity. Plato would have had no use for artistic nonconformity or bohemianism. Art is a discipline; it serves a moral end and can never be considered as a mere plaything of the senses or as a flight of egoistic expression.

The charge has been made that Plato feared the artist and his power as a threat to his own monolithic state. It would seem that Plato did have a lively respect for the power of artists, but it is doubtful that he feared them as agitators against political control. Rather did he realize their considerable potential for either encouraging virtue or debasing men by appeals to the passions. It was this conviction that prompted Plato to turn art into a buttress of the state and even to regulate the activities of artists.

Education as moral instruction has a significance beyond the salvation of individuals. It is required in order to prevent the destruction of the harmony of the polity, since that harmony rests on the universal recognition of virtue. Ignorance is the greatest threat to the just state. We might today heartily agree with this premise, but our thinking and Plato's are somewhat different. Reduced to the barest simplicities, we generally view the aim of education as providing the means of making men wise so that they may make intelligent political decisions. Surely education and ethics are not in this view interchangeable ideas. For Plato, however, the purpose of education is not to provide all men with the wisdom to make political decisions, but to provide all men with the wisdom to realize that only the truly wise should be entrusted with political judgment and to abide by their commands. Education, in the Platonic sense, is as much insight into limitations as insight into potentialities.

A large portion of the *Republic* is devoted to a discussion of what most commentators have called Plato's theory of *communism*. This is an emotionally charged word fraught with understandably ugly connotations. However, when applied to the *Republic*, the word "communism" bears only the remotest resemblance to the communism of Marx and Engels, to say nothing of Lenin and Stalin. Plato's social prescriptions are described as communistic because they advocate the communalization of property and the family.

Plato was apparently firmly convinced that familial ties and the private ownership of property were incompatible with the austere pursuits of virtue required in the ideal state. Quite radically, therefore, Plato virtually abolishes these institutions in the *Republic*. At base, his reasoning is the same in both cases: private property and the family represent threats of divided loyalty to the state and hence to the community. Men quite evidently quarrel over the ownership of property and are preoccupied excessively by the subordinate institution of the family. Both pose the problem of diverting attention from the moral objectives of life to private and selfish ends. The *Republic* sharply departs from the casual diversity that marked contemporary Greek life and substitutes a degree of regimentation more suggestive of the military state of Sparta than the somewhat effete Athens of Pericles. Plato was an admirer of some aspects of the Spartan way of life, but decried Sparta's exclusive emphasis on military efficiency. If Plato conceived of the barracks state in the *Republic*, it was not in terms of a military establishment but of a monastic order. Regimentation—and Plato would not shy away from advocating it—is embraced not in the cause of corporeal power, but in the cause of social virtue.

Several facts should be kept in mind before discussing the *Republic*'s collectivist patterns. While the institution of private property existed in Plato's day, it did not have the sacrosanct mandate that developed under the impact of the "natural rights" philosophy. While Plato's abolition of private property was a severe measure, it did not then represent the total revolution that it now appears to be in the wake of Adam Smith and John Locke. Equally, there is some speculation that Plato was convinced that the commercial preoccupations of Athens contributed to its moral and political decay. Plato's communism embraced a rejection of property quite in the same spirit that communistically organized religious communities place property in the common fold.

Plato's uprooting of the family appears even more indefensible—Aristotle was especially unhappy over this feature of the *Republic*. Viewed across the centuries, the abolition of the family, with its ties of affection and mutual dependence, seems unthinkable. The nineteenth and twentieth centuries have been imbued with the romantic conception of marriage resting upon essentially sentimental love. Oddly enough, this is a comparatively modern idea. It certainly was not held by the Greeks, although they generally tended to treat women with gentleness and affection. The family as it must have been observed by Plato was not much concerned with what we have come to call "love." Love of country, even the love of a friend for a friend, was a higher form of love to the Greeks than love between the sexes. Consequently, it is not too surprising that Plato could espouse undivided loyalty to the state and the abolition of the secondary loyalties of family.

But does not Plato disregard human nature? What of the love of parents for their children? A man for his mate? In the *Republic* Plato feels no need to justify his prescriptions psychologically. The *Republic* is not concerned with the limitations of the practical or carnal; it is an extended allegory, graphically depicting the ideal polity. In the *Laws*, Plato acknowledges human proclivities, somewhat sadly, and reintroduces both private property and the family.

One of the more provocative phases of Platonic communism is the role of women. Women occupied a most limited state in Greek life. However well-treated in the main by Greek males, they were denied all political opportunities and informally exercised small influence (as contrasted with Roman womanhood, who frequently were figures to be reckoned with in the intricacies of Roman politics). Greek women were not considered suitable subjects for education and were relegated to a life of complete domesticity. There is no suggestion, however, that Greek women offered much complaint regarding this inequity.

Women in the *Republic* are emancipated from home and hearth. For one thing, there are no homes and hearths to which they can be assigned. But the status of women must be explained on other grounds. Plato's theory of the moral nature of the individual makes no distinction between male and female. Both must seek virtue; both must receive education. The limitation on the political participation of women is for Plato more a biological limitation than a metaphysical one. The race is propagated by women; child-bearing is women's most fundamental role. (Even here Plato does not want to leave anything to chance. Selected mating is considered the most rational approach to regenerate the species.) The role of motherhood naturally limits the degree to which women can share civic duties, but, beyond this reservation, women can perform duties equivalent to those of men. There is some suggestion that Plato may have been an admirer of Spartan women. Surely the women of the *Republic* are neither domestic helpmates nor elegant practitioners of feminine leisure.

The *Republic* has been described by no less a critic than Sir Ernest Barker as an "ideocracy"—in his own words: "the despotism of the Idea." [8] Despotic or otherwise, it is the striking and even histrionic exemplification of moral absolutism. Perhaps the best way to think of the *Republic* is to consider it as an elaborate and extended analogy. Platonic argument very often employs the mechanism of analogy as its principal device. [9] The *Republic* appears to be a sustained analogy in which the Platonic Idealism is clothed in the dress of government and society. Its value to the history of politics lies not in its actual prescriptions, but in the power and suggestiveness of its analogous argument.

Plato was not entirely satisfied to let the issue of politics lie with a

---

[8] Barker develops this theme in Chapter III of his *The Political Thought of Plato and Aristotle.*

[9] The use of analogies in Plato is provocatively discussed by Renford Bambrough in an article, "Plato's Political Analogies," in *Philosophy, Politics and Society,* Peter Laslett, ed. (New York: The Macmillan Co., 1956).

mere logical tour de force. The implications of the *Republic* were clear; they pointed toward more mundane recommendations. Consequently, Plato's speculations regarding justice did not cease with the *Republic*. On the contrary, this dialogue is often described as a product of Plato's youth. There was more to come. There was a "bridge" dialogue, the *Politicus* (sometimes referred to as the *Statesman*), and finally the great work of his waning years, the *Laws*.

There was a good deal of water under the bridge between the *Republic* and the *Laws*. They are separated by many years, and the *Laws* is sometimes labeled the creation of old age, weariness, disappointment, and pessimism. It is also alleged that the *Laws* indicates a marked weakening in Plato's powers—even senility is vaguely suggested. It is true that the *Laws* is not comparable as a literary work to the *Republic*; it lacks the latter's rhetorical sweep, grandeur, and poetic unity. At times this last dialogue (which was never fully completed in the opinion of most scholars) is dull, repititious, and lacking in clarity. But the allegation that it was produced by a bitter and discouraged old man seems superficial.

In the first place, the philosophic differences between the *Republic* and the *Laws* can easily be overestimated. The *Laws* is not a rebuttal to the *Republic*; Plato does not switch his position. On the contrary, the *Laws*, viewed carefully, is a logical outgrowth of the position assumed in the *Republic*. The difference between the two dialogues is not a significant ideological one, but one of form and purpose. If the *Republic* is an analogy, the *Laws* is a demonstration of how the principles of the ideal polity might be adapted to the needs of living men in a world of practical political arrangement. The *Laws* has been called Plato's "second-best state," since, like the *Republic*, it is a description of a hypothetical state. This phrase contains some truth, but it is also misleading. The state depicted in the *Laws* is more likely the *best state of its kind*. The *Republic* is a logical demonstration; the *Laws* is a direct attack upon the problem of worldly government.

From the argument of the *Republic*, Plato assumed that when all is said and done, political power must reside in the hands of a dedicated and educated élite. Practical considerations make the realization of the infallibly just élite of the *Republic* unattainable. The alternative is a compromise; the compromise is aristocratic rule in a "mixed state." A mixed state is one in which political control is partly

diffused and in which a pluralism of ends and interests is acknowledged. It is a "balanced" state, as opposed to the rigorous, monastic
absolutism of the *Republic*. Ideas regarding the formal governmental
organization of states and the conception of the mixed or balanced
polity are first contained in the *Politicus,* but they see full fruition
in the *Laws.*

Few people today read the *Laws* (few read the *Republic,* for that
matter, but it gets a fairly good play from students in courses on political philosophy and zealous attendants at Great Books sessions). It is
not usually included in collections of Plato's outstanding dialogues.
It is surely not as pleasant reading as the *Symposium,* as lofty as the
Phaedo, or as intriguing as the *Timaeus.* But Plato looked upon it as
his final great labor. It is not essential here to offer a synopsis of the
dialogue. We can be content with extracting its principal features.

One would do well by commencing with the dialogue's title. It
suggests that what follows is to be a treatise on law. This is perhaps
startling when one recalls that the *Republic* was constructed without
the benefit of law. Has Plato changed his mind about the necessity of
law? No, Plato emphatically upholds the need for law as a foundation for the just state, *assuming* the lack of the omnicompetent
philosopher-rulers who guided the *Republic*. In the *Laws,* he reintroduces law with rhetorical flourishes, calling it the "golden cord" that
pulls together the fabric of the state.

The argument for the absence of law in the *Republic* (that it
would undesirably constrict the operation of the all-wise rulers) is
reversed in the case of the *Laws*. Because the act of governing is a
high art at which flesh-and-blood rulers are never likely to be fully
proficient, the power of the ruling élite must be tempered by the
existence of law. Power unchecked by law is too great a temptation for
tyranny, which Plato so vehemently abhorred. Even though law might
not prove an errorless guide in human affairs, if it is properly conceived, it acts as a reliable guide and has the merit of preserving the
essential political harmonies.

What kind of law does Plato envision? The Platonic law is a
sweeping departure from the Greek concept current in the third or
fourth century, B.C. The Greeks were never a particularly legalistic
people. True, they had laws and Athens boasted of juries and public

trials, but Greek law was principally the sanctioning of convention, the quasiformalization of habitual ways of doing things. Nothing could have struck Plato as more foolish—or more pernicious. Perhaps the major theme of Plato's political thought is that political and social prescription must rest upon reason rather than upon convention. (One recalls the exchange between Socrates and Glaucon on this point.) Law is hardly an exception. It must have reason as its base. It must in fact be a surrogate for the transcendental wisdom of Plato's ideal rulers.

A distinction must be drawn here (at the risk of introducing another idea prematurely). The reason that informs law must be ethical. There can be no confusion on this point. It is not pure metaphysical insight; it is not a discovery of a "natural" order of law for the universe. In short. Plato's law is not what we will later call "natural law." Such a philosophy of law would be foreign to Plato, because wisdom consists for him of something more than the discovery of the natural order. It is the revelation of the realm of the ideal perfection, the province of souls. This discovery is certainly the result of reason, but that term is broadened in Platonic usage to include a range of human enlightenment that goes far beyond the purely analytic, the strictly deductive. Here we are considering what is at times a contradiction in Plato's nature: his austere regard for the validity of mathematics, side by side with his intense imaginative commitment to transcendental insights—indeed, his trust in what we would be apt to call "intuition."

Law is not convention (although in ancient Greek there was one word for both); nor is it the law of machine-like nature. Law is reason enumerated into regulations for social order and harmony, into safeguards for moral well-being. George Sabine coined a happy metaphor when he commented that in the *Laws* wisdom was "frozen" into law.

In the *Laws*, Plato's ideas of law receive rather detailed explication. Indeed, the picture of the state drawn here is one of considerable complexity and exactitude. Plato even locates it for us (on the island of Crete) and recommends a size for the proposed population (5,040). All the apparatus is designed to insure the restraint, the moderation, that must exist as the compromise alternative to the idealized arrangements of the *Republic*.

Plato describes a political organization that, while it rests on the foundation of law and supposedly insures control by the wise, gives greater amounts of freedom to the citizenry. Gone are most of the elements of Platonic communism; private property and the family are restored. Marriage is reinstituted—with what Plato deems appropriate controls. An intriguing feature of the *Laws* is Plato's continuing distrust of the commercial life. In this state, all such sordid activities are performed (under the most stringent regulations) by aliens, not citizens.

The spirit of moderation prevails, and the political stability of the state is maintained by a balance of interests, a plurality of principles, a diversity of classes based upon differences in property. The political machinery is rather conventional, constructed of a council and a magistracy, along with a participating electorate. The details are relatively unimportant, except we must stress that the end product of the intricate electoral machinery is aristocratic control. Just how, on the other hand, Plato insures the political ascendency of the wise and virtuous is uncertain. Critics have suggested that in the *Laws* power will rest in the hands of the prosperous, forming a property-minded oligarchy. There is nothing in Plato's writing to indicate that a self-satisfied bourgeoisie has an inside track in the matter of virtue. One of the nagging questions raised by the *Laws* is just who are in fact the élite, a question sharply answered in the *Republic*.

There are features of the state described in the *Laws* that impress the modern reader as anything but moderate. Plato appears to endorse a variety of thought control—and apparently is even insincere in his convictions regarding law. The sections that give rise to these forebodings are those dealing with religion. Plato's state is a theocratic absolutism, with all the instrumentalities associated in the modern mind with the dreaded Inquisition. There is a state religion, which demands unwavering compliance. Heresy is summarily punished. Atheism is punishable by death. And Plato creates a powerful official priesthood, which has a most ominous character since it provides the means for wholesale religious persecution.

Strangely, and perhaps sadly, Plato adds a curious epilogue to the carefully wrought structure of the *Laws*, a last-minute addition that may well destroy its essential validity. This closing paradox is his description of the Nocturnal Council. After rooting his polity in law, Plato suddenly appears to lose his sense of assurance and creates an extralegal, all-powerful body of elder statesmen who are beyond the very law he has so laboriously built. The Nocturnal Council comes as a sort of troubled afterthought by one whose firmest convictions, after all, lie not with the mixed state, but with the philosopher-rulers. Even his choice of a name for his *ultra vires* praesidium is regrettable. The brave day of the *Laws* must finally succumb to night.

The history of political thought has been described as a prolonged footnote to Plato. Matthew Arnold once shrewdly observed that all men could be divided into two groups: Platonists and Aristotelians. Most of the main currents of political ideas claim a wellspring in Plato, both ideas of freedom and justice and moral responsibility and those of authoritarianism and repression. Plato would be mightily alarmed by many of his self-proclaimed disciples, certainly by those who would deny what clearly remains as the Master of the Academy's essential message: The only legitimate power is virtue. Throughout the *Republic* and the *Laws*, through the meanderings of his mind, the most majestic and perpetual vision is that of a human society incorporating that principle.

Man's political institutions bear small resemblance to the tiny city-states of Greece or of Plato's conjecture. To this extent, he, like all philosophers, was a demi-captive of his age. Yet Plato's problems remain the world's problems—and perhaps this is a sorry commentary on the usefulness of political philosophy or philosophy of any description. But the fact that Plato's genius caused him to confront the same awesome problems that remain unresolved by us should not appear as too abject a defeat. Plato is an indispensable prime mover. We have built upon his insights. We have been taught by him how to judge and discard that which is spurious or unrewarding. And we have learned that each generation of men must reinterpret the ancient questions in the light of its immediate experience.

The contemporary political philosopher, Michael Oakshott, put this most gracefully when he said:

> Political philosophy cannot be expected to increase our ability to be successful in political activity. It will not help us to distinguish between good and bad political projects; it has no power to guide or to direct us in the enterprise of pursuing the intimations of our tradition. But the patient analysis of the general ideas which have come to be connected with political activity—ideas such as nature, artifice, reason, will, law, authority, obligation, etc.—insofar as it succeeds in removing some of the crookedness from our thinking and leads to a more economical use of concepts, is an activity neither to be overrated nor despised. If we pursue it, at least we may hope to be less often cheated by ambiguous statements and irrelevant argument.[10]

---

[10] The quotation is taken from Professor Oakshott's Inaugural Lecture at the London School of Economics and Political Science (1951).

. . . for further discussion:

These questions—and those that follow each chapter—are designed to stimulate your reflections on the ideas contained within the foregoing chapter.

1. In a letter to John Adams, Thomas Jefferson made the following evaluation of Plato's *Republic:*

   > While wading through the whimsies, the puerilities, and unintelligible jargon of this work, I laid it down often to ask myself how it could have been, that the world should have so long consented to give reputation to such nonsense as this?

   Do you agree with Jefferson's critique? Is it a fair summary? For what reasons have many intelligent persons over the centuries reacted with intense feelings to the ideas of Plato? Why has Platonic thought provoked such bitter rejoinders?

2. What lines of reasoning can be presented to refute Plato's contention that politics and ethics are the same? John Dewey, a famous twentieth-century American philosopher, argued that ethics is fundamentally the reconciliation of ends and means toward the realization of individual self-interest. How would Plato react to this position? How do you believe he would go about refuting Mr. Dewey?

3. Plato believed that political authority should belong to the wise. Do you think we would advocate today that political authority in America or Europe should be in the hands of university professors, scientists, and "intellectuals"? Assuming that these persons are "wise," do you think Plato would support the creation of a ruling intellectual élite? (Incidentally, why do you think such "wise" men occupy rather less than influential positions in our society?)

4. Plato argues generally that the average man's powers of reason are inadequate to permit him to make morally sound political judgments. If this is the case, is Plato guilty of an inconsistency when he suggests that political harmony results in part from the average man's realization of his proper function and his cheerful acceptance of it? Is this not an act of rational reflection at least as demanding as political judgment?

. . . for further investigation:

Agard, Walter, ° *The Greek Mind.* New York: Anvil Books, 1957.

Barker, Ernest, ° *The Political Thought of Plato and Aristotle.* New York: Dover Publications, Inc., 1959.

Bowra, Cecil M., ° *The Greek Experience.* New York: Mentor Books, 1960.

Grube, G. M. A., ° *Plato's Thought.* Boston, Mass.: Beacon Press, 1958.

Hamilton, Edith, ° *The Greek Way to Western Civilization.* New York: Mentor Books, 1948.

Jaeger, Werner, *Paideia: The Ideals of Greek Culture,* 3 vols., Gilbert Highet, trans. New York: Oxford University Press, Inc., 1943-1945.

Nettleship, R. L., *The Theory of Education in Plato's Republic.* New York: Oxford University Press, Inc., 1935.

Plato, *Laws,* 2 vols., R. G. Bury, trans. New York: G. P. Putnam's Sons, 1926.

Popper, Karl, *The Open Society and Its Enemies.* Vol. I, "The Spell of Plato." Princeton, N. J.: Princeton University Press, 1950.

Taylor, Alfred E., * *Plato: The Man and His Works.* New York: Meridian Books, 1956.

Toynbee, Arnold, * *Greek Civilization and Character.* New York: Mentor Books, 1953.

Voegelin, Eric, *Order and History.* Vol. III, "Plato and Aristotle." Baton Rouge, La.: Louisiana State University Press, 1957.

Zeller, Eduard, * *Outlines of the History of Greek Philosophy.* New York: Meridian Books, 1955.

---

* Indicates paperback editions in this and subsequent chapter bibliographies. No specific citation is given for the *Republic* or other dialogues (except the *Laws*) as these are available, both paperback and hard cover, in a wide variety of editions and translations. There are differing opinions as to the merit of these translations, although the author leans toward the Cornford translation. A splendid new one-volume edition of Plato's collected works, edited by Edith Hamilton and Huntington Cairns, features the work of a number of translators. (*The Collected Works of Plato,* Edith Hamilton and Huntington Cairns, ed., Bollingen Series LXXI. New York: Pantheon Books, Inc., 1961.)

2

THE UNIVERSAL

SYNTHESIS

If anyone has doubts about the importance of the relationship between teacher and pupil or underestimates the influence of the former,
one need only look at the development of Greek thought. Socrates,
the teacher, had Plato as a pupil. But Plato himself had a pupil, one
who became a giant—some would argue, greater than his master.
Plato's unusual protégé came from quite a different background from
that of the founder of the Academy. The son of a physician in distant
Stagira, *Aristotle* (384-322 B.C.) went, like many a student after him,
to study under an acknowledged figure in the intellectual world; he
journeyed to Athens to become resident at Plato's Academy. He
enjoyed it so much that he stayed twenty years, and it is reported
that during this time he followed Plato about, drinking in every word
and thought. Aristotle's first employment after departing from the
seclusion of the Platonic garden was the post of tutor to the young
Macedonian prince, Alexander.

This period of Aristotle's life—the sojourn at the court of Alexander's

father, the ambitious Philip—is something of an empty page. The fact
that we know little makes it a ripe area for speculation. What influence
did the philosopher exert on the military genius and world conqueror
whom history was to dub Alexander "the Great"? Historians have
examined Alexander's political decrees and concepts of empire in
hope of finding some traces of a fine Stagirian hand. While it is true
that Alexander did consciously attempt to fuse Hellenic and Persian
culture, in a rather bizarre sense, the fact of the matter is that Alexander appears to have profited little from his exposure to Aristotle—
though perhaps a bit more than Nero did from his tutor, the Stoic
philosopher Seneca. Certainly there is no evidence to suppose that
Aristotle ever entertained any notion of becoming a political adviser
to Alexander. Finding his duties in Macedonia at an end, Aristotle
returned to Athens and, like Plato, went into the school business,
founding the Lyceum in 355. There is left one more connection between Aristotle and his warlike pupil; the teacher outlived the pupil
by the space of but one year, as Alexander died in the prime of his
life in 323, while his old tutor died a year later, after having been
forced to flee his adopted city of Athens.

Aristotle was not a shadow of Plato. For good or ill, Aristotle made
no particular effort to emulate his master in all things. Genius invariably seeks its own individual ways, and in many areas Aristotle
could not have equaled his teacher. Plato was a superb literary stylist;
Aristotle's writing is frequently prosaic and even turgid in style.
Aristotle was not a poet in temperament. He could not rival Plato's
intense skill with reasoned argument—"dialectic" is the trade word—
although Aristotle made greater contributions than Plato to the development of what we call "formal logic." Aristotle lacked Plato's soaring
imagination and speculative sweep; the Stagirite was more earth-
bound and even practical of mind. Aristotle was never given to the
sort of mystic insight frequently noticeable in Plato.

But Aristotle had strengths of his own. In the first place, he was
more wide-ranging in his interests. He was a genuinely curious man.
While Plato was concerned with a relatively narrow spectrum of
concerns, Aristotle was the first thinker to attempt a comprehensive
survey of the full content of human knowledge. While much of what
Aristotle classified in the way of knowledge has become obsolete, the
scope of his task and the success he had in fulfilling it remain a tower-
ing testimonial to human enterprise. Aristotle wrote on every subject
from poetry to animal husbandry. He was versatile, curious, systematic,
and thorough.

One suspects that at heart, Aristotle was a biologist first, last, and always. His general approach to knowledge was in some ways similar to that of natural science—a subject that Aristotle virtually introduced into Western thought. His primary intellectual tool was observation; he was attuned to the world of experience, of natural phenomena, and of human affairs. His main criticism of Plato, indeed, was his neglect of the teachings of experience. This predilection for observation and investigation caused him to adopt other methods of reasoning than Plato's strict deduction. Aristotle reasoned that it was possible not only to deduce inferences from a given proposition, but also to infer a general conclusion from a number of specific, less general pieces of evidence. This approach has been labeled *induction,* and while Aristotelian logic is in the main deductive, he introduces into it the inductive method.

Nowhere is this investigatory mood more noticeable in Aristotle than in his approach to the study of politics. Consider again Plato's notion of the ideal state as a yardstick for political prescription. Aristotle, for his part, adopts a strikingly different method. In order to understand politics, he reasons, one must first know what politics is, and since political life is to be found in the world of men and not of gods, one must investigate the existing political arrangements. With the help of his students in the Lyceum, Aristotle consequently began to collect and study the constitutions of 158 Greek city-states. (Unfornuately, most of these have been lost to us, but in 1891 the constitution of Athens was unearthed and was a major historical prize.) The analysis of these city-state constitutions led Aristotle to follow the path of Plato and to write a major work on politics. For convenience, this work is labeled *Politics.*[1] It is very probable that Aristotle himself did not actually write it—or, for that matter, any of the other works in his collected writings. The likelihood is that they are transcriptions of his lectures and notes made by his students.[2] The *Politics* contains two

---

[1] Aritotle's *Politics* is a quite different book from Platos' *Republic* in that there is a good deal of detail in it. But it does not include as full a treatment of the ethical foundation as does the *Republic.* For this reason, it is wise to read Aristotle's *Politics* with a copy of his *Ethics* close at hand for reference.

[2] The works of Aristotle were left in a disorganized state. Early compilers had great difficulties in putting them into proper arrangement. The story goes that one of Aristotle's works defied classification—it dealt with such matters as ultimate reality and the nature of the cosmos—and the compiler did not know what to title it. After some thought, he placed it after Aristotle's *Physics* and labeled it *Meta-Physics* and the term became a standard philosophic classification for writing dealing with questions of being and fundamental causes.

principal themes: a rebuttal to Plato [3] and Aristotle's original thoughts on politics.[4]

Aristotle's criticisms of Plato should not be wrenched out of proportion. There is far more affinity between the two philosophers than there is difference. Aristotle never forgot his essential debt and did not depart fundamentally from the spirit of Platonic thought. This unity of outlook between the two should not be forgotten. There is no real difference between them as to ultimate political ends or moral purposes; the break comes on questions of how men ought to proceed toward the attainment of these ends. Aristotle had deep reservations, as we shall see, about Plato's communism and endorsed a much more positive view of law; but running throughout his political writing is a profound belief in the notion of harmony—a concept pivotal in Plato. Indeed, one can assert that this principle of political equilibrium or balance appears more significantly in Aristotle than it does in Plato. And for Aristotle harmony means moderation.

This represents a slightly altered view of harmony from that of Plato. To attain harmony, Plato was willing to employ what we might term radical measures. Using his own analogy of the ruler as a physician ministering to the ills of the polity, Plato obviously thought that frequently a strong purgative dose was in order. Aristotle places less faith in extreme measures, representing as they do in Plato the objectification of absolute principles. Harmony must be attained by moderation, and radical social experimentation is by definition immoderate. Aristotle's moderation cuts both ways; he is as suspicious of popular rule, for example, as he is of monarchic tyranny. To use a modern word, Aristotle avoids the doctrinaire.

The Aristotelian view of moderation is not prompted by any backsliding in his thoughts on the nature of the Good. He here rejects little of the teaching of Plato. He even develops the Platonic notion of individual moral fulfillment into a far more explicit doctrine. However, Aristotle grasps the fact that moral considerations, objective as they may be of themselves, are realized by real men in real circumstances. Put another way, Aristotle's concept of the pursuit of the Good is presented within the framework of two significant existing factors: social institutions and human nature. Plato paid slight attention to either of these; Aristotle attempts to reintroduce them into the discussion of politics. Pioneer that he was, Aristotle wrote the first known treatises on what we now call anthropology and psychology.

---

[3] Books II, III, VII, VIII.
[4] Books IV, V, VI.

Moreover, he was intensely impressed in his observations of the natural world by the evidence of *purpose* in the apparent chaos of real forms. While he generally accepted the Platonic notion of the world of Ideas superinforming the world of nature, Aristotle reasoned that there was a purposeful relationship between them. This is the idea of the *telos:* that the evolving of natural forms, and among them human creativity, was guided by a built-in sense of purpose moving toward the fulfillment of its destined forms. This doctrine of Aristotle's is frequently termed "efficient causation"—that a sequence of natural events proceeds from a first cause and contains within itself the eventual form of its realization. An acorn, for example, grows into an oak, but within that acorn all along was the potential form "oak." The cause that started the acorn on its sequence of changes had determined from the beginning that the eventual realization would be an oak tree. All nature, for Aristotle, contains this efficient causation, is constructed in conformity with the *telos*.[5]

If the world proceeds teleologically, there must be an operative connection, Aristotle reflects, between the Real and the Ideal. Such a relationship suggests that there must be a compromise in the conception of political organization. There is more difference, Aristotle argues, between politics and ethics than Plato would admit. Although the goal of government is the attainment of moral ends—or making arrangements suitable for the attainment of individual moral ends—the means to do this is a separate area of study from the ends themselves. It is here that human nature and social practice enter the picture. They cannot be denied in the consideration of political problems. Consequently, the point of departure for the construction of any political philosophy—even the ideal state—is law. To the end, Plato clung to his reservations about law, but Aristotle contends that law is and must be the foundation of the polity.

But before we consider Aristotle's view of law, one other observation ought to be made. In the separation of ethics and politics partially made by Aristotle, politics becomes a semi-independent area of thought. Plato talked about the "royal science" of politics, but he reduced political prescription to ethics. For Aristotle, politics can be conceived of as a true science, a vast project in the harmonious arrangement of human affairs. This assumes a range of quite practical

---

[5] Aristotle's teleological doctrine had great influence upon Christianity, as Aristotle assumed a "first cause"—a "prime mover unmoved." In Scholastic philosophy, this was developed into what is termed the "cosmological argument" for the existence of God.

considerations; questions arise as to the divisions of power in a government and the legal responsibilities of legislators.

What is law? However one chooses to define it, one element is pervasive: Law must be some variety of rules designed to facilitate human relations. While we frequently think of law as an arbitrator in private disputes, this notion would have been as foreign to Aristotle as to any Greek. Law, for Aristotle, is concerned with the basic relationship between superior and inferior, between a legally constituted authority and those over whom he exercises that authority. Consequently, law becomes rules of differing types governing relationships between those in legal authority and those who obey. There are a number of such relationships: father and child, sovereign and subject, state and citizen. All of these are legal relationships. It follows that law permeates society, is omnipresent in society.

Society in the Aristotelian view is the natural state of man. Man did not construct society for his purposes (as Hobbes and others will later argue); society became a fact when mankind became a fact. Man is a social creature; a man outside society, as Aristotle once observed, would be either a beast or a god. Man as an innately social being is involved, by virtue of his membership in society, in legal relationships. The law is inescapable—whether the state be Real or Ideal.

Aristotle expresses this idea with considerable vigor:

> A social instinct is implanted in all men by nature, and yet he who first founded the state was the greatest of benefactors. For man, when perfected, is the best of animals, but, when separated from law and justice, he is the worst of all; since armed injustice is the more dangerous, and he is equipped at birth with arms, meant to be used by intelligence and virtue, which he may use for the worst ends. Wherefor, if he have not virtue, he is the most unholy and the most savage of animals, and the most full of lust and gluttony. But justice is the bond of men in states, for the administration of justice, which is the determination of what is just, is the principle of order in political society.[6]

Reduced to its simplest terms, Aristotle's view of the nature of political life rests upon two primary assumptions. One we have noted in the above quotation, namely, that the state must rest upon law. Coupled with this presumption is the conviction that, while the state contains both communities and families, the state is the fundamental and primal social organization. Aristotle underscores this point several times in the *Politics:*

---

[6] *Politics* (Oxford trans.), 1253a.

... the state is by nature clearly prior to the family and to the individual, since the whole is of necessity prior to the part.[7]

Every state is a community of some kind, and every community is established with a view to some good; for mankind always act in order to obtain that which they think good. But, if all communities aim at some good, the state or political community, which is the highest of all, and which embraces all the rest, aims at good in a greater degree than any other, and at the highest good.[8]

The Aristotelian concept of law can be defined as universal moral obligation. While this morality is essentially Platonic in character, Aristotle departs from his teacher in certain particulars. He differs principally in asserting that there are varieties of virtue and that the Platonic insistence upon the similarity of individual and corporate virtue is an oversimplification. In the first place, there may be drawn a distinction between what we might call "everyday" virtue and "intellectual" virtue. Aristotle draws the distinction this way:

Virtue, then, being of two kinds, intellectual and moral, intellectual virtue in the main owes both its birth and its growth to teaching (for which reason it requires experience and time), while moral virtue comes about as a result of habit, whence also its name is one that is formed by a slight variation from the word (habit).[9]

Since, like Plato's, Aristotle's fundamental ethical equation is wisdom = virtue and since wisdom is acquired by the use of reason, Aristotle deduces that there are varieties of reason quite as there are varieties of virtue. Consequently, the problem of governing justly, for example, involves a different type of wisdom than, let us say, a father must display in the moral education of his children. Law covers all moral obligations arising out of human relationships, but it takes different forms and applications. Law is universal in that it applies to the full range of moral obligations. But it is also subjective; it dwells in the human heart and can best be described in terms of a moral rather than an objective, absolute edifice.

Law, being such a spirit of moral obligation, is manifested by community will, the moral consensus of the citizenry. But here there arises the problem of how law can enjoy any substantial continuity, stability, if it is expressed through a collective moral consensus. This is explained by Aristotle by summoning up, once more, the idea of the *telos*. Law is stabilized through tradition, through the continuance of

---

[7] *Ibid.*, 1253a.
[8] *Ibid.*, 1252a.
[9] *Nicomachean Ethics*, 1103b2.

conventional patterns of human behavior (i.e., moral virtue). Such conventional observance is not the mere course of expediency or the substitution of the irrational, as Plato feared, but rather the laws of nature, the totality of the spiritual force of law purposefully coursing through the affairs of men. Nature speaks through convention; it does not war with it, argues Aristotle. The laws of nature and human reason coincide. Stressing as he does growth and purposive change, Aristotle asserts that social custom contains elements overlooked in Plato's condemnation. The moral and reasonable side of human nature expresses itself in human arrangements. "All men have an inclination toward justice," Aristotle alleges. Traditional institutions articulate the machinery of reason and should not be ill-advisedly cast aside.

Law must replace the rule of men as the cornerstone upon which the state is built. Aristotle is suspicious of Plato's infallible rulers even in theory. It is foolish, he implies, to talk of god-men; men charged with the task of governing are not only fallible, but they face tasks which call for specialized skill. Practical attainment of the science of politics requires that law replace transcendental insight as a point of departure; "divine madness" is an illusion. The law must bend all into the harmony of the *polis;* no one can be above it; the law must be sovereign.

It is true that for Aristotle the end for individuals and the end for the state may be the same (Aristotle terms this *eudaemonia* or "happiness," but it is in fact a refinement of Socratic virtue), but the business of assuring collective happiness or moral fulfillment requires, first, a sense of common identification with the sovereignty of the law and, second, participation in political life. To meet the first requirement, Aristotle develops the concept of the constitution, and, for the second, he advocates equality of political participation among those of equal competence. The ideal community, he argues, should be a community of equals and, even in a less-than-ideal state, wide disparities in social station and political status should be avoided.

The Aristotelian ruler, consequently, must be subject to the law, and this law should be manifested in a series of mutually understood ground rules between the ruler and those he rules. By Aristotle's definition of law—the acknowledgment of reciprocal moral obligations— both parties enjoy a legal status. This is and must be mutually understood. Aristotle argues that Plato's belief that men will willingly and unquestioningly abrogate all political judgment to rulers flies in the face of human nature. Dignity and a sense of reciprocity of obligation are essential to the relationship of ruler to subject. Moreover, Aristotle makes it clear that he feels collective wisdom to be superior to individual wisdom. The *polis* must be a pooling of political talents.

But it is not indiscriminate pooling. Aristotle introduces a concept of the "citizen" that makes of it quite an exclusive title. As we have seen, a distinction is made between freeman and slave (Aristotle defines a city as a community of freemen) and apparently Aristotle accepts this as a natural state of affairs.[10] What is a citizen? Is it a good man? Yes, says Aristotle, but he must be more than that. "It necessarily follows," Aristotle writes, "that the virtue of all citizens cannot be the same; as the business of him who leads the band is different from the other dancers." [11] The citizen must both command and obey; in less cryptic language, the citizen as described by Aristotle is a member of an educated, propertied, and leisured class. The citizen belongs to a distinct social stratum whose position insures both a relative freedom from the demands of self-interest and adequate leisure to pursue the "intellectual virtues." Among this class of citizens there must be a thorough equality. Equality among equals is a basic premise of Aristotle's mixed state. To the citizens, then, falls the chore of practicing the science of politics.

These somewhat restricted politically privileged citizens are confined by the constitutional character of the state. These constitutional limitations are, in essence, the following: (1) rule for the collective good, (2) obedience to the lawful regulations of the state, and (3) the rejection of coercion and rule by consent.

These are rather broad lines of authority, and, on the assumption that just rule to some extent must be the product of experiment, Aristotle advisedly does not choose to be more concrete. Further, Aristotle conceives of political institutions in terms of growth. Unlike Plato, he places reliance upon the wisdom that accrues from experience. Error is to be expected in all human endeavors, and politics is no exception. The aim of the rational state is to moderate and control political error, to minimize its consequences. The pervading harmony of the state—built upon the common moral purpose—can be sturdy enough to withstand the occasional buffeting and can grow significantly by the accumulation of experience. This is particularly true if the proper spirit of the *polis* is maintained. If there is a sense of political identification and participation, the unity of jointly held

---

[10] Says Aristotle: "Since then some men are slaves by nature, and others are freemen, it is clear that where slavery is advantageous to any one, then it is just to make him a slave." (*Politics*, 1255a).

[11] *Ibid.*, 1277a.

ends, adversity will not cause the adoption of extremes or radical departures from the traditional wisdoms.

For this reason Aristotle advocates the development of a vigorous public opinion. In this respect, he divorces himself from the authoritarianism of Plato. Aristotle discloses a point of view that has been described as "relativism." For him, the wise course in politics may be one resulting from compromise, from the "middle way," from the reconciliation of opposing views. This is "relativistic" in that it proposes that political judgment is not like a geometric proof; there are no "right" or "wrong" answers, pure and simple; solutions are only *relatively* wise or foolish.

But while the means of effecting political ends may be relative, the ends are unvarying. Like Plato, Aristotle insists that ethical concerns are the concerns and ends of the state. Moral fulfillment by the community of individual souls is the purpose for which a polity exists. The art of attaining this communal fulfillment, Aristotle explains, the art of politics, indeed, involves the cohesive use of moderation to attain perpetual harmony. For this moderation Aristotle employs the well-known phrase, "the golden mean."

> It is clear that a state is not a mere society, having a common place, established for the prevention of mutual crime and for the sake of exchange. These are conditions without which a state cannot exist; but all of them together do not constitute a state, which is a community of families and aggregations of families in well-being, for the sake of a perfect and self-sufficing life. Such a community can only be established among those who live in the same place and intermarry. Hence arise in cities family connexions, brotherhoods, common sacrifices, amusements which draw men together. But these are created by friendship, for the will to live together is friendship. The end of the state is the good life, and these are the means towards it. And the state is the union of families and villages in a perfect and self-sufficing life, by which we mean a happy and honourable life.[12]

It is evident from this that Aristotle holds views about marriage and the family that are strenuously opposed to Plato's austere connubial communism. This is true, of course, and we will consider Aristotle's specific objections a bit further on. The fundamental feature of Aristotle's departure from strict Platonic thought is the conviction that political prescription cannot fly in the face of human nature, of the verities of human behavior and organic composition. The difference can be drawn this way: One gets the impression that Plato was aware of human nature but considered it as a regrettable limitation; Aristotle,

---

[12] *Ibid.*, 1281a10.

on the basis of a like discovery, suggests that human nature may contain many desirable elements, many aspects of natural wisdom, and should be respected and taken into account in political calculations. Society itself may have a built-in wisdom, conjectures Aristotle. The schism here between Plato and Aristotle is teleological; Aristotle's concept of purposive change and growth renders human nature and social practice far more significant. The golden mean must serve as a fulcrum for the balance of the Ideal with the Real.

The conceptual side apart, what kind of a political system does Aristotle propose? He begins by reflecting on Plato's classification of governments found in the *Politics*. Briefly, this classification is three-fold: First, there is the rule of one, called "monarchy"; second, the rule of the few, called "aristocracy"; and, third, the rule of the many, called "democracy." All of these forms, Aristotle concludes, can degenerate into tyrannic facsimiles of the originals. Monarchy can become autocracy; aristocracy can be subverted to oligarchy. Democracy, being for Aristotle an "unconstitutional" form anyway, is corrupt by definition.

The classification of governments—which is essentially a description of the locus of power—raises the question of the legitimacy of political authority, the legal assumption of power. It is not enough, argues Aristotle, to pass over this issue by saying that the basis of political authority is moral principle. While true, the real catch is to bring this about, to see, in other words, that power falls to the virtuous. It is on this ground that Aristotle dismisses democracy as a possibility for the just polity. If political authority belongs justly to the virtuous, any system for the disposition of power that fails to take into account the diversity of moral standards among men is clearly incompatible with justice. Rule by the many reduces moral authority to a point barely discernible. And since the only effective political system is a just one, democracy will quickly deteriorate into either mob rule or the seizure of power by immoral opportunists.

If we are left, then, with monarchy and aristocracy as the only possibilities, the problem is to maintain the virtuous in power. Aristotle frequently makes the distinction between "constitutional" and "un-constitutional" states on the basis of whether power is wielded by the "good" men. The perpetuation of constitutional government cannot rest upon force or hereditary right (as was common in Aristotle's day). Further, it is not practical, he reflects, to put too much trust in the Platonic solution that the ruled, if educated properly, will consciously and willingly abide by the rule of the just. The safer, more expedient way, is to maintain constitutional government by a balance of political and social forces. In his theories regarding the mixed state or constitutional government, Aristotle implies that permanent social harmony rests upon a division and balance of forces, not upon a division and balance of functions, as Plato envisions. What sorts of "forces" does Aristotle mean? Primarily, he means social classes. These social classes, however, are divided not upon a division-of-labor principle, but upon the distribution of property (he calls this the "oligarchic principle"), softened somewhat by the moderating influence of family ties.

The constitutional state, then, rests upon a social hierarchy. This appears as a rather rigid "caste" system at first glance, but it is far less inflexible than Plato's "gold," "silver," and "brass." Several assumptions render the social stratification more moderate. First, political activity, like all civilized pursuits, must be the product of leisure. The citizens must have the means to procure the leisure needed for the attainment of self-cultivation and, in turn, political participation. In Aristotle's good society, the manual toil must be performed other than by the citizenry, either by slaves or by hired foreign labor.[13] Freed from the chores of hewing wood and drawing water, all classes comprising the polity share equally in the leisure and have equal opportunity for self-development and political action.

Secondly, no one class has a monopoly on political power. No class rights are recognized. Aristotle's "leisure class" encompasses all the citizenry, and no class is specifically entrusted with—or trained for—political leadership.

Thirdly, Aristotle's polity embraces the principle of "equality among equals." Surely all men are not equal, he would observe, but, among men of equal attainment, equality of political influence must exist. (This concept was to see actual fruition in the Roman Republic and later in the ideology of British "whiggery.")

Fourthly, Aristotle does not propose a closed society; his society features mobility. This mobility can be evidenced in two areas. One can progress upwards in the hierarchy on the basis of ethical competence. The aristocracy is one of virtue and ability. (The Aristotelian view has long intrigued political thinkers, and most ages have seen some form of the theory of "natural aristocracy." This ideal has con-

---

[13] It is interesting to note that Aristotle's argument on this point was pressed into service with gusto by the pro-slavery writers in the pre-Civil War period in the United States. It was a substantial feature of the attempt to "revive the Greek democracy."

tinued in the United States from Thomas Jefferson to Babbitt and Santayana and in Britain from Burke to Churchill.) Property divisions, too, are not fixed, and Aristotle might perhaps be described as the original "free enterpriser." He does offer a vigorous defense of private property, but he feels the need to limit individual wealth and deems "interest" to be immoral.

All these moderating conditions are forms of social division emanating from what Aristotle terms the "democratic principle." Aristotle's terminology is not always as consistent as one might wish, and he appears to shift the meaning of the word "democracy" considerably. Sometimes he means by it a limited popular participation, and then at other times he seems to use it as a term to describe moral leveling. Aristotle's mixed state combines, as we have seen, both oligarchic and democratic elements. However, the prevailing spirit is aristocratic, but with Aristotle's own concept of aristocracy. In modern jargon, Aristotle's is a bourgeois aristocracy, an élite of middle-class proprietors. The class that appeals most to him as a bulwark against radicalism is a propertied class, notable for its large size and inclusiveness rather than for its compactness and exclusiveness. In many ways, the gentry of Aristotle's polity bear small resemblance to what we have grown to associate with the term "aristocracy." Plato's philosopher-rulers—or even the guardians—seem more familiar aristocratic figures with their restricted membership, rigid code of behavior, and private élan.

Aristotle, fearing extremism more than any other danger, appears to place his trust in an economically satiated and politically dedicated upper middle class. His chief objection to monarchy is not its theoretic base, but its reliance upon the wisdom of one man and its lack of the socially unifying element of participation. Popular democracy he can dismiss as doing violence to the principle of rule by the virtuous. The extent to which Aristotle sees some connection between virtue and property ownership, as Plato seems to do in the *Laws*, is apparent but not altogether clear. Others who followed Aristotle, however, claimed to have seen an unmistakable connection. (Among these can be numbered many of the founding fathers of the American republic.)

Aristotle, having analyzed the problem of power, turned to the question of the division of government. His conclusions are at once familiar and, considering their antiquity, striking. Once more, his preoccupation with balance is observable; both democratic and oligarchic influences appear. There are three major divisions of government, he concludes, and they are "deliberative," "administrative," and "judicial." It is not difficult to extrapolate these into "legislative," "executive," and "judicial." Like more modern political theorists, Aristotle suggests that these are "natural" divisions, not merely expedient ones, and that they spring from different balances of forces in the polity. Montesquieu would say the same thing in the eighteenth century. Clearly, the deliberative branch has a more popular base than does the judicial, and the administrative branch must represent still a different aspect of political participation from the other two.

But however government is organized, its objective of growth toward communal virtue rests upon two premises. The first is the need for the polity to be more than a mere collection of social artifacts, to be the unified embodiment of the collective aspirations of the citizenry. The polity must be all-encompassing. At the same time, the polity must rest upon a variety of diverse social institutions of which the family, for Aristotle, is of prime importance. One can detect little basic disagreement between Plato and Aristotle on the first premise, but on the second Aristotle has diverged fundamentally from his teacher.

We have already indicated Aristotle's reaction to the Platonic communism of the *Republic*. Since it is not possible to offer here a full description of Aristotle's attack, his reply to Plato on the abolition of the family will suffice to illustrate the general line of thought.

Aristotle contends that if the family is to be sacrificed for the sake of statewide unity, as Plato demands, the exact opposite condition will result. Unity is not built upon so vast a scale as a state; it must be nurtured on a far more intimate scale. How can a citizen be expected to have a sense of unity with the state without having an intervening sense of unity with, or loyalty to, his family and his immediate associates? To destroy the family would be to court disunity, wrenching men asunder from their natural and personal loyalties. The unity of the state, argues Aristotle, is built upon the foundation of family and social unity.

Further, the family is a product of nature and is not, therefore, to be discarded, for all that is natural is purposeful. What, then, are the natural purposes of the family? Aristotle replies that they are the moral education of children and the increase of virtue resulting from the connubial associations of man and wife. Also, family ties and obligations provide an outlet for the increased development of the individual. In slightly broader scope, Aristotle argues that the diversity of elements that comprise a state cannot be successfully harmonized by the state alone. Any such attempt would produce an unnatural and futile uniformity. The end of the state cannot be sheer unity; the end must be happiness through moral fulfillment. And unity taken to the extremes of Platonic communism would be destructive of communal happiness. Basically, Aristotle's refutation rests on the belief that the polity is a unity which arises out of complementary diversity. To Plato, the polity must be the embodiment of the solitary Idea.

While it is true that the differences between Plato and Aristotle can be overstated, as we have already mentioned, one can point to places of substantial variance. These differences arise, some from disparities of temperament, some from metaphysical assumptions. To Aristotle, nature was a great, complicated, yet logical plan, unfolding its purpose slowly to human view. The basic wisdom was natural wisdom increased through the observation of phenomena, a wisdom rooted in nature but developing through experience. The state and the arts of the political leader are not in another category apart from this schema. Political wisdom, therefore, must be anchored, too, in observation and experience. While Aristotle tacitly accepts Plato's judgment that politics and ethics are one, his entire drift of reasoning suggests otherwise. Certainly the art of political decision-making is not formally intellectual, let alone geometric. It is an attempt to reconcile the principles of virtue with the volatile flux of human affairs. The wisdom of the statesman is not transcendental, intuitive, or even essentially deductive; it is *empirical*—knowledge gained through experience.

Throughout all of Aristotle's political writing there lurks his idea of efficient causation, which we have already examined. His preoccupation with the problem of causation has two general effects upon his political theory. First, it causes him to have a regard for the significance of growth and habitual causative relationships, and it prompts him to use caution in his judgment of what he observes. Who knows, he might say, what the end product is destined to be?

Secondly, this teleological view imposes greater limits on the range of political choice. While Aristotle is not a determinist in any sense, there is nonetheless always before him that proposition: "If *A*, then *B*." This proposition limits what the statesman can do, causes him to operate within more fixed boundaries than the more speculative statesman of the Platonic imagination. We are creatures of nature after all, muses Aristotle, and that is as it should be, for wisdom resides in the natural order. No, retorts Plato, we are captives of nature only insofar as we choose to admit nature's mastery. True wisdom is outside nature; nature is but a sham copy of true reality.

These are sweeping generalities and contain the shortcomings of all such pat rhetorical devices. Nonetheless, they do convey a profound difference in emphasis. Perhaps this is why Aristotle is the most influential thinker in Western history. Here is the counsel of reasonableness, of worldly understanding, the generations have said. Here is true insight into the world as it exists. Aristotle is the universal thinker, perhaps.

But it is not because Aristotle appears so down to earth that he has made such an impact; in the last analysis, it is because he was the first to view in its far-flung grandeur the virtual totality of the universe and to see it not as mystery or brute force, but as an interlinking and reciprocating "grand design." Bravely, Aristotle sought to bring all natural knowledge into one system, to create a universal synthesis. That he failed is of relatively small importance; no one yet has succeeded in so grandiose a cosmological feat. Its merit rests on the imprint it has left on our intellectual tradition, especially on our political heritage.

In no known age has Aristotle been without disciples, from Francis Bacon to Jacques Maritain. Perhaps the best characteristic of Western political thought is its commitment to the "golden mean." Here is Aristotle still doggedly at work today.

. . . for further discussion:

1. Aristotle defends slavery on the grounds that it is necessary in order to provide adequate leisure for the moral growth of citizens. Do you think Aristotle, if alive today, would take the view that the machine now replaces the slave in turning the wheels of society? How do you think Aristotle would account for the fact that while modern technology has created multitudes of labor-saving devices, the corresponding leisure provided does not appear to have elevated the moral tenor of society?

2. Aristotle appears to favor a "middle class state." Why? Why is it that most Americans and Englishmen consider themselves members of the middle class by choice? Do you think that the possession of property causes men to hold more moderate or more cautious political opinions?

3. At first glance, one is inclined to agree with Aristotle that Plato in some instances disregards human nature and the practical problems of social life. But is this a fair charge? How do you think Plato might answer some of Aristotle's criticisms—those regarding the family, for example? Compare for a moment the social views of Aristotle and Plato with contemporary opinions in the same area. From what you know of Freudian psychology, for example, which viewpoint—Plato's or Aristotle's—would be most in agreement with Freud? Why?

4. Aristotle has been described by some as the first philosopher to center attention on the individual man. He has been described as the progenitor of all individualistic social theory. Yet Aristotle took an ethical position not vastly different from Plato's, emphatically argued for an organic view of society, and linked individual moral fulfillment with social moral well-being. Can these reflections on Aristotle be reconciled?

. . . for further investigation:

Aristotle, *Complete Works*, J. A. Smith and W. D. Ross, eds. New York: Oxford University Press, Inc., 1908–1931.

———, *Politics*, W. Ellis, trans. New York: E. P. Dutton & Co., Inc., 1912.

———, *Politics*, B. Jowett, trans. 2 vols. New York: Oxford University Press, Inc., 1885.

Hamburger, Max E., M*orals and Law: The Growth of Aristotle's Legal Theory*. New Haven, Conn.: Yale University Press, 1951.

Randall, John H., Jr., ° *Aristotle*. New York: Columbia University Press, 1960.

Ross, William D., ° *Aristotle*. New York: Meridian Books, 1959.

Windelband, Wilhelm, ° *A History of Philosophy*, J. E. Tufts, trans. Vol. I. New York: Torchbooks, 1958.

Many of the titles contained in the bibliography for Chapter One are applicable to Aristotle as well.

3

THE GOOD LIFE
RECONSIDERED

The death of Alexander the Great left the world holding its breath. It had all happened so fast. Now the civilizations of the Mediterranean needed time to stop, take stock, and assimilate all the rapid changes wrought by the Macedonian conqueror. This was the Alexandrian Age—and the word "alexandrian" has a connected meaning when applied to art or literature. It means a style of art lacking in originality that seeks to copy and repeat an earlier model. This description is very apropos of the intellectual climate following Aristotle.

The great Athenian schools of philosophy were to continue, but under different management. The fire and excitement of the Academy and the Lyceum were gone, and the magnificent originality of the Greek mind was passing, too. Yet in spite of the general decline, and while no great figure arose of the stature of Plato, considerable philosophic wrangling went on. Factions grew up, and rival schools were established. These philosophic coteries had as their primary

point of difference matters of ethics—and a far more personal view of
ethics than was ever held by Plato or Aristotle.

This shift of view is the key to understanding the Stoic and Epicurean doctrines. The question asked by Zeno, the Stoic, or Epicurus
was: How should I live? This would have been a tangential question
for Aristotle, let us say. To him, the significant question would have
been: How should men live? One must not overdo this alteration of
emphasis, but the singular quality of these post-Aristotelian schools
was that they approached the moral dilemma from the standpoint of
the individual and his rather personal moral nature. They were far
more introspective and much less analytic than their distinguished
predecessors. Both Stoics and Epicureans also flirted with mysticism.
There is some mystic quality in Plato, as you know, and this can be
traced to a number of sources, but in the Stoic allegories, for example,
this mystic bent is far more pronounced. With the Epicureans, for all
their antireligious convictions, there is the idea of a quasimystic
transcendence or peace that comes from ascetic detachment—an idea
not at all unlike several Oriental religions. However different the Stoics
and Epicureans were, they both embraced a concept of something
extrarational, although Stoicism, for its part, laid claim to rather
rigorous logical injunction.

The school of the Stoics was founded by Zeno (336?–264? B.C.) probably around 300 B.C. The Greek word for porch is stoa, and Zeno so
frequently held forth on a convenient porch that his followers were
dubbed "Stoics." Actually, Zeno had belonged to a philosophic circle,
the Cynics, whom we shall discuss briefly a bit further on, and decided to strike out on his own. The word "stoic" should not be unknown to you, incidentally, even if you are not familiar with the
background of it. It is a rather common word in English (e.g., "She
has a very stoic attitude about visiting the dentist.") meaning great
forbearance, the ability to absorb misfortune or discomfort without
complaint, "carrying on" in the face of adversity, and so on. This
"stiff upper lip" posture was indeed part of the Stoic philosophy. The
story is told of the Roman Stoic philosopher, Epictetus (60?–120?),
a slave owned by a sadistic master who tortured him for pleasure. On
one occasion, when the master was subjecting his slave to the rack,
Epictetus glanced up and said in a friendly, calm voice: "I do believe, dear master, that if you persist in bending my leg in this fashion,
you shall surely cause it to break." Such was the Stoic spirit.

But dignified forbearance was only a small part of the entirety of Stoic thought. Actually, Stoicism underwent three quite distinct phases in its development. First, the early period under Zeno, where Stoicism is rather mystic, personal, and almost evangelical. The second phase entailed the impact of Platonism upon it, making of it a doctrine far more sophisticated and rationalistic. Finally, in its last phase, Stoicism was transplanted into Roman society, as much by Cicero as anyone else, and here it became the unofficial religion of the Roman intelligentsia and upper classes. At this time, Stoicism became an urbane, tolerant, and most cosmopolitan code of life. Perhaps the most dedicated Stoic of them all was the Roman emperor, Marcus Aurelius.[1]

There are two aspects of Stoicism that we must consider: its ethical propositions and the implications of these in terms of ideas regarding law and politics. It is in Stoicism that we first encounter that formidable phrase, *jus naturale*—natural law. The basic ethical postulate of the Stoics was: individual well-being through virtue. Virtue, then, was the goal of human endeavor for them as it was for Plato, but there are significant differences. First, for the Stoics, virtue and well-being were not synonymous; virtue was a state the attainment of which permitted individual well-being. Virtue, then, became operational in the sense that the practice of it led to human happiness. This represents a shift in both goals and means from the Platonic concept of virtue as an end in itself. Further, the Socratic virtue-knowledge equation was abandoned. For the Stoic, virtue was not attained by knowledge, but by the restraint of the will. Now of course Plato argued that man must learn to control his grosser appetites—this is one of the prime chores of education, as you will recall—but sheer discipline of will could not, unenlightened, lead to virtue.

If virtue was to be attained, contended the Stoics, human proclivities for evil must be restrained by training, and this training took two general forms: the training of the will and religious instruction. The aggressive will—perhaps not unlike the Freudian id—must be brought to heel by inculcating the rigid code of duty and encouraging patient forbearance even to physical pain. As we shall see in a moment, the Stoic *Weltanschauung* was of a world of "wheels within wheels," a series of interlinking levels and strata. Human society was built upon the principle of reciprocal duties and obligations; everyone must do

---

[1] *The Meditations* of Marcus Aurelius (121–180) are the best place to get an understanding of Roman Stoicism. It is a fascinating book, written by one of the truly noble men of the ancient world.

his part, as it were.[2] The highest form of human expression was the
discharge of duties, performing the tasks allotted by Providence. (There
is more than a touch of determinism in this notion.) Each man, then,
discharging his duties and practicing the attendant self-controls would
lead to the existence of a social harmony of mutual affection and
respect—some translators have used the word "concord" to express
this idea. In a sense, the Stoic view of the polity is a trifle like a
frontier community, each man contributing his special skills to the
common effort and defense, be he a blacksmith or a preacher.

But duty, patience, and forbearance were not enough for the Stoic.
It was equally important to acknowledge the sovereignty of Providence. The Stoics were somewhat vague as to theological matters,
although they conceived of a dualistic universe.[3] Gone was the
ancient pantheon, but there was no literal replacement in Stoicism.
There were hints of monotheism [4]—as in Aristotle——and it could
certainly be reasonably argued that the Stoics advanced the notion
of pantheism.[5] God, Providence, Divine Power, or what you will,
nature, like man, was a product of God, although the theological
specifics were largely lacking—and became even vaguer under Roman
influence.

Man and nature created by God made man and nature linked by a
common inheritance. Moreover, to the Stoics, God was rational, not
a figure of caprice or barbaric whim or vengeance, and man, as His
product, shared this rationality. Man and God could understand each
other through their mutual reason.

To pursue this line of thought further: If man is the product of God,
then not only do man and nature share an inheritance, but men,
all men, have a common ancestor. All men must be brothers, since
they are fathered by God. This is a surprising view for Greeks to hold.
They had long maintained the distinction between Greek and non-

---

[2] Such a view reoccurs in almost every age—Edmund Burke in the eighteenth
century will call upon each man to learn to serve and love his "little platoon."

[3] *Dualism:* a belief that the ultimate nature of the universe consists of two
orders of existence. In this instance, a conception of two worlds, one "natural,"
the other "divine." This conception is traceable to Platonic metaphysics.

[4] *Monotheism:* the belief in one God. Frequently attributed to Judaism, historical research tends to substantiate the fact that monotheism appeared in Egypt
under the reign of *Amenhotep IV.* Several discussions are available, not the
least of which—nor probably the most careful—is Sigmund Freud's *Moses and
Monotheism.*

[5] *Pantheism:* the belief that God exists in nature. He does not possess anthro-
morphic form, but exists omnipresently in the elements of nature.

Greek—to whom they referred merely as "barbarians." The Romans maintained a similar ethnocentric point of view until late in the Imperial Period. Universal as Plato and Aristotle were, neither really ever considered any civilization that was not Greek, and, for his part, Aristotle was untroubled by the institution of slavery. Now the Stoics argued that there exists a brotherhood of man.

There were immediate political consequences of such a view, and the Stoics accepted them and built upon them. If there was a universal brotherhood, then the entire world was a single great city created by Providence. The fact of brotherhood demands a political order that is worldwide, that encompasses all men—a world state. All dreams of the world state, and we have had more than a few in our century, trace back to this original Stoic conception. It should be remembered that this world community, this political concord of all men, would rest upon the Stoic concept of virtue. It would not be a political marriage of convenience, but merely obedience to Providential ordering of nature and man.

If the world state is in obedience to the plan of Providence and God and man are rational, the underpinning of the world polity is not mere loose acquiescence, but response to law. There is a universal law, the Stoics maintained, that is eternal, immutable, ever-present, and everywhere applicable; they termed it natural law (*jus naturale*). Natural law forms the apex of a hierarchy of laws which should govern man. There must also be a law of the world (*jus gentium*), and this should be constructed by human reason employed as a means of determining the character of natural law. Since the natural law is universal, so should the world law be.

The Stoics realized, however, that differences exist between peoples, between Greeks and Semites, Romans and Carthaginians. There should, consequently, be room for the preservation of customary practices and traditional local jurisprudence (provided it does not contravene natural law). There must be a second law, suited to regional variation, and the Stoics termed this "local law," or *jus civile*. Such law is frankly based upon custom, not upon reason, and world law must always possess the higher mandate.

It is all well and good to talk about something called "natural law" and to build visions of a law in the sky that is eternally the just dictates of Divine Providence, but it can be significant only to the extent that it is both known to exist and known as to content. If there is a natural law, what does it say? Here the Greek Stoics become both less communicative and more hesitant. They do not provide us with an account of natural law, and their defense of its existence is essentially a defense of the rationality of nature and an admission of the necessity for acknowledging the existence of a higher authority. Even if nature could be demonstrated to be rational in its make-up and processes, would this require *prima facie*, natural law? The Stoics assumed that it would and let the matter drop. They were never legalistically oriented and made no effort to develop a body of jurisprudence from their premises. This they left to human reason—and, as it happened, to the Romans.

As we shall see when we meet Cicero, Greek Stoicism had a marked impact on Roman intellectuals. In the second century it became a fashionable view in polite Roman circles. But by the time it had its vogue in Rome, Stoicism had undergone considerable change from its original doctrine. It became increasingly legalistic, and in the hands of its Roman interpreters it became much less personalistic and ascetic. Virtue was still Stoicism's major theme, but the Romans tended to view it in terms of civic virtue rather than personal piety. Indeed, Stocism became considerably more attractive as it became less austere. Kindness, nobility, public service, taste, and learning became part of the Stoic creed, which evolved into a distinctly aristocratic "religion." Part of its popularity can be explained by the general cynicism in which traditional religion was held by educated Romans. The gods and their domestic foibles and pastoral banalities had ceased to do anything but amuse the cultured Romans of the late Republic. Even imperial fervor could not resuscitate the gods.

As Stoicism extended its hold as a personal credo for Roman patricians, it also began to influence Roman political thought in two vital areas: the concepts of the Empire and of the law. In 212 A.D., by the Edict of Caracalla, citizenship was extended to all those under Roman hegemony, and such citizenship entailed the protection of the Roman law. The notion of *pax romana* had Stoicism as its roots. Rome became determined to create a universal empire—not merely out of national pride or territorial greed, but because Rome yearned for the civilized tranquillity such an order would bring. She very nearly accomplished it.

The Stoic influences on the creation of Roman law are immense. The fundamental ground of Roman law was the *jus naturale*, and while the Greek Stoics were satisfied to leave such law primarily conceptual, the Romans endeavored to create a system of jurisprudence that would incorporate the natural law and make law-giving a rational art. The result was the birth of one of the two great legal systems still extant in the Western world. We will examine the origins and growth of this law in the next chapter.

Stoicism is remembered most for its influences upon more enduring philosophies and religions, of which Christianity is one. While there are numerous points of similarity between the Stoic view and Christianity, much of what we identify with Christianity is attributable to the influences of Stoicism upon a religion whose major impetus came from Rome and whose principal early leaders were the products of Roman civilization. To Christianity Stoicism gave a cosmopolitan flavor, broadened its appeal from what Gilbert Murray calls a "religion of the urban proletariat" [6] to a faith embraced equally at all levels of Roman society. Such Roman Stoics as Seneca have frequently been described as "pre-Christians." If neoplatonism played a vital part in the intellectual molding of St. Augustine, Stoicism was an evident influence on Gregory and Ambrose if in no other way than by shaping their general cast of thought. It is argued that Christianity as it initially was introduced into Rome might have made no greater impact than a number of contemporary oriental religions had not it been for its affinity to Stoicism and the widening influence of the latter.

Marcus Aurelius in his *Meditations* provides a veritable handbook for the Stoic. One can sense the spirit of conviction in his words:

> Every moment think steadily as a Roman and a man to do what thou hast in hand with perfect and simple dignity, and feeling of affection, and freedom, and justice; and to give thyself relief from all other thoughts. And thou wilt give thyself relief, if thou doest every act of thy life as if it were the last, laying aside all carelessness and passionate aversion from the commands of reason, and all hypocrisy, and self-love, and discontent with the portion which has been given to thee. Thou seest how few the things are, the which if a man lays hold of, he is able to live a life which flows in quiet, and is like the existence of the gods; for the gods on their part will require nothing more from him who observes these things.

> Adorn thyself with simplicity and modesty and with indifference toward the things which lie between virtue and vice. Love mankind. Follow God. The poet says that Law rules all. And it is enough to remember that law rules all.[7]

---

[6] For an entertaining discussion of this general topic, you might like to read Gilbert Murray's *Stoic, Christian and Humanist.* Also recommended is H. J. Blackham's *The Human Tradition.*

[7] Marcus Aurelius, *Meditations*, pp. 144-145, and 213.

Stoicism was not the only Greek ethical creed competing in the intellectual market place. Old Athens had its "angry young men" as do most generations. Like the discouraged students that circled the feet of Jean-Paul Sartre after World War II and made "existentialism" a popular word, disillusioned young Greeks of the third century B.C. clustered around the person of *Epicurus* (342?-270? B.C.). He taught them that the only sensible aim in life was the pursuit of the pleasurable. Ethics maintaining that happiness or pleasure is the base of morality have become known as "hedonism." Epicurus was the first announced hedonist. At first glance, this appears to be a prescription for gay and carefree debauchery—not a new idea to the Greeks—and the apotheosis of "wine, woman, and song." Such was not at all the case. The creed of Epicurus—Epicureanism—was severe and called for the avoidance of most earthly indulgences, save those carefully and tastefully selected. The Epicureans espoused not rich indulgence, but withdrawal and ascetic contemplation, because not only was the pursuit of the pleasurable involved, but also the avoidance of the painful. "If you do not participate, you are less likely to get hurt," would be one way of phrasing their advice. Life should be lived withdrawn from the chaos of the world with its painful struggles and frustrations. Better to sit alone in a secluded garden, tasting an occasional grape and avoiding emotional turbulence.

Like the word "stoic," the term "epicurean" is frequently encountered in our language, meaning the discriminating faculty for fastidiously selecting food, drink, and amusement. The word "epicure" has the same stem—it describes one who is an authority on such sensual delights as cookery and wine. The followers of Epicurus, however, were little interested in such luxuries. For them, it was a case, in the language of the *Rubáiyát*, of "a jug of wine, a loaf of bread, and Thou beside me, singing in the wilderness"—except that the "Thou" was likely to be omitted.

If the proper moral attitude of men is to embrace pleasure—of an ascetic sort—and to avoid pain, moral conduct can be described in terms of expediency. The moral injunction is reasonably simple: Do that which permits you to embrace the pleasurable. The circle is half-run from the counsel of Socrates. It is another generation of Greeks.

Epicureanism was also a sort of quietistic rebellion. It was in revolt against the old myths and the heretofore venerated religions. These

were labeled as dangerous superstitions, dangerous because they taught a spurious moral lesson. Nature was not the artifact of Divine Providence or of the gods or of ideal forms; it was a brute biological fact, explainable in terms of materiality. The Epicureans embraced a thoroughgoing materialism [8] and injected into this picture of the world the concept that nature is constructed of a vast multitude of atomic particles. The forms of nature, then, are chains of these atomic entities in constant flux. Interestingly enough, this view produced a startlingly modern concept of physical evolution. The full treatment of this idea is found in a long verse catalogue of the universe written by the Roman Epicurean, Lucretius (96?-55 B.C.), *De Rerum Natura* or *On the Nature of Things*. This is an astonishing book.[9] Its scope and even its sense of scientific prediction mightily intrigue the modern reader. It is by far the most lofty product of the Epicurean school.

The premises of the Epicureans held considerable import for social and political thought. The proposition that the universe could be best discussed as physics and not as metaphysics and that moral good was individual assessment of the calculus of pleasure and pain made it rather clear that the state—all organized government—had a far more limited role to play than that conceived by the Platonists, Aristotelians, or Stoics. Indeed, government could have but one primary function and that was to provide the security and order upon which individual pursuits depended. Therefore, law was conceived merely as a means of restraining invasions of privacy. Theodore Roosevelt was giving voice to a rather Epicurean view when he commented: "Your freedom to swing your fist ends where my nose begins." Indeed, government was a necessary evil and could in no sense be deliberative. It was to keep the peace. If these pronouncements appear vague and even a little simple-minded, it is because the Epicureans—again unlike those in the Socratic tradition—did not view politics as a "royal science" and thought of it, if at all, as an appendage to be dealt with as hastily as possible. How far the pendulum had swung from the organic sense

---

[8] *Materialism:* the belief that the only reality is that of matter or substance. It is what Eliseo Vivas called the "bumpable universe"—all that is real is subject to contact by the human senses.

[9] The most stimulating commentary on Lucretius is found in George Santayana's slender and charming book, *Three Philosophical Poets* (the other two are Dante and Goethe). For those interested in becoming familiar with general philosophy, Santayana's book may serve as a most useful introduction, as he contends that virtually all the mainstreams of Western philosophy can be found in the work of these three poets.

of social and political unity to the subjective individualism of the Epicureans and the Cynics (whom we shall mention shortly).

The Epicurean notion of physical evolution, of atomic growth, suggested the same view of society. An earlier Greek, Heraclitus (535?–475? B.C.), is reputed to have said (although it also appears in Aristophanes): "Whirl is King." This the Epicureans also believed and felt that social institutions were ephemeral things, likely soon to alter and pass. The Stoic preoccupation with the earthly commonwealth seemed to the Epicureans to be a foolish waste of time.

With the exception of Lucretius and a few others, the Epicurean doctrine appears to have had little appeal to the Romans. This is quite understandable; the sons of Romulus were activists and legalists, not hermits and contemplative idlers. However the Latin spirit might become imbued with altruism or idealistic visions, it was always in terms of concrete reform, empire-building, law-making, or serious attention to political problems. The Romans worked at what they did —even in their arts, which always lacked the sense of leisurely, detached elegance notable in Grecian art. The boisterous Latin character spurned the implicit social decadence of Epicureanism—and even when the Romans became decadent themselves it was in a rather sordid Dionysian mood, not as a cold, eviscerated withdrawal.

Cynicism, a movement contemporary with Epicureanism, embraced a point of view even more detached than that of the followers of Epicurus. It, too, bears a resemblance to the twentieth-century French existentialists like Sartre and Camus—even a similarity to the much publicized American beatniks. Cynicism was a philosophy of escape, pure and more than a little simple. It pushed individualism beyond Epicureanism to virtual self-sufficiency and opposed social institutions on principle, preferring to hold a vision of a cosmopolitan, egalitarian utopia. Lurking behind the Cynic position was a rather complete nihilism—the contention that there are no valid grounds for the establishment of truth or, for that matter, moral principle. A frequent concomitant of a nihilistic view is the necessity for anarchism —the abolition of government on the grounds that it is evil. The Cynics were both nihilists and, essentially, anarchists, apparently untroubled by the fact that nihilism in its denial of the existence of moral principle would also seem to be inconsistent with a belief that government must be eliminated on the ground that it is evil—clearly a moral judg-

ment. Diogenes, a minor figure among the Cynics, is well-known for his diligent. lantern-lit expedition in quest of an honest man.

Students of the history of political ideas usually pass over another significant intellectual school of the Greco-Roman Age presumably on the grounds that this philosophical movement did not address itself to political theory. While this is true, it had much to do with setting the mood of the time and hastening the growth of Christianity. In the third century, principally in the cultural center of Alexandria, Egypt, a group called the Neoplatonists gained prominence—particularly Plotinus (205?-270), the most important of the school. Like the other post-Aristotelian movements that preceded it, Neoplatonism was not primarily concerned with the arts of politics, but rather with problems of ethics. But ethics, in Neoplatonism, took the form of fervent religiosity, into which mysticism was blended, to the extent that it is difficult to decide whether Neoplatonism should be classified as a religion or as a philosophy.

Neoplatonism was the product of considerable borrowing from previous philosophies grafted onto the metaphysics of Plato—always with the exception of Epicureanism, which it sought almost feverishly to refute. Some scholars have described Neoplatonism as eclectic,[10] but this is true only to a degree, since the doctrine clings resolutely to a sense of religious commitment and to the Platonic cosmology.[11] Its debt to Plato aside, Neoplatonism adopted the same subjective orientation as had Stoicism; the individual was the starting point for conjecture. Further, Neoplatonism had deep reservations—like most mysticism —about the significance of the world of experience, the day-to-day phenomena of life. As well, it adopted in large measure the ethics of the Stoics.

It is not necessary to delve into the specifics of Neoplatonic belief other than to make several germane observations. First, Neoplatonism was a majestic declaration of ideals clothed in arrestingly transcendental garb, and in the hands of a first-rate thinker and writer such as Plotinus it had great beauty and sincerity. It touched the Roman world and left its imprint on such a giant as Augustine, and its lofty and poetic mood has since been felt by such modern figures as Emerson, Newman, and Santayana. Secondly, it gave the most intense ancient expression of the dignity of the human person and its essen-

---

[10] *Eclecticism:* practice of incorporating what appears best from a variety of systems.

[11] *Cosmology:* that portion of metaphysics concerned with the nature of the universe, whose orderly character it assumes.

tial sanctity, and in so doing it stressed the differences between man and the remainder of nature. Thirdly, Neoplatonism provided a persuasive argument for the existence and indispensability of revelation as a means of knowledge. Although revelation looms not overly large in Plotinus and the earlier Neoplatonists, such transcendental insight into the Divine—essentially the same idea that we are familiar with in Christian literature—became a salient principle. The Neoplatonic suprarational order assumed the human soul to be a kind of intermediary between the "real" and the "intelligible" worlds—between the world that we know and that which possesses true reality in the Platonic sense. The soul, rather than reason or the physical body, was conceived of as the touchstone of reality.

Although not an era much given to the formal writing of political philosophy, the age that followed the passing of Aristotle laid the foundations for the growth of social and political thought still lively in the melee of ideas that surrounds us. From the imaginative moral conjectures of disinherited Greeks, we can now face coming to grips with the voluminous political tradition we have inherited from Rome. From ethics we may move to law, but running through the preoccupations of men are the ancient concerns, well expressed by Stoics, Epicureans, and Neoplatonists, regarding the moral end for man.

. . . for further discussion:

1. From your reading of the opening sections of the *Republic,* what sort of arguments would Socrates put forward to refute the hedonism of Epicurus? Oscar Wilde, the British playwright, espoused the "New Hedonism" around the end of the nineteenth century. What other types of hedonism can you think of?

2. Lucretius, in Book I of *On the Nature of Things,* makes this observation:
   . . . nothing is ever gotten out of nothing by divine power. Fear in sooth takes such a hold of all mortals, because they see many operations go on in earth and heaven, the causes of which they can no way understand, believing them therefore to be done by divine power.

   To what extent do you think Plato would agree and disagree with Lucretius' contention?

3. What effect might the ethics of Epicureanism have upon the development of law?

4. The attainment of a utopian order of existence, a perfection realizable in the temporal realm, has been a theme running through all human thought,

Occidental and Oriental. To what extent does this utopian ideal occur in Stoicism, Epicureanism, and Neoplatonism? What are the differences in approach? Is it possible to make any generalizations about utopianism from these three viewpoints?

. . . for further investigation:

Bailey, Cyril, *The Greek Atomists and Epicurus*. New York: Oxford University Press, Inc., 1928.

Bevan, Edwyn, *Stoics and Skeptics*. New York: Oxford University Press, Inc. 1913.

Blackham, Harold J., *The Human Tradition*. Boston, Mass.: Beacon Press, 1953.

Lucretius, *On the Nature of Things*, W. Leonard, trans. New York: E. P. Dutton & Co., Inc., 1916.

Marcus Aurelius Antoninus, *The Meditations*, G. Long, trans. New York: Burt Franklin, n.d.

Murray, Gilbert, *Stoic, Christian and Humanist*. Boston, Mass.: Beacon Press, 1950.

————, *The Stoic Philosophy*. New York: G. P. Putnam's Sons, 1915.

Turnbull, Grace, ed., *The Essence of Plotinus*. New York: Oxford University Press, Inc., 1934.

4

THE LAW OF GOD
AND THE LAW
OF MAN

It is generally supposed by many historians that civilizations have "life histories." [1] They have infancies, adolescences, maturities, and, finally periods of decline, a hardening of the cultural arteries. Rome provides a classic case. Passing through brash adolescence, pushing her neighboring states about, she finally reached nationhood by destroying the opulent city of Carthage after three exhausting wars. Proving themselves the military masters of the central Mediterranean, the Romans began to take on the more pacific graces of a mature civilization. As we have noted in the preceding chapter, the Roman intelligentsia became much intrigued by the doctrines of the Greek Stoics. To a large extent, this new interest in philosophy and its companion art, law, arose out of the rejection of Roman religious primitivism. The old religion with its vegetative and martial symbols well served a simple and uncomplicated warrior-state, but it lacked the

---

[1] Numerous historians have been convinced that history is best explained in terms of recurring cycles. Nietzsche, Spengler, and Toynbee are among the best known examples.

qualities required to underpin a maturing commonwealth. The problem of a philosophical-legal base for Roman society was further complicated by the growing necessity to administer conquered territories acquired during the expansionist activities of the Republic.

The effect of the Stoic tradition was felt in two areas: the growth of a legal code and the development of religious ideas that would eventually shape Roman attitudes toward Christianity. At first, it was in the area of law that these Greek ideas took root. As has been noted earlier, Roman Stoicism stressed both humanitarianism and a sort of "public welfare," in contrast to the more austere and personalized credo of the early Stoics such as Zeno.[2] Above all, the Romans were much taken with the idea of a "natural reason" existing at all times for all men. If they did reject the Greek Stoics' obscure theology, they retained this notion of reason as being the common and accessible standard of all mankind. Surely if there were to be means of wisely administering human affairs, it was by turning to this universal reason. With this Zeno would have certainly agreed, even though he did not visualize it in terms of a universal law. It must be remembered that the Romans were never far in their thinking from the issue of political administration. If universal reason existed, it certainly implied a universal law. And this law had the attractive characteristic of being forever and ever the final word.

Here was Law, existing somewhere—perhaps in the sky or in the ether. In any event, it was *not* a human product. It existed independently of what men thought about it; it could not be altered by men. It was an ageless code; whether the creation of God, the gods, or nature, the Romans did not know, but it troubled them little. The problem of law, they reasoned, was one of discovery. The *jus naturale* existed; the job was to investigate it. Happily, the human species came with a built-in device for this discovery: reason. But how could one be sure that human reason would always discover the identical principles? At this point the Roman theorists paused in their reflections and begged the question [3] in a manner thoroughly un-Greek (if you

---

[2] There was much revision of the early Stoic doctrine within Stoicism itself. Of greatest influence on Roman thought was the writing of Panaetius of Rhodes (second century, B.C.).

[3] Begging the question is a common fallacy in argument. In logic it is described as a device contrary to the rules of coherent reasoning in which the response to a given question or statement is implied within the question itself. Example: "Should we exchange our precious freedoms for the bread and circuses of the welfare state?" Therefore a distinction between forms of reason, one of which is already designated as "right," clearly "begs the questions."

hold up Plato and Aristotle as the Greek mean). They held that there was something called "right" reason (presumably to be contrasted with something called "wrong" reason). Because there was a natural link between the law of nature and human reason, there arose from a like origin "right" reason, which could never be misleading. All men's reason, therefore, would lead them to the identical conclusions. It is perhaps unfortunate that such "reasonable" concord has eluded mankind, but the Romans were convinced that a new *humanitas* could be built upon the cornerstone of natural law.

The discovery of natural law did not prove in fact to be as self-evident as it might have appeared in theory. This is arrestingly seen in the development of a legal profession in Rome. Early in the Republic the "each man his own lawyer" system prevailed; judges were in no sense legal professionals, and their adjudications were based on the precept of the equitable and fair—*ex aequo et bono*. This was not only a quite informal standard of judgment, but a thoroughly subjective one as well. This method might have proven very satisfactory save for the fact that natural law was not as universally self-evident as the Stoic-influenced Romans had envisioned. Obviously, the means of discovery were more complex, the eternal truths more deeply veiled from human sight than had been thought.

Reason, then, became somewhat more specialized, and the discovery of a natural law began to assume the aspect of a professional quest. "Lawyers" began to appear, not only in the role of pleaders, but also as judges presiding over civil and criminal disputes. Gradually the natural law became manifest as the result of no small amount of legal scholarship and serious reflection undertaken by these early Roman lawyers. Their skill and dedication should not be underestimated. The system of law they built was perhaps the crowning achievement of Roman civilization. These founders of the legal profession enjoyed the facility and discipline characteristic of Latin culture, and this was tempered by the Stoic sense of dedication and humanitarianism. The Roman law, as it was carried by the crushing force of the legions, had an enormously civilizing effect upon the Western world.

As yet, however, the Roman law was still an informal body of principles, understood generally by the lawyers themselves. But if the natural law was the eternal law, could not this law be written down and combined into a great code of law? This would simplify the job of the judge. His duty then would consist of comparing the facts of the case with the code and adjudicating on the basis of such a comparison. Under the reign of Justinian (483-565), the Roman

Emperor of the East,[4] this great project, the codification of the Roman law was undertaken. Justinian's lawyers, principally Trebonian, labored long and finally produced the *Digest* in 533.

The *Digest* represented the creation of an enduring legal system.[5] These Roman codifications comprise the corpus of what is now termed "Civil Law" [6] and is the basic legal system under which all of Europe, with the exception of Great Britain, is generally governed. The success of this codification can be measured by the fact that only one major revision of it has occurred—the Napoleonic Code of 1804. (One of the fifty United States continues to be governed in part by Roman law via the Napoleonic Code: Louisiana.)

The Roman lawyers were interested in problems of jurisprudence, not political philosophy. But they were mightily influenced by such philosophy. They were particularly led by the most celebrated Roman of the Republic, the noble Cicero (well-known, and perhaps painfully so, by Latin students the world over). Cicero represents the best of that produced by what is termed the "Republic," and, indeed, he fought strenuously to save the ideal of the Republic in the face of the onslaught of oriental-style despotism. He even lent his moral support to the plot that culminated in the assassination of Julius Caesar in 44 B.C. Ironically, he himself was foully murdered by his political enemies.

Cicero (106-43 B.C.)—his full name was Marcus Tullius Cicero—was not born into the upper stratum of Roman society. He was a member of the "Equestrian Order," which made him a "knight" in more modern terminology. He had good connections and was an eager student, and his education included a period of study in Greece. His command of language brought him to the forefront of the legal profession and subsequently into the Roman Senate, where he managed with great adroitness to ride out the sporadic shifts of political power during

---

[4] Under the impact of barbarian invasions, the Western Roman world had become submerged by the middle of the fifth century. But in the East, another "Roman" empire at Constantinople held out until the eleventh century. Justinian not only codified the Roman law, but partially succeeded in his attempt to reunite the old Roman Empire by conquest.

[5] The *Institutes*, a sort of handbook to the Roman law, were also prepared in 533. The *Digest*, the *Institutes*, plus some other material were combined to form the *Corpus Juris Civilis*, the basic Roman law.

[6] The term "Civil Law" (capitalized) refers to the systems of law basically Roman in origin. It should not be confused with "civil law" (lower case) referring to noncriminal proceedings.

his lifetime. Although not specifically linked with the March Assassination (he did not fight with the Republican forces at Philippi), with the passing of the Republic his career was at an end, and his life was taken by a political ambuscade not long afterward.

Cicero was not an original political philosopher in the sense of introducing startling new ideas. He cannot rank in this category with Machiavelli or Hobbes, for example. Rather does Cicero's importance lie in his synthesization of other men's thought and in his ability to spread these ideas through the medium of his most able pen. His writings are of particular interest to the historian of ideas, as well as to the political theorist, since they reflect the values of the period of the Republic.

His political writing—titled, interestingly, the *Republic* and the *Laws*—like most of the political philosophy of the West, was written to further some specific political purpose. This provides a departure from the tradition of Plato and Aristotle, for whom political writing was generally both an abstract project and one designed to cope with fundamental problems and definitions. Cicero was seeking to pump life back into the dying Republic, to revivify its moral temper and its sense of civic responsibility. There was an aloof, almost puritanical streak in Cicero. Influential as he was, he always held back from partisan involvement and remained separated in semiseclusion from the sordid affairs of other men. This Stoic detachment was at once his strength and his weakness. It was his strength in that it permitted him to remain immune from some of the degenerating influences of the Latin life of his time, and it was his weakness in that he did not fully appreciate the impossibility of returning to the brave days of the early Republic.

What had really destroyed the Roman Republic had been the collapse of the mixed state (much as Aristotle had conceived it) as a result of sweeping social change. Yet Cicero sought to restore the mixed state in the face of these social facts. What had caused the estimable balance of the Republic to totter was the rise of the political rabble, manipulatable by opportunists who, as military heroes, became dictators when supported by the unpropertied plebeian element. Even though this trend had not yet reached the excesses that it would under the weaker emperors, the Republic had seen the rise of Marius, Sulla, Pompey, and, finally, Julius. All had brought the constitutional government of Rome to crisis—and principally through popularity. The Republic was shattered by the acceptance of *vox populi* as *Vox Dei*.

Cicero sought to redress the balance, and his principal tool was a romanized Stoicism. With this doctrine he would sound the clarion call of moral commitment, duty, and self-discipline. In practice, these reforms meant for Cicero the return of political control to the aristocratic faction.[7] Such a concept of dedicated aristocracy was soon to be swept away by imperial absolutism, yet it formed the basic governing spirit, if not the principle, for Cicero as it had for Aristotle.

In his effort to redefine the mixed constitutional state, Cicero invokes a philosophy of law more systematized and more comprehensive than any prior to his time. He offers an elaborate description of the natural law. In part, he writes:

> There is in fact a true law—namely, right reason—which is in accordance with nature, applies to all men, and is unchangeable and eternal. By its commands this law summons men to the performance of their duties; by its prohibitions it restrains them from doing wrong. Its commands and prohibitions always influence good men, but are without effect upon the bad. To invalidate this law by human legislation is never morally right, nor is it permissible ever to restrict its operation, and to annul it wholly is impossible. . . . It will not lay down one rule at Rome and another at Athens, nor will it be one rule today and another tomorrow. But there will be one law, eternal and unchangeable, binding at all times upon all peoples; and there will be, as it were, one common master and ruler of men, namely God, who is the author of this law, its interpreter, and its sponsor. The man who will not obey it will abandon his better self, and, in denying the true nature of a man, will thereby suffer the severest of penalties, though he has escaped all the other consequences which men call punishment.[8]

Much of this description is borrowed, more or less wholesale, from late Stoicism, but some aspects of Cicero's general theory are more original. He departs not at all from the Stoic conception of law as the product of divine ordering with its correspondence with the rational nature of man. Present, too, is Stoic concord, rephrased by Cicero in terms of "commonwealth," the moral community of mankind.

It is in the area of the role of popular mandate that Cicero advocates principles which clash head-on with the Platonic-Aristotelian tradi-

---

[7] It is perhaps worth a moment's thought that the artistocracy's sturdiest defenders are often not themselves born into it. To name only a few, Cicero was not a patrician; Burke came from the middle class; Alexander Hamilton's coat of arms bore the bar sinister; Disraeli belonged to an ethnic minority group frequently persecuted in Europe.

[8] Cicero, *Republic,* Book III, Section XXII.

tion. In the first place, Cicero held that all human beings are categorically equal. True, some men are wiser than others and should, individually, have a greater voice on questions of public policy, but men are equal in terms of their essential natures and their possession of reason. This is a view of human equality not unlike that held by the medieval Church. It is not a prescription for social leveling or radical popular democracy; it is rather a metaphysical assertion about the universality of human nature. Being equal in this sense, all men are equally subject to natural law and can avail themselves of its implied protection. In opposition to Aristotle, as it certainly is, in asserting a comprehensive equality, this doctrine is not, at the same time, a proposal to abolish political distinctions between persons. Cicero viewed equality in an abstract sense, not in practical terms of leveling all to one common stratum of political and social prerogative.

The natural law being the divine plan, the state is not above the law, contends Cicero, nor is it merely the embodiment of the law. The constitutional state is below the law, which regulates all men, all states, and the relationships between men and states. Since the state is subordinate to the natural law, the state cannot at will proceed to act at variance with it. Laws of a governmental character—*jus civile*—rely for their validity upon the natural law and, hence, if the law of the state contravenes the higher law, it is invalid. Cicero is not very specific as to the appropriate actions if the state does proceed to act in defiance of natural law. Who is to be the arbiter? There is surely no provision for the citizenry to undertake rebellion against an unlawful state.[9]

This raises the interesting question as to where the natural law resides. It is not enough to answer that the natural law exists in letters of fire writ large upon the heavens. What Cicero argues is that the natural law does *not* reside *in* the state. The natural law resides in nature, but finds its expression in the collective reason of men, through the people of the state, if you will. Therefore, since legitimate power depends upon the law, political authority resides in the collective body of the citizenry. In this sense, the state and its positive law are the common holdings of all, and political rule must arise from the moral community where rests the authority of the higher law. The state is a public affair—*res publica*—and all citizens are "stockholders."

One can easily grasp the directions that Ciceronian thought is

---

[9] No one would seriously argue that a citizenry was legally entitled to rebel against illegitimate authority until the *Policrates* of John of Salisbury in 1159.

taking. It sounds like a preview of the eighteenth century. Its emphasis upon the commonwealth as the locus of political authority and its concept of the legal state as acknowledging the higher sovereignty of natural law move political thought into a new era. The legalistic cast given by Cicero and the Roman lawyers to the question of political power colors all political thought until the late Renaissance. The ideals of the constitutional republic advanced by Cicero were soon submerged in the gory history of the Empire and the chaos of feudal decentralization, but their impact upon the corpus of Roman law kept them indirectly alive, especially as that law was perpetuated by the canon law of the medieval Church, wherein Thomas Aquinas and others would revive some elements of Ciceronian thought. He was the first definitely to espouse the proposition that just rule arises from the people who are governed.

Six centuries pass between the era of Cicero and the *Digest* of Justinian, but the intervening period, particularly the second and third centuries, A.D., saw the Roman law grow into a cogent and refined system. The Justinian Code, as we have noted, rested upon the *jus naturale*, but also incorporated subordinate levels of law.[10] Beneath the *jus naturale* was *jus gentium*—the "law of nations." This should not be confused with what we now call "international law;" the *jus gentium* was rather the law common to all men, irrespective of their cultural practices or civil law. The third level of law, the *jus civile*, was the actual legal enactments of states and the traditional social observances of peoples. These levels of law were clearly hierarchical; all law flowed from natural law, and all civil law had to consist of the application of the broader principles of natural law to specific civic concerns. Obviously there is no reference in the Justinian Code to traffic regulation, but this would be a superfluous criticism of it from the standpoint of a Roman lawyer. As a need to regulate motor vehicles arose, a political community formulated necessary law, but the principles of such law would have no sanction outside of natural law and would be formulated upon it. All positive law is based on natural law.

From Cicero's concept of equality the Justinian Code developed a doctrine that we would be apt to call "equality before the law," which has become an integral part of both common and civil law. Even mentioned are something called "rights." These are not the "natural rights"

---

[10] The terminology which follows is that found in Cicero's writing.

of John Locke, but the Justinian Code assumed that, given the common brotherhood of men—*universitas*—all men, having status before the law, have rights which involve the protection of that law. This is not a right to something (e.g., freedom of speech, assembly, etc.), but a right to be protected from injustice, to receive fair treatment, and, broadly, to be entitled to one's due, including life itself. Even slavery became legally regulated. The Justinian Code led to many specific reforms, but its longer range impact was to place, in principle, unequivocal legal limits upon the exercise of power. This was a far different approach from the use of the Nocturnal Council.

Seneca (4? B.C.-65 A.D.), like Cicero, acknowledged an intellectual inheritance from the Greek Stoics. True to his Stoic orientation, Seneca bore adversity with dignity—and he had much to put up with. His was an unhappy life, and perhaps his philosophy bears the stamp of his introspective gloom. Being the tutor to the Emperor Nero was hardly a choice assignment. The pious Seneca was not even permitted to die in a quiet and leisurely fashion; he was compelled to take his own life. It is noteworthy perhaps that two of the three thinkers discussed in this chapter met with violent ends. This might be put forth as evidence that philosophizing is a risky business or at least that philosophers are hardly immune from the trials and dangers of the common market place. As comedian Mort Sahl has put it: "Philosophers are people who would be in jail if they were politicians." Philosophers often are politicians, and not infrequently have they resided in jails or worse.

But Seneca had no wish to be a politician; he was just unfortunate enough to be associated with the paranoiac Nero. Nero himself is one to be pitied, if you are broad-minded, as he was the victim of a home life so depraved as to defy description—or at least such a description as would stay within the bounds of propriety for a standard textbook. Seneca longed for a life of detachment and uninterrupted repose. Like many who are of a sensitive nature, he was appalled and disillusioned by what he saw about him. One might hazard the opinion that being an observer of the domestic contretemps of Nero would be enough to appall even the insensitive. In any event, Seneca reveals a deeply ingrained pessimism and a sort of subdued horror at the depravity of which man is capable.

Such reactions occasioned in Seneca both a rejection of the world of temporal affairs and a Ciceronian faith in the powers of civil government. While these ideas are interlinked, it may be best to consider them apart. It would have been understandable for Seneca's disillusionment to take the form of recluse-like withdrawal. Such was not the case, due mainly to his notion of the nature of evil. His deep-seated impression that temporal existence affords vast opportunities for human depravity prompted him to revert to a religiously conceived Stoicism, to which he added an almost pre-Christian belief in the fragile significance of worldly existence as contrasted with the status of the soul after death. But this preoccupation with the eventual condition of the soul did not mean for him a rejection of the world. The world presented an arena for the propagation of evil, which could and must be combated by human dedication to moral ideals and to religious faith. Evil became for Seneca something more than the absence of good; it was a formidable force against which men of good will and purpose struggle. And it was the duty of the good man to struggle and to repel the entreaties of evil, an evil capable of the corruption of individuals and societies.

Civil society and the arrangements of government were inadequate to the chore of containing evil and keeping chaste the morals of men. Governments could not make men good; they could not even do much to provide the conditions under which men could grow morally. Here, Seneca reflects, Cicero placed too much trust in worldly institutions. What could governments be expected to do? They could play only a negative role; they could enforce moral rectitude by coercion. They could curb overt sinning. Greed, passion, and lust must often be curbed by governmental interference. (Seneca doubtless would have approved of antismut ordinances and early tavern closing.) Law, too, was an instrument of moral regulation; but in a broader sense law and government were mere devices, in themselves without faith in the existence of a higher order of providence, faith in something more than *jus naturale,* even without faith in the loose theology of the Stoics and Neoplatonists. According to Seneca, God is more than a mere Lawgiver; He is the Creator of "worlds within worlds," and in this conviction Seneca returns to the older Stoic dualism, but embellishes it and adds to its dimensions.

For Seneca there was first the dualism between the natural world and the supernatural realm of divine providence. But upon this fundamental dualism there rested another. Within the temporal world itself there were two orders. The first of these was the civil state. The second was a vaster and more significant community, the moral commonwealth. It was almost a religious brotherhood; it was a refurbishing of the Stoic idea of the universal commonwealth, but it contained a much more intense theological spirit. It was the realm of God's intervention into the world. Seneca's "two commonwealths" stand midway between the Stoic position and that of Augustine, who depicts a similar dualism in Christian terminology in *The City of God.* The important distinction to retain is that Seneca's moral commonwealth is clearly separate from such civil institutions as governments. It is more significant because its base is in God's nature. Further, it operates outside the realm of man-made society; its purposes are not equivalent to the purposes of even a just government.

This schism is of extreme importance both historically and ideologically Seneca's ideas are a bridge between the temporal rationalism of the Greco-Roman Period and the theology-centered culture that blossomed with the rise of Christianity. The Roman moralist was moving toward the separation of Church and Empire that marked the beginning of the medieval age. His vaguely emerging view of the dual commonwealth had three significant consequences: first, if human society involves a dual commonwealth, individual members of that society face the problem of dual membership. A man is at once a member of a civil society and of a religious brotherhood. But what if this dual membership implies differing obligations and loyalties? Which membership enjoys first call? Seneca implies clearly that the religious community is preëminent, but if this is the case, a drastic alteration has taken place in the most essential premises of Greek and Roman political philosophy. Where is the *polis?* What has happened to the principle of citizenship and the unreserved participation of the individual in the sociopolitical community? Man has been split apart.

Secondly, Seneca's two commonwealths imply a sharper separation of social functions than he likely envisioned. If we pursue his reasoning to its inevitable conclusion, no other dictum is possible than that the civil authority ceases to be a moral agent except in the negative sense of suppressing vice and chastizing evildoers. Such a separation reduces secular political authority to the limits of keeping order and supplying necessary, if mundane, community services. It denies to the state the role of ultimate principle of moral order that it had assumed from Plato to Cicero.

Lastly, if Seneca's second commonwealth requires devotion and adherence, this presupposes some measure of authority—although Seneca himself does not press it this far. A dual commonwealth suggests a dual structure of organization. So long as Seneca remains essentially a Stoic, convinced of the adequacy of the individual ethic and humanitarian sensitivity, the idea of authority need not intrude. But with later Christian thinkers, the dual commonwealth demands the creation of ecclesiastical authority and organization, and out of this springs the Church as a semiautonomous realm within the society.

In the last analysis, Seneca's importance lies in his heralding a religious consciousness that would envelop Europe for a thousand years. His philosophy well launches the assault on the secularism of the Greco-Roman world; his view of a mandate higher than the political begins the process of reshaping the definition of the state. This conviction that the state operates within operational limits imposed by the existence of a more legitimate religious commitment arises from a radically revised estimation of human nature. Seneca hints that man is a "fallen" creature, much in the same vein as does later Christian theology. If man for Plato and Aristotle was either wise or foolish, man for Seneca could not be discussed in terms of wisdom. Wisdom, indeed, was a rather pallid virtue. Man shared a common inheritance from God, but man was also universally prone to do evil, to lapse morally, to fall from grace. His redemption was not intellectual; it was spiritual. Moreover, frequently the very instrumentalities of the worldly order, such as governments, schools, and so forth, were responsible for the fallen state of mankind, since they bemused men into thinking that their spiritual communion was of trifling importance. Seneca went so far as to argue in his *Letters* that man's fall could be traced to his corruption from a prehistorical state of natural innocence.[11] Societies and governments meant fleshpots and temptations. In any case, man's moral redemption could not be accomplished through the possession of wisdom; no matter how enlightened the government, no matter how cultivated the society, these institutions belonged to the civil commonwealth and could not effect moral renovation. The state could not make men good; it could only partially curb them from being bad.

If the civil commonwealth could not redeem man, how was the

---

[11] The French eighteenth-century philosopher Rousseau would expand on this idea and carry it to rather rhapsodic extremes. Too, it is curious to note the prevalence throughout Western thought of the idea of knowledge as a corrupter of human innocence. Even in Greek mythology it appears (e.g., the punishment of Prometheus). It is common in many Christian theologies, particularly in more primitive Protestantism. The Devil is depicted as a purveyor of knowledge (Lucifer means "Light-bringer"). The common word "erotic" refers to lust and sensual indulgence, frequently connoting aberration. Yet its Greek stem *eros* or "worldly love" prominently included a love of wisdom and learning.

religious community to do so? The Christian Church after Augustine
had a firm answer. Man could not redeem himself; he was the product
of the Original Sin of Adam. Only God through His Grace could
effect redemption. The religious commonwealth, however, realized in
the Church, was a divine agency and combined both didactic and
punitive functions designed to preserve man so that he might receive
the blessings of Grace. The idea of good works remained, and the
religious commonwealth assumed a variety of social responsibilities
shaped to ameliorate man's moral shortcomings—activities previously
encompassed by the state.

Seneca, however, was far less specific than this; he was not yet
armed with the elaborate metaphysic of Christianity. His concept of
the religious commonwealth did not include Grace, but rather a sense
of spiritual communion among men that might lift them up from
worldly sins. It was an interesting blend of Stoicism with elements of
Neoplatonism. Seneca's thought was severe in tone and, consequently,
unpopular. His depiction of the spiritual world lacked the dramatic
imagery of a St. Paul. His supernaturalism was tentative and lacking
in concreteness as compared with the vividness of the early Christians.
Seneca's following was made up of introspective and sensitive intellectuals, not the urban slum-dwellers who marched singing into the
Colosseum convinced of the promised paradise to come for believers.
Yet Seneca, more perhaps than any other man in the crumbling Roman
world, articulated the coming separation of Church and Empire.

Seneca had seen Imperial Rome in full flower, past her intellectual
prime but still clothed in elegance. St. Augustine (354-430), the
Bishop of Hippo, watched from his North African bishopric the
Eternal City's downfall and actual destruction at the hands of Alaric
in 410. He watched a world collapsing, a world of classical splendor
and pagan philosophy, and he foresaw the creation of a Christianized
Europe. He himself had belonged to both worlds and, being of a
vigorous and assertive temperament, lived in each to the fullness of
his being. His origins were pagan and his early inclinations decidedly
worldly. He was born in a Roman colony not far from Carthage, and
his early years were given over to conventional pleasure-seeking and
less conventional scholarship. As a young man, Augustine flitted about
with a variety of philosophic positions, arriving essentially at Neoplatonism. In his remarkable and candid book, the Confessions,
written after he embraced Christianity, Augustine describes this im-

mature period of intellectual wandering, his pervading doubts, and even his follies. The turning point in his development came when he journeyed across the Mediterranean to be a pupil of the great Ambrose of Milan; [12] it was as a result of this experience that he joined the Christian Church. He was returned to North Africa as a priest and, after becoming Bishop of Hippo, spent the remainder of his life writing and most conscientiously waging war—both philosophic and actual—upon a variety of current heresies. He was at once a thinker and an activist.

There is a completeness and tidiness about Augustine's view of the world that is lacking in Seneca's, and it grows from Augustine's Christian training. He need not draw back from the miraculous, the prescient, or the incredible. Observes Augustine:

> . . . Cicero chooses to reject the foreknowledge of future things, and shuts up the religious mind to this alternative, to make the choice between two things, either that something is in our own power, or that there is foreknowledge,—both of which cannot be true; but if the one is affirmed, the other is thereby denied. He therefore, like a truly great and wise man, and one who consulted very much and very skilfully for the good of humanity, of those two chooses the freedom of the will, to confirm which he denied the foreknowledge of future things; and thus, wishing to make men free, he makes them sacrilegious.[13]

After chiding Cicero on his logical circumspection, Augustine offers this counterargument:

> Now, against the sacrilegious and impious darlings of reason, we assert both that God knows all things before they come to pass, and that we do by our free will whatsoever we know and feel to be done by us only because we will it.[14]

From the fragments above you can perhaps catch a clue to one of the most provocative characteristics of Augustine's thought. It is his attention to the question of human nature. There is a curious feature about his major work, *City of God,* and that is that his description of

[12] Ambrose (340?-397) deserves further mention in his own right. As Bishop of Milan in the latter half of the fourteenth century he combined the qualities of an ecclesiastic and a shrewd politician. And the times demanded the latter. His particular fame rests on his resolute championing of the autonomy of the Church and its freedom from interference by temporal authorities. In this struggle he was both bold and implacable, and his belief that the Church had its own independent sphere of authority even brought him into conflict with the Emperor Valentinian from which he emerged unhumbled.

[13] Augustine, *City of God,* Book V, Chapter 9.
[14] *Ibid.*

the world proceeds both up and down—that is to say, he constructs
the order of the world from the premise of God's sovereignty on the
one hand and then builds upward by asserting that the order of the
world is equally the result of the nature of human beings, such nature
of course being of divine origin as well. From this the impression is
clear that God is immanent in the Augustinian world; He pervades
it from top to bottom.

Augustine's view of human nature is the result of a combination of
influences. Reinhold Niebuhr has described Augustine as the "first
great realist in Western history." [15] By this, he implies that Augustine
was the first to grasp comprehensively the complexities, the passions,
the myriad acrimonies that are present in human behavior. Whether
or not Augustine was the first is an academic question, but it is certainly true that he had seen the less attractive sides of life at close
range and had few illusions about the difficulties involved in the
moral, religious, and political management of human beings. This
certainly gave Augustine an acute sense of human evil, but it neither
caused in him a barren pessimism nor a rejection of worldly concerns.
He was not even as exercised over the passions of the flesh as was
Seneca and retained a rather wholesome respect for the temporal
side of human nature. If human flesh is heir to sin, then Augustine
condemns pride, vanity, and egocentricity as the paramount corruptions. He once commented that it was less sinful to be a "woman of
the streets" than a pious matron, absorbed in her sin of pride and
moral vanity. Rather does Augustine extol the power of love, true
love having its genesis in the love of God and of God's creatures. In
this way, he avoids splitting human nature into a "soul" and a "depraved flesh," a dualism too frequently encountered in some Christian
moralists. If man is to be divided, it must be not on the basis of soul
versus body, but upon the basis of "good souls" and "evil souls." The
evil soul is one essentially turned toward love of self and not toward
love of God and humanity. This is a somewhat personalized view of
evil, and Augustine dodges any description of the world as a battle-

---

[15] A distinction should be made between the political and philosophic meanings
of the term "realist." In the more popular political meaning, a realist is one who
generally takes a hard-boiled view of political and social affairs. He is one whose
views are uninhibited by sentimentalism or moral predispositions; he is frequently
highly sensitive to the factor of power. In philosophy, on the other hand, a realist
is one who embraces realism, a broad conviction regarding the nature of knowledge
that maintains that universals exist and that perceived objects have an objective
existence independent of the perceiver.

ground between institutionalized Good versus institutionalized Evil.[16] Yet the individual person is the arena for a struggle between an evil will and the love of God. Augustine has frequently been misread on this point, primarily because some commentators have taken too literally his view of evil as a will, the implied difference between body and soul, and the distinction between the "Earthly" and "Heavenly" cities. It would perhaps be better to say that man has two loves—himself (which is essentially evil) and God (Who is essentially good).

From this base, Augustine argues that man belongs to two communities: an Earthly City founded upon egocentricity and a Heavenly City resting upon the love of God. It is true that Augustine refers to the Earthly City as the realm of Satan and vaguely identifies it with earlier pagan empires, but the Earthly City—the kingdom of evil—is not an institution; it is an historical-theological conception. It is historical because history itself is an account of the struggle of the Earthly City to turn men from their view of the City of God, where peace and redemption await. Likewise, the Heavenly City, the City of God, is a society existing not in time-space, but in the universal spirit of divine love that will in the end vanquish egocentricity and avarice. Its victory is inevitable; God's commonwealth will in the end prove irresistible because such is God's plan for the world.

There are several more concrete conclusions drawn from this schema by Augustine that affect the actual ordering of political institutions. In the first place, according to Augustine, all attempts at political organization are doomed to failure unless they are founded upon the rock of Christianity. Moreover, justice without the Christian mandate is impossible. The Heavenly City, while it cannot be fully realized on this earth, must serve as the basis for civil society. All else is evil; all non-Christian civilizations are but satanic pawns, because they fail to embrace the love of the Christian for God. Government, then, arises from the concept of the Heavenly City, and in this way the two cities are intermingled in the affairs of men in the same fashion as men belong to both.

---

[16] In this connection, it might be added that Augustine sought to refute the Manichean heresy, a theological persuasion in which he was briefly interested early in his life. Manicheanism was the concept that the world was being contested for by two powerful adversaries, Good and Evil, and that they were essentially evenly matched and that the issue was still in doubt. This view of evil was vigorously rejected by the Christian Church, which viewed Satan and his host not as equal belligerents with God, but as tempters indirectly serving the omnipotent God.

If lasting and beneficial political arrangements must be founded upon the vision of the Heavenly City, what about the Church? There is some dispute among scholars as to the degree to which Augustine viewed the Church as the embodiment of the City of God.[17] A fair appraisal might be that Augustine did not think of the Church as the Heavenly City set down on this planet but that he did conceive of the Church as the indispensable social institution instigated by God as the prime means of furthering the eventual coming of the Heavenly City. Augustine makes it clear that "history" means the history of the Christian Church. There is no question about the fact that the Church was a far closer approximation of divine will than the state, and, although Augustine does not say so, the state would seem to serve much less lofty ends. Beyond this, Augustine was a fervent advocate of Church organization and the furtherance of its institutional influences. The Church, for him, was the instrument of salvation, since it both taught the love of God and represented the total community of those who were joined to God. The destiny of man was the destiny of the Church.

The *City of God* exerted massive influence on the Church's development and provided ecclesiastical weapons in the later battles against secular authority. The power of Augustine's message cast all European institutions into the Christian mold, and where he hesitated to press his reasoning into the area of temporal political affairs, there were others who would do so and who would preserve the vision of the dual commonwealth on into the modern period. Long after Rome had perished and nationalism had dismembered the Catholic religious community, the forces set in motion by Augustine remained visible. After all, as late as the eighteenth century there was the "Holy Roman Empire"—but, alas, as Voltaire supposedly pointed out, "it was neither holy nor Roman nor an empire." But the Bishop of Hippo dealt a crushing blow to the concept of the state as a moral agent—even Hegel and cohorts could not long revive this classical outlook.

If Augustine had convinced the thinking world that there were two commonwealths and that men belonged to both, the puzzling question was: "To which does a man owe his first loyalty and obedience?" If

---

[17] Roman Catholic writers tend to interpret Augustine as maintaining that the Church was the Heavenly City transplanted, while Protestant analysts take the position that he made a visible distinction and even laid the foundation for the eventual Reformation.

Augustine had not in fact intended to depict temporal authority and ecclesiastical authority as the Earthly City and the Heavenly City, there were others who viewed the dual commonwealth in this way. The world was for them divided between the Church and the State. But which was to be foremost? At first it appeared that a political scramble for power might be avoided. Surely there was apparent division of labor. The Church was interested in the care of souls, and the State was concerned with the social and political activities of its subjects. Could not the two coexist? [18]

In the long run the answer was "no." Divided authority is always a delicate business, as, indeed, the United States discovered in the growth of its federal system. A number of factors brought the truce, always a shaky one, to an end. Popes and bishops became inordinately ambitious in ways not quite in keeping with the priestly virtue of humility. Further, the Church soon branched out into areas distinctly secular, such as the management of land holdings, diplomatic representation, the launching of military projects, and the accumulation of extensive wealth. Then, too, there was the problem of the wicked ruler, the prince who chose to violate the moral precepts of Christianity—at least as they were articulated by the clergy. From the other side, secular rulers cast envious eyes at the political opportunities afforded by bringing ecclesiastical affairs under their aegis.

As this question affected the majority of people, the Christian principle of obedience and forbearance had to remain a guide. In the last half of the sixth century, Pope Gregory I decried the wickedness and tyranny of despotic rulers, but held that the Christian must not take it upon himself to disobey temporal authority even if that authority were used in an unjust and oppressive fashion. Christians were used to suffering and, indeed, their preoccupation should be with the afterlife and its rewards. Life in this world was a time of trial and testing; "rendering unto Caesar the things that are Caesar's" required that the secular rule go unquestioned, although such obedience need not be more than passive acquiescence, silent forbearance. Advocating private judgment, it was felt, could usher in all manner of dangerous precedents. Gregory further exhorted bishops to refrain from med-

---

[18] A temporary solution to this problem was provided by Pope Gelasius (?-496), who proclaimed papal independence on the basis of the "Doctrine of the Two Swords": The spheres of the Church (*sacerdotium*) and the State (*imperium*) are separate and need not impinge and both were autonomous. He did suggest, however, that since the Church was in charge of souls, it followed that it must be in charge of the souls of the rulers, too. Gelasius' claims were later expanded and the balance upset.

dling in political affairs; but this was a rather hopeless admonition.

If the Christian's duty was summary obedience to political authority, however despotic, this did not solve the issue of primary loyalty. Suppose that a ruler demanded acts jeopardizing the soul of the individual. Should the subject obey? Surely a man's immortal soul came first, the clergy asserted. And who, they asked, is logically in a position to decide when a given act constitutes a violation of the mandate of God? Here the issue of ultimate authority came to the fore.

The most telling argument in the ecclesiastical armory, however, was the proposition that since rulers, too, have souls, the care of these is also within the scope of the Church. Bishops, then, were the moral and spiritual judges of temporal rulers. But the reverse was surely the case insofar as the Church sought to act outside its declared province, in areas wholly unrelated to their sacred mission. Who but the Church, however, could define the limits of its mission? Who could and should finally decide what is ecclesiastical and what is secular?

These were formidable arguments, given the basic premise of a dual commonwealth. The secular rulers would make reply—not in the parochial logic of churchmen, but in the empirical language of historical momentum and political reality.

. . . for further discussion:

1. Natural law is one explanation for the rise of law in human society. It rests law upon a concept of a rational universe. Do you think this is a valid assumption? What arguments can you think of to refute the notion of natural law? What differences do you think might be suggested between natural law as Cicero thought of it and "laws of nature" as Newton might have conceived them? What alternative explanations could be advanced to account for the development of law?

2. Cicero maintained that all men are equal and yet that this metaphysical equality need not imply political equality. This view was accepted by the Middle Ages, too. But is this a consistent position? If men are naturally equal and political institutions, like society itself, are also natural, how can political inequality be logically defended?

3. Seneca and the early churchmen were much preoccupied with the matter of evil. They were not satisfied with the Greek notion that evil was the absence of good. But if evil is not the absence of good, it must be something. What are the possible explanations for the nature of evil? Is evil, however defined, a necessary concept to be kept in mind in framing political theory? If politics is the pursuit of power and such a pursuit of

power is contrary to the Christian ideal of humility and simplicity, is not politics inherently a "fallen" activity, more in the province of Satan than of God?

4. Is the "problem of evil," in the Augustinian sense, a political problem?

. . . *for further investigation:*

Augustine, *City of God,* M. Dodds, trans. 1887. Vol. II of *A Select Library of Nicene and Post-Nicene Fathers of the Christian Church,* 14 vols., P. Schoff, ed. New York: Charles Scribner's Sons, 1886-1890.

Bailey, Cyril, ed., *The Legacy of Rome.* New York: Oxford University Press, Inc., 1924.

Cairns, Huntington, *Legal Philosophy from Plato to Hegel.* Baltimore, Md.: The Johns Hopkins Press, 1950.

Declaureuil, J., *Rome the Lawgiver.* New York: Alfred A. Knopf, Inc., 1926.

d'Entreves, A. P., *Natural Law.* New York: Hillary House Publishers, Ltd., 1951.

Grant, Michael, * *The World of Rome.* New York: Mentor Books, 1961.

Greene, William C., *The Achievement of Rome.* Cambridge, Mass.: Harvard University Press, 1934.

Jolowicz, Herbert F., *Historical Introduction to Roman Law.* New York: Cambridge University Press, 1952.

Pickman, E. M., *The Mind of Latin Christendom.* New York: Oxford University Press, Inc., 1937.

Sabine, G. and S. B. Smith, eds., *On the Commonwealth: Marcus Tullius Cicero.* Columbus, Ohio: Ohio State University Press, 1929.

5

THE MEDIEVAL
PANOPLY

Although historians have done their best to dispel the idea, the notion persists that the Middle Ages comprise a sort of vacant section in the human record. The phrase "Dark Ages" sticks in the mind, summoning up images of feudal chaos, barbarism, decline of art and the gentle graces, and, even more significantly, the virtual cessation of intellectual activity. The picture is not only overdrawn, but is in substantial error. It is in fact possible to describe the medieval period as an era of great energy and even of the spirit of reform. Henry Adams, a man of many sides, had what could best be described as a love affair with the eleventh century, and he minced no words in picturing the vigor and even restless creativity of that time:

> Never has the Western world shown anything like the energy and unity with which she then flung herself on the East, and for the moment made the East recoil. Barring her family quarrels, Europe was a unity then, in thought, will, and object. Christianity was the unit.

Mont-Saint-Michel and Byzantium were near each other. The Emperor Constantine and the Emperor Charlemagne were figured as allies and friends in the popular legend. The East was the common enemy, always superior in wealth and numbers, frequently in energy, and sometimes in thought and art. The outburst of the first crusade was splendid even in a military sense, but it was great beyond comparison in its reflection in architecture, ornament, poetry, colour, religion, and philosophy. Its men were astonishing, and its women were worth all the rest.[1]

Whether or not one chooses to agree with Adams' glowing appraisal of the merits of the eleventh century, he is certainly correct in commenting that "Christianity was the unit." It is understandable, then, that the spirit of reform and change which eventually reached its peak in the thirteenth century and paved the way for the glories of the Renaissance occurred within the framework of the puissant Church. Reforms within the Church triggered reforms in the secular realm. The founding of Church communities, especially the Benedictine abbeys at Cluny and Citeaux, provided models of Christian decorum and communal harmony that cast a curious rebuke to the indulgent, corrupt, and comfort-loving ecclesiastical hierarchy. The sterner admonitions of Augustine were remembered. Eventually this zeal for internal reform would blossom into a serious challenge to papal authority[2] and later into the Reformation itself.

Coupled with both reformist tendencies and a mounting intellectual restlessness within the Church, the energies of the Middle Ages were directed toward upsetting the happy compromise of the Two Swords, the neat division of the world into the realms of the spiritual or ecclesiastical and the secular or imperial. As we have already seen, the supporters of the Church position sponsored the subtle argument that, while the two realms are independent, priests, being charged with the care of souls, must prevail over kings and princes.

This argument did not go unmet. It went unassailed for as long as it did primarily because there was no one to question the higher authority of the Church over matters directly governmental. The Church had the vast advantage of being a going concern, a well-oiled instrument of influence, and, as Adams pointed out, it was the unifying factor in a divided Europe. Opposing the Church's will on an

---

[1] Henry Adams, *Mont-Saint-Michel and Chartres* (New York: Mentor Books, 1961), p. 45.

[2] Internal reform of Church organization reached its fullest extent in the fifteenth century with the Conciliar Movement, which would have limited papal authority by a form of canonical "constitutional government" featuring a General Council as the executive head. Perhaps the best-known name associated with this movement is Nicholas of Cusa.

operational level were the fragmented political entities created by feudalism and the tenuous grip held by kings on vanishing and reappearing kingdoms.

Early attempts to assert the imperial position against the authority of the Church (almost invariably in the person of the Pope) involved the investiture problem—who had the authority to create bishops? It should be remembered that this was no mean prize. Bishops were far more than kindly old pastors shepherding their dioceses; they were political figures of influence, and it was a matter of vital need for shaky kings and emperors to buttress their positions by the appointment of sympathetic and loyal bishops. Indeed, "Prince-Bishops" were feudal magnates controlling both the political and ecclesiastical administration of large blocks of Europe. So-called "lay investiture" had been a customary perquisite of monarchs until Pope Gregory VII banned the practice in 1075. Emperor Henry IV,[3] supported by his own publicists, asserted that the monarch's authority was derived directly from God and that in consequence it was beyond the right of the Church to question such authority. The Emperor was answerable to God, not to popes. The issue of investiture was really a superficial one and was susceptible of compromise, but the deeper issues lying at the root of the dispute were to occupy the attention of Europe for a half-dozen centuries to come. Was the Church to be independent of secular authority, a political realm unto itself? What was the authority of the monarch, and what were the limits, if any, to his powers?

Against this backdrop of institutional struggle and released reformist energies, the main political ideas of the medieval period emerged. It must be recalled that as yet these ideas were not yet distilled into "pure" political theory. If the Greeks and the Romans were convinced that political ideas were variants of the broader theme of ethics, the thinkers of the medieval period were equally convinced that political considerations were but a part of theology. We have yet to encounter the notion that political philosophy involves unique conceptions separate from moral or religious thought. We must be content for a time with discerning the flow of political ideas as it is channeled through the language of ethics and theology.

---

[3] Henry enjoyed the title of "Holy Roman Emperor" and claimed to deserve acknowledgment as the secular ruler of Christian Europe. In fact, the Holy Roman Empire, a concept stemming from the investment of Charlemagne in the eighth century, was a myth, and Henry IV clung to a federation of German principalities as his domain.

But theology was far from being a settled body of dogma. The Middle Ages are a delight for anyone inordinately fond of the niceties of dispute; perhaps the thirteenth century is the high water mark in the history of elaborate argumentation. While it is sadly nothing but a myth that at this time scholars argued on the question of how many angels could stand on the head of a pin, the fabled debate does convey some of the flavor of the argument of the period. This restless intellectualism and vivid sense of controversy were centered about those astonishing institutions, the new universities, the pride of the thirteenth century. Paris, Bologna, Oxford, and other college towns became arenas in which the ideas of the age were born and matured. In truth, these were astonishing institutions. Founded as appendices to the Church, they soon became organs with a strong corporate sense—even a fierce independence—and the devotion to individualist values that was characteristic of the philosophic revival of the thirteenth century. Rapid in growth and free in spirit, the medieval universities became like water taps, flooding Europe with scholars developed under their influence. These influences are important in themselves; the universities bred doctrinal flexibility, a keen interest in the new "science," and even a secularism more real than apparent. Moreover, it was in the universities, especially Paris, that philosophy emerged as a separate branch of knowledge, finally shorn from the tree of theology.[4] With philosophy pushing out, then, as a distinct field of inquiry, men arose proud of the distinction of being philosophers. The period shone with now famous names: Thomas Aquinas, Duns Scotus, Albertus Magnus, Roger Bacon—to list but four.

But was the distinction between philosophy and theology an actual one? Were philosophical questions entirely discrete from ones involving God, Grace, Divine Law, and so forth? The answer is obviously "no." It would have been unthinkable to suppose at this time that the speculative content of philosophy could proceed without the tacit assumption of the Christian view of creation. But within this limit, philosophic battle raged unabated, and by the end of the thirteenth century political questions had moved to the forefront of the new philosophy.

What provided the primary impetus for these political as well as

---

[4] Such a schism did, in fact, formally take place at the University of Paris. After a long dispute, the Faculty of Theology was separated from the faculties of law, medicine, and arts.

philosophic speculations was the translation of Aristotle into Latin.[5] It would be difficult to overestimate the impact of Aristotle on the intellectual scene. He reshaped the medieval mind and gave it a sense of direction, while substantially revitalizing a flagging Christianity. But medieval thought was receptive to Aristotle because it was conditioned for it. The teaching of the Stagirite found a ready soil because the ground had been prepared. In the first place, the key to medieval thought might well be described as an abiding interest in the role of the *person* and the examination of the nature and capacities of the human being. Aristotle's preoccupation with a similar humanism made his thought immediately understood and appreciated by medieval scholars.

Secondly, medieval thought had by the thirteenth century taken on a distinctly rationalistic tone. The Church reformers, concerned with canonical law and corporate structure, had approached their tasks with a deductive method which fit in well with the systematic exposition of Aristotle. Was it chance that Aristotle's *Logic* was the first of his works to be translated?

Thirdly, Aristotle was the first philosopher of science, and science was in process of a rapid "rediscovery" in the medieval world. Aristotle's fascination with the machinery of the universe was seconded by an age suddenly reaware of the mysteries of the natural world.

Lastly, the split between philosophy and theology notwithstanding, the medieval intellect was groping hesitantly toward synthesis, toward a unification of knowledge, toward a master plan combining the human faculties. Before the reintroduction of Aristotle, medieval scholars had been busy in attempts to classify human knowledge, and Aristotle was not only the philosopher of synthesis, but he provided the schema as well. The medieval thinkers took it over, adapted it for their own purposes, but essentially accepted the grand design as Aristotle had conceived it.

Out of the intellectual reawakening, then, out of the move for reform, out of the break-off of philosophy, out of the reappearance of Aristotle, there came the dominant philosophy of the late medieval period: *Scholasticism*. It is a broad concept of thought, complete with subschools and the usual heresies. It produced doctrines that run the

---

[5] By the end of the thirteenth century the translation was complete. The *Politics* is believed to have been translated in 1260 by William of Moerbek at the express suggestion of Aquinas.

gamut of human concerns; it rendered judgments on metaphysics and
city planning, on the task of the ruler and the education of children.
Political thought appeared late in its development, largely due to the
continued assumption that political questions are invariably predicated
on theological or metaphysical ones. It is impossible, and for our purposes unnecessary, to examine Scholasticism in all its varied aspects,
but an attempt should be made to outline the main features of its
approach to the subject of political philosophy.

All the Scholastic thinkers appeared concerned about five aspects
of political thought: (1) unity, (2) the status of the individual, (3)
law, (4) authority, and, (5) the structure of the state.[6]

By *unity*, they meant unity of two sorts. First, they were convinced
that the first principle of the universe was Unity, that Unity being
God. In a less metaphysical sense, this principle of oneness, which
Otto Gierke has described as the "Constitutive Principle of the
Universe,"[7] is apparent in the world, which, while it exhibits many
diverse elements, is in fact a whole, the parts being subordinate to
the principle of unity. This line of thought can be pressed further to
argue that while the "plural" world moves toward the Unity (God),
elements of this plurality contain their own partial unities. Thus, for
instance, mankind is a partial whole distinct from individual men.
Gierke comments:

> Mankind is one "mystical body;" it is one single, and internally con-
> nected "people" or "folk;" it is an all-embracing corporation (*universi-*
> *tas*) which constitutes that Universal Realm, spiritual and temporal,
> which may be called the Universal Church (*ecclesia universalis*),
> or, with equal propriety, the Commonwealth of the Human Race
> (*respublica generis humani*). Therefore that it may attain its one
> purpose, it needs One Law (*lex*) and One Government (*unicus*
> *principatus*).[8]

This, as you can see, is the flowering of an idea found in Greek
Stoicism and in Augustine, but as evolved by the Scholastics it becomes highly elaborate, reinforced as it is with Aristotle's concept of

---

[6] The term "state" may be misleading. By "state" the Scholastic meant self-
governing political units, not national states in the modern sense. The national
state did not appear until the sixteenth century. To the Scholastics, a state might
be a "free city," a principality, a feudal fief, or even a small manorial holding. One
historian has commented that in this period political fragmentation had gone so far
that often a feudal baron controlled only what territory he could see from his
bedroom window.

[7] See Otto Gierke, *Political Theories of the Middle Ages* (Boston, Mass.:
Beacon Press, 1957).

[8] *Ibid.*, p. 10.

causality, with the concept of *universitas* integrated with concepts of law and political authority. It also presupposes a rather intricate set of interlinking hierarchical principles in which government and society are constructed with gradations of authority and dependence upon divine law. We shall observe this schematic concept of the social order in greater detail when we survey the theories of Aquinas.

Yet by no means is the political thought of the Scholastics a monolithic authoritarianism. Indeed, both the ideas of *representation* and *popular sovereignty* appear in the writings of Aquinas. Further, the Scholastics conceived of an individual man as being a partial whole in himself and of the Aristotelian ideas of the *telos* as being as applicable to an individual as to any other natural form created by God. A man must fulfill himself; he must utilize to the fullest his capabilities; but he is under obligation to do so. But—and this is an important "but"—the end for man is God, and the realization of the destiny of an individual rests only on his being a part of the greater whole of mankind and, beyond that, of the universal order that God ordains. This concept of society is even more sweepingly organic than that of Aristotle, since it rests upon a thoroughly articulated idea of the divine law. Such law would limit the rapacious inclinations of secular monarchs, and, while it does not imply any absolute "rights" for individuals—apart from their membership in the Commonwealth of the Human Race—Scholastic thought, in its insistence upon divine law and the sacredness of the person, never wavers in its demand that the individual always be treated by the state or the community as an end, never as a means.

The Scholastic concern with *law* is not difficult to trace. The Church had from its early beginnings taken the Roman Law to its bosom and, enlarging on it, had created an imposing body of canon law. This cast the Christian philosophies of the period into a legalistic frame. It provided a very easy idiom in which to work. But beyond the historical continuity, theology had moved ever closer to the Greco-Roman concept of natural law. In a nutshell, Christian theology since its day of evangelical fervor and catacomb meetings under the Roman persecution had been moving away from the oriental elements in the belief. It was a slow process from revelation and dramatic disclosures to "right reason" and deductive demonstrations of the existence of God. The dogma of the Church became fixed in an essentially rationalistic vein. God was rational; He could be discovered rationally and His existence demonstrated rationally; and He constructed His kingdom upon this earth rationally. A reasonable, rational universe suggests one governed by law—natural law. Hence, since the medieval period, Christianity and natural law have coupled hands.

Next came the question of *authority*. It is the Scholastics who first confront us with the idea of *sovereignty*—the power to decide unchecked by a higher legal will. It does not clarify the situation much to advance that God is the Sovereign Power, because the question immediately becomes: Who shall exercise the will of God? In whom does God rest ultimate political authority? It was generally assumed by the Scholastics that the political order—the *state*—was created by Divine Will to fulfill an ever-increasing role. The Scholastic philosophers were less specific on the manner in which the state actually came into being, some advancing a theory not unlike the "contract" theory of the Enlightenment. The argument over just how the Divine Sovereignty was to be distributed followed along the lines of earlier disputes about papal versus imperial prerogative. The bone of contention was whether sovereignty passed directly from God to monarchs or was transmitted to secular rulers *through* the papacy. This difference divided the Scholastics.

But the Scholastics were far from divided on the question of the role of the state *vis-à-vis* the obligations of rulers to the ruled and the basic nature of authority. Here they were in agreement. Clearly the fundamental duty of the state was to the general well-being, the creation of conditions that would permit the fullest development of man in service of God. The state, being instituted by God, must serve the needs of the human community, not the other way around. And the Scholastic philosophers made it plain that the rulers, the sovereign monarchs, exercised their authority only on behalf of the general good and that their powers were delegated expressly for this purpose by God. The oft-quoted dictum that "public office is a public trust" is not far from the Scholastic idea. As you might infer, this view of authority presupposes that sovereignty is not a fixed, unalterable possession. Rather is it a functional implement, a dynamic tool forged for the general good—and capable of being withdrawn from those who fail to observe the strictures of the divine law.

Beyond these basic considerations, Thomas Aquinas was forcefully to extend the doctrine and to devise a concept of authority both striking in its boldness and thorough in its examination of the political problem. It is in the writings of Aquinas that we come upon the careful examination of the structure of the state and the interrelationship between the ordering of political affairs and the role of Christianity.

St. Thomas Aquinas (1225-1274) was one of those all too rare giants in the history of thought. It can be argued that he was the first figure since Aristotle to match the Greek's sweep of mind and comprehensive grasp of the integrating principles of knowledge. Thomas' influence was and is immense—in 1879, the corpus of his philosophy was announced to be the official dogma of the Roman Catholic Church. Philosophers yet today are happy to designate themselves as "neo-Thomists" or even just as "Thomists." His impact on the intellectual growth of European society is perhaps unequalled by any other single figure. He is still reverently spoken of as the "angelic doctor." The contemporary philosopher, Jacques Maritain, has said of him: "The apostle of the mind, the doctor of truth, the restorer of the intellectual order, St. Thomas wrote not for the thirteenth century but for our time. His own time is the time of the spirit, which dominates the ages." [9]

A nobleman's son, Thomas was educated as a Benedectine, but in 1244 joined the Dominican Order, that potent and energic brotherhood which was aspiring to be the school for the Church. After study in Paris and a philosophic apprenticeship at the feet of the German Scholastic, Albertus Magnus, Thomas attracted the attention of the scholarly world by his dogged defense of Christian orthodoxy in a dispute with one of the heresies of the day, Averroism. [10] Aside from the more or less routine duties of a highly placed ecclesiastical academic, Thomas dedicated much of his life to a gigantic exposition of the Christian religion, the *Summa Theologica*, a task interrupted only by his death.

The simplest beginning one can make in surveying the thought of Aquinas is to acknowledge his debt to Aristotle. The great Dominican himself makes this unequivocal. He is a follower of Aristotle; his monumental defense of Christianity proceeds from the primary assumptions of the founder of the Lyceum. Even his method of exposition parallels Aristotle's somber and deliberate style. But the most significant connection between the two rests on their identical view of the imperative need for conceiving the natural order as a universal synthesis, a harmony of parts combining into a grand whole, obedient

---

[9] See Jacques Maritain, *St. Thomas Aquinas: Angel of the Schools* (New York: Sheed and Ward, 1931).

[10] *Averroism*, named after its progenitor, Averroës, was a Muslim interpretation of Aristotle which held that faith and reason were irreconcilable since they were by nature two entirely separate spheres of thought.

to law and moving forward in an orderly fashion to their ultimate purposes. The world of Thomas was a rational order, made so by the teleological principle—indeed, by *the* teleological principle—Divine Will. In this regard, Thomas goes beyond his forerunner, Aristotle, in effecting a synthesis between the metaphysical and natural orders by introducing the additional factor of faith as inseparable from reason. In order to understand the "grand design," Thomas, like Aristotle, set about to construct a comprehensive summation of human knowledge, but this would need to be supplemented by the additional ingredient of faith.

The political thought of Aquinas is a logical outgrowth of this conception of reason as an approach to the knowledge of God, reinforced by faith that the universe is rational and purposeful. The aim of society, then, is what the Scholastics conceived of as the creation of conditions permitting both the fullest possible development of the moral capacities of the individual and the individual's progress toward a fuller knowledge of God's nature. Underlying this view of the avenues to the knowledge of God or of nature or of self-knowledge is the repeated theme of *progress*, purposeful progress made through the exercise of reason. Aquinas himself puts the thesis succinctly:

> It seems natural to human reason to advance gradually from the imperfect to the perfect. Hence, in speculative sciences, we see that the teaching of the early philosophers was imperfect, and that it was afterwards perfected by those who succeeded them. So also in practical matters. Discursive rationality implies progress.[11]

The use of the word "natural" is not a mere accident. Aquinas holds that man is by nature a political animal. Society is natural, not contrived. Law is "natural;" Thomas' ethics are rooted in the notion that immorality consists primarily in the unnatural. He does not, however, use the term "natural" to denote the pure workings of the natural world. Natural behavior is not merely a response to physical urgings. Thomas even departs significantly from Aristotle by arguing that the natural order is not only teleological, but divinely ordained, and that the final cause of the natural order is not contained within itself, but within the mind of the Creator. For Aquinas, man, even with the highest performance of his rational faculties, must inevitably fall short of complete knowledge.

A political philosophy, then, must be an examination of the plan that God built into the natural order to meet the needs of mankind

---

[11] St. Thomas Aquinas, *Summa Theologica*, I-II, Question 97.

for political arrangement. Such a concept clearly suggests where one should begin, and Aquinas commences there—with an analysis of law.

According to Aquinas' own scheme, this consideration of law must consist of three parts: (1) the essence of law, (2) the different kinds of law, and (3) the effects of law. An examination of this sort would make clear such associated problems as the role of the ruler, the aims of the state, proper forms of government, and even the church-state dilemma. In short, Thomas attempts to derive both political prescription and ethical authority from a detailed explication of the nature of law. What kind of law? Here is Aquinas' problem. It is obviously not enough to answer by responding "eternal law" or something of the sort; the difficulty is to harmonize eternal law with human law, to reconcile the split inherent in Augustine and in earlier conceptions of *jus naturale*, and, also, to demonstrate that the law of man and the law of God both exist within the great synthesis, the rational order. Further, they not only exist side-by-side, but human law is logically derivable from divine law.

What, then, is the essence of law? For Aquinas the answer is reason. He says:

> Law is a rule and measure of acts whereby man is induced to act or is restrained from acting: for *lex* (law) is derived from *ligare* (to bind), because it binds one to act. Now the rule and measure of human acts is the reason, which is the first principle of human acts, as is evident from what has been stated above, since it belongs to the reason to direct the end, which is the first principle in all matters of action, according to the Philosopher.[12]

To define the essence of law as reason is not quite so obvious in its consequences as it might first appear. If law is reason, then an unreasonable act is clearly illegal. Or, as Aquinas puts it, "[if] what is commanded may have the nature of law, it needs to be in accord with some rule of law." This flatly denies the concept that law can be defined as the "command of the sovereign," a concept that has persisted in political thought from the dialogues of Plato to modern legal positivism.[13] How does such a definition affect the legal position of those entrusted to rule? A command is law provided that it coincides with evident reason. But this proposition involves Aquinas in two

---

[12] *Ibid.*, Question 90.

[13] The phrase "law is the command of the sovereign" is that of John Austin, the nineteenth-century British jurist who is discussed in Chapter 13. However, it seems possible that Austin was a close reader of either Aquinas or the Roman jurist Ulpian (170?-228), since Aquinas quotes Ulpian in the *Summa* as follows: "Whatever pleases the sovereign, has the force of law."

difficulties: (1) There must be some generally accepted criterion of reasonability, and, (2) if one defines law as reason and attempts to weigh a presumably legal act by a standard of reason, is one not arguing in a circle? Is one not really saying that a law is something that is legal? Perhaps Aquinas' definition is a tautology.[14]

But the wily Thomas is not to be taken in so obvious a trap. In the first place, he counters, there are various types of reason and, hence, various types of law. This presupposes standards by which to determine the nature of law. So much, then, for the objection regarding the reasonable criterion. Further, reason is not so subjective or quicksilver a category; it is discoverable and eternal. It can be set forth in orderly array. Its manifestation is law, and it follows that there are varieties of law quite as clear and immutable as reason. The base of reason is the mind of God; the foundation of law is the eternal law.

Aquinas offers a classification of both reason and law, dividing them into four forms: eternal law—Divine Reason; natural law—Divine Reason in nature; divine law—Christian revelation; and human law—regulations of human society. This classification is hierarchical. It flows downward. The indispensable fountain is eternal law—Divine Wisdom. Aquinas comments:

> A law is nothing else but a dictate of practical reason emanating from the ruler who governs a perfect society. Now it is evident, granted that the world is ruled by divine providence . . . that the whole community of the universe is governed by divine reason. Wherefore the very Idea of the government of things in God the Ruler of the universe has the nature of law. And since the divine reason's conception of things is not subject to time but is eternal, according to Proverbs viii, 23, therefore it is that this kind of law must be called eternal.[15]

In the treatise on law in the *Summa*, Aquinas asks the question: "Whether there is in us a natural law?" With this query he opens up the entire subject of natural law and the relationship between natural and eternal law. It is important to notice that in his question Thomas asks if the natural law is "in us." With this phraseology the Dominican introduces a definition of natural law that constructs it not only in terms of the rational ordering of nature, but also as a part of human personality. "Participation of the eternal law in the rational creature," he asserts, "is called natural law." Disobedience to law is, for the individual, disobedience to his essential nature. This conception draws a perceivable distinction between eternal and natural law by describ-

---

[14] *Tautology:* a statement comprised of a repetition of meaning.
[15] Aquinas, *op. cit.,* Question 91.

ing the latter as the province of man, he being a rational creature. In Thomas' words:

> Even irrational animals partake in their own way of the eternal reason, just as the rational creature does. But because the rational creature partakes thereof in an intellectual and rational manner, therefore the participation of the eternal law in the rational creature is properly called a law, since a law is something pertaining to reason. Irrational creatures, however, do not partake thereof in a rational manner, wherefore there is no participation of the eternal law in them, except by way of similitude.[16]

Divine law consists of revelations by which God directly instructs mankind and reveals His ordinances. The law of Moses may be taken as an example. This is quite evidently law of a different sort; it is independent of the hierarchy of Aquinas' classification and possibly even contradictory to it. On the one hand is natural law, which is identifiable as natural reason, and on the other is divine law as a direct injection of God's will. Aquinas anticipates some demurrer to this section of his classification as he pointedly raises the question: "Whether there is any need for divine law?" He answers:

> By natural law the eternal law is participated in proportionately to the capacity of human nature. But to his supernatural end man needs to be directed in yet a higher way. Hence the additional law given by God, whereby man shares more perfectly in the eternal law.[17]

The divine law raises more philosophical questions than it does those strictly concerned with political thought. Aquinas' conviction that reason (natural law) and faith (divine law) are complementary and never in opposition is arguable, to say the least, but what is intriguing in his discussion of divine law is the spirit of moderation, even tolerance, that pervades it. Divine law is the revelation of perfection only to be found in Christianity, but, says Aquinas, the natural law is in man regardless of his religious attachments, and hence the just society and polity, built upon natural law, are not invariably Christian, nor need they be. Obedience to law is not exclusively Christian behavior, although the divine law offers the additional knowledge of God to the Christian believer. Thomas goes so far as to maintain that a just ruler need not be a Christian and that the ruler's failure to embrace Christianity is not grounds for disobedience on the part of his subjects.

---

[16] *Ibid.*, Question 91.
[17] *Ibid.*

Thomas' explanation for the existence of human law is the need
for the ordering of practical affairs, and he quotes Cicero on this point:
"Justice has its source in nature; thence certain things came into
custom by reason of their utility; afterward these things which
emanated from nature and were approved by custom were sanctioned
by fear and reverence for the law." He postulates that natural law
provides the principles, but the details of actual applied law are
matters of human concern and, further, that "practical reason" is
engaged with matters which are "singular and contingent" and that
a flexible and workable code of human regulation is necessary. He
even intimates that human law may not always be ideal. This, however, is not a valid charge against it, as "it is not necessary for every
measure to be altogether unerring and certain, but according as it
is possible in its own particular genus." Elsewhere Thomas observes:
"Human laws cannot have the inerrancy that belongs to the demonstrated conclusions of sciences." But he leaves not the slightest doubt
that human law rests solely and completely on natural law. Human
law divorced from natural law is no law at all.

What is the effect of law? Is it, for example, the rendering of justice? Aquinas does not use the term "justice" in the broad Platonic
way; his definition [18] follows closely upon Aristotle's.[19] Law is
equated by Thomas with reason, and justice—which, although a major
virtue, is but one of many results of natural reason—becomes the
character of "right" human relationships. "The proper effect of law,"
writes Thomas, "is to lead its subjects to their proper virtue." But in
a more particular sense, the effect of law (beyond the Aristotelian
end of happiness founded on virtue) is involved with the examination of two main topics: (1) the role of the ruler and the relationship
between the ruler and the ruled, and (2) forms of government.

There are two streams in Aquinas' thought on the ruler-subject
relationship. The first is that the ruler exercises a trust; the ruler
becomes lawmaker for the general good with the aim of making his
subjects virtuous. His authority is a limited one. He must obey the
natural law; he must promote the general welfare, as it were. Even
his power is derived, according to Thomas, from the sovereignty
inherent in the rational order. Further, Thomas stresses that justice is

---

[18] Aquinas defined justice as "a habit whereby a man renders to each one his due
by a constant and perpetual will," *ibid.*, Question 58.

[19] Aristotle's brief definition: "Justice is a habit whereby a man is said to be
capable of doing just actions in accordance with his choice." (*Ethics*, V. 5.)

primarily equality and that the ruler must respect this juridical equality in such matters as the inviolability of contracts, property, and the
privileges of the person. No one to date had scored the evils of tyranny
with the vigor of the Dominican. In *De Regimine Principum* (*On
Kingship*), Thomas writes that "tyranny is the worst form of government." And further, he observes, "a government becomes unjust by
the fact that the ruler, paying no heed to the common good, seeks his
own private good." Tyranny is the unavoidable outcome of the growing selfish interests of rulers. The worst feature of tyrannical rule is
that in following a path of wickedness, of disobedience to law, the
ruler creates wickedness in his subjects, which leads to the corruption
of the polity.

If Aquinas is eloquent against the excesses of unjust rule, he is not
prepared, on the other hand, to argue that such conduct amounts
legally to a forfeiture of the ruler's authority. This is the second
stream, the theme of *obedience*. He makes his justification in the
following terms:

> A tyrannical law, though not being according to reason, is not a law,
> absolutely speaking, but rather a perversion of law; and yet insofar
> as it is something in the nature of a law, it aims at the citizens being
> good. For all it has in the nature of a law consists in its being an ordi-
> nance made by a superior to his subjects, and aims at being obeyed
> by them, which is to make them good, not simply, but with respect to
> that particular government.[20]

Thomas' insistence on obedience, particularly obedience to secular
authority, is rooted firmly in the developed Christian attitude toward
the difference between the subjugation of the body and the subjugation of the soul. Thomas explains that, in matters of "internal
will," human obedience is only to God, but in "matters concerning the
disposal of actions and human affairs," the subject owes obedience to
the ruler, regardless of the tyrannical dispositions of the latter. But
the soul will remain free in any event, and within the internal will it
is the right, the duty of the subject to resist the wicked ruler. It is not
up to the subject to judge the acts of rulers; that is the prerogative of
God, and, indeed, Aquinas suggests that tyrants will in due course
receive their just deserts at the hands of divine judgment. Lurking
behind this idea, although Thomas does not extend his reasoning as
far as some other religious divines, there is the feeling that physical
life on this earth is transient and comparatively insignificant and that
human beings should practice obedience in the face of secular oppres-

---

[20] *Op. cit.*, *Summa*, I-II, Question 92.

sion, since this persecution may be God's method of testing the Christian will.

Tyrannicide or rebellion are manifestly rejected. Aquinas concludes, however, that in certain instances the oppressive practices of a tyrant reach such proportions that some action against him is justifiable. Such action, on the other hand, can never be justified as a result of individual opinion or private instigation. He terms this "private presumption." The opposition must be lawful in that it conforms to the standard of natural law. It must avoid violence, and, most important of all, it must be collective action. Elected rulers can be deposed for flagrant abuses even before their terms are completed, since they then place themselves outside the lawful relationship of subjects and rulers. About the putting aside of kings Thomas is less specific.

Assuming this bond of obedience from the ruled and love and communal dedication from the ruler, along with steady movement toward the realization of the virtuous community, how is government best organized? In principle, Aquinas' response is a repetition of Aristotle, even to adopting the classification of "good" and "bad" polities. Like his Greek mentor, Thomas is dubious about democracy and equates the excesses of popular rule with majoritarian tyranny. Dignity or excellence are held to be the standard in either a monarchy or an aristocracy, while an oligarchy is primarily concerned with material gain and a democracy is pro-freedom. Like Aristotle, Thomas recognizes the penchant for tyranny in each form.

In his search for the best regime, Aquinas departs to some degree from Aristotle's views and in so doing provides the rationale for several centuries of defense for the institution of monarchy. While he makes much of the fact that conditions greatly affect the judgment of governments and that all general statements in this connection must be examined in the light of practical circumstances, the author of the *Summa* says that "the best regime of a community is government by one person."

His choice of monarchy as the best form is the result of his conviction that, all other things being equal, the preservation of peace and order is the most critical function of a ruler. The single sovereign is very likely better able to do this than a cabal of aristocrats or a board of elected officials would be. In his own language, Thomas puts it this way:

> It is evident that several persons could by no means preserve the stability of the community if they totally disagreed. For union is necessary among them if they are to rule at all; several men, for instance,

could not pull a ship in one direction unless joined together in some fashion. Now several are said to be united according as they come closer to being one. So one man rules better than several who come near being one.[21]

The elevation of peace and order to be the first objective of government results from Thomas' concern for the need for unity. Order establishes unity, but this order is not a product of coercion; nor is monarchy desirable because it places the power to coerce in a single hand. The One is more conducive to the establishment of order than the Many because the One is more capable of self-unification. The One is better able to act with consistency and decision. Assuming that the single ruler, then, is dedicated to the promotion of the general good, as he must be in a true monarchy, Thomas holds that the ties of unity within that polity are *love*, the love that the monarch has for his subjects and that which they return. The monarch leads not only by wise decree, but also by love, dignity, and moral example. Aquinas contends further that the monarch must be a superior moral being, indeed, a sort of embodiment of the moral aspiration of the society.

But he candidly admits that monarchies can get into difficulty. In truth, "uneasy rests the head that wears the crown." He points out that in well-administered kingdoms, the population often grows lethargic because the governmental machinery operates so well. Also, monarchies sometimes fail to sublimate the ambitions and energies of a society when it contains a number of men of virtue and ability. In short, whatever the theoretical advantages of monarchical rule, it has one serious defect: the absence of a sense of participation. Men either lose interest in or militate against that in which they cannot share.

"What is the alternative?" reflects Thomas. Describing it as the best "practical" alternative to monarchy, he gives a blueprint for the mixed state. The problem of the mixed state is balance—as Aristotle so carefully pointed out. Aquinas therefore suggests that the principle of participation be introduced, at the same time preserving the merits of a full-bloom monarchy. Such a mixed state would retain the institution of kingship, but would become a limited monarchy. The plan for such a "constitutional monarchy," to borrow a modern phrase, incorporates some ideas of Aristotle, but it most closely resembles the *Republic* of Cicero. In places Aquinas seems to move along the road toward a doctrine of popular sovereignty, suggested in Cicero, but in the end his mixed state is still a monarchy with some concessions made to participation but no significant shift of authority. The king, a divine

---

[21] St. Thomas Aquinas, *De Regimine Principum*, Book I, Chapter 2, Section 18.

instrument, a shepherd in the secular fold, remains the abiding ruler for Aquinas.

Drawing together the strands of his political thought, it is apparent that the Dominican scholar has erected a monumental concept of a Christianized political order. From the historical standpoint, this vision whose influences on the political development of Western society are still noticeable was a pulling together of major elements of Greek thought, Roman political theory, and the Christian religion and an incorporation of them into a majestic account of a rational and humane universe. Yet beyond the obvious historical ramifications of Thomist thought, what actual contributions did he make, and to what extent have his ideas been able to withstand the turmoil of subsequent controversy?

His influence was probably threefold. He gave a rationalistic cast to political thought that has never been completely demolished, although it reached its high tide in the Enlightenment. He wedded the contemplation of political problems to law so firmly that such an amalgamation is still apparent in continental Europe. He was responsible for a tradition of toleration and moderation which, although eclipsed from time to time, has never fully departed from either political thought or religious conviction. He Christianized the character of political life to such an extent that only the full emotional fury of the French Revolution seriously dislodged this orientation.

It is true, also, that Aquinas' conception of political authority as resting upon natural law did not escape the bombardment of later philosophers. His concept of obedience even to unjust rule was soon to pass; monarchy was in the end a losing cause. His mixed state, too, was not to survive the revolutionary shocks of republicanism versus royal absolutism (although it very nearly did in England). It is even fair to say that Thomas' over-all synthesis of faith and reason did not stand up against the searching critiques of the eighteenth and nineteenth centuries. But his philosophy summed up much that was noble and enlightened in the medieval age, an age in which the human mind emerged as a finely honed instrument.

Thomas Aquinas left a legacy in his intense legalism, and this legalistic penchant grew among those who followed. Thomas' dream of the unified society enlarging so as to encompass ever larger political circles faded. Oddly enough, inherent in Thomas' Christian-centered philosophy was an unmistakable tone of secularism that has been attributed to his intellectual kinship with Aristotle. Too, monarchs were consolidating their power positions and were no longer "shadow kings" of semifictional empires. This legalism, secularism, and the marked increase of the power of earthly princes had produced some startling effects by the fourteenth century.

Quarrels persisted between popes and civil authorities, but the tide was running away from papal superiority. In a thoroughly argued contest of will between Philip the Fair of France and Boniface VIII over the issue of universal papal sovereignty as against the rights of kings, an intense feeling of national identification, even among the French clergy, permitted Philip to assert his independence. This collision was distinctly a power struggle, and the French monarch emerged as a formidable figure, principally because of the increasing sense of loyalty exhibited toward kings rather than toward the Church by large masses of the population. The written exchanges between papal advocates and supporters of royal power became decidedly more sophisticated, infinitely more legalistic, and, in the case of some of the supporters of *imperium*, far bolder in their attacks on the ecclesiastical institution. It would have been disheartening for Thomas to learn, no doubt, that the bulk of these anti-Church tracts were composed by lawyers. While it is evident in these volleys and counter-volleys that the goal of national states was replacing the dream of Christian empire, the revolt against the sacerdotal monopoly on political thought lay deeper.

Many were torn by divided loyalties, such as *John of Paris* (dates unknown), at once a churchman and a lawyer and also quite a devoted subject of the French king. He vigorously argued the case for the proposition that his king was not subject to the authority of the popes. The main implication of his arguments was that the political realm is an independent entity, free from ecclesiastical supervision and able to order itself.

Further and more extensive argument for secular independence followed. *Marsilius of Padua* (1290?-1343) in his *Defensor Pacis* set as his goal a redefinition of the extent of the spiritual domain, firmly placing the Church under the authority of the civil state. His instrument for this surgical operation was Aristotle, this time substantially shorn of Thomistic religious significance. In point of fact, Marsilius revived the Averroist argument that had aroused Aquinas to action, namely, that while one can grant the truth of Christian revelation, it is quite another category of knowledge than philosophy and that the latter must proceed in a state of separation from theological considerations. To put it concisely, Marsilius was prepared to say that, spiritual considerations granted, they were beside the point and consideration of political arrangements must be carried forth on more rationalistic grounds. The full explication of where this line of reasoning takes him in the *Defensor Pacis* is provocative, and Marsilius' discussion of the self-sufficient state is often astonishingly prophetic. It is worth a closer look than we can give it here.

The job of decimating the Thomistic synthesis was undertaken as well by *William of Occam* (1300?-1349?). William's point of attack was Aquinas' reconciliation of faith and reason. Holding the rationalism of Thomas inapplicable in areas which were within the province of faith alone, William strove to enlarge his separation between reason and faith to include a schism between secular and ecclesiastical authority, restricting the sacerdotal to nonpolitical functions. This was in fact an assault on papal absolutism, and he endowed secular monarchs with an enlarged sovereignty expressly for the purpose of curbing what he felt was an insidious concentration of power in the person of the pope. Regardless of the basic aim, the effect of Occamism was to confirm the growing separation of political thought from theology, the split between the concerns of the soul and the political management of human beings.

The pattern of political speculation from the early scholastics to William of Occam is not hard to grasp. Commencing as a running debate on the relationship of Church to State, the medieval period gradually altered the focal point of deliberation to the relationship between ruler and ruled, whether the ruler be pope or prince. From the disputes over jurisdictional boundary lines there came forth starker issues of power, sovereignty, authority, and resistance. And to probe yet deeper, was not the radical issue behind it all the very foundations on which politics rested? What was that foundation to be? Ethics? Theology? Natural reason? Law? Or yet something else?

. . . *for further discussion:*

1. Aquinas was convinced that faith and reason are not hostile but complementary. How would you choose to define "faith" and "reason"? Do you accept Aquinas' supposition that they are interactive? Whatever definition of faith one cares to use, there must arise the question of the role of faith, if any, in gaining knowledge in general and in political questions in par-

ticular. Does "faith" have a role in political theory? If so, what is it? If not, what other forms of reason are appropriate to the consideration of political issues?

2. The problem of the extent to which the citizen *ought* to obey his government is as alive today as it was in the thirteenth century. Suppose a government advocates the use of a nuclear deterrent contrary to the conscience of certain of its citizens. To what extent can that government call upon the loyalty of those citizens, and to what extent are they morally bound by law? Can a citizen in a region practicing racial discrimination by legal statute reject the law and use extralegal means to correct what he believes to be an injustice?

3. Thomas' argument for monarchy is that an individual is a more unified agent of decision than a group. Putting aside the questions of whether one-man decisions are good or bad and whether nonparticipation in political decision-making is injurious to a healthy society, is it true that one man can make decisions in a more efficient manner than can a group?

4. Justice Oliver Wendell Holmes, Jr., once wrote: "The jurists who believe in natural law seem to me to be in that naïve state of mind that accepts what has been familiar and accepted by them and their neighbors as something that must be accepted by men everywhere." Do you believe this to be a fair judgment?

. . . for further investigation:

Adams, Henry, * *Mont-Saint-Michel and Chartres*. New York: Mentor Books, 1961.

Bigongiari, Dino, ed., * *The Political Ideas of St. Thomas Aquinas*. New York: Hafner Publishing Co., Inc., 1953.

Carlyle, R. W. and A. J. Carlyle, *A History of Medieval Political Theory in the West*. New York: Barnes & Noble, Inc., 1909-1936.

Copleston, Frederick C., * *Aquinas*. Baltimore, Md.: Penguin Books, Inc., 1955.

Coulton, George G., * *Medieval Panorama*. New York: Meridian Books, 1955.

Wulf, Maurice de, * *Philosophy and Civilization in the Middle Ages*. New York: Dover Publications, Inc., 1953.

Gierke, Otto, * *Natural Law and the Theory of Society, 1500-1800*, Ernest Barker, trans. Boston, Mass.: Beacon Press, 1957.

———, * *Political Theories of the Middle Ages*, F. W. Maitland, trans. Boston, Mass.: Beacon Press, 1958.

Leff, Gordon, * *Medieval Thought*. Baltimore, Md.: Penguin Books, Inc., 1958.

Lewis, Ewart, *Medieval Political Ideas*. New York: Alfred A. Knopf, Inc., 1954.

Maritain, Raissa, *St. Thomas Aquinas: Angel of the Schools*. New York: Sheed and Ward, Inc., 1931.

Pegis, Anton C., ed., *Basic Writings of Saint Thomas Aquinas*. 2 vols. New York: Random House, Inc., 1945.

Taylor, Henry O., *The Medieval Mind.* 2 vols. Cambridge, Mass.: Harvard
    University Press, 1949.
Troeltsch, Ernst, * *The Social Teachings of the Christian Churches,* 2 vols.
    O. Wyon, trans. New York: Torchbooks, 1960.

6

THE FIRST POLITICAL
SCIENTIST ?

The title of this chapter introduces the quite controversial notion that politics is a science. This is a lively issue today; university departments divide over describing themselves as departments of "Political Science," "Government," "Political and Moral Philosophy," or merely as departments of "Politics." The quibbling over labels actually represents a far more profound argument over the entire character of the study of political affairs. We will have a look at some of these arguments in Chapter 18.

But however one views the study of politics, as a science or as an art or as something else, we have discovered so far in our tour of political ideas that these ideas are interrelated, for good or ill, with other modes of thought, ethical, theological, or metaphysical. Could not political principles be conceived independently? Are all political questions reducible to moral or spiritual concepts? Could the study of politics be a separate investigation?

Niccolò Machiavelli (1469-1527) thought it could. He was convinced that political theory rested on precepts quite separate from the traditional philosophic ones. In this sense, he might well deserve the title of "First Political Scientist." His claim to the classification "scientist," while remote in a literal sense, could be pressed by pointing out that Machiavelli's entire approach to the nature of the political was empirical. For him, the real stuff of day-to-day political intercourse was the proper subject for study and had to be observed objectively, dispassionately, the observer being as free as possible from ethical, religious, or philosophic bias. Machiavelli's cast of mind was essentially scientific. The job was to collect the data and frame conclusions.

This was a radical departure in a civilization steeped in the Scholastic conception of political arrangements as subordinate to ecclesiastical ends and incorporating Greek ideas of the moral fulfillment of individuals and society. Startling as Machiavelli's shift of direction might have been to a Renaissance mind fathered by Scholastic philosophy and wedded to a revival of Greek humanism, it was, in fact, this same Renaissance that produced the apparently amoral emphasis in Machiavelli's approach. As an epoch, the Renaissance pushed the fascination with the individual far beyond the medieval limits. It glorified the exuberant creativity of the individual; it worshiped even the eccentricities and excesses of individual appetite. It drank deep of luxuriant self-indulgence, artistic and political. The Borgias, combining skill and vice (as, indeed, the Tudors later did), exemplified an era unwilling to suffer stuffy moderation or cautious reflection. It was an age dominated by personalities, some bloody and avaricious, some transcendentally inspired, but all drawn in the brighter colors of the palette.

It was a time of enthusiasm, and enthusiasm usually finds itself accompanied by cynicism. If the Renaissance was an era of discovery, of seeking out new frontiers, of grandly elaborating on the scientific zeal of its medieval precursors, so was it also a time of brilliant disillusionment, elegant contempt, and cynical disregard of restraint. While it was an age torn between piety and libertinism, it was not a rebellious one as it lacked the motivations of the Reformation and the Enlightenment. If it was appalled by the lack of moral sentiment in Machiavelli, it was more for his candor than his apostasy. He had given the word to what a growing segment of the fifteenth-century population was both thinking and doing.

But Machiavelli has shocked succeeding generations quite as much as he did his own, and possibly a good deal more deeply. His very name has been incorporated into the language to denote cunning,

scheming, amorality, and devious design. Shakespeare referred to him
so. He has been called the "Prince of Villains," the "Anti-Christ," [1]
and the most dangerous influence in Western political thought. He
was admired by such a questionable character as Benito Mussolini.
Even some contemporary appraisals of him are unflattering and depict
him as a substantially immoral influence.[2]

If the name Machiavelli summons up the mental image of a ruthless
Renaissance courtier, crafty, predatory, possibly with a black, forked
beard, his actual character and life will come as a disappointment.
Connected with the Florentine Court of the Medicis and the victim
of fluctuating personal fortunes, Machiavelli nonetheless lived out
his days with notable circumspection and even a sort of "shopkeeper"
resignation. He was surely no court intriguer after the pattern of
"historical" fiction. He was the son of a lawyer and the scion of a
family whose origins were aristocratic, but whose worldly fortunes
were at an ebb. History does not reveal to what extent the home life
of the Machiavellis proved formative on their distinguished offspring.
Unlike the case of Schopenhauer and his mother, we know nothing of
young Niccolò's traumas. His education, likewise, is purely a matter
of speculation. He appears to have secured a minor bureaucratic post
in Florence in 1498, and he did manage to have a fairly noteworthy
career in the service of the city with which he is so intimately associated. He rose to the ambassadorial level and served at various times
as envoy to the major cities of Italy. He was an employee, therefore, of
a self-governing free city, and his political orientations were distinctly
republican.

His rise to the exalted state of ambassador appears to have been
the result of his eminently capable and subtle mind. It is evident, too,
that Machiavelli's prime asset in political life was his ability to judge
character and to act and advise on the basis of his observations. This
insight could be put to good use in Renaissance Italy, a patchwork of
petty states existing in an atmosphere of perpetual suspicion and
ceaseless and energetic intrigue. To stay alive as an ambassador was
no mean feat—it was not unusual for a state to declare its warlike
intent by poisoning the emissaries of its projected antagonist. No life
for the fainthearted or slow of wit, the diplomatic service.

---

[1] Others to receive this encomium have been Aristotle (bestowed by Martin
Luther, incidentally), Spinoza, and Kant. It was in one case self-designated—
Nietzsche.

[2] A recent illustration is the views of Leo Strauss.

While in the capacity of a diplomat, Machiavelli had ample opportunity to exercise his powers of observation on some of the most
diverse figures in European history. He seems to have taken a special
interest in Pope Julius II. But the man who intrigued him most in the
Italian landscape was Cesare Borgia; many students of Machiavelli
believe that his most widely read book, *The Prince,* had Borgia as its
inspiration. Cesare Borgia is worth a book by himself, but it would be
of greater interest to a student of military science, diplomatic history,
or the erotic lives of would-be conquerors than to a student of political philosophy. Duke Cesare does indeed resemble Machiavelli's
Prince in some respects; he was thoroughly ruthless, passionately
ambitious, cunningly skillful, and flamboyantly immoral. But he
sought to unify the bickering Italian states (a vision of Machiavelli's),
and he was probably the best military leader south of the Alps
(Machiavelli was intensely interested in military art [3] and at one time
in his life organized and trained the Florentine militia). Above all,
Duke Cesare believed in glory—and that Machiavelli's Prince held to
be the highest aim.

Ambassador Machiavelli's fortunes waned. As a result of some
intricate political and military maneuvers which are too lengthy to
deal with here, the Pope managed to restore the Medici family as
rulers of Florence. To power came one Lorenzo de Medici—descend-
ant of the ruler of the same name dubbed "The Magnificent." Machiavelli's position was rather uncomfortable at this juncture, due to his
having been vaguely associated with certain extreme prorepublicans.
An investigation followed which resulted in his being submitted to
torture—and Renaissance Italy must be listed as one of the high
(or low) points in the history of the art of forceful persuasion. Having
been found innocent of any substantial crime and undaunted by the
rack, Machiavelli attempted to curry Lorenzo's favor with a literary
effort dedicated to Lorenzo "The Magnificent." This was the now
famous essay on rulership, *The Prince,* written in 1513. It little
impressed the self-centered Lorenzo, and Machiavelli surrendered the
life of a courtier for more or less comfortable seclusion in the country.
He turned to literary pursuits, and the products of this period include
poetry, plays, essays, and his most significant work: the *Discourses on
the First Ten Books of Titus Livius.* Although a popular revolt sent
the Medici packing in 1527, it was too late for Machiavelli, who died
late that same year.

---

[3] Machiavelli wrote a military treatise under the title *The Art of War.*

If it were possible to summarize in a word the central theme of Machiavelli's thought it would be *power*—how to build it, keep it, and extend it. We have already noted that in viewing power, Machiavelli strips from it any concern with morality or Christian principle. He is engaged solely in the business of describing and analyzing what he takes to be the central core of all political action. But it is fair to ask whether there is any justification for the premise that power is the central core of all political life. There is ample defense for the view that the base of political life is either morality or theology, but how can Machiavelli justify his thesis that the base is power?

In order to offer this justification—which Machiavelli makes only implicitly—the Florentine accepts two assumptions, and the latter one is undeniably a value judgment. First, he argues, it is surely true that if you examine politics as they are in fact carried on, you cannot help but observe that all who practice the art appear to be motivated by a yearning to accumulate power. Why do men and states struggle? Why do they seek to impose their will upon others, as certainly they do? The answer would seem to be an impulsion to gain and hold and extend power. While Machiavelli does not provide us with a psychological explanation for it, he assumes throughout that men are naturally so disposed. It is the unarticulated assumption that runs through the entirety of his reflections. He makes this clear in the close of his description of Cesare Borgia:

> Reviewing thus all the actions of the duke, I find nothing to blame. On the contrary, I feel bound, as I have done, to hold him up as an example to be imitated by all who by fortune and with the arms of others have risen to power. For with his great courage and high ambition he could not have acted otherwise . . .[4]

But power in the Machiavellian view is not sheer domination; the resolute pursuit of power and the resulting power politics he examines are not evidence of some neurotic will to power. It is not a matter of some messianic *mystique;* rather is the urge to power inextricably linked to the notion of *glory.* The ruler chases power and glory; the glory is personal and is reflected in the glory of the state. While Machiavelli does write in *The Prince* that if the ruler must choose between being loved and being feared, prudence should dictate the latter; the ruler must never on any account behave ingloriously. The Prince must never *appear* small, though he may need to rely on petty acts. In a well-known passage, Machiavelli counsels:

---

[4] Niccolò Machiavelli, *The Prince,* Chapter 7.

For it may be said of men in general that they are ungrateful, voluble, dissemblers, anxious to avoid danger, and covetous of gain; so long as you benefit them, they are entirely yours; they offer their blood, their goods, their life, and their children, as I have said before, when the necessity is remote; but when it approaches they revolt. And the prince who has relied solely on their words, without making other preparations, is ruined; for the friendship which is gained by purchase and not through grandeur and nobility of spirit is bought but not secured, and at a pinch is not to be expended in your service.[5]

If, then, the constant in Machiavelli is the appetite for power-glory, what is the value judgment implied? It is that power and glory are worth possessing, and it is interesting to note that in Machiavellian thinking they are worth having for their sake alone. Most advocates of a similar proposition—that the base of politics is power—assume that power is a means toward some express end. Power means ability to reform, to convert, to expand, or to fulfill an economic or even ethnic aim. Not so with Machiavelli; power is worth having just for itself, and this is all the more true since power and glory are virtually one. This is Machiavelli's first principle, so to speak, and it underlies both *The Prince* and the *Discourses*.

Power is sought by individuals, and it is the motive force of men generally, whether they yearn after dukedoms or after the comforts of a mere petty merchant. Consequently, Machiavelli's view of the political struggle is an entirely egocentric one. George Sabine has well referred to Machiavelli as the "political theorist of the 'masterless man.' " Given this view, is it at all suprising that Machiavelli should toss aside as irrelevant any notion of society as a moral whole? Indeed, if the final objective is power and this is sought in a thoroughly egoistic manner, whatever moral judgment exists has already been supplied. The question, then, becomes one of means, not ends.

It is no wonder, therefore, that the great bulk of Machiavelli's writing is a discussion of means, liberally spotted with historical examples of successful means. His most celebrated treatise, *The Prince*, is a detailed summary of means, political, military, psychological, and even economic. Much has been made by some scholars of the differences in outlook between *The Prince* and the *Discourses*. While it is a fact that *The Prince* was composed in order to placate Lorenzo de Medici, these alleged inconsistencies have been overemphasized. *The Prince* does not read like a hypocritical book, in the first place, and the

---

[5] *Ibid.*, Chapter 17.

high regard displayed in the *Discourses* for the old Roman Republic or the Swiss democracies does not alter the basic continuity of the two works. One suspects that those who wish to find these dissimilarities are those who are shocked by the candor of *The Prince* and would prefer to find in the *Discourses* something more ostensibly charitable.

Perhaps you will find *The Prince* a "shocker," but that is rather doubtful. In the first place, there is hardly anything in that volume that a well-informed inhabitant of the twentieth century hasn't encountered before. Four centuries of hammer-and-tong politics separate us, and perhaps the highest tribute that can be paid to the wily Florentine is that he reads like a description of contemporary political life. Perhaps, in another sense, the eternal appeal of Machiavelli is that it is a strange and even exhilarating experience to see in print what one has secretly thought all along.

If we grant that *The Prince* is a more extreme statement of his ideas (perhaps written under practical stress) than the *Discourses,* and we can summarize the differences between the two by agreeing that in the *Discourses* Machiavelli openly admires democratic republics, enlarges on the need for popular consent, stresses more emphatically the problem of inculcating national unity and improving leadership, and, most provocatively, advocates the idea of national armies, then it will be possible to treat the ideas of Machiavelli as a whole rather than to flit to and fro between the works. This is not said to disparage the *Discourses.* As a work, it is far richer both in thought and in detail than *The Prince* and, in general, is a more reliable guide to Machiavelli's opinions.

Although Machiavelli's writing consists of completely unsystematic reflection and pithy admonition, it is possible to extract four primary themes. These are not discrete, but are interwoven, and it is difficult to consider one without reference to the others. The themes are: (1) the problem of holding the state together in the face of universal human weakness, (2) the techniques of effective statecraft, (3) the problem of morale and national spirit, and, (4) the forms of political organization.

Machiavelli paints a bleak picture of the human character. Men are selfish, easily corrupted, avaricious, disloyal, irresolute, cowardly, untruthful and vengeful—the Florentine actually uses all these terms to describe the proclivities of mankind. How can a ruler, then, either maximize his own power or bring glory to his state? He does so, Machiavelli suggests, by adopting techniques that successfully cope with these lamentable human shortcomings. The first problem of the ruler is to secure his own position, since weakness breeds disunity and the aims of the state cannot be realized without common purpose. Machiavelli comments:

> Men, in attempting to avoid fear themselves, give others cause for fear; and the injuries which they ward off from themselves they inflict upon others, as though there were a necessity to oppress or be oppressed.[6]

Power he conceives to be a quantity that if gained in some amount by one is lost in a proportional amount by another. In consequence, only the strong ruler can hold a society together, since without the virtue of his strength it might shatter itself upon the conflicting ambitions of the many.

Just why men are as Machiavelli seems to think they are he leaves unanswered. Perhaps he assumes that the matter is self-evident. He does, however, to some extent blame Christianity for this fault and his thoroughgoing paganism, indubitably Roman in its spirit, anticipates similar vituperations by Nietzche in the nineteenth century. His main criticism is identical to Nietzsche's, as we shall see in Chapter 15. The argument is that Christianity is a conspiracy of the weak, whereby what are defects are turned into virtues, and the total effect of this is that men are taught to admire weakness, humility, smallmindedness, low cunning, and hypocrisy. Machiavelli blames Christianity for the sorry state of Italy, with special dislike for the influence of the papacy. He admires strength and assumes, consequently, that only the strong, secure in their personal strength, can afford the luxury of openness, frankness, magnanimity, and nobility of conduct. Christianity clearly breeds the doctrine of the weak, he asserts, conspiring and agitating against those who are their superior beings. His indictment appears in the second book of the *Discourses:*

> ... the pagan religion deified only men who had achieved great glory, such as commanders of armies and chiefs of republics, whilst ours glorifies more the humble and contemplative men than the men of action. Our religion, moreover, places the supreme happiness in humility, lowliness, and a contempt for worldly objects, whilst the other, on the contrary, places the supreme good in grandeur of soul, strength of body, and all such other qualities as render men formidable; and if our religion claims of us fortitude of soul, it is more to enable us to suffer than to achieve great deeds.
>
> These principles seem to me to have made men feeble, and caused them to become an easy prey to evil-minded men, who can control them more securely, seeing that the great body of men, for the sake of gain-

---

[6] The *Discourses,* Book I, Chapter 46.

ing Paradise, are more disposed to endure injuries than to avenge them.[7]

The ruler would seem to have a moral role—although Machiavelli would not call it that—and that is to pursue glory. But he is forced to deal initially with his own people, predominantly lacking in the appropriate virtues, and then with other rulers who, either like his own people, are crass and low-minded or else are competitors, seeking after glory and power at his expense. If the ruler's aims are justifiable, then the methods employed are to be judged only on the basis of their success. Any technique applies; its pragmatic success is the only criterion. Machiavelli has thus given to political philosophy the most uncompromising statement of the dictum that "the end justifies the means."

This leads us to an examination of statecraft, the means, the techniques. *The Prince* is a handbook (and a very compact one) on that subject, a compendium of advice on how the ruler must adopt a double standard of conduct in dealing with his citizens. Any means are to be commended—and Machiavelli does not flinch at murder or an assortment of cruelties—but the first rule of statecraft is *self-discipline*. The ruler never acts without a purpose, never loses sight of his ultimate goals. He does not act out of caprice, impulse, anger, or revenge. The totality of his public acts (Machiavelli gives free rein to the private diversions of princes) must be a matter of careful, reasoned calculation. The ruler must be in complete charge of himself, with his head the sovereign and his heart held in necessary abeyance. Machiavelli even counsels against too rapid shifts in policy; he titles one of the chapters of the *Discourses:* "It is Imprudent and Unprofitable Suddenly to Change from Humility to Pride, and from Gentleness to Cruelty."[8] While he advises that it is better to be feared than loved if it comes to that choice, he recognizes that beyond the sheer impact of coercion, the obedience of terror, the ruler must instill a sense of public emotional identification to his cause if he is to realize his purposes. The art of statecraft is not the management of a "concentration camp" state. Madness would be the worst preparation for the successful prince. Machiavelli warns that the downfall of rulers is often the result of their need for and attempt to secure popular good will in time of crisis without establishing it first in periods of peace. He acknowledges the need, even of the absolute monarch, for some form of consensus.

---

[7] *Ibid.*, Book II, Chapter 2.
[8] *Ibid.*, Book I, Chapter 41.

Beyond self-discipline, it is possible to isolate perhaps five other principles that Machiavelli advocates as sound characteristics for successful rulers. One of these is *energy*. The ruler must never be lethargic. Power is in constant flux, and the ruler must never relax his attention, his vigilance. He is invariably busy, active, and watchful. He must always preserve the initiative; he must act so as to keep potential enemies off balance.

Decisiveness is indispensable. The prince who vacillates when his cool, calculated judgment tells him to act is doomed. When called upon to act, the ruler must act with inexorable resolution, with apparent daring and unhesitating force. When the sword is drawn it must be thrust; when not being used it should be kept in its scabbard.

Yet another cardinal virtue in statecraft is *flexibility*. Machiavelli observes that men may be deceived in general matters, but rarely so in particulars. This works two ways. The prince must never find himself bound to rigid conceptions, but should be prepared to shift with the winds of circumstance. Problems are best solved by an examination of the situation at a given moment. The rule may be Machiavelli's initially, but it is assuredly a maxim of statesmen down to the present. This flexibility also implies caution, patience, and the ability to "ride with the punch." Machiavelli advises his princely pupil not to stick his neck out too far:

> . . . when any evil arises within a republic or threatens it from without, that is to say, from an intrinsic or extrinsic cause, and has become so great as to fill everyone with apprehension, the more certain remedy by far is to temporize with it, rather than to attempt to extirpate it; for almost invariably he who attempts to crush it will rather increase its force, and will accelerate the harm apprehended from it.[9]

Next, the ruler must strictly adopt a *system of reward and punishment*—Machiavelli's suggestions are startlingly like the introduction to a book on dog training. The citizenry must be instantly and fully rewarded for obedience and constancy, swiftly punished for recalcitrance.[10] The following quotation is included as a good example of Machiavelli's thought processes:

> A prince must also show himself a lover of merit, give preferment to the able, and honour those who excel in every art. Moreover, he

[9] *Ibid.*, Book I, Chapter 33.

[10] Writes Machiavelli: "When it happens that someone does something extraordinary, either good or evil, in civil life, he [the ruler] must find such means of rewarding or punishing him which will be much talked about." (*The Prince*, Chapter 21.)

must encourage his citizens to follow their callings quietly, whether in commerce, or agriculture, or any other trade that men follow, so that this one shall not refrain from improving his possessions through fear that they may be taken from him, and that one starting a trade for fear of taxes; but he should offer rewards to whoever does these things, and to whoever seeks in any way to improve his city or state. Besides this, he ought, at convenient seasons of the year, to keep the people occupied with festivals and shows; and as every city is divided either into guilds or into classes, he ought to pay attention to all these groups, mingle with them from time to time, and give them an example of his humanity and munificence, always upholding, however, the majesty of his dignity, which must never be allowed to fail in anything whatever.[11]

The concluding sentence in the passage above sets out the final principle: *dignity*. This the ruler must preserve at all costs. Put another way, he must never lose face. Machiavelli exhorts rulers to "display a courage and dignity similar to that of the Romans." Dignity and majestic display are of paramount importance, as Machiavelli argues, "for men in general judge more by the eye than by the hands, for everyone can see, but few have to feel."

When self-discipline, energy, decisiveness, flexibility, a system of reward and punishment, and dignity are summed up as the ingredients of statecraft, there is perhaps one vital quality lacking. It is complete dedication to expediency. There is no better way to describe this attitude than to employ Machiavelli's own language. The following excerpt is one of the most striking passages in *The Prince:*

A prince being thus obliged to know well how to act as a beast must imitate the fox and the lion, for the lion cannot protect himself from traps, and the fox cannot defend himself from wolves. One must therefore be a fox to recognize traps, and a lion to frighten wolves. Those that wish to be only lions do not understand this. Therefore, a prudent ruler ought not to keep faith when by doing so it would be against his interests, and when the reasons which made him bind himself no longer exist. If men were all good, this precept would not be a good one; but as they are bad, and would not observe their faith with you, so you are not bound to keep faith with them. Nor have legitimate grounds ever failed a prince who wished to show colourable excuse for the non-fulfillment of his promise. Of this one could furnish an infinite number of modern examples, and show how many times peace has been broken, and how many promises rendered worthless, by the faithlessness of princes, and those that have been best able to imitate the fox have succeeded best. But it is necessary to be able to distinguish this character well, and to be a great feigner and dissembler; and men are so simple and so ready to obey present neces-

---

[11] *Ibid.*, Chapter 21.

sities, that one who deceives will always find those who allow themselves to be deceived.[12]

The art of statecraft is the tool of the prudent prince. Prudence
would dictate as well that the prince cannot remain powerful without some popular consensus, some feeling of national unity to support
him. In short, one of the tasks of a ruler is to build morale. Public
morale appears to Machiavelli to be constructed of two aspects:
admiration for the ruler and patriotic identification. It is one of the
objectives of the prudent prince to create this sense of admiration. By
"admiration," affection is not necessarily implied. Public affection is
not of itself injurious, but it must not form the sole foundation upon
which the prince's reputation rests. More important is a sense of awe,
an appreciation of the ruler's fame and accomplishments. "Nothing
causes a prince to be so much esteemed," advises Machiavelli, "as
great enterprises and giving proof of prowess."

There are other things, too, that a prince can do to heighten the
general spirit of unity and well-being. He should, from time to time,
"give some outstanding example of his greatness in the internal
administration." Machiavelli also recommends that the prince be open
and unequivocal about political alliances, about declaring himself
"in favour of someone or against another." By being a neutral, one
never gains friends or allies, and neutrality never raises the fervor of
the citizenry.

But the most successful device of all to stimulate public morale and
unity is war. War is depicted by Machiavelli as the shortest route to
power and glory—but it should never be employed hastily or without
careful judgment.[13] The fundamental value of going to war, aside
from the spoils, is the salutary effect warfare has on a civil population.
War not only arouses the patriotic sentiments, but it provides a means
of centering public attention on an obvious and frequently absorbing
crisis. There is much less likelihood, the Florentine argues, of conspiracies against the power of the prince if the state is kept involved
in a long procession of enterprises, the foremost among them being

---

[12] *Ibid.*, Chapter 18.

[13] "Every one may begin a war at his pleasure," Machiavelli muses, "but cannot
so finish it. A prince, therefore, before engaging in any enterprise should well
measure his strength and govern himself accordingly; and he must be very careful
not to deceive himself in the estimate of his strength, which he will assuredly
do if he measures it by his money, or the situation of his country, or the good
disposition of his people unless he has at the same time an armed force of his own."
(The *Discourses*, Book II, Chapter 10.)

the waging of war. After describing the success with which this tactic was employed by Ferdinand of Spain, Machiavelli adds cryptically:

> ... he has continually contrived great things, which have kept his subjects' minds uncertain and astonished, and occupied in watching their result. And these actions have arisen one out of the other, so that they have left no time for men to settle down and act against him.[14]

Much of what has already been said is entirely germane to the matter of patriotism. Machiavelli constantly reminds the reader of the patriotic keenness of Rome during the Republic. Aside from the secondary explanations, the Roman Republic is cited as an example of the fact that patriotism results from a strong feeling of what we might now call "national purpose." That is why the ruler must constantly find purposes to which the energies of the state can be put. Machiavelli repeatedly stresses that the key to military victory is the morale of the soldiery (for this reason, as well as others, he shows vast contempt for the mercenary). This patriotic dedication should attach itself both to the state and to the person of the state's ruler, since for Machiavelli they are in large measure the same. Here is his statement of the patriotic attitudes he deems ideal:

> For where the very safety of the country depends on the resolution to be taken, no considerations of justice or injustice, humanity or cruelty, nor of glory or of shame, should be allowed to prevail. But putting all other considerations aside, the only question should be, What course will save the life and liberty of the country? The French follow this maxim by words and deeds in defending the majesty of their king and the greatness of France; for nothing excites their impatience more than to hear anyone say that such or such a thing is discreditable to the king. For they say that their king can suffer no shame from any resolutions he may take, whether in good or ill fortune; for whether he be victor or vanquished is a matter that only concerns the king.[15]

When we approach Machiavelli's views on the structure and operation of states, we run headlong into those apparent inconsistencies that have so long captured the attention of Machiavelli scholars. For here there arises the apparent dichotomy between Machiavelli as an admirer of absolute monarchy on the one hand and self-governing republics on the other. Enigmatic, too, is his notion of law. How is it possible for a man to be an enthusiastic devotee of Duke Cesare Borgia and simultaneously argue on behalf of equality and even freedom of discussion? How can one place much credence in his en-

---

[14] *Op. cit., The Prince,* Chapter 21.
[15] *Op. cit., Discourses,* Book III, Chapter 41.

comium on law when he tells rulers that the best course is to practice the shady ethics of the fox?

In order to make any sense at all out of these seeming paradoxes, it is necessary to examine just what Machiavelli did say on the subject of republican government and popular liberty.[16] In the first place, he himself suggests a way out. Despotism, he submits, is vital only in the creation of a state or in its reform after a lengthy period of corruption. This doesn't seem a very promising means of resolving the dilemma, since Machiavelli appears unable to cite any states that are not sufficiently corrupt to require the despotic remedy, save the Roman Republic (and possibly the Swiss agrarian communities of which he speaks rather unauthoritatively). Why is the Roman Republic exempted from this otherwise uninterrupted list of corrupt states? The strong purgative of absolutism was unnecessary in the Roman Republic because of the high level of individual virtue (in Machiavelli's definition). He has already made the point clear that contemporary influences have destroyed the old Latin virtues. How, then, can one build a state along the lines of the Republic? What is involved in Machiavelli's contradictions is not a wavering philosophic clarity or shifting loyalties, but vacillating degrees of pessimism. What Machiavelli seems to say to us is: "This is what we've got. It's not very attractive, and the only way that it can be managed is by the following practical means " But *if* men were not as they in fact were at the beginning of the sixteenth century in Italy or as they were uncorrupted in the "old days," *then* we might take quite a different course. Machiavelli seems to have never been completely disillusioned by the corrupt political world in which he moved. His cynicism falls short of being a total attitude. The glories, real and imagined, of the Roman Republic with its patrician quality, intellectual freedom, and high regard for personal honor held out to him the hope of realizing again its attainments. The *Discourses* themselves lie somewhere between the contemporary degraded realities and bursts of enthusiasm for the ideal of a free military republic. Even from chapter to chapter, this tug of war exists.

But Machiavelli was too much of a realist to hold much hope for a renewal of republican vitality, though this does not prevent him from speculating on what other courses might be taken. In this mood, Machiavelli endorses legality, even legal limitations on the ruler. He advo-

---

[16] Machiavelli uses the word "liberty" frequently. When he does so he makes reference to the freedom of the state *per se*, not in terms of individual liberty or freedom of choice.

cates plural control in preference to despotic rule; he recommends elections and free public discussion of issues; he counsels against rule by
force and terror. What he envisions is not quite a proletarian state, but
he does show a fondness for what might now be termed "freedom of
opportunity." Scope must be allowed for the strong and able; his adumbrated suggestion of an élite is one of individual merit, of patriotism,
and of service. There is a covert detestation of hereditary aristocracy.

Somehow one is never really convinced by these occasional bursts of
liberality, however. They appear too much as nostalgic sighs over a
past Latin splendor. Machiavelli's cynicism may not be complete, but
it is in the end convincing. Once again, in the field of international relations, he is torn between a passionate advocacy of Italian unification
and of the sovereignties of princes. Thus he often wishes for the con-
querer—another Borgia who could unite not only Romagna, but all
Italy. But he reads his times well. He can clearly see that what is coming is the national state. He draws the proper inferences from the emergence of Spain and France. It is ironic that Italy, his motherland, was
to wait four hundred years, until the days of Cavour and Massini, to
realize this end. Machiavelli gives us, in fact, the first tentative description of that political entity which has dominated political consideration in the modern period—the nation-state. It is born in the sixteenth
century, passes through the adolescence of the French Revolution, and
reaches maturity in the nineteenth century.

The figure of Machiavelli and his place in the mainstream of human
thought have yet to be fully decided. He raises too many questions.
He is the author of too numerous antitheses. If you stop to reflect, these
perplexities flood in upon you. Does what he has to say hold any meaning beyond his immediate historical era? Was he an immoral scoundrel
whose influence has been only to demean political thought and practice? Was he the originator of a new and still vital mode of political
thought? Was he, in fact, the first political scientist?

Much can be discarded in the thought of this Florentine politician
as being an effect of the Italian Renaissance climate. Among these by-
products are three that may be of significance. First, he is overoccupied
with the problem of keeping power, of relentlessly fending off would-be
usurpers. His view of rulership is too much colored by the metaphor
of the wolf pack. While there is surely some justification for this concern, he allows it to override other factors. He misjudges the possibilities of other forms of political stability, owing partly to his lack of

understanding of the nature of institutions. Secondly, he is not notably scientific in his approach, as he fails to take into account the full range of his data. He assumes that the only essential problem in politics is the technique of rulership, and he arrives at this position by means of a most inadequate psychology. He overemphasizes and oversimplifies human motives. In so doing, he disregards the impact of economic and social pressures and changes. His political theory rests on a narrow psychologism—and one that he has developed from observation of a period in political history marked by its preoccupation with personal aspirations and individual defects. Thirdly, he misinterprets what is growing up under his very nose: social and political alterations wrought by a rapidly developing science. He fails to understand causal relationships between invention and social change. He does so in the limited military sense, holding, for example, that artillery is a mere gadget and missing the point that cannon can do more than pound holes in fortress walls, that they can alter the structure of cities and their governments. Cannon, the printing press, the physics of Newton, all would leave their imprint upon future political life.

Is Machiavelli an immoral scoundrel? This is a pleasant sort of academic parlor game. If one says he is, then there are the rewards of self-righteousness. If one holds that he isn't, then there is the titillation of being touched by the same attractive suggestion of moral turpitude. Too much of Machiavellian criticism seems to run in this vein. The fact is that Machiavelli is a moralist in the strictest sense of that word. He predicates his political philosophy on a moral judgment, namely that men tend to be bad. Now a moralist is one who weighs issues on the basis of their moral component. This is what Machiavelli initially does. If we say that his view of politics is stripped of moral considerations, what we mean is that he does not allow customary notions of good or bad, right or wrong, to influence either his observations or his political recommendations. But this is not to say that his view is immoral. Quite the contrary, the very cynicism of Machiavelli proceeds from a moral assumption, from a reflection on the moral state of human beings. Morality is not an instrument for Machiavelli, nor are politics aimed at making men good (probably impossible, he could comment), but his very amorality grows from his own subjective moral evaluation of human nature.

If this is so, then the question is rather: Is Machiavelli a "bad" moralist? Is he either wrong in his moral judgment or (a slightly different issue) the author of ideas detrimental to what we may choose to describe as moral? The argument that The Prince is a handbook for villains, that dictators have plotted their cruel persecutions by reading Machiavelli in candle-lit cellars must remain a matter of speculation. Further, the question of whether Machiavelli was a writer of political ideas whose effect was destructive of good morals in politics must rest on one's own concept of political morality. This much, though, can be said: It is certain that he was sincere and did not think of himself as an exponent of immortality. It is questionable anyway whether any body of political ideas is in itself dangerous. If Machiavelli or anyone else raises a severe challenge, it is invariably met with a vigor increased by the confrontation. In this sense, it would appear reasonable to assert that Machiavelli's influence has been more salutary than pernicious.

His contribution—and it is not inconsiderable—was the casting of political philosophy in a new light. Shorn of attitudinizing, politics were examined as by a researcher staring at a bubbling beaker. While it is true that Machiavelli's empiricism and his actual methodology appear both crude and impure to an age treated to the display of more sophisticated forms of both, the Florentine broke forever the exclusive hold established by a tradition of political writing that preferred metaphysics to observation. He cleared the way for the freedom and rationalism of the Enlightenment by inculcating a spirit of discovery in social affairs that matched a like urge in the material sciences.

Was he the first political scientist? In retrospect, we can realize that this is a sham question, a parrying with words. Machiavelli was certainly not a scientist—and perhaps no seeker after political truth can or ever will be. But one thing is certain: He was a student of something called *politics,* and, even with Aristotle considered, he was the first of that sturdy genus. Crane Brinton put this in sharp focus when he wrote:

> Machiavelli is the scientist in his initial and very self-conscious stage. He is going to get at what really lies behind all these fine words men write about politics and ethics. He is not going to be content with a few random reflections on these matters. He will study systematically certain problems, not to find out what is right, but just to find out what is. He does not wholly succeed in keeping an even temper, in being as detached as he should be. Above all, he fails in general—though there are signs that he sees the factor concerned—to realize that men's ethical ideas and ideals, even though they do not stand in simple causal relation to men's deeds, stand in *some* relation to men's deeds. In other words, Machiavelli makes the mistake still repeated by some of our deliberately hard-boiled writers on politics and morals;

he writes off men's professions of good just because they do not wholly live up to them.[17]

. . . *for further discussion:*

1. If Machiavelli were alive today and observing the operation of a state government in virtually any one of the fifty states of the United States, do you think he would write another book substantially incorporating the same ideas that he gleaned from Renaissance Italy and put into *The Prince?* What advice might Machiavelli give to the following people: The Republican State Chairman in Georgia, James Hoffa, Pandit Nehru, any ambassador to the United Nations?

2. Machiavelli raises the broad issue of motive in relation to political activity. Political life, the yearning for public office, has attracted all types of men in varying kinds of political systems. What explanations might be advanced to account for this urge to acquire political position? Is it at all possible to reduce this list of motives to one central one? Do you think that the same men who now exercise political power would have done so under other conditions? in the Renaissance? under feudalism? in the last century?

3. Carl Sandburg has created an image of Abraham Lincoln as a kind of popular saint, rural of origin, humanitarian of nature, and lofty of principle. With no view of depreciating the stature or ability of Lincoln, some scholars have criticized this conception as sentimentalized and fictitious (Edmund Wilson, for example). Indeed, it is possible to argue that Lincoln best exemplified in the history of the American presidency the Machiavellian precepts of statecraft. What characteristics, if any, can you find in Lincoln's political techniques that are reminiscent of Machiavelli's admonitions?

4. In the last analysis, do you think Machiavelli viewed power as an absolute end in itself or as an indispensable means to some other end (e.g., the glory of the ruler and state, the ascendancy of the nation)? Is this a valid question? Would Machiavelli have thought so?

. . . *for further investigation:*

Brinton, Crane, *Ideas and Men*. Englewood Cliffs, N. J.: Prentice-Hall, Inc., 1950.

Burnham, James, *The Machiavellians*. New York: The John Day Company, Inc., 1943.

Croce, Benedetto, *Politics and Morals*, S. J. Castiglione, trans. New York: Philosophical Library, Inc., 1946.

De Santillana, Giorgio, ed., * *The Age of Adventure*. New York: Mentor Books, n.d.

---

[17] Crane Brinton, *Ideas and Men* (Englewood Cliffs, N. J.: Prentice-Hall, Inc., 1950), p. 361.

Höffding, Harald, * A *History of Modern Philosophy*, B. E. Meyer, trans. Vol. I. New York: Dover Publications, Inc., 1955.

Machiavelli, Niccolò, * *The Prince* and the *Discourses*. New York: Modern Library, Inc., n.d.

Morley, John, *Machiavelli*. New York: The Macmillan Company, 1897.

Symonds, John A., *The Renaissance in Italy*. New York: Modern Library, Inc., 1935.

Young, George F., *The Medici*. New York: Modern Library, Inc., 1930.

7

WORLDLY EMPIRES
AND THE VOICE
OF DISSENT

Presenting Dante in a chapter following one on Machiavelli commits the sin of historical juggling. In strict chronology, *Dante Alighieri* (1265-1321) well precedes Machiavelli in the parade of Renaissance luminaries. But when one is faced with confusing currents of thought, the exact progressions of history should often be altered in the interest of clarity.

Dante, far more than Machiavelli or even Aquinas, provides the ideological foil for the high drama of the Reformation. Dante's dream of *De Monarchia* reads like an elaborate wish, even a sort of nostalgic meditation. Machiavelli had created too powerful an antithesis for Dante's vision to survive, and the battering rams of Luther and Calvin would complete the demolition. Yet if the soon-to-arise Reformation is to be compared meaningfully to any political-ecclesiastical concept, the logical selection is the imperial dream of Dante.

Dante is not the first poet-philosopher. Lucretius preceded him and many would follow—Goethe, Hölderlin, Coleridge, Emerson, Nietzsche, and Santayana, among others. Doubtless most poets are "philosophical" from time to time, but rarely does the poet possess, or wish to possess, the rigorous discipline required of the truly philosophic mind. It is alien perhaps to the poet's intense subjectivity. There are philosophers who write poetry (Santayana is the best recent example), poets who attempt serious philosophy (Coleridge will illustrate), and, too, those who never quite emerge as either original philosophers or first-rate poets (dare we suggest Emerson here?). Dante, one feels, remains at heart an artist, with all the strengths and shortcomings implied by that laudatory title.

Since we are already guilty of erecting Dante as a "straw man," we must not now obscure the major point of the chapter: that all notions of a widening European polity with its foundations on a universal church are shattered with the Protestant Reformation. Luther and Calvin thunderously announce *finis* to that homogeneity. But one of the most intriguing statements of the idea is found earlier in Dante's *De Monarchia*

Like many others of his age, as we have seen in Chapter 5, Dante was an antipapalist and wrote his lone political essay in order to expound the idea that power flows directly from God to the secular ruler. But Dante, unlike many of his contemporaries, was not a sympathizer with the existing imperial cause. He states:

> It is therefore again manifest that this liberty [free will] of all our liberty, is the greatest gift bestowed by God on mankind; by it alone we gain happiness as men; by it alone we gain happiness elsewhere as gods. But if this be so, who can say that humankind is not in its best state when it can most use this principle? [1]

It may be somewhat surprising on the basis of the above-quoted argument that Dante declares that "he who lives under a monarchy is most free." Dante's advocacy of monarchy has little or nothing to do with any admiration for the trappings of the system or the conviction that monarchs necessarily possess extraordinary gifts. He simply believes that the main political vice is dissension and the best way to deal with it is to establish a monarchical system. Behind it all, for Dante, is the issue of how to establish peace, both within states and between states. To him, the *pax romana* is a model to be studied and partially copied. Partially copied is enough; while the structure of imperial Rome, its administration and organization, might be

---

[1] Dante, *De Monarchia*, Book I, Chapter 12.

adapted with a few alterations here and there, the Roman Empire was after all a pagan creation. Dante was certainly not, like Machiavelli, a convert to paganism.[2]

The hope is the establishment of a new *pax romana* based upon the administrative framework of the old Roman Empire, but wholly Christianized. Dante's view is of a universal Christian society—that means Europe, of course—made fact by the existence of an imperial system. He remonstrates: "Oh, race of mankind, what storms must toss thee, what losses thou must endure, what shipwrecks must buffet thee, as long as thou, a beast of many heads, strivest after contrary things!"[3]

Dante's ambition for spiritual and political unity was to be dashed in a violent earthquake. Europe would be rent apart by religious conflict; the bitterest wars yet seen in the West would turn Germany into a charnel house for nearly thirty years. Thousands would die and dynasties would fall before the wrath subsided.

It all began quietly enough. In 1517, a German priest and theology professor, Martin Luther, disenchanted with some aspects of the established Church, penned his objections and tacked them to the door of a church in Wittenberg. Luther's epistle—the ninety-five theses—was the initial act in a drama entitled the Reformation. Europe became split into two camps, armed camps in both the ideological and literal sense.

Surely this massive onslaught could not have been the result of the disaffection of one priest, however dramatic his excommunication as a heretic. Luther's personal rebellion, while provocative, is only tangential to the basic causes responsible for inducing half of Europe to spurn the Catholic faith and to adopt the new dogma—Protestantism.

It is not accidental that Luther was a German or that he was protected by the German princes or that he gave unstinting support to his secular benefactors. One of the primary causes of the Reformation was certainly the political struggle with Rome. The Catholic Church was hardly a body of mere theologians; it was a political force and did not hesitate to assert what it claimed to be its prerogatives. The

---

[2] Dante describes faith as knowledge beyond reason: "The other conclusions and means are made manifest by the Holy Spirit, who by the mouth of the Prophets and holy writers and by Jesus Christ, the co-eternal Son of God, and His disciples, has revealed to us supernatural truth of which we have great need." (*De Monarchia*, Book III, Chapter 16.)

[3] *Ibid.*, Book I, Chapter 15.

feeling of national consciousness paralleling the growth of states in the sixteenth century was understandably anti-Rome if not anti-Catholic.

Further, feudalism as a social system was dying for a variety of reasons, not the least among them being the rise of the mercantile class. The feudal scheme could not really accommodate itself to the appearance of a middle class, well-to-do, urban, industrious, and self-assured. Moreover, this mercantile class, besides triggering social change, shook up the theological placidity as well. For a quartet of reasons, this bourgeoisie grew restless within the Catholic Church. First, it chafed under the hierarchical assumptions of the Roman Catholic faith, dependent upon the concept of priestly authority. The mood of the new middle class was more egalitarian and much less fond of sacerdotal pomp.

Secondly, the primary preoccupation of the merchant class was property in one form or another. The admonition of the Church to divest oneself of riches while bishops enjoyed the spoils of Church wealth rankled the burghers.

Thirdly, the mood of the new class was hard-working and essentially pious. Like all middle classes throughout history, this one, too, admired industry and personal rectitude. We might refer to its members as "upright citizens." In any case, they were intensely critical of the not inconsiderable moral corruption of the Roman clergy. They resented the ease with which some moral corners could be cut.

Finally, the new bourgeoisie was nationalistic, not pan-European. It was a peaceful sort of nationalism; it was a desire to be left alone so that they might get on with the business of becoming prosperous. A European imperial system held no allure for a merchant class having no wish to be taxed for the convenience of a remote emperor.

To put the whole matter simply, the middle class was lacking in a theology that suited its needs. Protestantism, particularly Calvinism, supplied it. Someone has said wryly that Luther's teachings were ideally suited to the requirements of German aristocrats; Calvin's to the needs of Swiss shopkeepers. While it is true that Luther's new religion was endorsed and defended by princes and barons, the impetus of the Protestant Reformation was supplied by the emerging middle class.

The rebellion of Luther set off these latent hostilities. But the shape of both events and doctrines to come were to be forged significantly by the man himself. *Martin Luther* (1483-1546) is one of those persons about whom it is impossible to be indifferent. Aggressive, self-confident, bellicose, even imperious, Luther either appeals as a giant of courage and a seer of transcendental visions or he repels as a bigot and a moral compromiser. In any case, he is a complex and even contradictory figure. This divergence of view on the character of Luther (and, indeed, on a number of other Reformation leaders—e.g., Calvin and Knox) is a reflection of Luther's basic orientation, the fundamental disagreement between himself and the Catholic Church. At bedrock Luther was a mystic, and the schism arising out of the Reformation was due primarily to Protestantism's disavowal of the theological rationalism of Catholicism and its replacement by the concept of knowledge of God through immediate, personal mystical experience.

This is obviously not the place to describe the theological issues presented by the Reformation, but the political consequences of the Reformation are better understood against the background of the theological quarrel. Luther, then, eschewed rationalism in favor of transcendental experience, the direct intuition of God. This, of course, made religion a far more subjective matter than it had been before. Now, "every man his own theologian" was not far from the fact. Personal freedom in making religious decisions suggests a similar freedom in political decision, although both Luther and Calvin deny this. The abandonment of rationalism and a presumed objective, constant, and universal rule (i.e., natural law) and its substitution by revelation were bound to have numerous direct effects on political thought.

What did Luther himself have to say on the problems of politics? All of his pronouncements on politics (and they are scattered through a number of his works) are really variations on the theme of *duty*. Where does the reform Christian's duty lie? And in this question lurks the dilemma that constantly confronts Luther, a dilemma reducible to a simple proposition: Man has a duty only to God, not to priests, yet man must unquestioningly obey the secular rule, says Luther. But this implies that Luther is taking the position that man is spiritually free and politically captive. Why does Luther take this position? Is it a tenable argument?

Interpreting Luther is troublesome because of the contrasts in his nature. He is at once an eloquent apostle of freedom and a convinced aristocrat who says that the "common people are Satan." "A worldly kingdom," he wrote, "cannot stand unless there is in it an inequality of persons, so that some are free, some imprisoned, some lords and some subjects, etc." [4] Luther's belief in spiritual freedom we will assume to be consistent with his theological premises. His doctrine of secular obedience is also consistent, but with premises of a different sort. In essence, the two conclusions are not causally related. Luther's argument for spiritual freedom proceeds from his concept of the soul; his argument for obedience proceeds from the political realities of the sixteenth century. Luther knew full well that he was engaged in a test of strength with Rome that was no mere academic dispute. It was a political struggle that required the creation out of the rebellious German princes of a political front to match the secular arms available to Rome. This required an exchange of commitments: secular power in support of Lutheranism for Luther's affirmation of princely authority. In order to prevail against the appeal of a Dante-like imperial system, Luther sought to shore up the national state, and he did in fact openly appeal to German patriotism and suspicion of "Italian" ambitions. A formidable man was Luther; not every man would, as Luther tells of himself, rout the Devil by heaving an ink pot at him.

This ambivalent attitude toward freedom did evidently cause Luther some internal disquiet. He was a man of intense feelings and convinced of the rightness of his introspective urgings. Such impulses led him to condemn the Peasants' Revolt in 1525 in language of remarkable severity.[5] Yet he did not see or did not choose to see the relationship between the political purposes of this revolt and his religious message. This willingness to accept political absolutism on Luther's part stems from his different appraisal of the individual-society relationship. Luther was violent in his rejection of Aristotelianism and in his opposition saw man as a spiritual individual and society as a totality of spiritually autonomous persons. Society had nothing to do with the spiritual nature of man; man was not a social or political being in this older sense. Consequently, beyond individual human souls, there was only temporal arrangement divested of real significance. Therefore, Luther's view of the individual was far different from the medieval one. It was more otherworldly, less socially oriented, but far more radically "individualistic." Luther could dismiss, as he did, much concern for the popular welfare. Political arrangement had

---

[4] Martin Luther, *Admonition to Peace: A Reply to the Twelve Articles of the Peasants in Swabia.*

[5] He recommended giving the "mad peasants" an opportunity to surrender and if they did not, "then quickly grasp the sword."

nothing to do with moral fulfillment, either in the case of persons or societies. God gave authority to princes directly, as Luther argues, primarily to maintain order and to be instruments of divine chastisement.

His doctrine of passive obedience to worldly authority was rooted in yet another conviction. Luther's religion was quietistic and benign. The temporal life of man was described in terms of a brief period of trials and troubles, leading eventually to the reward of eternal life for the faithful. The importance of this life was deëmphasized. The tribulations of wicked rule, then, must be borne, according to Luther, and complaint can be made only to God. Suffering is the lot of men on this earth and persecution by tyrants cannot be excepted from the general ordeal. It is for the Christian to bear these burdens silently and obediently, while awaiting succor from God, Who alone is capable of punishing and rewarding.

Whatever misgivings Luther may have had regarding the conciliation of freedom and obedience, he considered his position to be an eminently tenable one. That other major figure of the Reformation, Calvin, agreed with him in principle. However, later Protestant thinkers—especially when political measures were being employed to suppress the promulgation of their religious beliefs—resolutely took the stand that theological freedom and individualism had as their logical consequence political freedom and individualism. However Luther might have wished otherwise, it was inevitable that his act of rebellion against Rome and the rationale upon which it was based would be expanded to include a mounting justification for rebellion against secular absolutism. But to describe this snowballing effect now would be to rush the narrative. Calvin is yet to be heard from.

John Calvin (1509-1564) possessed a voice that, metaphorically speaking, reverberated throughout Europe. It was a loud voice, compelling in sheer volume of influence. It gathered more converts than did the preaching of Luther. Calvin's long-range impact was probably greater as well, even if only for the reason that he undertook to turn his attention to a broader collection of concerns. His influence was deep, and many observers find it still operative in a host of contemporary attitudes toward such diverse matters as economic theory, public morals, the status of women, advertising, and club membership, to say nothing of religion.

If Calvin's teachings made such an impression, it is largely the result of the man himself. Somehow the word "cyclonic" seems apropos for Calvin. Unlike Luther, he was invariably in a frenzy of activity; he was an endless producer of writing, a driving organizational administrator, a militant general of a religious army, always a relentless crusader. He seemed to possess unlimited resources of energy and resolve. A modern psychologist might describe Calvin as being compulsive—and some modern critics have gone further to describe him as paranoid. He did appear pursued, either by the Furies or by the voice of God, depending on one's private judgment of Calvin. Inexorable, inflexible, unwilling to brook the slightest divergence of view, Calvin was often vindictive, and the charge of cruelty and wholesale persecution has been leveled against him.[6]

A French lawyer, Calvin embraced the break with Catholicism, and his heretical activities forced him to flee to Geneva—that sanctuary for the dispossessed. Save for one temporary expulsion from that Swiss city, he remained there for the rest of his life. On Geneva he imposed what was a virtual ecclesiastical dictatorship, a "rule of the saints." The best description of this community under Calvin is to be found in R. H. Tawney's engrossing book, *Religion and the Rise of Capitalism*. Tawney relates that Calvin "made Geneva a city of glass, in which every household lived its life under the supervision of the spiritual police." Yet that fervent Calvin disciple, John Knox, was moved to describe Geneva under Calvinist domination as "the most perfect school of Christ that ever was on earth since the days of the Apostles." It is clear that fanaticism was an ingredient added to the political life of the West by the religious controversies arising from the Reformation. This fanaticism was primarily Calvinist in origin, but it soon became widespread. Luther, for all his diatribes against "mad peasants" and the immoralities of Rome, was not given to the sort of compulsive militancy that absorbed Calvin. Lutheranism was essentially a personal salvation; Calvinism was an evangelical faith. It existed on the momentum of spreading its gospel, converting, conquering. The spirit of Calvinism was activist, its organizational framework basically military in tone.

Calvinism as a creed demanded of its adherents two qualities above all else: *discipline* and *piety*. Both were required in extreme measure by Calvin. Only by discipline could the faith be maintained and

---

[6] There is disagreement as to how many persons died from torture or burning under Calvin at Geneva. The figures range to over two hundred in some accounts. The best source, Preserved Smith, puts the figure at fifty-eight during the years 1542-1545.

spread, and only by the practice and enforcement of piety could the Christian glorify God. The emphasis on discipline and, especially, piety might suggest to some that Calvinism was much concerned with the moral welfare of the individual. Such was not the case, however. All was done to glorify God; God's grace alone could save men, and individuals were powerless to help themselves. Piety was not practiced for its moral import, but for the fact that it represented obedience to what Calvin construed to be God's law.

This belief in human helplessness was linked to a similar belief in essential human depravity, the result of Adam's transgression. A further Calvinistic embellishment was the doctrines of *election* and *foreordination*. Very briefly, these doctrines amount to the following propositions: Human salvation results only from the intervention of God's grace. God grants salvation to some and denies it to others, not on the basis of acts in this life, but on the basis of His own unknown designs. God does not necessarily withhold His grace from His chosen ones in this life, but rather "elects" them in the present life. There are visible signs of God's election—one man's fields may prosper and his fortunes multiply, while another's decline. Foreordination applies to the establishment by God of a body of saints—on earth, in this life—whose purpose it is to lead the faithful and protect and extend the church.

Such doctrines contain immediate implications for social and political thought. Socially speaking, Calvinism was the hoped for gospel of the commercial classes; it actually endorsed the acquisitive dispositions of the merchant-citizen. It went further than accommodating the middle-class virtues of hard work, thrift, business acumen, and social mobility based on property; it preached that God's favor was indicated by material prosperity. And it is far from accidental that conversions to Calvinism were heaviest in the urban trading centers of Northern Europe. Calvinism was the faith of the new urbanite.

More directly political, the doctrine of foreordination implies the establishment of a *theocracy*.[7] Calvin denied this in theory, but accepted it in practice, and he was more or less bound to do so for the sake of dogmatic consistency. If, to put it in a much oversimplified fashion, God ordains saints to safeguard the flock, then it follows that the separation between church and state must necessarily be a token one, if existent at all. What Calvin proposed to do—and he leaves us

---

[7] *Theocracy:* a political system organized so that political authority and ecclesiastical authority reside in a common governing body, and political participation is restricted to practicing adherents of the church.

in no doubt—was to resolve once and for all the wrangling between secular and ecclesiastical authority. Discussing the necessity of bringing these two powers into their proper relationship, Calvin comments:

> I am under necessity of doing so, especially while, on the one hand, frantic and barbarous men are furiously endeavoring to overturn the order established by God, and, on the other, the flatterers of princes, extolling their power without measure, hesitate not to oppose it to the government of God. Unless we meet both extremes, the purity of the faith will perish.[8]

Calvin's avoidance of "both extremes" led him to a theocratic position, a point in the road quickly reached by many of his disciples.[9] But it might be well to inquire just why within Calvin's theocracy there remain the two separate skeletons of civil and church government. Calvin puts the need for some type of civil government this way:

> But if it is the will of God that while we aspire to true piety we are pilgrims upon the earth, and if such pilgrimage stands in need of such aids, those who take them away from man rob him of his humanity. As to their allegation that there ought to be such perfection in the church of God that her guidance should suffice for law, they stupidly imagine her to be such as she can never be found in the community of men. For while the insolence of the wicked is great, and their iniquity is so stubborn that it can scarcely be curbed by any severity of laws, what do we expect would be done by those whom force can scarcely repress from doing ill, were they to see perfect impunity for their wickedness? [10]

The civil authority was to be an instrument of law—Calvin, the ex-lawyer, never lost his regard for law, and the *Institutes* preserves a legalistic tone. But what was the function of law to be? Calvin had a simple answer: Law is a means of curbing impiety, heresy, idolatry, and other forms of backsliding; it is the method of preserving purity by wielding the stick of punishment. Law must maintain the "purity of the faith." And Calvin is prepared to go even further than Plato was in his darker moods in the *Laws* to act against the corruption of the faith:

> For in the minds of many the love of equity and justice grows cold, if due honor be not paid to virtue, and the licentiousness of the wicked

---

[8] John Calvin, *The Institutes of the Christian Religion*, Volume III, Book IV, Chapter 20. The *Institutes* is Calvin's chief work. It has been called the "Protestant *Summa.*"

[9] Well-known examples of this theoretic philosophy and practice are the early Puritan colonies founded in New England.

[10] Calvin, *op. cit.*, Chapter 20.

cannot be restrained without strict discipline and the infliction of punishment. The two things are comprehended by the prophet when he enjoins kings and other rulers to execute "judgment and righteousness" (Jer. xxi. 12; xxii. 3). It is righteousness (justice) to take charge of the innocent, to defend and avenge them, and set them free; it is judgment to withstand the audacity of the wicked, to repress their violence, and punish their faults.[11]

If the aim of law—and the stream of civil authority—is to safeguard the faith, it is plainly not wholly a secular matter. What is the faith? What acts jeopardize it? How is wickedness to be judged? Who are the innocent? Answers to these questions demand a criterion certainly beyond the conventional scope of civil jurisdiction. If civil authorities are to punish on the basis of theological strictures, it is either necessary that civil authorities be in fact saints or that civil punishment be left in the hands of the clergy. What Calvin suggests theoretically is a dedicated élite of Christian magistrates, virtual lay apostles, who exercise temporal power in support of the faith. But is it not difficult to maintain a distinction between such a magistrate and a leader within the church proper? Moreover, is it the most efficient arrangement? Would it not be simpler to dispense justice from the altar and be done with it? Many of Calvin's followers thought so and, indeed, Calvin himself functioned in both roles at the same time.

It is evident that Calvin did not really solve the church-state problem, other than to imply the desirability of a theocratic solution. What is interesting to note is that Calvin shies away from any inkling of "popular sovereignty" as suggested in Cicero or the writings of some of the Scholastics. For him, sovereignty is directly conferred upon what he calls the "Magistrate." He does not mean by this that the Magistrate must be a single individual. In the main, he is hostile toward monarchy and prefers an élitist concept, with power belonging to a small ruling council. Calvin's point of view has been described as aristocratic, but this is a dubious usage since his élite features none of the public service ideals usually associated with aristocracy. This ruling junta, ecclesiastical in fact if not in title, is endowed with absolute power; its accountability is only to God. What Calvin proposes— and put into practice in Geneva—is a stern authoritarianism. If the closed state can be imagined, Calvin's is a good approximation. Its restrictive character rests on theology; law is the machinery of compliance.

[11] *Ibid.*, Chapter 20.

Calvinism was a revolutionary doctrine not because it sought to overturn the familiar ruler-ruled relationship, but rather because it wished to redefine the base upon which political society rested. It drastically altered the aims of the polity, shifted the concern about social institutions from the multipurpose view of the Scholastics to one of singleness of purpose. Although Calvin seems to be far more engrossed in the problems of secular institutions than Luther, even he attributes only transient meaning to their nature and operation. To reduce this revolutionary difference to its most radical expression: Calvin looked at political arrangements as something one artificially imposes from above, while the Aristotelian tradition assumes that political organization is something that arises from beneath, an expression of the natural order, the result of the widening development of the *telos*. If Calvin's God is undiscoverable by means of reason, then it is not remarkable that Calvin saw no justification for the assumption that the natural order is in any way directly linked to a rational divine plan. God does what He chooses. He elects; He damns; He changes the shape of things at will. His ways are inscrutable, and it is blasphemous for Calvinists to argue that man has a right to expect God to be consistent by human standards of that quality. Not only is nature a mere temporary arena for human trial, it is unreliable and even dangerous, filled as it is with Satanic pitfalls and temptations of the flesh. To entertain the idea either that political institutions are natural or that man is divinely endowed with social obligations is unthinkable for Calvinists, since it assumes both God's unknowable purposes and the existence of some relationship between man and God other than personal revelation. These assumptions held by Calvinists, when joined to their evangelical ardor, amounted to a revolution in political and social ideas.

If the revolutionary elements in Calvin's philosophy were theoretical, they were made fact by several of his leading adherents. Under their direction, Calvinism became a creed for political revolution. Swept away was Calvin's personal disdain for political agitation; such reserve vanished with the belief in the necessity of obedience. Freedom of conscience (in that rather schizophrenic Calvinist sense) meant freedom to disavow and overthrow governments and dynasties. Calvinism had always been a militant persuasion, but now it became an international pressure group which did not hold back at the employment of the sword. It brought on a vengeful and sometimes sinister response from the Roman Church—the Counter-Reformation and the

Inquisition. Religious wars broke out in France; England was split by a civil war fought between rival shades of nominally Protestant devotion. There was a new radicalism in the Calvinist movement, a radicalism foreign even to the authoritarian mind of John Calvin.

No more zealous admirer of Calvin lived than John Knox, for example, but Knox's Calvinism called for popular conspiracy against the Catholic house of Stuart on the ground that rebellion against an heretical ruler is not merely a legally sanctioned act, but a solemn duty. Knox passionately inveighed against his Catholic enemies and even exhorted his faction to take up arms and put the followers of Rome to the sword.

The struggle between the Huguenots in France and their Catholic antagonists—which included such unspeakable horrors as the St. Bartholomew's Day massacre—reached such a frenzy of hatred and sanguinary lust that even the more moderate of Calvin's disciples, his biographer Beza, for example, turned their backs on his doctrine of obedience. Persecution produced a flood of polemical tracts, revolutionary and eloquent, and there was a curious aspect of this inflammatory rhetoric. The Calvinists, both in Scotland and France (and later in England), found themselves immediately under attack not only from Catholics, but from Catholics (or Anglican Catholics) *in power*, those holding political authority. The Protestant rebuttals were aimed not merely against the competing theology, but against the existing authority that was suppressing them. Calvinist writers, then, began more and more to shift the weight of their barrage to the generally existing forms of royal absolutism. "The Enemy" was no longer the pope; it had become the crown.

The arguments leveled against the authority of the monarch were varied, and in the next chapter we shall consider the controversy of the "divine right" as the basis for kingship. One of these antimonarchical tracts deserves mention, because it illustrates the main ideas of the Reformation and because its principal motif is the right to resist.

The *Vindiciae contra tyrannos* is unusual among the classics of political thought if for no other reason than that its authorship has not been definitely established. There has been considerable scholarship devoted to authenticating its authorship, but there is no general agreement.[12] In any case, it appeared in France in 1579 and was certainly the product of the Huguenots. The pamphlet, as we would probably classify it today, is noteworthy for its boldness, general originality, and insight. It deserves methodical study because it contains in embryo many of the ideas that appear in fuller plumage later on. Three of these are manifest in the *Vindiciae* in unmistakable shape: (1) sovereignty's residence in the collective body of subjects, (2) the social contract, and, (3) the right of revolution.

In form, the *Vindiciae* is a response to four hypothetical questions: (1) Is obedience required to a ruler violating the law of God? (2) Is it lawful to resist a ruler who acts in violation of the church and against its interests? (3) Is resistance lawful against a ruler who is oppressive and who is acting against the state, and, if so, who may resist and in what fashion and by what justification? (4) Should a ruler aid the people of a neighboring state who are being oppressed by a tyrant, particularly on religious grounds?

Some of the questions elicited well-known answers, responses one might expect looking back over the literature of antipapal writing and Reformation ideas. Indeed, the *Vindiciae* is in part straightforward Calvinism. But in sections of the work, particularly the famous Part III, the anonymous author begins to deal with political matters that exhibit little direct connection with Calvinist theology. The most striking of these political asides is the discussion of contract. Discourse on the subject of the contract theory was to keep political philosophers occupied on into the nineteenth century. In this early form, the idea of contract involves two separate phases or, possibly, even two distinct components. The primary contract was an agreement between God and mankind to form the church. This idea is not quite so prosaic as it might now seem. Calvinism had been moving toward a sort of contract theory concerned with the matter of free will; now it appears as an explanation for the establishment of the church—which is taken to mean the only real human community.

The second contract was between king and subjects. It established the political community; it created the state. The author of the *Vindiciae* explains:

> In this pact, it was a matter of creating a king; for the people made the king, not vice versa. It cannot be doubted that in this contract

---

[12] The *Vindiciae* was signed by the *nom de plume* Stephanus Junius Brutus. Like speculations over who wrote the works of Shakespeare, there are numerous candidates for the authorship of this work. Hubert Languet (the choice of Sir Ernest Barker) and one Phillipe du Plessis-Mornay are currently heading the list, but there are others—Theodore Beza and Francis Hotoman among them.

the people had the part of stipulator, the king that of promiser. And the part of the stipulator is deemed more advantageous at law. The people, as stipulator, ask the king whether he will govern justly and according to the laws; the king promises that he will. The people then respond that they will faithfully obey him while he governs justly. The king, therefore, promises absolutely, the people conditionally; if the condition is not fulfilled the people are absolved from every obligation.[13]

The concept of the contract as stated above is clear enough, but the difficulty springs from the *Vindiciae's* vacillation as to the source of monarchical power. "In a word, all kings were in the beginning elected," reads the *Vindiciae*. Elsewhere: ". . . it is God who establishes kings." How does this square with the idea of the people as ultimate possessors of sovereignty? Does God choose and man remove? Surely this is not feasible. Perhaps the solution lies in the concept of the peoples' choice as God's will—*vox populi, vox Dei*. The *Vindiciae* is not certain. It is still in the theological web. But however vague and even bizarre some of the arguments might appear in the *Vindiciae*,[14] it is not hard to see where the major thesis is leading. The contract idea, imprecise and even fanciful, does provide a tenable premise upon which to rest an advocacy of limited sovereignty. The effect is to provide a quasilegal justification for the trimming of the royal wings, while at the same time maintaining the basic Christian or, more specifically, Protestant orthodoxy. Hobbes, unencumbered by theological obeisances, would later press aspects of this general argument to more radical terminations and then reverse the whole conclusion.

The repeated message of the *Vindiciae* is that government must exist on the basis of consent. It is the first unequivocal statement of this thesis. This consent is held so fundamental that its absence is full justification for rebellion. Consider this remarkable passage:

> As thus the law of nature, the law of nations, and civil law command us to take arms against tyrants, no other reason can properly dissuade us. No oath or other pact, public or private, interposes to prevent us. It is, therefore, permitted to any private person to eject an intruding tyrant.[15]

---

[13] *Vindiciae contra tyrannos*, Part III.

[14] Many have held that the entire idea of an original contract is an absurd fiction. Even the *Vindiciae* is sensitive on this point: "Even if the formalities of a contract never have taken place, are we not sufficiently taught by nature herself that kings are established by the people on the condition that they govern well?"

[15] *Vindiciae contra tyrannos*, Part III.

The phrase "any private person" stands out. Did not Aquinas also hold that a ruler can be legitimately deposed if he transgresses the natural law? Yes, but Aquinas, as well as all others prior to the *Vindiciae*, held that such a deposition must result from the collective action of the subjects, *not* individual wills. The provocative feature of the *Vindiciae's* doctrine of resistance is that it incorporates the Reformation's elevation of the individual conscience. The duty to resist is an individual act of mind and will, since, indeed, the tyrant himself must be judged as an individual criminal. The *Vindiciae* contends:

> He [the ruler] is as much more vicious than the ordinary bandit, murderer, or oath-breaker, as it is more serious to offend against the many or all than against particular individuals. If these private offenses are deemed infamous and are punishable by death, is it possible to devise a penalty worthy of a crime so atrocious as tyranny? [16]

The tyrant is more than a criminal, he is also a traitor, argues the *Vindiciae*.

> It follows that the tyrant commits a felony against the people—the lord of the fief; he is guilty of treason against the kingdom or empire; he is a rebel. He has thus violated the same laws that the ordinary criminal violates and merits a far severer punishment.[17]

As the *Vindiciae* exalts the people and depreciates the monarch, it does not do so in order to lay the foundation for some democratic theory of the state. The tract is not a preamble to a constitution of a popular government. If the people *establish* monarchies, it does not necessarily follow that the people should rule. The very idea of the contract would tend to deny this. The king has a legitimate function, provided he acknowledges the covenant. Even when the monarch commits a tyrannical abuse, the proper check upon him should come from what the *Vindiciae* describes as the "electors, patricians, peers, and other nobles." They have the responsibility for watch-dogging the ruler; the *Vindiciae* refers to them as "co-guardians" and to the king as "chief guardian." These officers of the state, presumably a body of aristocrats, are to be the major safeguard of justice in the state sketchily drawn in the *Vindiciae*. "If they undertake to save the commonwealth," the *Vindiciae* explains, "and defend it with their powers, they are protectors, guardians, and, in a sense, kings themselves." Consent, then, advanced as the proper base of a just government, does not yet imply participation or continuing representation.

---

[16] *Ibid.*
[17] *Ibid.*

The concept of the contract will, however, ultimately include the recommendation of popular involvement in the act of governing.

The Reformation had permanently redirected the course of European political thought. It had written a final chapter to many of the fondest convictions of the medieval age, and it had provoked the creation of new ones. Its vigor, even in its frequent extremes, hastened the coming of the Enlightenment in the century that followed. If the Reformation itself had been a strenuous rejection of the medieval values, it brought about value proposals of equal force and significance. And, as is almost invariably the case, it carried with it the germs of the ideas that would ultimately be used to attack it. In retrospect, the effects of the Reformation on political philosophy can be isolated without great difficulty. In substance, they are these:

1. The Reformation presented the first comprehensive exposition of *irrationalism* [18] seen in the West since the pre-Socratic Greeks. Prior to Luther and Calvin there had been a virtually unbroken chain of intellectual development which rested on the assumption that the primary source of human knowledge lay in the operation of reason. This was as true of the Christian Scholastics as it was of the Greek Stoics. What the Reformation had done was to assault this rationalistic orientation by asserting that, on the contrary, the primary source of human knowledge was not reason, but divine revelation. Knowledge, then, was not an objective, discoverable body of truths (e.g., natural law), but rather personal intuitions of God through His intervention. However the Enlightenment worked to rebuild the edifice of rationalism, it never wholly succeeded. The Reformation, even after undergoing marked metamorphosis, contributed to the continued presence of irrationalism as a potent influence in the subsequent history of political ideas.

2. The Reformation offered a new account of the relationship between the individual and society. The Aristotelian organic society was incompatible with the Reformation view that the sole significant relationship was God-to-man; it allowed no supplemental man-to-man relationship in the sense that that relationship is a part of a divinely ordered scheme. Society, to Luther or Calvin, was a collection of autonomous souls. Political arrangements, obedience, law, etc., were

---

[18] The word "irrationalism" properly used does not refer to mental disorganization or unreasonable convictions. Rather does it refer to the denial that reason is the most certain form of knowledge.

all temporal matters that were merely transient devices, all devoted to otherworldly ends. Man was not a social being, and he owed obligation to society only to the extent that he found it necessary to enter a compact for the protection and propagation of the faith. There was nothing natural, mystic, or organic about societies or states. They were man-made constructs, erected to further piety.

This was the beginning of the "new individualism." Society was beginning to be seen as a collection of individuals—whether they be "souls," or predatory mammals, or creatures endowed with "unalienable rights." Is the whole greater than the sum of its parts? The effect of the Reformation was to reopen the question.

3. The Reformation shattered the monopoly of the moralistically oriented philosophy of the classical age. It did so by radically reappraising the whole nature of ethics. The Greek aim, accepted by the medieval thinkers, of government as moral preceptor or as an agency for fostering conditions favorable to moral growth was inconsistent with the Reformation view that such salvation rested only on God's grace. True, Calvin would use the monopoly of the state to enforce piety, but this is not the same as either encouraging moral behavior or implementing moral growth. The aim of the Calvinists was distinctly negative in this sense. One was pious in order to assure oneself of the possibility of salvation—impiety equaled damnation. But piety in itself grants no assurance of salvation. This reserved the whole matter of ethics to mysticism and reshaped moral philosophy root and branch by redefining moral responsibility. Ethics became highly simplified; ethical principles were either self-evident and enforceable or beyond human ability to comprehend. This narrowed the scope of moral speculation drastically. It affected the entire development of ethical thought in the next century and had the effect on political philosophy of turning it toward law and psychology for its fundamental concepts.

4. The religious strife that trailed in the wake of the Reformation introduced the element of systematic intolerance into the history of thought. There had been persecutions before, a thousandfold, but they were caused by factors other than the conviction that a human being holding differing religious views must be either converted or slain. Such an idea was really quite shockingly un-European until the sixteenth century. Tyrants by the legion had existed; madmen like Nero and Caligula had persecuted a religious minority, and Charlemagne had spread Christianity at the point of a lance. No parallel exists, however, between the attitudes of the Greeks, the Romans, and the

medieval Europeans and the post-Reformation use of the machinery of the state to crush wholesale doctrinal defection. This institutionalized intolerance provoked some most brilliant thought in rebuttal—and it also left a hideous legacy to the political record of the West.

5. The Reformation ushered in an era of secularism. It is perhaps paradoxical that this should be true, but the preoccupation with religion that permeated all aspects of life in the sixteenth century created a powerful recoil in the seventeenth and an even more extensive secularization of thought in the eighteenth centuries. The Reformation had not only made religion too bloody to suit many, but it also made it far too grim, authoritarian, dour, and colorless. These attitudes propelled the Counter-Reformation, but they were also a spur to a rising humanism and a repugnance for religious dogmatism.

Oddly enough, Protestantism itself, with its aversion to sacerdotalism, had tended to secularize worship and to reduce the aura of ecclesiastical remoteness to the point where both fragmentation of doctrines and variation of private opinion had encouraged an increasing spirit of independence from any religious commitment. The Protestant view of sin as inescapable and irremediable had effects other than inducing contrition and piety; it turned some toward moral nihilism.

Above the smoke of religious combat, eyeing the battle with a careful scrutiny, sat the kings of Europe, aware that the cannonballs that had once been aimed solely at Catholics and Protestants were beginning to pass uncomfortably close to their royal heads. There was no cause for real alarm, they concluded, for, after all, theirs was a divine sinecure. "L'état, c'est moi," Louis of France was to say, but he also, in a less optimistic moment, would have a motto cast into the barrels of his cannon: "The last resort of kings."

. . . for further discussion:

1. Most political ideologies have nothing but good to say about something called "freedom." The democracies of the West use the word with almost deadening repetitiveness; communism, too, glorifies its own notion of freedom. The problem of definition is monumental, but so is the problem of accounting for the origins of freedom. Why is man free? What sort of explanations can you think of to support the contention that man either is naturally free or ought to be free? The Reformation did a good deal of talking about "free will." Does this have anything to do with political freedom?

2. If Calvin believed that the law ought to be used to enforce piety, are current squabbles over book and motion picture censorship examples of Calvin's point of view being debated? Are enforcing piety and maintaining governmental regulation of materials allegedly detrimental to the public morals the same thing? Is this ever a justifiable exercise of governmental authority? Some would argue that freedom cannot consist of the right to debauch oneself, and others that the public has no right to abridge one's right to make private judgments on the moral content of literature or art. Is the issue of freedom involved here?

3. Only one President of the United States was not a bona fide member of a religious denomination. This is a far lower percentage than exists in the public at large. Discounting the issue of just how "religious" presidents and other politicians in fact are, virtually all of them make considerable public show of their devotion to religion, even though the United States is a pluralistic, rather secular society, and the separation of church and state is fundamental to the Constitution. What conclusions would you draw from this fact as to the remaining influence of religion on politics?

4. Early Protestantism was very much immersed in the tug of war of worldly politics. Since the Reformation and the ensuing religious conflict, organized religion has, in the main, grown aloof from actively taking sides on avowedly political questions. Is this a good thing or ought religious organizations to play a more forthright role in the debate on political ideas and issues?

. . . for further investigation:

Brinton, Crane, *Ideas and Men*. Englewood Cliffs, N. J.: Prentice-Hall, Inc., 1950.

Calvin, John, *Institutes of the Christian Religion*, John T. McNeill, ed., 2 vols. Philadelphia, Pa.: The Westminster Press, 1960.

Dante, Alighieri, *De Monarchia*, F. J. Church, trans. New York: The Macmillan Company, 1879.

Gilson, Etienne, *Dante the Philosopher*. New York: Sheed and Ward, 1948.

Luther, Martin, *Collected Works*. Philadelphia, Pa.: A. J. Holman Co., 1915-1932.

————, *Reformation Writings of Martin Luther*, B. L. Woolf, trans. New York: Philosophical Library, Inc., 1953.

Smith, Preserved, * *The Age of the Reformation*, 2 vols. New York: Collier Books, n.d.

Tawney, Richard H., * *Religion and the Rise of Capitalism*. New York: Mentor Books, n.d.

Taylor, Henry O., *Thought and Expression in the Sixteenth Century*, 2 vols. New York: Frederick Ungar Publishing Co., 1959.

Weber, Max, * *The Protestant Ethic and the Spirit of Capitalism*. New York: Charles Scribner's Sons, 1948.

8

THE TWILIGHT OF
THE KINGS

Thomas Hobbes set out to rescue the monarchy and succeeded in bulldozing away the last defenses of the divine right argument. He put his not unformidable dialectical sword at the disposal of the Stuart dynasty, and in his zeal he cut away the ground upon which they stood as absolute monarchs.

Hobbes was born into a world of royal absolutism. The best political system was conceived to be benevolent despotism. States were kingdoms; countries were the private preserves of dynastic inheritance. Even among those critical of royal privilege, many would argue that royal absolutism was the best form of government that was obtainable in practice; others would maintain that the formal arrangement of government was a trivial matter, administrative skill and devotion being the paramount consideration. The Scholastic tradition supported, in the main, the royal prerogative, and the legalists, following Bodin's preachments on sovereignty,[1] rallied to the banner of monarchy. Patriotic sentiment upheld divine right. The territorial consolidation of states, largely accomplished by the sixteenth century, buttressed the monarchical institution.

But even in the midst of unfettered royal grandeur, certain concessions were evident. Kings were conceived to be bound to support the general good rather than personal aggrandizement; they were expected to be hard-working and dedicated. They themselves realized that popularity was imperative, and they openly sought general support. But time was running out for the legally unrestricted monarch. The assault of the Protestant publicists and antiroyalist pamphleteers was mounting. Yet, on solely legal grounds, the advocates of divine right appeared to have a reasonably good case. Five centuries of discussion of the rights of those subjected to tyrannical rule had failed to destroy the essential rationale for the divine right doctrine. The difficulty, however, was that, although the rationale was old, the explicit doctrine of the divine right of monarchs was comparatively new and more or less contrived out of historical necessity. The theory followed the need; the divine right argument was fundamentally a justification for the centralization of power under the figure of the king, a necessary phase in the development of national states and the imposing of order upon a chaotic feudal society.[2]

Apart from the argument of its historical necessity, the divine right

---

[1] *Jean Bodin* (1530-1596) in his *Six livres de la république* (1576) attempts the first systematic treatment of the subject of sovereignty. He defines it as the supreme power, beyond restraint of law. It is perpetual, limitless, and not subject to change. Among the features of sovereignty are the ability to make law and to wage war. It is restricted by only three factors: God and natural law, constitutional arrangements when applicable, and private property.

Bodin develops a theory of the state which identifies it as a unique expression of sovereignty and distinguishes states, as single-form political entities, from governments, as "agents" of states. He further deals with the questions of citizenship and relations between states and between the state and its integral parts. He also advocates religious toleration and political moderation.

Bodin is considered to be the founder of "historical jurisprudence" and to be responsible for the modern concept of the sovereign state. He established a tradition of natural law carried on by Althusius, Hugo Grotius, and Pufendorf.

Bodin deserves attention, especially for students of international law. A good source is J. W. Allen's *Political Thought in the Sixteenth Century.*

[2] Take the famous case of the Magna Carta (1215): The issue between King John and the barons was whether John through his kingly office could impose a system of "national" control upon the decentralized baronial feudalism. History, at least popular history, has tended to be hard on John Lackland, but revered as the Magna Carta is, a good case can be made for John as a perceiver of the drift of history.

of kings was defended along two general fronts. One was the tried and true theological justification—we are familiar with it—which was trotted out with appropriate scriptural evidence. The second line of defense was more original and certainly more imaginative. It was a mystical conceptualization of the office of king which asserted that the theory of divine right was suprarational and beyond the ordinary limits of understanding. It was all a "divine mystery," a special dispensation that could neither be discussed nor described in the workaday language of political intercourse.[3] Only the king himself could understand or explain it. This had the marked advantage for the royalists of barring further debate on the matter. But further debate arose —and mounted in volume.

Part of the outcry against royal absolutism we have looked at in the last chapter. But what caused Hobbes to come running like the fire brigade to the defense of the monarchy in England was the multisided assault that was commencing on the English crown in general and on James I, the first Stuart, in particular. *Richard Hooker* (1553-1600), in his *Laws of Ecclesiastical Polity* (1594), had set out to defend the Anglican Church and to prove the obligation of obedience on the part of Nonconformists, particularly the Presbyterians. In order to make his vindication a telling one, Hooker felt obliged to outline the nature and origins of commonwealth, the true "public society." What Hooker in fact did was reconstruct natural law, in a manner not unlike that of Aquinas, and then derive from it an altogether un-Scholastic account of the rise of political organization. Hooker's account of this latter phenomenon is reminiscent in part of the *Vindiciae contra tyrannos*. His belief in the primal existence of natural law did not imply that man was originally in a state of political organization. Rather did there exist an original society in which the natural law was operative and in which human reason prevailed, but it included no form of political order. Because of man's imperfect (or, perhaps, inadequate) reason and because man's needs could not be met by solitary existence, human beings formed, by an act of conscious will, a political society, a commonwealth. In Hooker's own words:

> But forasmuch as we are not by ourselves sufficient to furnish ourselves with competent store of things needful for such a life as our

---

[3] Undoubtedly the clearest statement of this view is a treatise by James I entitled *The True Law of Free Monarchies* (1598).

nature doth desire, a life fit for the dignity of man, therefore to supply
these defects and imperfections which are in us living single and solely
by ourselves, we are naturally induced to seek communion and fellowship with others. This was the first cause of men's uniting themselves
at first in public societies; which societies could not be without government, nor government without a distinct kind of law from that which
hath been already declared. Two foundations there are which bear up
public societies; the one, a natural inclination, whereby all men desire
sociable life and fellowship; the other, an order expressly or secretly
agreed upon touching the manner of their union in living together.
The latter is that which we call the law of the commonwealth, the very
soul of the politic body, the parts whereof are by law animated, held
together, and set on work in such actions as the common good re-
quireth.[4]

Hooker's prepolitical society—not unlike the "state of nature" to be
discovered in Hobbes and, in a different fashion in Locke [5] clearly
implies both compact and consent. While the main theme of the
Laws of Ecclesiastical Polity is the validity of the national church, of
the uniformity of religious and political obligation in England, the
portent of Hooker's schema is distinctly antimonarchical. Hooker
himself does not panic before the implication; he suggests that to
"fathers within their private families" nature has extended "supreme
power." But a king and a father are not the same, Hooker reflects, nor
do they have similar powers. Kings, he tells us, "not having the natural
superiority of fathers, their power must needs be either usurped and
then unlawful; or, if lawful, then either granted or consented unto
them over whom they exercise the same." [6]

Hooker's lucid statement on the matter of a prepolitical state of
man and his unswerving defense of the indispensability of consent
did not comprise the only contributions he made to the English mind
of the sixteenth century. If Hooker's wellsprings were not directly in
the medieval age, his nearest intellectual forebears were Bodin and
the continental lawyers. In this, Hooker represents a bridge between
the extensive examination of law on the continent and the rise in
England of a political thought centered on legal premises. Contemporary with Hooker and accelerated by him was the emergence of
theory concerned with the broad problem of *constitutionalism*.

---

[4] Richard Hooker, *Laws of Ecclesiastical Polity,* Book I, Chapter 10.
[5] Histories of political philosophy invariably mention that John Locke acknowledged his debt to Richard Hooker by referring to him as "the judicious Hooker."
Locke having paid his debt to Hooker, the author herewith acknowledges his debt
to academic custom with this reference.
[6] Hooker, *op. cit., Ecclesiastical Polity,* Book I, Chapter 10.

Among the splintering religious sects bickering about theological banalities, there was an increasingly influential circle of men immersed in the *common law*. Hooker himself had said that the laws of the political society must be built upon the customary practices of a people. A lawyer of the stature of Sir Edward Coke would argue that this was the very basis of law and that its guardians were not kings, but "priests of the law."

Here we must pause in the narrative long enough to consider briefly what the common law was all about. The Roman law had followed the Roman legions, which had subjugated most of Britain and held her under their sway for four and a half centuries.[7] It is a curious fact that while Roman law had been successfully implanted everywhere else that Roman authority had become entrenched for any appreciable period of time, this had not proved to be the case in Britain. The lack of any real inculcation of Roman culture in Britain is itself an interesting historical riddle. But what had remained in Britain was a rude form of law that had been imported by Germanic tribes and infused with Celtic customs. At base, this law was tribal law; it was a loose body of practices that had grown from customary means of dealing with such day-to-day predicaments as horse stealing, adultery, a warrior's obligation to his chief in battle, clan taboos, and so forth. It was altered but little by the rise of feudalism and was not materially reshaped by William and his Norman barons. But as a body of legal principles, it did enlarge in scope and became increasingly fixed.[8]

Essentially this law was rooted in custom and, hence, in social consensus. Its ultimate appeal was not to abstract reason, or to a "higher law," or to a written code. It was a law of social utility. Judges turned in their decisions to existing practices (as evidence of general moral consensus), to a rather vague concept of "reasonableness," and, increasingly, to prior decisions of other magistrates.[9] By the beginning

---

[7] Britain was first invaded under Julius Caesar in 54 B.C. and the legions were not withdrawn until 407 during the reign of Honorius.

[8] The best illustration of this is the so-called "Law Merchant" of the Middle Ages. In England, guilds and tradesmen, weary of cut-throat competition and shady practices, established a code of laws designed to regulate the conduct of commerce and trade. The Law Merchant had a deep impression on the growth of the common law.

[9] This is the doctrine of *stare decisis*—let the previous decision act as a guide. The common law, since it did not rest upon any "eternal truths," developed through the unfolding of firm principles in actual legal decision. Common law is frequently referred to as "case law" as opposed to "code law," which is identified with Roman

of the seventeenth century, a distinct and comprehensive legal profession had been developed. This professionalism had a number of effects on the further growth of the common law. It tended by extensive use of precedent to crystallize the process of legal growth; it led to the composition of a number of commentaries on the common law that became, in fact, a part of the corpus of that law; and, finally, it made the common law more and more the exclusive province of the lawyers, a realm they guarded with zeal, a mounting independence, and no small measure of learned authority. The common law was becoming, as is so often remarked, "what the lawyers say it is."

One can easily see that, if this is how things stood at the beginning of the seventeenth century, the common lawyers were commencing to think in terms of constitutional arrangements in the state and limitations on royal power. If, for these lawyers, the law did not rest upon either theological grounds or upon natural law, justifications for divine right were absurd. Law was concerned with relationships between persons—especially the common law, with its "adversarial" foundation [10]—and all these relationships and persons were subject to the broad legal jurisdiction. On what grounds could a king be exempt? Was it not a question of determining the legal relationship between king and subject, both of whom were answerable to law—but not to a divine law in the hereafter or a set of "natural" commandments? The problem of political authority, then, was a problem of constitutional arrangement under law.

Further, the common lawyers, historically minded as they were, saw the divine right claim as a newly foisted aberration having no just historical precedent. Even primitive societies, at least in Europe, featured no such exotic despotisms. On the contrary, the older concept was one of mutual obligation and enforceable privilege. It was within the framework of these ideas and in this intellectual climate that the quarrel between James I and Sir Edward Coke took place.

Sir Edward Coke (1552-1634) pressed the monarch with the assort-

---

law, the other great legal system in the West. One might say that the mood of common law is empirical, Roman law rationalistic. The distinction between common law and Roman law on the basis of their reliance on codes and statutes has become somewhat blurred by the role of modern legislation.

[10] The common law is an adversarial system in that all proceedings are involved with an actual clash of interests between two genuinely concerned contesting parties. The court acts in the role of adjudicator or even referee. In the Roman system, the court plays a far more active part, hence the Roman law is said to be an "inquisitorial" system. The common law's ancient precept is that the contestant with whom justice rests will prevail. (One recalls the trial by combat of feudal times and the admonition: "May God defend the right.")

ment of arguments sketched above, but he also extended the range of the legalist claim. He was not content to allege juristic limitations on royal authority, but sought to establish the doctrine that it was in fact the courts which formed the nucleus of government. With an argument not greatly dissimilar to John Marshall's statement of judicial review.[11] Coke maintained that if the nature of government is that of a legal distribution of powers, then who, in the last analysis, is the logical arbitrator in disputes regarding these powers? The answer was plainly the lawyers, institutionalized into courts. What Coke did not perceive was that, although the case against the absolute monarch was a cogent one, the recourse was not likely to be rule by the judiciary, but rather the emergence of the legislature as the source of law. The Parliament, old in name but youthful in the powers accumulated, paradoxically, under the despotic Tudors, was to be the chief gainer from Coke's surgery on the divine rights claim. There was some hint of this in Hooker's noncommittal observation that consent was a continuing feature of the just commonwealth and that it implied some representation, some participation in the formulation of political ordinances.

Into the melee came *Thomas Hobbes* (1588-1679). The son of an eccentric clergyman,[12] Hobbes was befriended as a youth by a merchant relative who underwrote his education at Oxford. Afterwards, Hobbes sought scholarly serenity as a tutor with the Cavendish family, a tranquillity he enjoyed only in his early years. The relationship between Hobbes and his employers was a mutually happy one, and this connection provided him with an *entrée* into circles of the intelligentsia both in England and on the continent. His talents were acknowledged, and they ranged from translation of the classics into verse and later to mathematics and science.

---

[11] John Marshall, Chief Justice of the United States Supreme Court, held in *Marbury v. Madison* that the Supreme Court could hold acts of the legislature unconstitutional and hence void on the grounds that, since the Constitution was a legal document, it was reasonable to suppose that the final authority on its meaning must be the highest judicial body in the nation. See *Marbury v. Madison*, 1 Cranch, 137, 176-180 (1803).

[12] There are numerous tales of the rather unconventional behavior of Hobbes *père*. One account has it that Vicar Hobbes physically assaulted a clerical colleague and fled, completely disappearing and abandoning his wife and family. (See Sir Leslie Stephen's *Hobbes*.) Another entertaining family anecdote has it that Hobbes' mother delivered him prematurely as a result of her fright over the coming of the Spanish Armada. Hobbes himself once remarked that he and terror were born twins.

In his later life, Hobbes found himself caught up in a web of political circumstance. His support of Charles I made it necessary for him to flee England after the Parliamentarians had won the day. He shared exile with the Cavalier refugees and served briefly as a tutor to the Prince of Wales, who was to become Charles II. The publication, in 1651, of Hobbes' great political treatise, *Leviathan*, shocked the royalists profoundly, and Hobbes, forced to take flight again, returned to England and took his chances with Cromwell's Protectorate. Granted amnesty, his position once more became difficult when the Stuart house was restored in 1660 and the Interregnum came to an end. While Charles II bore him no ill will and was well-disposed toward scholars and scientists, Hobbes' views disturbed the religious leaders of the kingdom, who looked upon him as a dangerous heretic. Pressure convinced Hobbes of the desirability of retirement, and he ended his days quietly engaged in the project of his youth, classical translation.

This turmoil and often bitter and petty disputation, coupled with Hobbes' oft-quoted observation that life was "solitary, poore, nasty, brutish, and short," creates the impression that Hobbes was a brooding egotist, a warped quarrelsome personality whose authoritarianism sprang from a deep resentment against the world. He was not. Hobbes was a placid and generally friendly individual who led a private life in which his bellicosity (directed toward some French philosophers and Oxford mathematicians) was the exception rather than the rule and was provoked by issues hardly central to his general philosophy or his political thought. Hobbes, like Machiavelli, was an espouser of consistent egotism in political theory, but he was not himself an "evil genius" or an embittered hater.

Hobbes, like Plato, Aristotle, and Aquinas, sought to construct a general philosophy in which political ideas were to play a major role. As is so often the case, these political ideas were dependent for their intelligibility and coherence on the remainder of Hobbes' thought. *Leviathan* proceeds from the foundation Hobbes laid in his general exploration of philosophic principles.[13] He came to philosophy rather late, for the simple reason that his philosophy was the outcome of his exposure to mathematics and science, particularly physics. In

---

[13] Hobbes' full exposition of his philosophy is contained in a trio of works: *De Corpore* (1655), *De Homine* (1658), and *De Cive* (1647)—or "Physical Nature," "Human Nature," and "Society." Although the first two followed the publication of *Leviathan*, it is clear that Hobbes himself had his essential position outlined before *Leviathan*. While it might appear from the publication dates that he worked "backwards," that is, from social thought to metaphysics, a study of the development of his ideas suggests otherwise.

1634 he met Galileo, among others, and his imagination was suddenly charged with the implications of the new scientific outlook and the possibilities latent in mathematics. At forty years of age, Hobbes resolved to become a mathematician and scientist. While it is safe to say that he overestimated his success in this venture, his absorption led him to attempt a philosophy whose main orientation was an analysis of physical nature. It is clear that Hobbes' philosophy was, in consequence, a natural philosophy and one that contained three sharply defined, but closely connected, parts: the physical universe, the nature of man, and the nature of society. It was an orderly, coherent, and even geometric development, and Hobbes, for whatever other shortcomings can be found, had the merit of tight logical development and pronounced clarity.

If society must be accounted for in the light of propositions relating to the nature of the universe and human nature, then social philosophy must rest on metaphysics and psychology. The notion that political philosophy had its ultimate roots in metaphysics was an old idea (at least as old as Plato), but Hobbes' conception of metaphysics was a striking departure from philosophic orthodoxy. Of even greater significance was his invocation of psychology, suggested at times in Aristotle, rather recklessly appealed to by Machiavelli, but never treated as a systematic category until Hobbes. His psychology was both new and radical, because it asked a different question. Hobbes sought the answer to the question: What makes an individual human being behave as he does? This is quite different from a Scholastic investigation into the nature of man as a collective entity.

Hobbes' metaphysic is a thorough materialism. The natural order is a complex of matter regulated with the precision of a machine. The metaphor of the universe as a machine is perfectly applicable to the Hobbesian view. The machine of nature is a complicated apparatus, but it, like all machines, combines the principles of *motion* and *regularity*. Its motion is constant and not erratic; both in terms of function and structure, the material entities that comprise the natural world are regulated by laws. These "laws" are not divine ordinances, but the physical principles discovered by such men as Copernicus, Galileo, and, later, Newton. These principles are indispensable to the operation of the machine, without them the stars would collide and the tides rush upon the shore with senseless caprice. The secret of the nature of these principles, relates Hobbes, is mathematics.

Now if one conceives of nature as being a gigantic machine, constructed of physical forms and operated in accordance with mathe-

matically discoverable principles of force and motion, it is possible to
speak of these physical "rules of conduct" as "natural laws"—or better,
"laws of nature." But this is clearly not what is meant by "natural
law" in the traditional sense. In the first place, orthodox theories of
natural law presuppose teleology. Hobbes makes no such assumption.
There is no reason to allege, he maintains, that, merely because the
universe subscribes to rules of physical motion, there need be an
eternal purpose or a final cause. Nor does Hobbes—except in the lip-
service sense—trouble to inquire as to the origin of the natural order.
Does the existence of an orderly physical universe prove *per se* that
it is the product of a guiding intelligence, Aristotle's "prime mover
unmoved"? For Hobbes, there is no reason to posit unknowable categories to account for all this. Such speculation is beside the point.
Natural law, then, in the theological context, is a chimera, and Hobbes
attacks it by substituting the idea of pure physical-mathematical laws
to account for natural phenomena. Further these laws are shorn of any
moral intent. Traditional natural law is a body of moral commandments, a divinely ordered system whose purpose is ethical and
eschatological.[14] Natural law provides moral norms. Hobbes' laws of
nature provide norms, too, but they are not concerned with ethical
dictates. It is a law that the planets of the solar system circle the sun,
but such a law is clearly uninformative as to the moral consequences.
The axioms of Hobbes are therefore nonteleological, nonethical, and
nonjuristic in the sense that it is impossible to derive positive human
law from the processes of nature.

If it is true that the Hobbesian conception vividly denies the postulates of the natural law theory, it is equally true that Hobbes' system
requires that his laws be binding on natural forms. Today, we might
phrase it as: "One may break the law of trespass, but one can't break
the law of gravity." Natural entities, Hobbes points out, conform to
and perform according to a pattern of principles that are both consistent and discoverable. Now human beings are undeniably natural
entities, so it follows that they behave in accordance with laws. From
his mechanistic view of the universe, Hobbes proceeds to apply his
ideas of physical law to human nature. His aim is to discover the laws
of human behavior.

Hobbesian psychology is too extensive to be treated here in any
detail, but for our purposes it is enough to consider his theories regard-

---

[14] *Eschatological:* pertaining to doctrines concerned with theological-meta-
physical finalities, such as death, immortality, the future of the soul, divine judgment, etc.

ing human motivation. Hobbes' conviction that the universe can be described in terms of geometric analysis of motion carry over into his psychology. He defines the emotional life of human beings in terms of motion—movements toward and away from objects of sensual awareness. These motivations must be considered in two aspects: (1) All motivation is entirely egoistic, that is, its aim is the increase of individual self-gratification; (2) all motivations are involved with physical sensations. Richard Peters has called Hobbes' doctrine of human motivation "psychological hedonism." [15] Self-satisfaction is the goal of all human motivation, and it is gained through the disposition of the senses. Hobbes breaks these motivations down into two main groups: *appetite* and *aversion*. While he deals with this matter in detail, it is sufficient to point out that, by "appetite," Hobbes means physical pleasure or the endeavor to secure it. By "aversion," he means the avoidance of threats to the physical well-being of the individual (death, pain, discomfort, etc.). Both are powerful motivations, often complementary. The end product of these psychological impulses is to make the human being a predatory creature and to make self-preservation the fundamental human concern.

Before we chart the implications of these theories for society and politics, it is wise to reflect just how revolutionary this psychology was in its time. The most startling departure is its extreme individualism. The human being stands alone as a solitary egoistic physical entity; the individual becomes the primary object of study, and social prescription must proceed from a knowledge of his discrete nature rather than the other way around. Secondly, human motivation is described solely in physical terms; man behaves in accordance with his biological requirements rather than his reason or his spiritual consciousness. Man becomes, in short, an animal, and, for Hobbes, what separates him from the wolf or the hawk are his rational faculties. But these rational abilities do not constitute the origin of his motivations; they merely enable him to use his reason in the pursuit of goals that are sensual, physical, and essentially animalistic.

Man did, in fact, once live as an animal, Hobbes contends. By "animal," Hobbes does not imply an evolutionary explanation, but

---

[15] See Richard Peters, *Hobbes* (Baltimore, Md.: Penguin Books, Inc., 1956), Chapter 6.

rather that in some prehistorical epoch human beings lived in a pre-
societal state. Man was a solitary predator living in the midst of a
savage struggle for survival—"a war of all against all." This is Hobbes'
conception of the original state of nature. Here ruled the law of bloody
fang and claw; kill or be killed was the order of nature. No quarter was
asked and none given. The strong devoured the weak at will. Constant
and unending conflict was the human lot. Hobbes forcefully gives a
picture of this primeval world:

> To this war of every man against every man, this also is consequent,
> that nothing can be Unjust. The notions of Right and Wrong, Justice
> and Injustice have there no place. Where there is no common power,
> there is no Law; where no Law, no Injustice. Force, and Fraud, are in
> war the two Cardinal virtues. Justice, and Injustice are none of the
> Faculties neither of the Body, nor Mind. If they were, they might be
> in a man that were alone in the world, as well as his Senses, and
> Passions. They are qualities, that relate men in Society, not in Solitude.
> It is consequent also to the same condition, that there is no Property,
> no Dominion, no *Mine* and *Thine* distinct; but only that to be every
> man's that he can get; and for so long, as he can keep it. And thus
> much for the ill condition, which man by mere Nature is actually placed
> in; though with a possibility to come out of it, consisting partly in the
> Passions, partly in his Reason.[16]

What was the "possibility to come out of it"? How does Hobbes
explain the transition from the original state of nature of political
society? In the first place, the primary preoccupation of man in the
state of nature was survival (it remains always as man's primary concern, says Hobbes, although in political society it tends to translate
itself into a concern for security). But there were differences in strength;
the weak lived in perpetual terror of destruction by the strong. Man,
unlike the lower animals, possessed reason, and it occurred to the weak
that if they cooperated in their mutual defense they would be able to
overwhelm the isolated strong. This was the beginning of society, the
banding together of the weak in order to survive. As Hobbes puts it:
"For as the strength of body, the weakest has strength enough to kill
the strongest, either by secret machination, or by confederacy with
others, that are in the same danger with himself." [17]

This was self-preservation (the first rule of nature), but it was also
rational self-preservation. The motivation was of the passions, but the
method was of the reason. But it is upon the establishment of this community for mutual security that a number of problems present them-

---

[16] Thomas Hobbes, *Leviathan*, Part I, Chapter 1.
[17] *Ibid.*

selves. The survival of the members of such a society (Hobbes calls it a commonwealth) depends on the group's acting as a unified force, virtually as a single individual. The society must become a corporate body. The only way to do this is for the individual members to relinquish their rights to freedom of action. Explains Hobbes:

> That a man be willing when others are so too, as farre-forth, as for Peace, and defence of himself he shall think it necessary, to lay down this right to all things; and be contented with so much liberty against other men, as he would allow other men against himself.[18]

The act of the individual's renunciation of private action takes the form of a covenant, which is both an initial consent that establishes the corporate unit and a perpetual obligation of obedience on the part of the individual. The individual has no right to abrogate the contract except under certain express conditions that we shall examine later. In a loose sense, the covenant or contract is an exchange by which the individual gets protection and security for the surrender of individual freedom. Put another way: Individual sovereignty possessed in the state of nature is relinquished in favor of the establishment of a corporate sovereignty. But, in fact, the corporate unit cannot really act as a sovereign; it cannot act as a single person. Instead, sovereignty must be conveyed to one who acts on behalf of the commonwealth.[19] The contract must create a single sovereign capable of decisive action both to protect the society from without and to insure order and unanimity within. This sovereign must be absolute, since only with unlimited power can he exercise the threat of punishment that is essential to the maintenance of order in the face of the predatory inclinations of men. "Covenants without the sword," Hobbes observes, "are but words." The commonwealth, then, becomes the sovereign, the sovereign the commonwealth; the sovereign speaks for the commonwealth, makes laws for it, can punish it, and, indeed, can legally do anything he wishes *except* violate that provision of the covenant which states that he must provide for the safety and security of the commonwealth.

But so far we have been speaking in terms of small corporate bodies emerging from the "war of every man against every man." We are not

[18] *Ibid.*, Chapter 20.

[19] The sovereign can be a plural ruler (e.g., a council or legislature), but Hobbes places little or no trust in them, and for all practical purposes the sovereign is a single individual ruler. Hobbes defines the sovereign as: "One Person, of whose Acts a great Multitude, by mutual Covenant one with another, have made themselves every one the Author, to the end he may use the strength and means of them all, as he shall think expedient, for their Peace and Common Defence." (*Leviathan*, Part II, Chapter 6.)

yet describing the state. The state is created by the same process as the
original corporation, except that it is made up not of individuals but
of corporate structures whose sovereigns, in order to survive, have
themselves entered into yet another covenant creating a greater sovereignty. Eventually this process of amalgamation of sovereign entities
reaches the point where the state is created—or at least what. was
known as the state in the seventeenth century. Over the state, then,
there rules a sovereign with precisely the same powers and functions,
many times magnified, that the sovereign originally possessed over the
tiny corporation. The modern sovereign, therefore, is a monarch of
unlimited authority; he has no superiors either beyond the state or
within it. It is thoroughly reasonable, Hobbes argues, that this is so.
The sovereign cannot acknowledge an external superior, for to do that
would be to violate the contract that created him. His duty is to protect
the state at all costs and by any means. If the sovereign acknowledged
an internal superior, he would clearly no longer be sovereign either
by definition or by the terms of the legal contract. Hobbes' all-powerful
sovereign cannot have a superior within the state, for to admit that
would be to destroy the state itself. Without a head, the state becomes
merely a mob of individuals, each pursuing his self-gratifications as
ruthlessly as need be. There is only one alternative to the sovereign,
Hobbes reiterates, and that is anarchy, a return to the law of the beasts.
Power can never successfully be divided without rending apart the
structure of the state; order and disorder are the alternatives, and order
is always preferable. There is really no such thing as bad government,
Hobbes would say, only strong and weak government, and the latter is
really no government at all since its weakness prevents it from doing
that for which it was created: protection and maintenance of order or,
in one word security.

Here is the central characteristic of Hobbes' leviathan state. It is a
unitary corporation, built upon the consolidation of institutions and
embodied in a legally unrestricted sovereign ruler. But the role of the
Hobbesian sovereign—"the Mortall God"—is not as rosy as one might
think at first glance. If sheer power is the most significant category in
Hobbes' view of survival, the sovereign is compelled to play a constant
game of power politics. The ruler's only justification for his position is,
in the final analysis, power. He can be overthrown by the attack of
other states. Since Hobbes holds that the state is the highest form of
"rational self-preservation," the world of international politics must
represent a continual struggle for survival. Too, the sovereign is the
legal ruler only so long as he remains powerful enough to impose his

will. If he is insufficiently powerful to maintain himself in the face of internal dissension, then he ceases to fulfill the requirements of the contract. Hence, there can never be either limited powers or divided sovereignty. Since sovereignty is the ability to legislate without restriction, asserts Hobbes, to divide it is impossible. How can something be limited or shared that is by definition ultimate? If the state is in fact the sovereign, then any incursion upon sovereignty means the dismantling of the state, or worse, its disappearance into primordial anarchy. Hobbes, in a cogently worded passage, nails home this argument:

> But the Rights and Consequences of Sovereignty are the same in both. His Power cannot, without his consent, be transferred to another; He cannot forfeit it; He cannot be Accused by any of his Subjects, of Injury; He cannot be Punished by them; He is Judge of what is necessary for Peace; and the Judge of Doctrines; He is Sole Legislator; and Supreme Judge of Controversies; and of the times and Occasions of War and Peace; to him it belongeth to choose Magistrates, Counsellors, Commanders, and all other Officers, and Ministers; and to determine of Rewards and Punishments, Honour and Order.[20]

Hobbes advises rulers not to shirk power or to "obtain a Kingdom" by accepting less power than is necessary to maintain the peace. This is but one of the many pitfalls the state should try to avoid—Hobbes calls them "diseases of a Common-wealth"—and the author of *Leviathan* counsels rulers much after the fashion of Machiavelli. In brief, Hobbes' "diseases" are as follows: (1) Private citizens exercising judgment as to whether public acts are good or bad; (2) The belief that whatever a man does against his conscience is necessarily a sin; (3) The contention that "faith and sanctity" are reached not by reason but by revelation (Hobbes calls this "supernatural Inspiration or Infusion"); (4) The idea that the sovereign is subject to civil law; (5) Private citizens enjoying the right of private property even in the face of the demands of the sovereign; (6) A concept of divided authority.

Has the private citizen no legal recourse in the Hobbesian state? Virtually none, save in two instances: first, when the sovereign chooses to extend privileges (and these are retractable at will) and, second, in the event that an outside sovereign can succeed in deposing the ruler by force. If this is the case, then the covenant is void, since the ruler has failed to perform his function and the people are free to acknowledge the sovereignty of the conqueror.

The feature that gives Hobbes' picture of the state such a stark

---

[20] *Ibid.*, Book II, Chapter 7.

appearance is the absence of the restraining character of law. Hobbes'
ruler is beyond law—using that term in any ordinary sense denoting
law as obedience to generally known principles. The ruler in *Leviathan*
is as *ultra vires* as Plato's Nocturnal Council. What is arresting about
Hobbes' concept of sovereignty limited only by naked power is that
it is so at variance with the gathering spirit of constitutionalism in
England. It might be alleged that Hobbes' legal despotism was influenced by a wish to provide an effective curb on the antimonarchical
theories of the common lawyers, Coke in particular. He does in fact
pummel Coke with obvious relish. He mocks Coke's mysticism about
the subterranean reason of the common law. He drives a wedge
between law as used to describe natural forces and law as a civil
instrument. In the latter use, law must simply be the power to command. No other form of law stands up to the test of strenuous analysis,
Hobbes contends. Law is the sovereign speaking, and his commandments are limited only by his power to enforce them.

In this way Hobbes avoids any discussion of the normative problem of law—whether laws are good or bad and what standard of
judgment is valid. Even Machiavelli was concerned with the effects
of legal pronouncements by his prince and in this way implied that
laws are either effective or ineffective in furthering the welfare of the
ruler. Hobbes makes no such judgment; for him, the overriding necessity of the power monopoly of the ruler as a means of securing order
forestalls any concern with moral criteria. All law is essentially good,
and a law that sends persons to the torture rack as a result of monarchical whim is not only no less legal than a humane law, but it is no less
just. One can then surmise that Hobbes considers law a question removed from justice, even if he denies it. Law is coercion, but coercion
for a purpose—just as, for Calvin, law was a coercive instrument for
quite another purpose. For Hobbes, that purpose is the maintenance
of social order, the preservation of rational control as contrasted with
an irrational combat between individuals. So a moral judgment enters
via the backdoor, as it often did with Machiavelli: Men must be
coerced for their own good, since, undisciplined, they revert to un-
bridled and ruthless egoism. That is bad, and order is to be preferred
to disorder.

The total effect of Hobbesian theory on the development of political
thought is immense. His influence in this field has remained long after
his eclipse as a systematic philosopher. Like Machiavelli, Hobbes still

evokes replies from those disturbed by the relentless denial of many
of the cherished beliefs and hopes of libertarians. Hobbes particularly rankles those of the Christian persuasion. Let there be no doubt,
his references to God and Christianity notwithstanding, that Hobbes
is among the enemies of religion and far more significantly so than
cynics like Machiavelli, for example. Hobbes challenges the basic
ground upon which Christian theology stands. Hobbes' scientific materialism is, then, a comprehensive early statement of a position still
vigorous in thought, namely, that to conceive of the world or many
worlds in terms of supernatural entities and forces is to posit fantasies
in the face of hard, factual human knowledge. The case against Hobbesian materialism, as against most materialisms, rests on a denial of
the adequacy of the materialist's description of the universe and a
rejection of the materialist thesis that one exhausts the categories of
existence by classifying material objects. Hobbes' materialism in particular is rather crude and unsophisticated and is open to serious
question. But for its day it was a lusty challenge to theistic dogma.
It hit hard at the church not only from the social or political angle,
but also at the very roots of belief. Hobbes most forcefully attempts to
reframe the whole character of belief. Religious belief, Hobbes proposes, is not a rational undertaking, but a sort of popular tonic. Hobbes
compares it to "wholesome pills for the sick." [21] Religious belief has
a useful function not because it is true, but because it serves desirable
social ends, because it is a force for social solidarity. Religion must
be promulgated as a national myth; it should be "swallowed whole,"
since it cannot endure the process of being chewed. If it were chewed,
it would be "for the most part cast up again without effect." Institutionalized religion, the church, must be but a corporate segment of
the state and subject always to sovereign will. And while Hobbes
calls for punishment of heretics and the imposition of the state orthodoxy, he never gives to religion the serious import found, say, in
Plato's Laws. Hobbes begins the habit of not taking religion very
seriously; he damns it by inattention, heralding the coming of the
Enlightenment mind. If religion does provoke Hobbes to vituperation,
it takes the form of anticlericalism, which suggests as well the
philosophes of the eighteenth century. Hobbes' influence channels
British political thought into a distinctly secular direction and infuses
into it a naturalistic temper that is still in evidence.

Hobbes' extreme individualism had two general results: (1) It

---

[21] It is intriguing to wonder to what extent Karl Marx is indebted to Hobbes for
his famous remark that "religion is the opiate of the people."

shattered the monopoly enjoyed by theories of organic society and
(2) it encouraged subsequent theorists to analyze politics from both
a psychological and an empirical point of view. It laid the foundation
for the contention that the aim of political institutions is to serve the
individual—a notion unthinkable to Hobbes personally, but thoroughly
implied in his psychology. It ushered in the idea that the needs of a
polity and the needs of an individual are not necessarily identical
and may even be in conflict. Again, such a conclusion would do violence to the specifics of Hobbes' theory, yet the sheer radicalism of
the egocentric psychology compels such an observation.

Hobbes created for himself a monster. The leviathan was built to
serve very specific ends, but it backfired. Where it sought to justify
the monolithic state, the barracks community, it did in fact provide
the basis for theories of popular government resting upon reforma-
tions of Hobbesian psychology. Where it endeavored to deny individuals any rights whatsoever, its concept of the genesis of political
society led to the conviction that individuals had natural rights resulting from a mechanistic view of nature. And, above all, where Hobbes
had set out to rescue the monarchical institution, he nearly demolished
it. His redefinition of natural law and his materialism explode the
divine right myth; his concept of sovereignty and power reduce to
nothing the mystique of kingship. Little wonder the Stuarts and their
advocates trembled and denied him. Thomas Hobbes was surely no
conservative, if by that one means an admirer of established institutions, a gradualist, or a spurner of extremes. On the contrary, he was
a dedicated radical—even if he didn't fully realize it himself. Virtually
all radical political thought in the West can be traced in part to
Hobbes. He gave birth to the concept of the single purpose, the
"complete overhaul," the revolutionary alternative.

In less general terms, Hobbes' development of the contract theory
based on universal egoism was to provide the essential premise for
another century of political speculation, albeit speculation emanating
both from a very different idea of the state of nature and from a
redrawn contract. His concept of society as a rational construct, an
artificial compact, would remain largely unchallenged (except by an
occasional figure like Burke) until the nineteenth century. Likewise,
his reflections on the law of nature were equally pervasive. Hostile as
he was to *jus naturale*, Hobbes in no way destroyed the idea of the
universe governed by orderly process or causal laws (which Hume
would attempt to refute), and in this way he acts as a bridge between
the theologically oriented "natural" lawyers and the empiricists like

Locke who founded political philosophy on natural rights. Hobbes failed, however, in his self-imposed assignment. He did not rescue absolute monarchy. He had let the cat out of the bag, and political radicalism was free to prowl.

The Civil War in England, like internecine strife everywhere, was conducive to the rise of extremist elements. Even the managers of the Parliamentary cause against Charles Stuart soon found themselves too conservative for the tastes of many of the rank-and-file who felt that they had thrown off the yoke of oppression forevermore. What started as a squabble over unlimited royal authority had grown into a full-scale collision between royalists and republicans, and it became increasingly apparent that the end result might be strife between those advocating aristocratic republicanism and those demanding sweeping social and political reshuffling. Those followers of Oliver Cromwell whose religious deviation was the most pronounced entertained equally radical ideas regarding the reform of the state. Cromwell and the victorious moderates had trouble keeping these more extreme elements in line. But force was used with typically Cromwellian decisiveness.

Two groups were prominent in these reformist agitations: the *Levelers* and the *Diggers*. It is startling to peruse the demands of these splinter groups, since they so aptly articulate what were eventually to become cornerstones of modern popular government. The Levelers in particular advocated what could fairly be called the universal rights of man, asserting that these rights were bound up with the creature existence of human beings and that they were beyond political action to deny—they were a human "birthright." These human rights called for a reform of society in which there would be equal representation in government. universal suffrage, a republican form of government, and protection of property. The label "Leveler" is accordingly appropriate.

The Diggers, on the other hand, influenced by the writings of *Gerrard Winstanley* (1609?-1660?), [22] were more utopian in tone, and, while accepting the main tenets of the Levelers, they sought to establish a communistic system of joint ownership of property. The rationale for this collectivization of property was that private property encouraged greed, the bane of man's existence.

---

[22] The principal exposition of the Digger position is Gerrard Winstanley's *Law of Freedom* (1652).

These cries for reform were answered by a moderate and more cautious republicanism endorsed by the Parliamentary leadership, themselves men of property and concerned with the establishment of legislative superiority, not kicking over the social traces. It was they who dubbed the reformers, those seeking to reduce all men to a common social status, "levelers." Further, they were uneasy not only over the socially equalizing tendencies of the Levelers and the threat to property posed by the Diggers, but also over the hostility that both groups showed to the leadership of Parliament. The radicalism of the Levelers and the Diggers, beyond the question of universal human equality, posed a criticism of political institutions, Parliamentary or monarchical, that in turn raised the issue of stability and permanence in political organization.

Foremost among the moderate republicans was *James Harrington* (1611-1677). His contribution was in the form of a utopian tract entitled *Oceana* (1656), which depicted a fictional commonwealth that not surprisingly is identifiable as England. Its message is largely economic, and it claims that economic factors underlie political power and that only economic balance can preserve social and political harmony. Property, reasons Harrington, consists principally in land, and hence agrarian policy lies at the heart of good government. The aim of such policy must be the distribution of land in such a manner as to prevent a concentration of ownership in a few hands. He then proceeds to discuss a constitution that would embody this idea. After reiterating the need for reason to reign over passion and for the ascendancy of law,[23] Harrington outlines a government based upon consent and popular participation, in which the legislature, the "senate," is the prime organ:

> Dividing and choosing in the language of a commonwealth is debating and resolving; and whatsoever upon debate of the senate, is proposed by the people, and resolved by them, is enacted by the authority of the fathers, and by the power of the people, which concurring, make a law.[24]

The commonwealth is to maintain political equality, states Harrington, by a perpetual law of agrarian balance. To insure this, it is necessary to have elections of legislatures, rotation of office, and the secret ballot. There is in Oceana's constitution, however, an elaborate social stratification that, while having the effect of diversifying rulership,

---

[23] It was Harrington who first said that the good state should be "an empire of laws and not of men."

[24] James Harrington, *Oceana*, Part I, Chapter 3.

explicitly limits suffrage. The leading role in Oceana is still to be played by the country squires (who in fact make up the bulk of the Parliamentary leadership), whom Harrington romantically calls "knights." While much of Oceana is fictional embroidery, quite sententious utopianism, and faulty economic theory, it both predicts much of the machinery of popular government to come and harbingers the drift of future political sentiment.

The absolute monarch was dead—even if Sir Robert Filmer didn't quite grasp it yet.[25] Louis XVI of France is reputed to have observed just before the French Revolution: "Après moi, le déluge!" And there was indeed a flood in the eighteenth century. It commenced in a torrent of intellectual activity, zest for freedom, exploration of libertarian alternatives in government, and philosophic heterodoxy. It ended in a maelstrom—with the shadow of Napoleon lengthening over it.

. . . for further discussion:

1. Hobbes' argument that self-preservation is the basic human motive is possibly quite convincing. There are modern psychologists who seem to suggest the same thing. And, too, Hobbes' discussion of *appetite* is not unlike what Sigmund Freud terms the "pleasure principle." If, however, for the sake of argument, we accept Hobbes' view about self-preservation and couple with it his view of the natural conflict between states, how will it be possible for the society to defend itself if individuals choose self-preservation instead of the risks of military service? Let us suppose that Hobbes answers this by saying that it is neither here nor there, since the sovereign will order them into battle. But what kind of efficient behavior can you expect from those who fight out of coercion or fear? Is this a factor in the ability of a society to defend itself? Was Machiavelli wiser than Hobbes when he recognized the question of morale and national feeling? Does Hobbes' psychology adequately take into account mass emotional factors? How might these affect his ideas about the state?

2. Is Hobbes' state of nature a remarkable description of primitive human life that is now confirmed by research into the probable life of prehistoric man?

3. If society is formed by a coalition of the weak to protect themselves against the strong in the state of nature, what happened to the strong? If they were killed off, what conclusions might one draw about the "survival of the fittest" idea? Perhaps the strong, seeing the light, joined into the society as supplicant members. Did they then assert themselves within

---

[25] Reference is made to *Patriarcha* (1680), Sir Robert Filmer's well-known and slightely a posteriori defense of the divine right of kings.

the society? Who is apt to be made Hobbes' omnipotent sovereign? Are the terms "strong" and "weak" of any use when discussing the acquisition of political power? Would you say that today the strong or the weak rule the world?

4. Hobbes makes no distinction between a "legitimate" rule and a "right" or historically efficacious one. Can a government be legitimate (legally exercising authority) and still be undesirable for the welfare of the state? Can a government provide a wholesome leadership without legitimacy? Is Hobbes justified in rejecting a criterion of legal legitimacy? Assuming the end result is benficial, does it make any difference how authority is acquired?

. . . for further investigation:

Gooch, George P., ° *English Democratic Ideas in the Seventeenth Century.* New York: Torchbooks, 1959.

Hampshire, Stuart, ° *The Age of Reason.* New York: Mentor Books, 1956.

Hobbes, Thomas, *Leviathan or the Matter, Form and Power of a Common-wealth Ecclesiastical and Civil,* Michael Oakeshott, ed. New York: The Macmillan Company, n.d.

Peters, Richard, ° *Hobbes.* Baltimore, Md.: Penguin Books, Inc., 1956.

Stephen, Leslie, ° *Hobbes.* Ann Arbor, Mich.: The University of Michigan Press, 1961.

Strauss, Leo, *The Political Philosophy of Hobbes.* Chicago: University of Chicago Press, 1952.

Warrender, Howard, *The Political Philosophy of Hobbes.* New York: Oxford University Press, Inc., 1957.

9

NATURE AND

HER LAWS

The spotlight remains on England. Toppling the absolute monarch from his seat of divine authority could not by itself settle the issue of what was to serve as his replacement. True, Charles II had been taught to respect the elected assemblage of the landed gentry and the merchant community in Parliament, and he had been carefully instructed about no religious nonsense—no Catholic need apply. But just how the Parliament was to govern and in accordance with what principles was far from resolved. Royal power had been limited by the blunt fact of the great rebellion, but there was disagreement as to just what these limits were and, more significantly, as to how the relationship between the individual and his government was affected by the creation of a "limited monarchy."

These were not the only disagreements that hung in the air toward the close of the seventeenth century. England was rapidly undergoing an economic revolution, not as dramatic as the Industrial Revolution of the nineteenth century, but in its own way quite as formative. The English aristocracy, down to and including the "squirearchy" of the countryside, by having early checked royal excesses, had prevented themselves from being drawn into the web of regular attendance at court. They were usually resident on and concerned mainly with the operation of their country holdings. Unlike the French aristocrats, the English gentry remained farmers at heart, more interested in agricultural fairs than court soirées. This not only had the effect of making them more independent of royal control, but it also placed them in a distinct economic position. The landed estates grew large and profitable; they were extremely valuable agricultural operations. Their owners, even gentlemen as they were, became interested in trade—not in selling pots and pans, but in preserving and enhancing their property and operating it on a profitable basis. The country gentry became involved in a new interest: "political economy," which Thomas Carlyle would later refer to as "the dismal science."

For a longer period of time, the merchant middle class had had a vested interest in things economic. Property and its political ramifications were their paramount concern. This tended to draw the landed aristocracy and the merchant class together in common cause. But this rising alliance resulted not only from mutual economic concerns, but also from historical factors. Unlike the continental practice, in the development of the English Parliament the lower ranks of the aristocracy (the knighthood and, later, the baronetcy) were lumped with the yeomanry or freemen.[1] Additionally, sons of noblemen in England were generally untitled—only the eldest son inherited the aristocratic appellation. This resulted in numerous gentlemen of aristocratic lineage going through life as "Mr. Smith"—and sometimes with precious little inherited domain. Customs of land ownership were more flexible in England than on the continent, and many members of the middle class who had acquired huge wealth had, by the end of the seventeenth century, bought manorial establishments and were living in the expansive manner of hereditary aristocrats. What was being created

---

[1] Compare this with the French Estates-General, in which the representation was based upon three "estates": the aristocracy, the clergy, and the politically enfranchised middle class. In contrast, the traditional division of the English Parliament into Lords and Commons placed the higher levels of the aristocracy (the Peerage) into Lords and the knights and middle class into Commons. The reason for this arrangement was originally in part economic, since the "communes" (whence the word "Commons" is derived) were local divisions for the purpose of tax collection and the knights' economic situation more closely resembled that of the freeholder than the baronial lord.

was a large well-to-do upper class, vitally concerned with property and economic matters and opposed to both royal influence on the one hand and popular leveling and social experimentation on the other. Coming into being was the tradition of English Whiggery, its roots in the Reformation, the Civil War, the growth of the common law, and, perhaps, an English disposition toward moderation, conservatism, and admiration for orderly process.

The religious question remained unresolved by both the Reformation and the struggle between Roundhead and Cavalier. Two conditions were apparent: a deep-seated fear and suspicion of a Catholic countercoup (the so-called "Jacobite Plot") and the quarrelsome fragmentation of the Nonconformist denominations.[2] Many in England, and particularly the avowedly Protestant Whigs, had misgivings about the Stuart family's religious inclinations. They seemed to sense a Catholic predilection, and in the case of James II this issue came to a head, resulting in his forced abdication. This was the "Glorious Revolution" of 1689. But the fear did not subside here, and it was rekindled by the advertised Catholic, Charles Stuart, who began an uprising in Scotland and a projected invasion of England that was only crushed by the battle of Culloden in 1746.

The passing of the Young Pretender did not cause the unrest to stop. Rival Protestant sects were perfectly willing to persecute one another if given a chance. This ill-feeling existed not only between Anglicans and Nonconformists, but also between Presbyterians and Anabaptists, and so on. In short, the age was one of intolerance, a mood of religious incriminations that jeopardized the tranquility of the state.

The foremost English philosopher of the seventeenth century, *John Locke* (1632-1704) was forced to take up the political cudgels over the issues of religious toleration, property, and the mixed constitution. Like Hobbes, Locke was an Oxford man; he acquired a medical education while in attendance there and set out to be a physician. Locke came by his liberal attitudes honestly; his family was Puritan, and Nonconformity was in vogue at Oxford during his student years. His service first as physician and later as secretary to Lord Shaftesbury, a peer of Whig sentiments, confirmed his convictions while exposing him to a wide intellectual community. Sharing the political fortunes of

---

[2] The term "Nonconformist" refers to those Protestant denominations in England outside the community of the Church of England. The term is still in use.

his employer, Locke became an exile in Holland for four years. Then, after Shaftesbury's death, he chose to remain in seclusion in Holland. The political upheaval of 1689 brought him back to England to defend the Glorious Revolution. Reëstablished, Locke quickly enjoyed both public and governmental favor. A friend and adviser to political leaders and an acquaintance of Newton, Locke was a gregarious personality. His personal outlook was moderate, optimistic, and congenial. He exuded a feeling of reasonableness.

This period of recognition and influence was to last for only five years, but the span from 1690 to his death included the publication of Locke's most meaningful work. It was during these years that the great *Treatises on Civil Government* and the *Letter on Toleration* appeared. But Locke's philosophical study and production go back much further. In the beginning Locke's interests were in strictly philosophical matters, centering first around Descartes and later around Hobbes' individualism. There is evidence that Locke had commenced work on his *Essay on Human Understanding* in the 1670's. But he was never a detached individual; his avowedly humanitarian instincts were never far from the surface, and the Revolution of 1689 prompted him to come to its defense. The two *Treatises on Civil Government*, begun even before his exile, appeared in print in 1690 in support of that cause.

The *Treatises* are a curious pair of essays in one respect. The first was written as a reply to Sir Robert Filmer's *Patriarcha* (See Chapter 9), which by this time hardly needed a rebuttal. Both *Treatises* were declared to be a refutation of Hobbes, but in fact they incorporated substantial amounts of Hobbesian argument. Locke paid tribute to Harrington; but it was to Hobbes that he owed his larger debt—not for Hobbes' conclusions, but rather for his underlying assumptions. Locke saw fit to adopt the root premises of Hobbesian psychology, and he accepted in very general terms Hobbes' account of the creation of society. Beyond this, the differences are striking. Hobbes posits the completely authoritarian state; Locke builds a theory of a democratic constitutional political community. As Harold Laski put it: "The great debate inaugurated by the Reformation ceased when Locke had outlined an intelligible basis for parliamentary government." [3] He had certainly outlined a political philosophy that became the pattern for the democracies of the West.

---

[3] Harold Laski, *Political Thought in England: Locke to Bentham* (New York: Oxford University Press, Inc., 1920), p. 13.

John Locke's political philosophy, while triggered by events and personal loyalties, was evolved gradually, proceeding from his investigations of the nature of human knowledge and his reflections on the writing of Hobbes, Hooker, and Harrington. From the beginning Locke was intrigued by the problem of knowledge, of how we come to have knowledge of the world about us. It is likely that an early interest in Cartesian philosophy provided an incentive, but Locke's conclusions strongly contradict those of the French philosopher. In short, his method was one of empirical examination, careful observation of phenomena—he has, indeed, been called the first critical philosopher.

Locke's analysis of the nature of human knowledge, obviously influenced by the psychology of Hobbes, holds crucial meaning for his political ideas. In the first place, Locke levels his main critical attack on the notion of "innate ideas." [4] Very simply, he denies that human beings come into the world with any built-in ideas; the human mind is rather, as he puts it, a *tabula rasa*, an empty tablet. The mind, instead of being shaped by its a priori content (as the Scholastics asserted), is nothing more than a learning mechanism. Whatever the mind becomes is the result of accumulated *experience*. We come into the world, says Locke, with nothing more than the equipment to sense and to ponder the inferences of our sensations. All knowledge is thus the product of the individual's contact with the environment, and it consists of sensations plus reflections. Explains Locke:

> Let us suppose the mind to be, as we say, white paper, void of all characters, without any ideas; how comes it to be furnished? Whence comes it by that vast store, which the busy and boundless fancy of man has painted on it with an almost endless variety? Whence has it all the materials of reason and knowledge? To this I answer, in one word, experience. In that all our knowledge is founded, and from that it ultimately derives itself. Our observation, employed either about external sensible objects, or about the internal operations of our minds, perceived or reflected on by ourselves, is that which supplies our understandings with all the materials of thinking. These two are the foundation of knowledge, whence all the ideas we have, or can naturally have, do spring.[5]

Locke's description of knowledge, contained in his *Essay Concerning Human Understanding*, is far more rigorous and extensive than is suggested here. But from this very fundamental conception it is possible to draw four important inferences:

---

[4] Locke uses the term "ideas" to represent the full content of human thought.

[5] John Locke, *An Essay Concerning Human Understanding*, Book II, Chapter 1.

1. When Locke denies the existence of innate ideas—of human nature's being built upon a common possession of preëxperiential knowledge—he immediately raises an ethical issue. He must derive a concept of morals that springs not from built-in moral absolutes in human nature, but from the realm of human experience alone. And if knowledge is the result of individual experience exclusively, then how can a moral order be established or even shown to exist in potential?

2. His ethics do not depart greatly from Hobbes. The "good" for Locke must be individual self-interest, and he accepts the essentially hedonistic description of "good" and "bad" in terms of the alternatives of pain and pleasure. But such an egoistic hedonism had led Hobbes to depict life as a deadly struggle, a perennial conflict of warring self-interests. In Hobbes, indeed, a similar ethical view had led to the very rejection of social morality. Yet Locke's ethical individualism comes out in a very different shape. What prevents Locke's ethics from being a "war of all against all" is his conviction that *rational* self-interest demands furthering the common good and that there exists a body of individual rights.

Locke's argument in favor of natural rights we shall examine a bit further on, but his suggestion of rational self-interest demands comment here. Locke shows marked evidence of a transition from the Hobbesian-oriented view of nature in terms of a priori principles to the investigatory spirit of empiricism. But isn't this queer talk for an empiricist? In fact, however, Locke is not a thoroughgoing empiricist, and the apparent inconsistencies between his empricism and rationalism (e.g., his doctrine of substance) have troubled later critics. But the point to be made here is that Locke's notion of reason involves:

3. "Associations of ideas," that stage beyond sheer observation. He defines reason this way:

> If general knowledge, as has been shown, consists in a perception of the agreement or disagreement of our own ideas; and the knowledge of the existence of all things without us (except only of God, Whose existence every man may certainly know and demonstrate to himself from his own existence) be had only by our senses: what room is there for the exercise of any other faculty? What need is there of reason? Very much; both for the enlargement of our knowledge and regulating our assent; for it hath to do both in knowledge and opinion, and is necessary and assisting to all our other intellectual faculties, and indeed contains two of them, viz., sagacity and illation. By the one, it finds out; and by the other, it so orders the immediate ideas, as to discover what connection there is in each link of the chain, whereby the extremes are held together; and thereby, as it were, to

draw into view the truth sought for, which is that which we call illation or inference, and consists in nothing but the perception of the connection there is between the ideas, in each step of the deduction, whereby the mind comes to see either the certain agreement or disagreement of any two ideas, as in demonstration, in which it arrives at knowledge; or their probable connection, on which it gives or withholds its assent, as in opinion.[6]

Locke's ponderous style aside, reason is identified with the consistent association of ideas and the coherence of inferences drawn from them. Such a process, Locke declares, should persuade men that if their individual well-being is to be furthered, it is necessary that they cooperate for the common good, the general welfare. How does such a view of "functional" reason affect Locke's conception of the laws of nature?

4. Clearly natural law cannot be either "law in the sky" or the divine order discovered wholly by abstract reason. For Locke, natural law is far from certain and demonstrable; it is largely a matter of opinion, of inferences drawn from human experience. Natural law is human observation of the workings of nature. This gives to Locke's view of nature a certain moral neutrality; it is a concept of nature as being decisive in human conduct, but leaving it to human ingenuity to tackle the issues of the moral order and political organization. Natural rights exist not in the sense of legal justification resting on the moral fabric of the cosmos. They are real because observation of nature convinces us that natural creatures enjoy certain prerogatives by virtue of their being creatures and that in the case of man these rights are in conformity with his unique composition and place in the scheme of nature. This theory is not to be construed in any Darwinian sense; Locke has not anticipated any novel hierarchical view of the natural order (man at the top of the mammals, and so on), but rather is it that man's participation in the natural world presupposes certain unchallengeable rights—the right to retain the fruits of his labor, for example. Locke is unfortunately vague in offering an exhaustive account of the origin and character of these natural rights and rather summarily dismisses the question either by describing them as "self-evident" or by incongruously supposing them to be found in the scriptures. They are most certainly less self-evident than Locke supposes.

These, then, are the main ideas that underlie the political recommendations contained in the *Treatises*. For the student of political

---

[6] *Ibid.*, Book IV, Chapter 17.

philosophy, it is the second treatise that provokes major attention. The first is a direct refutation of Filmer and a less direct critique of Hobbes; the second contains Locke's basic pronouncements on political thought. It is straightforward and relatively uncomplicated—and this directness of expression has undoubtedly heightened Locke's popularity; certainly he could never be accused of elegance of language.

The second treatise begins with yet another presentation of the pre-societal state of nature, far less brutal than Hobbes', but not vastly different. Man in this state of nature was not so much vicious as helpless. Men were, Locke tells us, both completely free and completely equal.[7] But their ends (preservation of life and property) could not be assured in such a state. There were always those who would transgress the law of nature.[8] Men could not with certitude enjoy the blessings of "life, liberty, and property."

Locke himself asks why men would be willing to alter the state of perfect freedom and equality:

> If man in the state of nature be so free, as has been said, if he be absolute lord of his own person and possessions, equal to the greatest, and subject to nobody, why will he part with this freedom, this empire, and subject himself to the dominion and control of any other power? To which, it is obvious to answer, that though in the state of nature he hath such a right, yet the enjoyment of it is very uncertain, and constantly exposed to the invasions of others. For all being kings as much as he, every man his equal, and the greater part no strict observers of equality and justice, the enjoyment of the property he has in this state is very unsafe, very insecure. This makes him willing to quit this condition, which, however free, is full of fears and continual dangers; and it is not without reason that he seeks out and is willing to join in society with others, who are already united, or have a mind to reunite, for the mutual preservation of their lives, liberties, and estates, which I call by the general name, prosperity.[9]

---

[7] Says Locke: "To understand political power aright, and derive it from its original, we must consider what state all men are naturally in, and that is a state of perfect freedom to order their actions and dispose of their possessions and persons as they think fit, within the bounds of the law of nature, without asking leave, or depending on the will of any other man." (*An Essay Concerning the True Original, Extent and End of Civil Government*, Chapter 2.)

[8] Again Locke: "The state of nature has a law of nature to govern it, which obliges everyone; and reason, which is that law, teaches all mankind who will but consult it, that, being all equal and independent, no one ought to harm another in his life, liberty or possessions." (*Ibid.*, Chapter 2.)

[9] *Ibid.*, Chapter 9.

Locke thus returns to the thesis of the contract, but he clearly implies two contracts, one to establish society and the other to create political order. Although Locke is regrettably cloudy on this point, it is discernible by implication that the civil contract precedes the political one and that the difference between them is primarily one of permanent and continuing consent. To the first contract, society, men are bound as long as society exists,[10] but in the case of the political contract, man must give continuing assent or the contract becomes void. In short. the political order rests upon a constant agreement—in the form of majority decision—to maintain it; government depends upon popular acquiescence to its existence.

Putting aside for the moment the question of when *ought* the people to disavow the political contract, the rest of Locke's ideas regarding the contract are concerned with the premise that individual rights are better protected in the public charge than if every man is allowed to guard his own in any manner he sees fit. The aim is always individual self-interest. That this seems reasonable to Locke is very apparent if one keeps in mind that he was concerned, above all, with one private right: *property*. At times on reading Locke one gets the impression that this is the sole natural right. By "property," he means something beyond real property; he means the products of a man's labor. A man is entitled to what he produces or gains. Locke even goes beyond this at times to equate "property" with "estate," meaning by the latter term not only a man's material possessions and products, but also his status in society, that ineffable aura that surrounds an individual's personal attainments. This is apparently a natural right, too. It would be hard to overestimate the significance of property to Locke; it is elevated to an almost sacrosanct status. Locke remains the first champion of private property. But too often his conception of property as the products of labor is forgotten or slighted. This is a notion about the nature of private property that can cut two ways. As Locke himself writes:

Though the earth and all inferior creatures be common to all men, yet every man has a property in his own person; this nobody has any

---

[10] Of society Locke writes: ". . . the power that every individual gave the society when he entered it can never revert to the individual again as long as the society lasts, but will always remain in the community, because without this there can be no community, no commonwealth . . ."

Speaking of the political order he contends: "When by miscarriages of those in authority it is forfeited, upon the forfeiture, or at the determination of the time set, it reverts to the society, and the people have a right to act as supreme and continue the legislative in themselves; or place it in a new form, or new hands as they think good." (*Ibid.*, Chapter 19.)

right to but himself. The labour of his body and the work of his hands we may say are properly his.[11]

To recapitulate: Locke supposes an original contract forming society and perhaps a supplementary one creating government, and both of these exist to insure the protection of private natural rights ("life, liberty, and property"). This abbreviated thesis is not as simple as a quick look might disclose—it is not altogether "self-evident." It poses a direct problem and invokes others. Is the idea of a contract as elaborate as Locke sets out a feasible one? And if it is, what moral justifications and implications must follow? What machinery of government does Locke suppose to be demanded by such a vision of the nature of state and society?

Locke was not the last to expound the contract. As we shall see, Rousseau will clothe it in mythical thunder-and-lightning. Perhaps, indeed, Rousseau pushes it to a *reductio ad absurdum*. But if this be true, is there not also an element of absurdity in Locke's notion? After all, Hobbes' state of nature could be defended by an appeal, however crude, to biology. Locke's cannot. On the face of it, it would seem a piece of fiction. Aristotle would have been deeply shocked by such a departure from empiricism—and yet Locke is described as an empiricist. What evidence is there in human experience to imply such a contract? On empirical grounds anyway, the whole idea is untenable—and Locke provides no real defense along this line. Surely he must have foreseen this difficulty. But it is a difficulty only so long as Locke's description is taken as a literal account of an unrecorded historical event. Does Locke mean it to be a sort of logical construct, an inductive conclusion drawn from his observations of human nature which provides a handy hypothesis? Perhaps. But viewing the contract theory in this fashion does not make it possible for Locke to get off the hook altogether. Creating myths, however serviceable, seems an odd occupation for an empiricist.

But Locke is never really a thoroughgoing empiricist.[12] This is nowhere more graphically exhibited than in the matter of natural rights. Like the contract, these natural rights are difficult to demonstrate in a manner satisfactory to a convinced empiricist. They failed to impress David Hume, for example. Locke's plea that they are self-evident is a candid confession of this obscurity. An appeal to the

---

[11] *Ibid.*, Chapter 5.

[12] The most striking case is Locke's belief that although knowledge is the agreement between ideas, the causal relationships between these ideas is not established by experience, but by direct intuition.

natural order will not do. There is no evidence that lower forms of life have any "rights" in any reasonable definition of that term. The claim from experience is a shaky one, too. There seems to be little justification for observing that individuals enjoy "self-evident natural rights." In what sense are they self-evident? Is not Locke, who so vigorously denies innate ideas, posing another set of innate qualities impossible of empirical verification?

Perhaps Locke's predicament follows from his failure to couch natural rights within an admittedly moral frame—perhaps he confuses the "is" and the "ought," to borrow language from Hume. "Natural rights *ought* to exist or are even compelled to exist by moral necessity" might be a strong argument, but this is not to say that they do in fact exist outside the ethical demand. Locke seems to assume their existence under the stress of believing in their moral indispensability. Locke might have put his case more forcefully in more overtly ethical language.

His view of moral philosophy is not at base much different from that of Hobbes. It includes the primacy of individual self-interest, a sensual quantification of pleasure and pain, and it assumes a universal egotism. Locke differs from Hobbes, however, in two particulars. First, he advances a natural rights doctrine, and, secondly, he argues that individual self-interest does not necessarily mean a "war against all." Instead, Locke maintains, man's rational faculties will tell him that the maximization of his own self-interest lies in advancing the "common good"—individual protection is best operative when all are protected. Cooperation, not conflict, is the reasonable means of attaining private satisfaction. Locke comes close to saying that universal egotism is mitigated by an almost instinctual human urge for cooperation and joint action.[13] His moral tenor is one of vibrant optimism, of deepseated belief in man's better nature.

If we assume John Locke's ideas of contract, natural rights, and morals, what sort of a political system do we discover? Locke's pervading influence on political thought can be quickly traced to these political recommendations. They are far more compelling than his creaking psychology and sometimes inconsistent metasociology. For convenience, we can take a look at these contributions under five

---

[13] One of Locke's intellectual descendants, the twentieth-century philosopher, John Dewey, would say precisely this.

headings: (1) the government as social agent, (2) equality, (3) majority rule, (4) legislative supremacy, and, (5) minority toleration.

Locke was the first widely read political philosopher regularly to insist that society and government are two entities and that government is an agent of society. It was created to serve the general good and deserves to exist only so long as it performs as a steward of the social welfare. Consequently, Locke chops away from the idea of government many of the medieval draperies that had been thrown about it so as to give it an almost supernatural appearance. He insists that the state is not omnicompetent but is accountable; he casts doubt on the thesis that order is *always* preferable to liberty, assuming that the latter can be enjoyed without the destruction of the former. He introduces to the general audience the concept of political arrangements as devices to promote individual happiness. And he popularizes the idea of governmental responsibility.

This does not mean, for Locke, that government ought to be powerless or even innocuous—he does not preach that "he who governs least governs best." Governments must make law and enforce that law; to do otherwise would be to jeopardize private rights. But law must be the end product of popular assent and some measure of general participation, and the enforcement of it must be subject to continual public scrutiny. Locke might well have said that "public office is a public trust."

Government operating on the basis of continuous consent demands the principle of political equality, reasons Locke. Of this equality he writes:

> Though I have said that all men by nature are equal, I cannot be supposed to understand all sorts of equality. Age or virtue may give a man a just precedency. Excellency of parts and merits may place others above the common level. Birth may subject some, and alliance benefit others, to pay an observance to those to whom nature, gratitude, or other respects may have made it due. And yet all this consists with the equality of which all men are in, in respect of jurisdiction or dominion, one over another; which was the equality I there spoke of as proper to the business at hand, being that equal right that every man hath to his natural freedom, without being subject to the will or authority of any other man.[14]

This does not sound much like a twentieth-century democrat. Locke was a seventeenth-century gentleman. He did not advocate "social leveling" or the "classless society." He was not a radical in the tradi-

---

[14] *An Essay Concerning the True Original, Extent and End of Civil Government,* Chapter 6.

tion of the Levelers or the Diggers. He observed the properties of social rank and the varying capacities of individuals.[15] He has been called a "spokesman for middle-class revolutions." But *political equality* he supported without reservation. For Locke, both the defense of private rights and the rule of continual assent required a base of political equality.

Continual assent meant, in practice, majority rule. Government was to be by show of hands. "It is necessary," Locke advises, "that the body should move that way whither the greater force carries it, which is the consent of the majority." It must be apparent that the Lockean doctrine of majority rule is a bit of a compromise in theory because majority rule is neither unanimous consent nor the continuing assent of all individuals. The problem is that participation in the body politic must assume some measure of deprivation of private decision, beyond of course the matter of "life, liberty, and property." Is the justification for this sacrifice to be merely on the ground that some individuals holding a particular view are in the greater number? Locke would most likely reply that this sacrifice of omnipresent private decision is a small price to pay for the protection of more critical rights. But the difficulty here is that the appeal of the individual against the state is made not to a moral standard, but only to the will of the majority who have it within their power to make law. And can we assume as well that a majority might not see fit to tamper with natural rights as readily as a despot? Locke endows majority rule with neither a special wisdom nor a mystic will, but rests majority rule on the largest total of collected self-interests. What real recourse is there against the majority? Apparently Locke did not see what John Stuart Mill would perceive sharply in the nineteenth century—that is, the tyrannical possibilities of majority rule unchecked by solid restraints.

However inadequate Locke's development of the majoritarian point of view, his statement of it can be considered as a foundation of democratic political philosophy. The majority must act, according to Locke, through a legislative body. His whole idea of legislative theory can be summed up as *legislative supremacy* and *limited representation*. Both ingredients are designed to create positive law while at the same time safeguarding private rights, particularly property rights. Locke makes it crystal clear that the legislature is "the supreme power in every commonwealth." He asserts that it is not only supreme:

---

[15] His theories are evident in Thomas Jefferson's somewhat unorganized idea of a natural aristocracy, for example.

. . . but sacred and unalterable in the hands where the community
have once placed it; nor can any edict of anybody else, in what form
soever conceived, or by what power soever backed, have the force
and obligation of a law, which has not its sanction from that legislative which the public has chosen and appointed.[16]

Law-making, then, is the exclusive function of the legislature. But
the power to enact laws, Locke contends, must have a reasonable
check—the most obvious line to be drawn being the invasion of private
rights by a legislature abusing its mandate. In such a case, Locke
points out, the public can act to replace or abolish the legislative body.
In his words:

. . . the legislative being only a fiduciary power to act for certain
ends, there remains still in the people a supreme power to remove or
alter the legislative when they find the legislative acting contrary to the
trust reposed in them.[17]

Locke's "legislative" is not quite the same as a modern popular
assembly. Believer that he was in majority rule, its is a mixture of
popular representation (delegates elected from the public at large)
and representation of property interests and traditional institutions.
It is a mixed legislature. "Things in this world are in so constant a
flux," Locke muses, "that nothing remains long in the same state."
This is true, he goes on to say, of the character of the body politic,
and for this reason it is prudent to balance the legislature with something more than sheer popular representation. This means, for him,
legislators who are not expressly responsible to constituents and thus
have no need to be responsive to changes in popular fancy.

Locke also envisions a government of distinct divisions—we would
now term this a "separation of powers." It is necessary, comments
Locke, to have an executive branch:

But because the laws that are at once and in a short time made, have
a constant and lasting force and need a perpetual execution or an
attendance thereunto; therefore, it is necessary there should be a
power always in being, which should see to the execution of the
laws that are made and remain in force; and thus the legislative
and executive power come often to be separated.[18]

Locke draws an interesting distinction between what he calls
"executive" and "federative" power. Executive power refers to the
execution of the acts of the legislature; federative power refers to

---

[16] An Essay Concerning the True Original, Extent and End of Civil Government,
Chapter 11.

[17] Ibid., Chapter 13.

[18] Ibid., Chapter 12.

powers impossible for the legislature to discharge, but necessary to the welfare of the commonwealth, such as diplomacy, war-making, and international affairs in general. It was mainly from Locke that the idea arose of the conduct of foreign policy as an executive function, although the legislature was either supreme or equal to the executive. Locke did not foresee, however, the tremendous impact of the courts on constitutional development; nor did he contemplate the judiciary as a separate organ of the state.

On the matter of the encouragement of toleration, John Locke exerted very considerable influence. In his day, the question of toleration chiefly concerned religious controversy, yet his point of view had effect on the whole issue of how far the state ought to go in permittting doctrinal disagreement—religious or political. In his *Letter Concerning Toleration,* Locke laid down what was for his time a far-reaching thesis:

> For the private judgment of any persons concerning a law enacted in political matters, for the public good, does not take away the obligation of that law, nor deserve a dispensation. But if the law indeed be concerning things that lie not within the verge of the magistrate's authority . . . men are not in these cases obliged by that law, against their consciences.
>
> . . . as the private judgment of any particular person, if erroneous, does not exempt him from the obligation of law, so the private judgment (as I may call it) of the magistrate does not give him any new right of imposing law upon his subjects, which neither was in the constitution of the government granted him, nor ever was in the power of the people to grant.
>
> Another more secret evil, but more dangerous to the commonwealth, is when men arrogate to themselves, and to those of their own sect, some peculiar prerogative covered over with a specious show of deceitful words, but in effect opposite to the civil right of the community.[19]

It is possible to argue that Locke raises more questions than he answers. Some have dismissed him as a compiler of other men's more original ideas. Certainly it is not difficult to detect circularities and inconsistencies in his logic. His thought frankly lacks the vigor and elegance of the Greeks, the speculative sweep of Aquinas, the passion of Luther, or the practical insight of Machiavelli. Yet his influence on Western political institutions is more directly to be seen than that of

---

[19] John Locke, *A Letter Concerning Toleration* (1689).

any of his more eloquent and sophisticated rivals. One has only to read the United States Constitution or the political history of Britain in the nineteenth century to see Locke's fine hand. Why?

Four factors seem to explain Locke's unusual hold on the political imagination. While these factors help to account for his popularity in the late eighteenth and nineteenth centuries, they also shed some light on why Locke's thought remains so alive today. In the first place, Locke's appeal to many is his consistent *moderation* (a similar quality has endeared Aristotle to the generations). Here is middle-of-the-road common sense, if you will, tempered judgment, and a refusal to accept extremist palliatives. Locke is a comfortable philosopher to cling to; he is safe, solid, and modestly humane.

Secondly, he made little or no effort to lay down dicta for the ages. Unlike Plato or Kant or Hegel, he was addressing himself to his time and its problems and he wrote not in the ringing phrases of the absolutist, but as a discourser on topical issues. He did not shun *contemporaneity;* his message did not arrive *ex cathedra.*

Thirdly, Locke was a dogged, almost stubborn advocate of *optimism.* This was a cheering, reassuring attitude. Man was both good and sensible, given an opportunity; with properly reasonable policies and habits of mind, things were bound to get better. Locke hinted that mankind might be on the threshold of a new era of understanding, freedom, and communal happiness. Such announcements came as welcome news. (Without depreciating Locke, it must be said that people tend to agree with those who tell them what they want to hear.) Locke heralded an epoch of democratic optimism that has begun to fade only now in the middle of the twentieth century.

Lastly, he gave new scope and a new definition to *individualism* and renovated the idea that the person was important. Proceeding from Hobbes' propositions, Locke constructed an individualism that gave susbtance and dignity to the nature and aspirations of individual men. He subordinated all the machinery of society to the interests of the single citizen, without demolishing the role of government or essentially weakening the command of law.

The winds of change had been blowing in France, too. Locke's philosophy and the revelations of Newton (the *Principia* appeared in 1687) added to the intellectual ferment. English institutions were admired—particularly by Montesquieu—and English philosophy digested. This period of assimilation covered the first half of the eighteenth century. But while English ideas were fed into the machine of Gallic cerebration, the product that emerged was quite different. The French were, after all, dedicated to the Roman law and English common law would have been an exotic flower indeed to import into France. Nor did the French enjoy the climate of political moderation and stability that marked English growth during the seventeenth and eighteenth centuries. They had a tradition of energetic fratricide. Moreover, the Gallic mind had no real affinity for the empiricism that had become the distinguishing feature of English thought. For better or worse, they were rationalists and inclined toward the dogmatism of political absolutism. But it might be remembered that although Newton was an Englishman, the mechanistic implications of his physics were obviously conducive to social and political theory that were equally mechanistic and inflexible.

In the front rank of French Anglophiles were *Charles de Secondat, Baron de la Brède et de Montesquieu* (1689-1755) and *Voltaire* (1694-1778). Both were resident in England for considerable periods; both were cultivated, urbane observers, personally detached from the mounting social tensions in France. Both were practitioners of *belles-lettres*—Montesquieu had gained fame with his *Persian Letters* and Voltaire is perhaps best remembered for *Candide*. Both were ardent democrats and libertarians. But the reputations of both rest more on literary grace than on political substance.

Montesquieu's *Spirit of the Laws* (1748), the most widely read French treatise on political ideas in the first half of the eighteenth century, is a sprawling conglomeration of rather disconnected ideas regarding science, geography, sociology (the term was yet to be invented, however), history, and government. Precise paraphrase is impossible, and perhaps one should shun even an attempt at summarization. The most arresting feature of the work is its deification of nature. Montesquieu makes nature the source of virtually everything imaginable and subordinates all human considerations to it. Nature also acts as a kind of oracle to which the products of man's invention can be referred for judgment. Specifically, nature provides a comprehensive yardstick for the measurement of justice, the correction of law. The conjoining of natural factors (even climate and topography) creates an environmental frame that imposes certain conditions on the evolution of society. Such factors are responsible, indeed, for forms of political organization and the convolutions of social practice.

Beyond this chaotic synthesis, Montesquieu is well-known for his misinterpretation of the English Constitution. He assumed that the mixed character of the British government amounted to a separation of powers in which legislative, judicial, and executive organs were employed as a means of balance, each checking the power of the others. In retrospect, it seems difficult to imagine how Montesquieu could have failed to appreciate the supremacy of the legislature in England, but this fact aside, the most peculiar feature of his theory is that this separation of powers is not a logical construction, but rather a natural division of governmental powers. Moreover, however erroneous his reflections, they were highly influential. One need only to consult a number of American constitutional instruments produced at the end of the eighteenth century to discover this. It might even be fair to say that Montesquieu's legacy is still causing painful second thoughts in the gradual metamorphosis of American government.

Voltaire, for his part, had no yearning to produce weighty political theory. Voltaire, the literary artist, was prompted to take up the political gauntlet over the issue of censorship. This led him to a personal vendetta against the curtailment of the freedom of expression, exchange of ideas, and academic toleration. His weapons were biting irony and a mordant, scourging wit. A number of hallowed institutions came to feel their sting, including the law, religion, and the prevailing political leadership. This passionate personal concern with freedom encouraged the growing political radicalism in France, but Voltaire himself remained an aloof iconoclast, far above the commoner brawls of politics.

A variety of radical theories followed. *Claude Helvétius* (1715-1771) argued for a reform based on scientific ethics. The Physiocrats revived hedonism and extreme economic individualism. *Paul Henri d'Holbach* (1723-1789) continued the adoration of nature, replacing Christianity with a materialistic creed notable for its paradoxically mystic atmosphere and urging that government was a wicked conspiracy. *Anne Robert Turgot* (1727-1781) proposed a mechanistic account of history. *Marie Jean de Condorcet* (1743-1794) depicted a new utopian age growing out of the increase in human knowledge and the democratization of institutions.

The optimism encouraged by Locke, the advances of science, the utopian notions of progress, the mounting urge for radical reform, the sentimental conceptualization of human nature, the fascination with the natural, all these currents spiraled into a deafening charybdis.

But the most strident and powerful call came from *Jean-Jacques Rousseau* (1712-1778).

Although the remark was made of Marat, the bloody manipulator of the Revolution, that "he was a creature whom nature rarely produces," the quip might well have been employed earlier for Rousseau. Certainly none of the traditional categories into which philosophers are neatly put would do for Rousseau. Even the supply of adjectives is probably inadequate. Indifference in the face of this incredible personality is out of the question. Genius or madman? Reformer or immoralist? Seer or scoundrel? Fighter for freedom or apostle of tyranny?

Agreement of any sort is impossible. Rousseau remains either a gospeler of human salvation or a perpetrator of immense wickedness. Take these examples of commentary:

Irving Babbitt, one of Rousseau's bitterest twentieth-century critics, has this to say of him:

> He is the first of a long series of aesthetic vagabonds who have found solace in a world of luxurious dreams, and often sought refuge in this world from a reality disenchanted by scientific analysis. This confusing of the contemplative life with revery is doubtless destined to become a matter of curious study when we see the romantic movement more from the outside and are less inclined than we are at present to take the romantic leaders at their own estimate of themselves. "I am in no wise tempted by the active life," says Rousseau, and thus he speaks like some sage or eremite; but as we read on we discover that he was the kind of hermit who, as Byron puts it, would have liked a "harem for a grot," and who entertained his solitude with the very images that St. Anthony sought to escape by leaping into the snow.[20]

A more sympathetic commentator, Harold Laski, has written thus:

> We have to remember that ours is the fruit of his decision. What he experienced in sorrow, we have inherited in knowledge; what he in his personal happiness lost, we in our collective tradition gained. For him it was a tragedy of bitterness which his utmost eloquence could hardly express. But for us it invokes the memory less of its sadder moments than those magic hours where we seem to share the hope of his enchanted dream.[21]

What did Rousseau think of himself? If one is convinced that he was suffering from severe paranoia—and there are quite a number

---

[20] Irving Babbitt, *Literature and the American College* (Chicago, Ill.: Henry Regnery Co., 1955), pp. 172-173. See also Babbitt's *Rousseau and Romanticism*.

[21] Harold Laski, "A Portrait of Jean-Jacques Rousseau," *Yale Review*, XVII, July, 1928.

who entertain this view—then the question is difficult to answer unless Rousseau were to submit *in absentia* to some long sessions on the analyst's couch. If one is inclined to take his self-appraisal as something more than the symptoms of paranoia, then Rousseau has a great deal to say and it is contained in large part in his *Confessions*. It is a remarkable book, shocking, frank, embarrassingly intimate, filled to the brim with egotistical posturing and what may well be melancholy sincerity. It is a narrative filled with petty crimes, seductions and remorse, wounded feelings, frantic misery, self-pity, and lurid indictments of his inconstant fortunes. Take this brief extract as a sample:

> You have seen my peaceful youth pass away in a tolerably uniform and agreeable manner, without great disappointments or remarkable prosperity. This absence of extremes was in part the result of my passionate but weak disposition, which, more easily discouraged than prompt to undertake, only quitted its state of repose when rudely shocked, but fell back into it again from weariness and natural inclination; and which, while keeping me away from great virtues, and still further from great vices, led me back steadily to the indolent and peaceful life for which I felt Nature intended me, and never permitted me to attain to greatness in anything, either good or bad. What a different picture I shall have soon to draw! Destiny, which for thirty years favoured my inclinations, during a second thirty thwarted them, and this continued opposition between my position and inclinations will be seen to have produced monstrous errors, unheard-of misfortunes, and all the virtues that can render adversity honourable, with the exception of strength of character.[22]

Rousseau's life began quietly enough in Geneva in 1712. But by the age of sixteen he had left home to seek the solace of the open road. He led a nomadic life, often becoming a protégé of sympathetic older women. He was apparently more interested in music than any other calling, and a new system of musical notation that he had devised prompted him to go to Paris in 1741. His contribution to musical theory was not readily accepted, but he did attract some attention among Parisian intellectuals and Diderot gave him a job working on his *Encyclopedia*. Rousseau began to write essays as well as music. In 1749 he won the prize of the Academy of Dijon and in 1752 scored a hit with an opera. About this time, Rousseau became convinced that he was the victim of various sinister conspiracies to ruin him—he blamed principally Diderot and his associates. These delusions of

---

[22] Jean-Jacques Rousseau, *Confessions* (New York: Modern Library, Inc., 1945), p. 283.

persecution did not prevent him from publishing two novels in the next few years, *La Nouvelle Héloïse* and *Emile* (both thinly disguised polemics against social conventions and contemporary education), and his *Social Contract*. The radical flavor of his novels made it necessary for him to flee to Switzerland and then to England, where he was befriended by the philosopher Hume. But Rousseau soon became suspicious that Hume was plotting his disgrace, and he returned to Paris, where he died in ignominy in 1778.

Although he died before the romantic movement reached its crest (in the first half of the nineteenth century), Rousseau embodied many of the chief characteristics of romanticism. He was a violent, even frenetic sentimentalist; for him, feelings were the principal guides to action. His individualism (and its antithesis, collectivism, which he also curiously espoused) was buried in a romantic belief in the ascendency of the ego. In Rousseau, this egoism assumes the shape of an all-encompassing will, primitive, dominant, infallible, glorious. He advocates almost a caricature of the romantic conception of nature. Nature is the eternal fountain, all-good, all-gentle, all-just, and all-beautiful. He outdoes even Wordsworth's hyperbole in summoning up the imagined perfection of the natural. Wickedness is defined as that which is contrary to nature, or at least to that which Rousseau thinks nature to be. This passionate primitivism leads him, not illogically, to extreme condemnation of civilization as corrupting, immoral, and degrading. Such a view almost necessarily means a rejection of intellectualism. The villains of the piece are academic intellectuals. They mar the innocent simplicity of the pastoral folk. Reason and knowledge are the enemies of the natural man or the "noble savage," as Rousseau occasionally calls him. The attainments of art, learning, and science spell ruin in the end, for they only corrupt virtue and make luxury and inequality possible. Certainly he is the patron saint of those suspicious and contemptuous of learning. In his *Discourse of the Arts and Sciences*, Rousseau cries:

> Virtue! sublime science of simple minds, are such industry and preparation needed if we are to know you? Are not your principles graven on every heart? Need we do more, to learn your laws, than examine ourselves and listen to the voice of conscience, when the passions are silent? [23]

When he turned to the great issue of political society, Rousseau proceeded with these thoughts, and they convinced him of several

[23] Jean-Jacques Rousseau, *Discourse on the Moral Effects of the Arts and Sciences* (1750).

political evils. First, political order itself is a form of slavery, because
it is unnatural. He begins the *Social Contract* with the famous lines:
"Man is born free and is everywhere in chains." Secondly, private
property is the basic cause of corrupt civil societies and the first and
foremost disease of man. Explains Rousseau:

> The first man who, having enclosed a piece of ground, bethought
> himself of saying, "This is mine," and found people simple enough to
> believe him, was the real founder of civil society. From how many
> crimes, wars, and murders, from how many horrors and misfortunes
> might not any one have saved mankind, by pulling up the stakes, or
> filling up the ditch, and crying to his fellows: "Beware of listening
> to this impostor; you are undone if you once forget that the fruits of
> the earth belong to us all, and the earth itself to nobody.[24]

Thirdly, all forms of inequality are immoral, since all men belong to
a common brotherhood; the human race is one vast community.
Fourthly, men, uncorrupted by institutions, are by nature good, peaceful, and congenial.

Rousseau commences his analysis of politics by presenting a picture of the "original state of nature" that is a virtual reversal of the
Hobbesian version. Men were happy, simple children, at peace with
themselves and with their animal coinhabitants of the earth. It was a
sort of Garden of Eden without Eve's naughty prank. But sin was
abroad in this paradise in the form of greed. This greed created private
property and destroyed the mutual trust of these innocent natural
men. The sense of human community was obliterated. Mankind became fragmented into jealous and crafty individuals.

What has to be done, argues Rousseau, is to reëstablish this community. But to do so requires a new social contract, one that will
preserve human freedom from exploitation. He frames the problem
in these terms:

> The problem is to find a form of association which will defend and
> protect with the whole common force the person and goods of each
> asociate, and in which each, while uniting himself with all, may still
> obey himself alone and remain free as before. This is the fundamental
> problem of which the social contract provides the solution.[25]

What is Rousseau's "solution"? It rests on a radical redefinition of
community. The social contract creates a community that is not a

---

[24] Jean-Jacques Rousseau, *Discourse on the Origin of Inequality* (1754).
[25] Jean-Jacques Rousseau, *Social Contract*, Book I, Chapter 6.

collection of individuals—the whole is once more greater than the sum of its parts. What is produced is a body politic that is itself a separate corporate being, a "moral" being, a living, viable political organism enjoying an existence quite distinct from the citizens comprising it, yet in which its members are completely immersed. On what basis can Rousseau argue, however, that a community in which men are but "an invisible part of the whole" is a separate being with a sovereign voice?

Rousseau's justification hangs on the introduction of the principle of the *volonté générale*, the general will. This is not a simple concept to define, since in Rousseau's writing it appears shrouded in almost mystical rhetoric. The general will is the will of the body politic, the collective will of the citizenry. But at the same time it is not a mere collection of individual opinions or judgments. It is not an adding up of an aggregate will. Instead, the act of communal living seems to produce, in Rousseau's judgment, a sort of common mind, a collective will, which incorporates yet transcends the collective wisdom. The act of collectivization by some sort of metamorphosis produces a community will.

To this general will, Rousseau ascribes virtually complete authority. The general will is infallible. Writes Rousseau:

> It follows from what has gone before that the general will is always right and tends to the public advantage; but it does not always follow that the deliberations of the people are always equally correct. Our will is always for our own good, but we do not always see what that is; the people is never corrupted, but it is often deceived, and on such occasions only does it seem to will what is bad.[26]

The general will is sovereign. Again Rousseau:

> If the State is a moral person whose life is in the union of its members, and if the most important of its cares is the care of its own preservation, it must have a universal and compelling force, in order to move and dispose each part as may be advantageous to the whole. As nature gives each man absolute power over all his members, the social compact gives the body politic absolute power over all its members also; and it is this power which, under the direction of the general will, bears, as I have said, the name of Sovereignty.[27]

The general will is the source of law. Rousseau explains:

> But when the whole people decree for the whole people, it is considering only itself; and if a relation is then formed, it is between two

---

[26] *Ibid.*, Book I, Chapter 3.
[27] *Ibid.*, Book I, Chapter 4.

aspects of an entire object, without there being any division of the whole. In that case, the matter about which the decree is made is, like the decreeing will, general. This act is what I call a law.[28]

This broad thesis raises a host of questions. Even assuming that Rousseau can in some fashion demonstrate the existence of his general will, how can the mandate of the general will be unerringly known? Who speaks in behalf of it? If the general will is always right—indeed, is itself the only criterion of rightness—how does it, in practice, counsel on matters of policy? All these questions Rousseau can dismiss by maintaining that the general will is made known through the will of the majority. But clearly the general will and the will of the majority cannot be the same thing. How, in fact, the general will speaks through a majority of the community suggests all manner of metaphysical complexities, but assuming that it does so, what Rousseau has done is make an absolute out of majority decision. For him, there is obviously magic in numbers.

That the majority is always right because it is the outward expression of the general will invokes four major questions: (1) What evidence is there that the general will motivates the majority and is not a mere rationalization of the power of numbers? (2) Assuming that not all political decisions are made on the basis of overwhelming unanimity, does the general will speak with the same authority if the majority is but a tiny fraction larger than the minority on a given issue? (3) To what extent does the majority impinge upon the rights of dissenters? (4) What reason is there to believe that an all-powerful majority might exercise its will in a less despotic fashion than an absolute monarch or an all-powerful oligarchy of entrenched aristocrats?

If these questions were put to Rousseau, one suspects that he might answer them in the following way: (1) The general will is an indispensable characteristic of a true society. It is the underlying principle of community that converts men into social beings. Its existence is as clearly manifest as the society it shapes. (2) The size of the majority is immaterial. The majority is not a mere numerical calculation. As men come together in true community, there is created an organic bond, a wisdom, that transcends the sum total of individuals. (3) The act of being involved in a community, responsive to the general will, renders men free of corruption and greed, thereby eliminating oppression. Rights are essentially rights to participate and not rights to abstain, and the minority has no recourse from majority decision.

---

[28] *Ibid.*, Book I, Chapter 6.

(4) The true community is a community of free men who live in virtue because they have been liberated from both the threat and the temptation of tyranny.

Whether or not Rousseau could sustain these arguments is questionable. Even those who have followed in his tradition, and there have been many, have drastically revised many of his tenets. Yet the flood of ideas that gushed forth from these doctrines was immense. Rousseau's influence, always potent, had both short- and long-range effects. In the short run, he virtually made the French Revolution a certainty, and he helped give it its doctrinaire and extremist cast. In the longer run, Rousseau spawned the modern phenomenon of nationalism. It is curious that this should be so. He was hardly a patriot himself in the accepted sense; he was surely no paladin of La Belle France. He was Swiss by birth, his orientations were cosmopolitan, and his residences varied. Yet the theory of the general will gave a completely new dimension to the emergence of the nation-state. Indeed, it added the word "nation." It made of the state a "thing," an organism with a mystic soul, a quasisacred communion of national souls. The time was propitious for such a concept, and it caught the popular imagination. It was a simple matter to convert the doctrine of the general will to the idea of the utter, unique self-sufficiency of the nation-state. From this, nationalism followed like a forest fire, bringing with it the rise of national armies, total war, and, not surprisingly, the virulent nationalism that fostered the totalitarian uprisings of the twentieth century.

Rousseau let off a bigger bang than he could ever in the wildest flights of his eccentric imagination have expected. He had fathered a revolution, but the upheaval in France was but one of many of a series of revolutionary conflagrations, intellectual and political, that could claim Rousseau as progenitor. Modern radicalism is essentially the product of his utopian extremism. On the other hand, a large portion of the totalitarian thinkers of the current century have their roots in Rousseau's inexorable general will. Rousseau, the apostle of freedom, the champion of individual egocentricity, had in fact only supplanted one tyranny by another. In the place of the hated aristocracy, the hierarchy of officialdom, he had substituted a popular dictatorship, not the less oppressive because it appeared to stand on a numerically larger base. Plato could have counseled him against this unhappy eventuality, and among the radical thinkers who came afterward, Mill pointed out the serious threat of a majority unchecked and galloping roughshod over minorities.

The paradox of Rousseau's sincere belief in freedom and the implications of a majoritarian dictatorship via the general will can be explained best by reference to his neglect of law. Like other radicals of one shade or another, Rousseau had deep suspicions about the law, being prone to regard it as an instrument of social control wielded by oligarchies in the interests of preserving property rights and the social status quo. This hasty dismissal of jurisprudence was unfortunate in the case of Rousseau, since it left his idea of the social order without any effective means of balancing interests and rights, power and just claims. Law may be enacted by the majority, but it must also rest on a consensus much more permanent and solid than the caprices of popular opinion. In this way, law frequently becomes the defender of those who buck the general will, the citizen *v.* his government and unpopular causes *v.* prevailing public passion. What Rousseau failed to grasp in his reformist zeal was the importance of social change and reform in England by means of constitutional revision. If Rousseau had been able to consult a crystal ball, he would have discovered that the growth of freedom in the West would be essentially a legal commentary, an enlargement of constitutional guarantees, and that freedom and equality, far from being consequent upon each other, would prove to be elements requiring a delicate equilibrium, a balancing act that is still going on in the democracies of Europe and America. But oddly enough, powers of prognostication are somewhat rare among utopian theorists, and Rousseau, whatever else he was, was the most dramatic, compelling, and irritating of all political dreamers, the builders of those idyllic earthly commonwealths that await man's vision and ingenuity in some unscheduled age to come. Who could argue that the growth of utopias lies in their literal attainability? But, too, who could argue that the fate of society rests upon random musings and sentimental hopes, however transcendental? The attraction of utopias probably lies in their optimistic and self-complimentary appraisal of human nature. Rousseau rhapsodized on man's innate goodness, albeit it seems he was intensely apprehensive about the intentions of those with whom fate brought him into personal contact. But the human saga must appear to the most perfunctory observer as a decided mixture of heroism and villainy, a gigantic "western" in which the forces of law and order may not necessarily emerge triumphant.

The Jivaros of the Amazon jungles collect human heads to adorn their huts, while members of a nominally civilized society have been known to use the skulls of their fellow men as ashtrays. Inevitably, a certain skepticism must intrude on the utopian dream.

. . . *for further discussion:*

1. Both Locke and Rousseau thought in terms of a state of nature. Yet in the case of Locke, private property was one of the most precious of natural rights, while Rousseau contended that greed created private property and destroyed the idyllic life of presocietal men. How do you account for this extreme difference of view about property, considering that the two men worked from a broadly similar idea about the creation of society? Who was right, Locke or Rousseau? Is there a middle position? If so, what might it be?

2. Locke maintained that the commonwealth ought to be founded on political equality, yet he did not suggest universal suffrage or equal representation. Is this inconsistent? Is it a tenable position to argue that all men share equally in the political community, yet are not entitled to have an equal voice in its management? Does popular sovereignty logically demand universal suffrage?

3. Rousseau was the author of a militant irrationalism. He maintained that feelings were to be trusted and obeyed, urges to be accorded priority. Reason, on the other hand, was superfluous or even misleading. How do you think current psychological opinion (either Freudian, Jungian, Gestalt, etc.) squares with Rousseau's view of personality? Freud, for example, did implicitly minimize the significance of conscious reasoning as a basis of behavior, but, on the other hand, he pointed out that men often do not act in their own best interest and have self-destructive and antisocial tendencies. From your knowledge of Rousseau and Freud (you might sneak ahead and look at Chapter 15), how would you compare their views on human nature?

4. What similarities do you think exist between the Frenchman, Rousseau, and the American, Walt Whitman? You might reread sections of *Leaves of Grass* and *Democratic Vistas* and a good critical analysis of Whitman.

. . . *for further investigation:*

Babbitt, Irving, ° *Rousseau and Romanticism.* New York: Meridian Books, 1955.

Barker, Ernest, ed., ° *Social Contract: Essays by Locke, Hume, and Rousseau.* New York: Galaxy Books, n.d.

Becker, Carl L., ° *The Heavenly City of the Eighteenth-Century Philosophers.* New Haven, Conn.: Yale University Press, 1959.

Filmer, Sir Robert, *Patriarcha,* Peter Laslett, ed. New York: The Macmillan Company, 1949.

Laski, Harold J. *Political Thought in England: Locke to Bentham.* New
    York: Oxford University Press, Inc., 1920.
Locke, John, *Treatise of Civil Government* and *A Letter Concerning Tolera-
    tion*, Charles L. Sherman, ed. New York: Appleton-Century-Crofts, Inc.,
    1937.
Montesquieu, Charles de Secondat, Baron de la Brède et de, * *Spirit of the
    Laws*, Thomas Nugent, trans. New York: Hafner Publishing Co., Inc.,
    1949.
Rousseau, Jean-Jacques, *Confessions.* New York: Modern Library, Inc., 1945.
———, *The Social Contract* and *Discourses*, G. D. H. Cole, trans. New York:
    E. P. Dutton & Co., Inc., 1950.
Strauss, Leo, *Natural Rights and History.* Chicago, Ill.: University of Chi-
    cago Press, 1953.

10

THE COUNSEL
OF CAUTION

The fluctuations of political ideas have frequently been compared to the swing of a pendulum. Such a simile must be prominent in a list of political clichés. But like many a wear-worn habit of language, it contains a palpable truth. If political ideas venture too far afield or ahead of the Zeitgeist,[1] a brake is applied. The Age of Enlightenment moved at blinding speed; it was exciting, exhilarating—and to many, disquieting. The old gods had indeed been given a thorough shaking, and in the intoxication of demolishing ancient fallacies and hoary tyrannies, Rousseau and his confrères had grown reckless and arrogant. The swing of the pendulum, the brake, the rebuttal to radicalism was inevitable. The full implications of the Revolution in France, etched in the gory doings of the Terror, could not go unnoticed and un-

---

[1] Zeitgeist: literally, "time-spirit," a word coined by Hegel to describe the predominating ideological temper of an epoch. In strict Hegelian usage, Zeitgeist is itself an existent entity, a manifestation of Absolute Spirit.

reproved. While it is understandable that French radicalism would appear most threatening to English institutions and the moderate temper of British political life, the philosophy of Rousseau did not, as we shall see, go unchallenged by Frenchmen. And on the English side of the Channel, long before the fall of the Bastille or the Tennis Court Oath, opposition was forming to liberal democracy as fostered and popularized by Locke.

There remained in England a considerable bloc of opinion highly skeptical of both French and Lockean egalitarianism. This bloc was in a curious political position, which rendered it largely inarticulate and ineffective. Its members could find little or no political expression in supporting the Tory faction in Parliament, since they had little liking for the Hannoverian kings and their centralizing tendencies. Consequently, they were (in the vague nomenclature of the times) Whigs rather than Tories, but this, too, was a restless and uncomfortable accommodation. These gentlemen comprised the landed aristocracy, the gentry of the countryside, and had few interests in common with either the more liberal and pro-French Whigs (Charles James Fox is a prominent example) or with the ultimate social aims of the commercial classes. They had no party and no spokesman—but they knew that they smelled the odor of radicalism, both foreign and domestic. They were a political faction of smoldering but silent discontent until they found their natural leader in Edmund Burke.

Edmund Burke (1729-1797) would not seem an obvious choice as the champion of the aristocracy, and, indeed, his leadership of this faction was neither openly acknowledged nor universally accepted. But he spoke for them and in defense of English tradition against continental rationalism. And his voice was the most considerable dialectical instrument in eigtheenth-century political life. Though he stoutly maintained a disdain for political philosophy and invariably defended the thesis that political thought was an invention of the moment dictated by immediate political realities rather than rigid systems, Burke in fact founded a creed that has since been called "modern conservatism."

Burke was born and educated in Dublin, the son of a lawyer. His career in British politics began unobtrusively as secretary to Lord Rockingham, a prominent Whig. From this beginning, the transplanted Irishman was to become the stormy petrel of the House of Commons, an orator of unrivaled power. But as a politician he never succeeded in attaining ministerial office or even in becoming a major party leader. To the end, the party wheel horses had a suspicion of Burke's uncompromising independence. Burke wound his way through the complex of Parliamentary combat, often the spokesman of unpopular causes (e.g., the conciliation of the American colonies), the center of controversy (e.g., the impeachment of Warren Hastings, the Indian administrator), but invariably unfettered in his judgments and forthright in his opinions.

Although Burke's preoccupation was with the actual issues of his day, consistent threads run through all his writing and correspondence. It is not difficult to extract these and arrange them into a corpus of political beliefs; varying as his stands were on Parliamentary questions, he departed not at all from his root philosophy. These basic tenets emerge quite consistently.

For convenience, it is practical to divide Burke's thought into two main areas of concern, although they overlap substantially. First, his defense of the aristocratic principle and, secondly, after the French Revolution, his almost frenzied effort to check the infestation of revolutionary ideas into Britain. He was partially successful in his first aim and considerably more effective in the latter—although at the time his condemnation was not immediately appreciated; it cost him numerous lifelong friends, his political reputation, and, finally, split the Whig Party. His indictment of the Revolution was contained in his *Reflections on the Revolution in France* (1790). This was the last major effort of the aging Parliamentarian, written under the stress of intense personal feeling and displaying some of Burke's most striking language, gloomy, prophetic, acid, lofty, and filled with almost Miltonic imagery. Burke is a rarity among the procession of political philosophers; his scope of mind was matched by his mastery of language. He would be remembered alone as a literary stylist, for he was perhaps the best practitioner of argumentation in English prose in the eighteenth century. Only Plato and perhaps Nietzsche are his peers in the art of literary craftsmanship.

His thought, up until his thundering denunciation of the French Revolution, was occupied with a wide range of problems, all stemming from his belief in the central necessity of aristocratic political control. Burke's concept of aristocracy was far more Aristotelian than Platonic; his was an accessible aristocracy of custom, of merit, of civility, of piety, and of service. It had none of the Olympian premeditation of the philosopher-rulers and, indeed, Burke's aristocrats were not philosophers, but men of affairs. Unlike Plato, Burke had no optimism regarding the efficacy of reason, and he rooted his aristocracy in the soil of tradition and sentiment rather than in rationalistic premises and scientific concepts. Burke is paradoxically at once a realist and a romantic, virtually a sentimentalist. For mathematics, pure or otherwise, Burke showed no noticeable admiration.

But it would be an artificiality to attempt to describe Burke's idea of an aristocracy in terms of some concrete conceptualization of a ruling élite. Burke never formulated such a concept. Rather did his defense of the necessity for aristocracy arise from his efforts to deal with a number of practical concerns; his aristocratic counsel is implicit, not explicit. But in general it is clear that the Burkean ideal of a governing class was of a superior English country gentry with its conceptions of personal honor, rural industry, service, moderation, religious orthodoxy, and national loyalty. It is very evident that he admired the Greek aristocratic model as well as the patrician dedication of the Roman Republic.

Burke's political thought proceeds from perhaps eight central ideas, assuming it is possible for our purposes to construct such a list: (1) the problem of progress and the nature of constructive change— the dangers of doctrinaire judgment; (2) the natural hierarchy and the necessity for prescriptive politics; (3) the organic society and the role of institutions; (4) the interrelationship of duty, discipline, and freedom; (5) the limits of reason; (6) the wisdom of tradition, custom, and beauty; (7) the moral basis of society; (8) history as divine purpose.

The act of entertaining propositions such as these by itself casts political thought in a mold far different from the one so emphatically imposed since Hobbes. Burke was not greatly concerned with the familiar themes of post-Hobbesian theory. He skimmed briefly over such formerly engrossing topics as natural law, natural rights, contract, representation, and forms of written constitutions. As a matter of fact, these questions can be rather quickly dispatched as far as Burke's thought is concerned, some recent scholarship notwithstanding. Burke was not a natural lawyer in the conventional sense of that term; he certainly belonged in the common law tradition and patently disavowed any rationalistic interpretation of either morals or jurisprudence. He certainly had no sympathy for natural rights as such. He occasionally used the language of the contract theory, but only as a figurative device. He opposed any attempt to reform government by sheer structural remodeling. He stood firm, for example, against a move to reform the representative basis of the House of Commons, although by current standards that House was not at all representative of the population. His argument was, in essence, that what makes a Parliament a good instrument of government is not who sends the representatives, but rather the quality and purpose of those sent. A good legislator, Burke asserted, serves the nation, not local interests. He had no use whatever for the fashion of written constitutions and vindicated at every opportunity the British Constitution, as it was, unwritten, prescriptive, mixed, and largely a collection of revered customary procedures.

These, then, are some of the issues in and for which Burke showed comparatively little interest or enthusiasm. He was provoked, as we have noted, by other categories of political ideas. By examining these in some detail, it is possible to see (1) how Burke's thought was at once a sharp departure from and renunciation of the mainstream of British political thought from Hobbes to Locke and a vigorous attack on Rousseau and the French *philosophes* and (2) how Burke laid the groundwork for what has since been called "conservatism."

Edmund Burke was not an enemy of change any more than what has come to be known as conservatism is an utter rejection of change. Burke, however, was preoccupied with the dangers of indiscriminate tampering with what he viewed as the most perfect of political creations, the English Constitution. Contends Burke:

> Our constitution stands on a nice equipoise with steep precipices and deep waters upon all sides of it. In removing it from a dangerous leaning towards one side, there may be risk of oversetting it on the other. Every project of a material change in a government so complicated as ours, combined at the same time with external circumstances still more complicated, is a matter full of difficulties: in which a considerate man will not be too ready to decide; a prudent man too ready to undertake; or an honest man too ready to promise.[2]

He was persuaded that progress was neither inevitable nor rapid and that realism dictated that the folly of reckless alteration was more to be feared than deliberate pace. Change in order to be constructive, argues Burke, is not born of theoretical planning, but of the gradual evolution of public sentiment and the modifications of institutions. Burke had a horror of "planners," whom he dubbed "sophisters, economists, and calculators," and he espoused a political adjustment unhampered by doctrinaire systems, a flexible balancing

---

[2] Edmund Burke, *Thoughts on the Cause of Our Present Discontents*, Part I.

responsive to the shifting demands of the moment. He railed against
political a priorism; he scorned French logic. In a word, "prudence"
was elevated to replace the abstract principles that dominated the
Enlightenment. "Prudence," Burke remarks, "is not only the first in
the rank of the virtues political and moral, but she is the director, the
regulator, the standard of them all. Metaphysics cannot live without
definition; but Prudence is cautious how she defines." [3] Prudence is
thus defined as a variety of political empiricism, a technique of continual improvisation relatively unaffected by dogmatism and systematic theory.

Such a view of prudent statecraft invariably resists change that has
as its motivating force either change for change's sake or change that
overturns the delicate equilibrium that in Burke's view must dominate
the political scene. Progress is a process accomplished by patient nib-
bling and by the gradual development of customary patterns. Progress
is not wrought by dramatic breakthroughs or ideological blitzkriegs.
Further, the entire idea of progress, the rhythm of change, is conceived by Burke to be affected by a number of unassailable limitations,
among which are the deficiencies of human reason, the importance of
tradition, the volatility of human nature, the true character of society,
and, last but far from least, his conception of the divine purpose. Like
those of political realists of all shades—from Plato to Machiavelli to
Hobbes—Burke's writings are filled with somber warnings regarding
the folly of ephemeral optimism. This is a frequently cited illustration:

> By this unprincipled facility of changing the state as often and as
> much and in as many ways as there are floating fancies or fashions,
> the whole chain and continuity of the commonwealth would
> be broken; no one generation could link with the other; men would
> become little better than the flies of a summer. [4]

Burke's picture of nature, both organic and human, is hierarchical.
There exist levels of complexity and of consequent responsbility. If
this pyramid-like organization of nature is to him apparent, in the
political sphere this type of hierarchy is not only self-evident but
vital. And it demands, thinks Burke, that political leadership be the
reward of virtue—good government results from allowing the able,
the meritorious, the "natural" aristocrats to have the largest say. Here
Burke's political philosophy is essentially patriarchal. Power must
always lie in the hands of a dedicated and talented élite whose prin-

---

[3] Edmund Burke, *Appeal from the New to the Old Whigs*, Part IV.
[4] Edmund Burke, *Reflections on the Revolution in France*, Part III.

cipal job is to guide the society, tactfully if possible, much in the manner of a knowledgeable parent rearing a brood of children, unruly and potentially capable of injuring themselves and each other. This conception of political leadership, Burke asserts, is neither a defense of entrenched aristocratic privilege nor an excuse for oligarchy. In the first place, Burke's ruling class is not a closed aristocracy.[5] It is reasonably accessible to men of talent, but closed enough that it rests on the disciplines of tradition that demand service and loyalty. It is a self-perpetuating "establishment," an institution born within the greater institution of the state. Burke's own definition, while rather lengthy, deserves inclusion here both because it is comprehensive and lucid and because it is as good a statement of a position still entertained as was ever penned:

> A true natural aristocracy is not a separate interest in the state or separable from it. It is an essential integrant part of any large body rightly constituted. It is formed out of a class of legitimate presumptions, which, taken as generalities, must be admitted for actual truths. To be bred in a place of estimation; to see nothing low and sordid from one's infancy; to be taught to respect one's self; to be habituated to the censorial inspection of the public eye; to look early to public opinion; to stand upon such elevated ground as to be able to take a large view of the widespread and infinitely diversified combinations of men and affairs in a large society; to have leisure to read, to reflect, to converse; to be enabled to draw the court and attention of the wise and learned, wherever they are to be found; to be habituated in armies to command and to obey; to be taught to despise danger in the pursuit of honor and duty; to be formed to the greatest degree of vigilance, foresight, and circumspection in a state of things in which no fault is committed with impunity and the slightest mistakes draw on the most ruinous consequences; to be led to a guarded and regulated conduct, from a sense that you are considered as an instructor of your fellow citizens in their highest concerns, and that you act as a reconciler between God and man; to be employed as an administrator of law and justice, and be thereby amongst the first benefactors to mankind; to be a professor of high science, or of liberal and ingenuous art; to be amongst rich traders, who from their success are presumed to have sharp and vigorous understandings, and to possess the virtues of diligence, order, constancy, and regularity, and have cultivated an habitual regard to commutative justice: these are the circumstances of men that form what I should call a *natural* aristocracy, without which there is no nation.[6]

---

[5] Practical politician that he was, Burke generally felt that such leadership in England must come largely from the landed gentry, the Whig families who were neither avaricious, royal privilege-seekers nor social levelers and experimenters.

[6] Burke, *op. cit., Appeal,* Part IV.

Not an easy requirement for membership. And Burke is insistent upon the appellation "natural." The character of society is hierarchical and regardless of circumstances of time and locale, the stratum of authority emerges. The problem is to insure that power is exercised by the legitimate leaders, those "instructor(s) of your fellow citizens." "The state of civil society," he writes, "which necessarily generates this aristocracy is a state of nature."

The duty of this natural aristocracy is not merely to mirror the public mind or wantonly to create havoc among the venerated institutions of the state. The aim for Burke, as it was for Aristotle, is equilibrium, harmony, and the collective moral-spiritual fulfillment. Moreover, the leadership is bound by sacred ties to the law, a law that incorporates the wisdom and the mellow heritage of the race. *But,* too, political leadership involves policy-making, guidance, and moral instruction. It must never be subjected to the pull of popular passion or corrupted by the temptations of personal gain. Such a sense of freedom and security requires that the leadership be aristocratic in character. Indeed, the very virtues Burke enumerates in the quoted passage are those traditionally associated with the better aspects of the code of the aristocrat.

This aristocratic thesis is clearly incompatible with any idea of majority rule as put forward by Locke or Rousseau. The primary difference between the position of Burke and that of Locke or Rousseau rests on philosophic grounds. Burke argues in favor of an absolute standard of moral good. Truth is truth; justice is justice. If this be so, Burke reasons, these moral absolutes exist independently of what men think about them. If there is a God-given scheme of right and wrong, then counting votes among the people on these questions is clearly superfluous. Indeed, advises Burke, it is worse than that, for majority rule would soon teach the people to become confused as to the eternal standards and would encourage the imposing of a human arrogance destructive of the moral fabric of the society. Burke puts his case this way:

> And the votes of the majority of the people, whatever their infamous flatterers may teach in order to corrupt their minds, cannot alter the moral any more than they can alter the physical essence of things. The people are not to be taught to think lightly of their engagements to their governors; else they teach governors to think lightly of their engagements toward them. In that kind of a game, in the end, the people are sure to be losers. To flatter them into contempt of faith, truth, and justice is to ruin them; for in these virtues consists their whole safety. To flatter any man, or any part of mankind, in any

description, by asserting that in engagements he or they are free, whilst any other creature is bound, is ultimately to vest the rule of morality in the pleasure of those who ought to be rigidly submitted to it—to subject the sovereign reason of the world to the caprices of weak and giddy men.[7]

Of course, the issue joined is twofold. Does an absolute moral standard exist? And: Who is to determine what it is? But if one agrees with Burke's proposition that such a standard does exist and that it can be known by men of knowledge, piety, and reason, then it follows logically that rule by majority will is senseless and that prudence would dictate entrusting political authority to those superior in wisdom and virtue.

Edmund Burke's view of the state is often clothed in language at once majestic and somewhat obscure. He comments that a "nation is a moral essence, not a geographical arrangement or a denomination of the nomenclator." A society, whose loftiest outward manifestation is the state, is a natural creation. Moreover, Burke likens it to an organism, a living and dynamic form that is at once a natural entity, a "moral essence," and a product of evolutionary development. The state rests on the foundation of a "prescriptive" constitution. By this word Burke means a national political character prescribed by time and created out of ancient experience. He refers to the English Constitution as an instrument of government whose "sole authority is that it has existed time out of mind."

The state represents the totality of the body politic, and in this confluence it attains a dimension beyond the mere elements comprising it. In this regard, Burke's state is not unlike Rousseau's community, but the vast and drastic differences between the two rest in the origins of Burke's envisioning. The state, for him, is the product of divine purpose in the natural order, the intuitive wisdom and practice of a self-conscious people. Burke, too, appeals to a variety of nationalism, but one both more subtle and more morally sensitive than Rousseau's. Burke's concept of nationhood is also far more complex, since it contains far more elements and is intricate in the balancing of its integral parts rather than being proudly primitive like Rousseau's community. Further, Rousseau's ideas, while nationalistic in application, are in theory universal. Burke makes a great point of national difference, since each state must be the outgrowth of unique cultural traditions; each state is a manifestation of differing anthropological facts. In this way, Burke has a far more modern sense of the

---

[7] *Ibid.*, Part IV.

role and character of the state, or, as he is fond of calling it, the
"nation." At the bottom of all Burke's speculations about the state
lies a belief in the organic state as a culmination of divine providence.
All the historical accidents that contribute to the shaping of a nation
appear to Burke to have a purpose. They are part of what he once
called the "divine tactic" of history. He says this in the *Reflections:*

> . . . a nation is not only an idea of local extent and individual
> momentary aggregation, but it is an idea of continuity which extends
> in time as well as in numbers and space. And this is a choice not only
> of one day, or one set of people, not a tumult and giddy choice; it is
> a deliberate election of ages and generations; it is a constitution made
> by what is ten thousand times better than choice. It is made by the
> peculiar circumstances, occasions, tempers, dispositions, and moral,
> social, and civil habitudes of the people, which disclose themselves
> only in a long space of time.[8]

Moral absolutism—and its frequent corollary, political authoritarianism—needs in some fashion to be reconciled with freedom. Burke must
certainly be numbered among the champions of freedom; he was no
friend of despotism, and he urged the causes of the American colonies,
misgoverned Indians, and the victims of religious persecution. Yet his
view of freedom is a rejection of the extreme individualism suggested
both in Locke and in certain of the French *philosophes.* The problem
of human liberty occupies a large part of Burke's attention, and his
reflections on it produce several tenets: (1) Liberty is a human
birthright. (2) There are no abstract rights of man. (3) Freedom
must exist within legality and order. (4) Liberty implies obligations
and duties. (5) Suppression of liberty, while regrettable, is not the
worst of all possible conditions of man.

It is impossible to be confused by Burke's writing regarding his
belief that liberty is the natural state of mankind. He specifically
rejects the idea that freedom is earned. "It is not," he comments, "the
reward of our merit or the acquisition of our industry." Yet liberty
does not arise from any abstract rights. Burke dismisses the "rights
of man" (Thomas Paine's phrase) with vociferous language, substituting a thesis that "rights" constitute a right to justice, to the fruits of
industry, inheritance, and, most general of all, "instruction in life and
consolation in death." Political equality he particularly denies to be
a right. Further, no right can be maintained that is contrary to virtue,
and "men have no right to what is not reasonable, and to what is not
for their benefit."

---

[8] Burke, *op. cit., Reflections.*

Charles Parkin has neatly put Burke's position this way:

> The natural social order is, in Burke's eyes, a state of *reason*, of moral reason. It is rational in the sense that by allowing the natural feelings their due expression, it prevents the emergence of will and passion, and enables the individual to maintain a calm, steady perception of the rights of others, and the limits set by obligations of his own. But when the harmony between self-interest and obligation is broken, assertive willfulness appears, and this is bound to lead to conflict in society, because will is in essence self-centered, does not recognize bounds, and is blind to the rights of others.[9]

All freedom depends for its existence on political order and social harmony; Burke often repeats the thesis that individual liberty may never trespass upon the preserves of other individuals. Freedom is a "partnership," Burke remarks, and he adds that "all men have equal rights, but not to equal things." He speaks of freedom as being social rather than expressly individual; individual acts can destroy corporate freedom. Freedom is not, he maintains, "solitary, unconnected, individual, selfish liberty, as if every man was to regulate the whole of his conduct by his own will." To preserve social freedom, order is vital and restraint legitimate. Liberty, for Burke, is not a carte blanche. Quite the contrary, it implies duties to be diligently discharged. Duties are moral injunctions, contends Burke, and are part of the order of nature. Some choices are voluntary, but the basic human relationships imply an involuntary consent. Burke likens this binding to the social web to the relationships imposed by the ties of parents and children. This is true, explains Burke, because " the presumed consent of every rational creature is in unison with the predisposed order of things." The "social ties and ligaments," as he puts it, culminate in the political order. As the state is an "ancient order," its nature prescriptive, its foundation is obedience to moral precept and acceptance of the elemental social and political duties and loyalties. Where there is no recognition of ethical claims on individual behavior, says Burke, there is no true liberty.

Such cognizance of political duties is not always the prevailing condition. Men are often swept by unseemly passions and irresponsibility. Put another way: Men are frequently prone to act irrationally. Liberty, insists Burke, can never rest on the renunciation of reason or the ill-considered destruction of venerable social amenities. If, indeed, such stark misfortune should overtake a state, the preservation of order

---

[9] Charles Parkin, *The Moral Basis of Burke's Political Thought* (New York: Cambridge University Press, 1956), p. 54.

and the defense of the constituted society must take precedence over
individual freedom. To allow men to act as beasts, reflects Burke, is a
greater error than to deprive them of their liberty. Of this liberty
he writes:

> We cannot forfeit our right to it, but by what forfeits our title to the
> privileges of our kind? I mean the abuse, or oblivion, of our rational
> faculties, and a ferocious indocility which makes us prompt to wrong
> and violence, destroys our social nature, and transforms us into some-
> thing little better than the description of wild beasts. To men so
> degraded, a state of strong constraint is a sort of necessary substitute
> for freedom; since, bad as it is, it may deliver them in some measure
> from the worst slavery of all—that is, the despotism of their own blind
> and brutal passions.[10]

Burke is obviously troubled by two broad assumptions of the
Enlightenment. One is that abstract reason can be relied on and,
secondly, that man's nature is essentially disposed to good unless corrupted by evil institutions. Curiously, his rejection of both these assumptions contains a vivid spirit of political realism coupled with an
orthodox Christianity with its convictions regarding supernatural wisdom and human depravity. As a practical matter, Burke has deep
reservations about primitive human nature. He has hints of the darker
side of human character garnered from his experience as a workaday
politician—and the French Revolution confirms his suspicions. The
perfectability of the species, Burke reasons, is most unlikely. His
theology provides a convenient metaphysical explanation. Burke believes that he sees Caliban lurking in the human personality, and he
means to restrain him. The best means, he decides, is the weight of
tradition and the instructional power of institutions and laws. Yet
such a determination never rises to zealotry in Burke; he never sinks
to that rigid moralistic absolutism notable in many who have been
convinced that social control is a necessary counterbalance to human
mischief. Here Burke, the man of affairs, asserts himself, blending his
profound moral predispositions with a spirit of empirical compromise
that is noteworthy in the unfolding of British politics. Burke narrowly
misses being either sanctimonious or despotic—but avoid it he does.
This sense of proportion, despite what his critics have often written
about the *Reflections*,[11] can be judiciously compared with that of

---

[10] Edmund Burke, "Letter to Mons. Dupont," October, 1789, *Correspondence,*
Vol. III.

[11] Anti-Burkeans have often leveled the charge that the *Reflections* were an in-
temperate and embittered harangue against social progress, the intensity of which
casts doubt on Burke's motives and judgment.

Aristotle. Both men are essentially seekers after moral betterment to be gained through political equilibrium. With both, the undeniably cautious estimate of human docility is balanced with a sense of the possible moral shape of man, once his potentialities are tutored in the ways of reason and civility. This Aristotle-like grasp of humanity rescues Edmund Burke from either arid cynicism or crude authoritarianism.

If the abstract rationalism of the "Parisian philosophy" was spurious for Burke, wisdom was to be found in a subtle blending of tradition, custom, and beauty. These three elements are infused into all his thought. The Burkean concept of tradition describes this as a divine convolution of history, the unique spirituality of the race coming to the surface, the focal point of loyalty, and the continuity of gentle, humane civilization. Custom means the process of trial and error, the significant process of social maturity and prescriptive wisdom. Beauty —and Burke at heart was a thoroughgoing aesthetic in his world-view— is the sublime ingredient that redeems the commonplace world of space-time by offering hints of divinity. True wisdom, as Burke defines it, is gleaned and absorbed from the recognition of this trinity. In application, this dictates a fervent sense of reverence, a reverence for the old, the established, the dignified, the well-burnished, the graceful. One of the most telling of Burke's many phrases arises from his regret that the radicalism of the Revolution had destroyed the "unbought grace of life." If wisdom is to be found in tradition, in custom, and in beauty, it is discoverable both on an individual and on a collective basis. Men can be wise, but nations, Burke observes, are more likely to be so. Wisdom is a collective property and a substance best encountered by immersion into the deepest depths of the nation. The taproots of wisdom lie far below the conscious level of men's reasoning powers; wisdom is as much the province of the heart as of the mind.

Burke's view of society as a moral organism differs from the Aristotelian model in one significant respect—and that very fact Burke uses to justify his schematic notions of history. Aristotle was not a Christian. The moral character of human life, let alone the pattern of society, is for Burke the result of providential purpose. Society and history are examples of God's infinite purpose in realization. Burke does not go so far as to say, as Hegel would later, that the state is a divine thing, a direct inspiration from the mind of the Almighty; but he does hold that the evolution of political order is in response to the divine tactic of history. Burke is not such a bigot as to dismiss out of hand the question of the legality and authority of the state by an appeal to God's inscrutable designs. Indeed, the bulk of Burke's ideas about the role of the state are most this-worldly in nature. Essentially, he revives Aristotle's argument that the state must serve the citizenry. The state becomes a moral agency, not a divine sword. Yet it is clear that in Burke's mind the added dimension of Christianity reshapes the character of the moral situation and gives to the state a scope and grandeur more comprehensive and potentially more formidable than the blueprint of Aristotle. History, too, becomes more teleologically involved, if less precise, and there is consequently invoked a certain incense-laden spell over the Burkean vision of history.

The last days of Burke's life were taken up with the great struggle, almost a private one, against the French Revolution. He realized one major objective: The Revolution was never to cross the English Channel. But his further attempts to discredit radicalism fell short of accomplishment, though his influence to a large extent modified and gentled subsequent radical experimentation in Britain. And, too, the writings of Burke remain as a sort of handbook for the unbroken procession of conservative thinkers who have followed in his wake. Today, in fact, his name is invoked on behalf of this or that doctrine far more than it had been for over a hundred years. What Burke sought to inoculate England against was *Jacobinism*[12]—and it seems that he is most read when various varieties of latter-day Jacobinism are rampant. By this term, Burke means the forces of rapacious egocentricity which propose extreme action and desperate, violent reform. It was in the Revolution in France that these influences had their day in full measure. Burke thunders his denunciation:

> It is not a question between France and England; it is a question between property and force. The property claims; and its claim has been allowed. The property of the nation is in the nation. They who massacre, plunder, and expel the body of the proprietary are murderers and robbers. The state, in its essence, must be moral and just; and it may be so, though a tyrant or usurper should be accidentally at the

---

[12] *Jacobinism* makes direct reference to the Jacobin faction in the post-Revolutionary period, notable for its extreme measures and violent purges. Burke quite objectively defines Jacobinism: "It is an attempt (hitherto but too successful) to eradicate prejudice out of the minds of men, for the purpose of putting all power and authority into the hands of the persons capable of occasionally enlightening the minds of the people." Burke uses the word "prejudice," incidentally, not in a derogative sense. "Prejudice" in Burkean language means inarticulate and unreflective predispositions or habits of mind having their origins in cultural traditions.

head of it. This is a thing to be lamented; but this notwithstanding, the body of the commonwealth may remain in all its integrity and be perfectly sound in its composition. The present case is different. It is not a revolution in government. It is not the victory of party over party. It is the destruction and decomposition of the whole society; which never can be made right by any faction, however powerful, nor without terrible consequences to all about it, both in the act and in the example. This pretended republic is founded in crimes, and exists by wrong and robbery; and wrong and robbery, far from a title to anything, is war with mankind.[13]

Burke, when assessed by hostile critics, is usually accused of the following: encouraging anti-intellectualism, masking a selfish and crass defense of the "establishment" by sophistry, excessive sentimentality, confusing the issue of reform with eloquent mysteries, opposing change in favor of a vague worship of antiquity, misreading the implications of the French Revolution, warping a proper estimation of human nature with religious mumbo-jumbo, fomenting national snobbery in particular and snobbery in general, and justifying totalitarianism.

Alas, we have now arrived at that stage in the narrative of political ideas where the jury is still out. The theories under examination remain current among us. These ideas must then be weighed as carefully as our resources allow. We must make our judgments; the verdict of history cannot now be appealed to. If it is true that we are the products of all that has gone before, it is even more true that we are direct products of the world that came into being as the impetus of the French Revolution merged, with the last shots of Waterloo, into the placid world of the Congress of Vienna. We are fond of calling this the "Modern Period," and the principal ideas that moved it are still reverberating in our century.

But what of Burke? The prime importance of Edmund Burke is the clarity of the alternative he advocated. In a real sense, the alternative he advanced still remains. We cannot entirely entertain the choice presented by Rousseau, but Burke's concept of the good political society remains in partial potential. The same can be said of Hegel or J. S. Mill or Marx. Their propositions cannot be adapted in toto to our situation, but the basic premises are available for employment even now. Burke's theory is difficult to fragment. One swallows it whole with relish or rejects it summarily. This is characteristic of the modern epoch. We are still so close that we are involved as much with

---

[13] Edmund Burke, *First Letter on a Regicide Peace*, Part V.

our emotions as with our reasoning faculties. And, too, the nineteenth century reveals a series of "total" prescriptions for political salvation. Burke, then, with his cohorts, is there for your examination and decision.

The voices of protest against the Jacobin philosophy were by no means restricted to England. France herself saw the rise of counter-theories, some illiberal and bitter, some reflective and cautious. This continental riposte can be surveyed by a brief look at three French-men: Count Joseph de Maistre (1754-1821), Louis Gabriel de Bonald (1754-1840), and Count Alexis de Tocqueville (1805-1859).

Maistre's outlook involved a far deeper commitment to both crown and church than did Burke's. Burke's affection for royalty was that of a Whig, after all, and his religious piety was Anglican, not Roman. For his part, Maistre pleaded for the return of absolute monarchy, of the ancient privileges, and of the influence of the church. His justifica-tion for this restoration rests on a divine tactic conception of history that does bear some resemblances to Burke's. Writes Maistre:

> It is necessary that the origin of sovereignty should manifest itself from beyond the sphere of human power; so that men, who may appear to have a direct hand in it, may be, nevertheless, only the cir-cumstances. As to legitimacy, if it should seem in its origins to be obscure, God explains Himself, by his prime minister in the department of this world—Time.[14]

His insistence on absolute monarchy is both medieval and extreme. To the crown, Maistre gives a sovereignty both divine in origin and unassailable in practice. It is vital, argues Maistre, to put back to-gether the shattered French state; the most horrid crime of the late Revolution was its atheism, but its second most serious result was the breaking up of the web of society. Only by the reimposition of the absolute monarch can the damage be repaired. True, muses Maistre, kings had behaved badly in the past. They had been irreverent and too given to the easy joys of this world, but these are not liabilities basic to the institution and are subject to correction. The choice for Maistre is between the severe alternatives of licentious confusion on the one hand and civilized order enforced by a divine sovereign on the other. Once that choice is made, the means adopted must be swift, effective, and inexorable. The omnipotent secular ruler, free to impose

---

[14] Joseph de Maistre, Essay on the Generative Principle of Political Constitu-tions, Book II, Section XXVII.

his will in order to insure the goal of order and piety, is the answer.

The crown is linked tightly to the altar; in Maistre, the "Two Swords" appear again. In a famous remark, he declares that the solution to the demoralization of France lies in "the Pope and the executioner." His clericalism is militant and uncompromising, made so by his gloomy awareness of human evil. He talks much of Sin (the capitalization is appropriate), and the depths and dimensions of this primordial taint suggest to him purgatives, political as well as ecclesiastical, that are startling in their severity. Suffering can be viewed, ponders Maistre, as beneficial; he does not blanch a whit at the excesses of the Inquisition. These strong draughts of moral tonic are obviously to be administered by a church organization, aided and abetted by a sympathetic and even obedient monarchical system. The rock of the state is the religious principle. He underscores this for emphasis:

> ... the duration of empires has always been proportioned to the degree of influence which the religious principle had acquired in the political constitution: *the cities and nations most addicted to Divine worship have always been the most durable, and the most wise; as the most religious ages have also ever been most distinguished for genius.*[15]

Once the divinely ordered control is established, the problem is one of unending vigilance against the agitations for change and reform. Reform is a hated word for Maistre. "The word *reform*," he counsels, "in itself, and previous to all examination, will be always suspected by wisdom, and the experience of every age justifies this sort of instinct."

Bonald, though sympathetic to the cause of the church, is more simply a vigorous monarchist. In principle he is one with Maistre, but while he is slightly less rigorous than his colleague, he is also more ingenious. Like Maistre, Bonald views the Revolution as a divine judgment, an act of retribution against its instigators who failed to acknowledge the truth to be found in the traditions nursed into being by the historical process. Bonald argues that language, the undeniable product of historical development, is a divinely established locus of all truth. He looks upon it as a sort of revelation. The unveiling of truth, the master plan of God, is to be found in the Word as it becomes known in history. The custodian of the Word is the church. Its co-guardian-administrator is the monarchical state.[16]

Tocqueville belongs in a different category from Maistre and Bonald.

---

[15] Maistre, *op. cit., Political Constitutions*, Book II, Section XXXII.

[16] See Bonald's *Théorie du pouvoir politique et religieux* (1796).

He is a thoroughgoing and careful moderate, although his anti-Jacobin sentiments are evident enough. His most celebrated work, *Democracy in America*,[17] illustrates his quest for equilibrium and his marked revulsion at extremism and social upheaval. His detestation of absolute systems is as deep-seated as Burke's. "I detest these absolutist systems," he remarks, "which represent all the events of history as depending upon great first causes linked by the chain of fatality, and which, as it were, suppress men from the history of the human race."

Unlike Burke, Maistre, or Bonald, who by then had departed the scene, Tocqueville's moderate sensitivities were aroused by the Revolution of 1848 rather than the more violent one of 1789. His liberality was tempered by an essentially aristocratic point of view, and he responded to the drift of the '48 experiment by an attack upon a majority rule unconfined by moral restrictions and efforts to introduce utopian planning. His counterproposal stresses traditionalism, limited suffrage, social balance, and a belief in an evolutionary, gradualist approach to social change. At base, Tocqueville is most disturbed about equality, an enforced social leveling that he thinks might be injurious to the creative excellence of a society. This theme runs through most of Tocquevillean theory. As he remarks: "In the principle of equality I very clearly discern two tendencies; the one leading the mind of every man to untried thoughts, the other inclined to prohibit him from thinking at all."

From Burke has come down the tradition of conservatism. The weight of his influence is clearly seen in the United States from John Adams and John Randolph to Orestes Brownson and Henry Adams. Burke's vitality is noticeable in our century from Irving Babbitt to Peter Viereck. But it was in his own country that the great Whig's admonitions took even firmer root. There followed a stream of conservative thinkers—both politicians and critics: Coleridge, Wordsworth, Arnold, Carlyle, Maine, Acton, Disraeli, and even Winston Churchill —to list but a few. One of Burke's most vocal twentieth-century admirers, Russell Kirk, offers this laudatory estimate of his influence:

---

[17] Tocqueville's *Democracy in America* (1835-1838) has received just praise as a remarkable commentary on political and social conditions in the United States in the early nineteenth century. In general, Tocqueville was enthusiastic about what he saw, particularly the spirit of freedom and energy. At the same time, he criticized a preoccupation with social equality, the vitiating effects of majority rule, and warned against the rise of demagogic popular rulers.

Our age, too, seems to be groping for certain of the ideas which Burke's inspiration formed into a system of social preservation. Failing these or some other genuine principles, our own epoch of concentration is sure to descend into sardonic apathy and fatigued repression.[18]

Maistre and Bonald, as well, left their stamp on the mind of the continent. In their wake followed Veuillot, Balzac, Maurras, Guizot, and Metternich, plus a substantial segment of Catholic thought in the nineteenth century. Tocqueville's influence was scattered, but significant; in France, he was followed by Taine.

If it is a fact that the pendulum of political sentiment swings from Left to Right and back again, from radical experiment to caution and retrenchment, then the conservative critics aroused by the Revolution in France may yet have a say in the affairs of our century. If modern conservatism is at all a going concern in our time, then much of the spirit of this attitude can be traced to the energetic convictions, valid or otherwise, held by the gentlemen described in this chapter.

. . . for further discussion:

1. A consistent vision of political philosophers has been rule by a moral élite, on whatever basis of morality an individual thinker might hold valid. How realistic is the notion that this aristocracy of excellence could ever be realized? To what extent is any political order dominated by the few? Are there any justifications to be made for the contention that superior morals, ability, or even manners should allow for a difference in political status?

2. Alexander Hamilton, a gentleman of aristocratic pretensions, once observed: "Man is a reasoning rather than a reasonable animal." Do you think Burke would agree? Do you agree? What difference does it make to political speculation?

3. Maistre argues that states most given to the observance of religious principles are also the most durable, wise, and productive of human genius. Do you think history bears him out? The United States is a pluralistic, secular society, incorporating in its Constitution the doctrine of the separation of church and state. It is therefore the antithesis of Maistre's ideas about the good state. Yet to what extent do you think Maistre's premise about religious states is accepted by a democratic society such as the United States? Mottos on coins and official papers aside, to what extent do you think a state like the United States, Britain, or Canada is an example of the truth of Maistre's thesis?

---

[18] Russell Kirk, *The Conservative Mind* (Chicago, Ill.: Gateway Editions, 1954), p. 61.

4. What reasons can you suggest for Burke's sympathy with the American Revolution and his antipathy for the Revolution in France?

. . . for further investigation:

Bredvold, Louis I. and Ralph G. Ross, eds., *The Philosophy of Edmund Burke*. Ann Arbor, Mich.: The University of Michigan Press, 1961.

Burke, Edmund, *Collected Works*, 12 vols. Boston, Mass.: Little, Brown & Co., 1865-1867.

Graubard, Stephen R., *Burke, Disraeli, and Churchill: The Politics of Perseverance*. Cambridge, Mass.: Harvard University Press, 1961.

Kirk, Russell, ° *The Conservative Mind*. Chicago, Ill.: Gateway Editions, 1954.

Maistre, Joseph de, *Essay on the Generative Principle of Political Constitutions*. Boston, Mass.: Little, Brown & Co., 1847.

Parkin, Charles, *The Moral Basis of Burke's Political Thought*. New York: Cambridge University Press, 1956.

Stanlis, Peter, *Edmund Burke and the Natural Law*. Ann Arbor, Mich.: The University of Michigan Press, 1958.

Tocqueville, Alexis de, *Democracy in America*, Henry Reeve, trans. New York: Oxford University Press, Inc., 1947.

Viereck, Peter, ° *Conservatism: From John Adams to Churchill*. New York: Anvil Books, 1956.

White, R. J., ed., *The Conservative Tradition*. New York: New York University Press, 1957.

11

THE IMPERATIVE OF
EXPERIENCE

In his lifetime, David Hume's reputation rested on a quite mediocre but popular history of England. His excursions into political writing were rather undistinguished and not very original. He professed an orthodox Toryism. These would seem somewhat singular recommendations for his inclusion in a history of political ideas. And to make matters even more puzzling, his announced political inclinations bear little relevance to his other philosophic speculations. Indeed, his work has in general been a source book for political radicalism.

But the answer to the query as to why Hume deserves space here is simple. He was guilty of three major philosophic "crimes":

1. The raising of substantial doubt as to the ultimate possibility of human knowledge.
2. Perhaps the most devastating assault ever penned against religion.
3. The assassination of what was left of natural law.

Surely this is enough to earn him a place in our narrative, as it won for him a unique position in the history of thought. Much of political philosophy is a commentary on morals, and Hume's ethical relativism [1] has had a lasting impact on the development of politics.

David Hume (1711-1776), born to a family of Scottish land-owners, became in his youth a victim of a "writing fever" that caused him to retreat into the solitude of France. Abandoning his studies at the University of Edinburgh, this spell of literary isolation produced his *Treatise of Human Nature* (1739). His continued philosophic production was not interrupted even by a diplomatic assignment in 1748 —a year later the *Inquiry Concerning Human Understanding* was published. The popular *History of England* (1754) assured him of a reputation and a steady income, and he turned to a leisurely life in his native Scotland, punctuated only by a brief venture into politics. A lengthy illness brought about his death in 1776.

Reference has already been made to an intriguing episode in Hume's life involving his unfortunate association with Rousseau. Returning from France in 1766, he offered haven to the hard-pressed Rousseau who had been forced to leave both France and Switzerland. Rousseau, however, proved a difficult guest, as he soon entertained the picturesque notion that his host was plotting against him. The resulting situation was as painful as it was ludicrous, and Rousseau retired to Paris where the interdict had been conveniently lifted. The incident is illuminating as well as wryly entertaining. Hume by nature was congenial, generous, stoic, and modest in habits. Those who knew him remarked frequently about his charm and warmth. Yet the temper of Hume's skeptical philosophy often creates the impression that its author was grim, dour, sardonic, and even rancorous. Such simply was not the case.

Hume's theories have a central core, namely, a devastating and searching critique of human reason. This exploration of reason leads Hume to entertain grave doubts about matters usually taken for granted. One of the conceptions most frequently accepted without much question is *causality*—the tacit assumption that there is a logically necessary relationship between certain events, that if *A*, then *B*, if you will. The orderly universe—the entire idea of natural law or laws of nature—rests, as one might well imagine, on the assumption of

---

[1] *Relativism:* the denial of the existence of universal truths.

causal relationship. But what really are the connections between things, asks Hume? Is human reason a reflection of a rational universal order? Hume doesn't think so. With considerable cogency he argues that what in fact are mistaken for causal relationships are merely associational patterns in individual minds. Causality, then, is a name given by men to the associational habits created in their own thoughts and confirmed by their own experience. Yet, Hume points out, much of philosophy has dogmatically asserted the existence of laws that in turn assume a logical ordering of entities and events, the existence of which is not susceptible of proof. He once observed that one could not validly contend that the sun would come up the next morning; all one could say was that one's experience indicated that it had done so insofar as one had observed and that this suggested the probability that it might do so again. Probability, not certainty, experience and habit, not causal laws and a priori ideas, are the frame of human thought. Explains Hume:

> The idea of necessity arises from some impression. There is no impression conveyed by our senses which can give rise to that idea. It must therefore be derived from some internal impression, or impression of reflexion. There is no internal impression which has any relations to the present business, but that propensity, which custom produces, to pass from an object to the idea of its usual attendant. This therefore is the essence of necessity. Upon the whole, necessity is something that exists in the mind, not in objects; nor is it possible for us ever to form the most distant idea of it considered as a quality in bodies. Either we have no idea of necessity, or necessity is nothing but that determination of the thought to pass from causes to effects and from effects to causes, according to their experienced union. . . .[2]

Hume advances the following propositions: (1) Causality is merely the result of mental associations, not logical necessity. (2) Observation leads not to certainty, but only to probability. (3) All knowledge, such as it is, is experience as contrasted with intuition, revelation, or rational understanding. (4) Sense and feeling are therefore more important than rationality. (5) Experience, sensation, feeling are all private phenomena, knowable only to individual beings, and therefore certainty regarding the objective character of the world is impossible.

This cursory list is hardly fair to Hume. It but crudely hints at the nature of his philosophy, but it will serve, perhaps, as a steppingstone

---

[2] David Hume, *A Treatise of Human Nature*, Part III, Section VII.

to a consideration of Hume's effect on ethics and politics. Ponder for
a moment the implications of the ideas above. Place these ideas side
by side with those of virtually any thinker before Hume, and you
will understand the depths of Hume's criticism of dogmatic philosophies. Hume's theory of knowledge not only denies any notion of
natural law or supernaturalism,[3] it also precludes any common recognition of the external world. Such a radically subjective view of
knowledge and, indeed, of human nature understandably produces
an ethical system vividly at variance with the humanistic morality that
was evident even among such representatives of the Age of Reason as
Locke and Voltaire.

Hume relegates instinct to a secondary role and describes reason
as a conscious but limited reflection on sensation. Morals, for Hume,
lie in the realm of sentiment. Good and evil possess validity only
insofar as they represent feelings, individual attitudes arising from
sensual experience. This is not meant to detract from the significance
of moral attitudes, Hume claims, but moral judgment does not stem
from a recognition of objective standards or relationships outside the
range of personal conviction.

He puts the issue sharply in the opening passages of *An Enquiry
Concerning the Principles of Morals*:

> There has been a controversy started of late, much better worth
> examination, concerning the general foundation of Morals: whether
> they be derived from Reason, or from Sentiment; whether we attain the
> knowledge of them by a chain of argument and induction, or by an
> immediate feeling and finer internal sense; whether, like all sound
> judgment of truth and falsehood, they should be the same to every
> rational intelligent being; or whether, like the perception of beauty
> and deformity, they be founded entirely on the particular fabric and
> constitution of the human species.[4]

In answering his own question, Hume locates morality in sentiment,
which is at times instructed by reason (perhaps "ratiocination" is a
more exact term than "reason") in the sense that reason (or ratiocination) can reveal the "several tendencies of actions." Moral validity,

---

[3] Hume comments in *The Natural History of Religion*: "The whole is a riddle,
an enigma, an inexplicable mystery. Doubt, uncertainty, suspense of judgment appear the only result of our most accurate scrutiny concerning this subject. But such
is the frailty of human reason, and such the irresistible contagion of opinion, that
even this deliberate doubt could scarcely be upheld; did we not enlarge our view,
and opposing one species of superstition to another, set them aquarreling; while
we ourselves, during their fury and contention, happily make our escape into the
calm, though obscure regions of philosophy." (Section XI.)

[4] David Hume, *An Enquiry Concerning the Principles of Morals*, Section I.

however, must remain a matter of personal approbation, modified by what Hume refers to as a humanitarian feeling for the collective happiness. Moral judgment depends in part on "some internal sense or feeling, which nature has made universal in the whole species." If morality is essentially feeling, the criterion of appropriate human action is *utility*—"the usefulness of any quality or action." Utility, described in Humean language, is "whatever mental action or quality gives to a spectator the pleasing sentiment of approbation."

The principle of usefulness here depicted is particularly interesting, because it suggests that the good of an action is not measurable solely in terms of self-satisfaction, but is also a matter of the approbation of spectators or the wider community contributing to a feeling of personal gratification. C. D. Broad has described the essential ingredient of Hume's ethics as "the emotion of *approval* or *disapproval*." Writes Broad:

> Now for Hume, the statement that "X is good" *means* the same as the statement "X is such that the contemplation of it would call forth an emotion of approval towards it in all or most men." The definition of "X is bad" would be the same with "disapproval" substituted for "approval." [5]

Like other advocates of self-interest in one form or another, Hume rescues his ethics from crude egotism by stoutly maintaining the existence of "common feeling," a sense of humanity, and a concern for more than individual welfare. Moreover, he contends that benevolence is a commendable moral trait even if only for the reason that it is conducive to a state of self-approval. Comments Hume:

> Now where is the difficulty in conceiving that this likewise might be the case with benevolence and friendship, and that, from the original frame of our temper, we may feel a desire of another's happiness or good, which, by means of that affection, becomes our own good, and is afterwards pursued from the combined motives of benevolence and self-enjoyments? [6]
>
> Or what theory of morals can ever serve any useful purpose, unless it can show, by some particular detail, that all duties which it recommends are also the true interest of each individual? [7]

There are two major inferences to be drawn from Hume's discussion of morals that directly affect both his concept of justice and those

----

[5] C. D. Broad, *Five Types of Ethical Theory* (Paterson, N. J.: Littlefield, Adams & Co., 1959), pp. 84-85.

[6] Hume, *op. cit., Principles of Morals*, Appendix II.

[7] *Ibid.*, Part II.

political philosophies that bear his imprint. First, morals are emotionally constructed attitudes toward qualities or actions. This does not
necessarily mean that morality is entirely a private or subjective
matter, however, because although sentiment or feeling is the prime
source of moral insight, reason acts as a technique for estimating consequences. Also, there are natural or instinctive characteristics that are
a part of the human psychological make-up. ". . . Rationality and
benevolence are part of the nature of men, in the sense that they are
a part of this innate constitution," to borrow the language of C. D.
Broad. These innate properties are in practice socially oriented and
employed. Hume's ethic is not a fierce and pessimistic individualism;
it is but partially subjective.

Hume propounds relativism in ethics by arguing along the following
lines: (1) The location of value is not in the object or act, but in the
feeling of the actor. (2) There are no ethical universals and no objective moral order. (3) Public or social morality rests upon utility and
custom rather than upon natural law or abstract moral ordinance.
These arguments need amplification.

X is valuable, in the Humean sense, if it is a source of approbation,
either personal or collective. Objects or actions do not enjoy intrinsic
value. Value, like taste, lies within the limits of personal emotion and
attitude. Charity is not in and of itself good; it is good only to the
degree that it is useful, i.e., creates an emotional response of approval.
Virtue is not, quite obviously, its own reward, and Hume is contemptuous of the term "virtue" in its more traditional meaning.[8]

It should be clear that Hume leaves no room for ethical universals
or absolutes since he denies the possibility of an objective moral order
resulting from causal necessity. Natural law he cannonades with volley
after volley of trenchant analysis, attacking the principle of causal
necessity and the supposition that anything can be known outside of
experience. But even beyond this rebuttal to moral absolutism, Hume
advocates an ethic notable for its flexibility and adaptability to prevailing social conditions. Nonetheless, it is most inaccurate to describe
Hume as anything but a defender of moral probity. He castigates
hypocrisy and almost rivals Plato in his insistence that moral behavior

---

[8] Hume had this to say about a number of "virtues": "Celibacy, fasting, penance,
mortification, self-denial, humility, silence, solitude, and the whole train of monkish
virtues; for what reason are they everywhere rejected by men of sense but because
they serve to no manner of purpose; neither advance a man's fortune in the world,
nor render him a more valuable member of society." (*Principles of Morals,* Section
VI, Part I.)

leads to happiness, while immoral acts deny happiness.[9] But the difference between the Platonic and Humean outlooks lies between an objective moral standard and moral custom generated by "fellow-feeling."

David Hume's moral relativism, born out of the shambles, either temporary or permanent, that he made of natural law, requires some substitute concept of justice, and Hume produces one that is both consistent and ingenious. He extends his moral precepts into an account of the origin and nature of justice. Since he has no metaphysical base on which to rest a theory of justice, he enlarges his concept of social moral awareness and couples it with an argument that justice is the result both of human shortcomings and of the limited productiveness of nature. "Increase to a sufficient degree the benevolence of man or the bounty of nature," Hume suggests, "and you render justice useless, by supplying its place with much nobler virtues and more valuable blessings." Justice is a needed but poor substitute for collective ratiocination and unrestricted supply of material goods. It is intriguing to contrast Hume and Plato on this matter. Plato's view of justice has become significantly narrowed in Hume's thought, as the latter obviously identifies justice with legal arrangement. Yet if we equate Humean justice with law, the Platonic idea that the legal state is a second best alternative is obliquely seconded by Hume. If all people were morally capable, legal restraint would be unnecessary and even troublesome, putting aside for the moment the question of competition for scarce property. Law, for Plato, was a surrogate for wisdom; for Hume it is a substitute for humanitarian feeling. It is curious that vastly differing moral evaluations such as those of Plato and Hume can, in fact, lead to somewhat comparable social recommendations. Hume asserts that "it is only from selfishness and a confined generosity of men, along with the scanty provision nature has made for his wants, that justice derives its origin." [10]

But let us assume that justice derives its origin from the need to protect private interests. How, then, is justice to be perpetuated when self-interest is not immediately threatened? Hume responds by claim-

---

[9] "But in all ingenuous natures," Hume reflects, "the antipathy to treachery and roguery is too strong to be counterbalanced by any views of profit or pecuniary advantage. Inward peace of mind, consciousness of integrity, a satisfactory review of our own conduct; these are circumstances very requisite to happiness, and will be cherished and cultivated by every honest man who feels the importance of them." (*Principles of Morals*, Conclusion, Part II.)

[10] Hume, *op. cit.*, *Human Nature*, Book III, Part II.

ing that while the origin of justice is the protection of individual interests, its continuance rests on the development of a moral conviction
of the desirability of justice. He is even willing to admit that this
second phase, the recognition of and obedience to justice, is in part
created by artifice. Put simply: The preservation of justice depends
on men's shifting from an approval of that which protects their self-
interest to a sense of pleasure and approbation in participating in
"such actions as tend to the peace of society." Hume puts it in the
following terms:

> . . . the sense of morality in the observance of these rules *follows
> naturally* and of itself; though it is certain that it is also augmented
> by a new *artifice* and that the public instructions of politicians and
> the private education of parents contribute to the giving of us a
> sense of honor and duty in the strict regulation of our actions with re-
> gard to the properties of others.[11]

But let there be no mistake. Hume's explanation for the obedience
of the individual to political order remains founded unequivocally
upon the continued contribution of government to individual and collective self-interest. Hume methodically attempts to refute the position that obligations are morally binding merely because they are in
fact obligations. He boldly asserts that "a promise would not be intelligible before human conventions had established it; and that even if
it were intelligible it would not be attended with any moral obligation." Appealing to the "general opinion of mankind," Hume suggests
that human beings sense that their political obligations are bound up
with service rendered to the public interest. He writes:

> If the sense of common interest were not our original motive to
> obedience, I would fain ask what other principle is there in human
> nature capable of subduing the natural ambition of men and forcing
> them to such a submission? Imitation and custom are not sufficient.
> For the question still recurs, what motive first produces those instances
> of submission which we imitate and the train of actions which pro-
> duces the custom? There evidently is no other principle than common
> interest; and if interest first produces obedience to government, the
> obligation to obedience must cease whenever the interest ceases in
> any great degree and in a considerable number of instances.[12]

The implications are most apparent, even though Hume himself makes
much point of the fact that only in rare instances is civil disobedience
justifiable on this ground.

---

[11] Hume, *op. cit., Human Nature,* Book III, Part II.
[12] *Ibid.*

THE INFLUENCE OF HUME

What is so radical about Hume's assumptions? Why has this nominal Tory been identified in retrospect as a precursor of social and political theories generally hostile to the traditional divisions of power and authority? The question can be put another way: If Hume is so careful an analyst, as his work abundantly shows, why does he not appreciate that these fundamental ideas lead not to conservatism but to radicalism?

In the first place, Hume is only sentimentally a conservative and an admirer of Burke—although he himself would hardly rate this an insignificant motivation. Too, Hume has respect for the weight of tradition, the authority of human experience, but for reasons vastly different from those of men like Burke or Maistre or Metternich. For Hume, experience is significant in and for itself, not because it represents the unravelling of some purpose beyond that direct experience. All of Hume's thought centers about the rejection of purpose, the rejection of organic society, the rejection of moral continuity. When Hume argues that men can be wicked he is asserting that individual men can depart from the path of the reasonable, the pattern of communal approbation. But man, as some quasimystic composite, does not exist for him; good and evil, even rationality and irrationality, do not exist as conceptual entities apart from the experience of individual men.

When Hume attempts to strike down natural law as nothing but subjective habits of association, when he seeks to explode the bubble of moral or spiritual universalism, he in fact brings into serious question the possibility of rational judgment. He maintains that no rules of the game exist by which political behavior can be judged save utility, but even this would-be utilitarianism takes on a moral aspect involving essentially only the individual agent of experience, the individual knower. Later advocates of utilitarianism will chant: "The greatest good for the greatest number." This Hume would reject. It would hint to him of the likelihood of judgments both dubious and doctrinaire.

His comprehensive skepticism regarding judgment, then, takes him to an advocacy of a far-reaching individualism, infinitely more radical in scope than the modest precepts of Locke. There can be nothing for man to cling to other than loose general approbation of shifting values. Life is purposeful only to the extent that it generates self-satisfaction. Even approbation is, after all, ego gratification, and morality becomes a device for making this gratification reciprocal.

From Hume two diverging ideological tributaries flow. From his psychological and moral individualism come the libertarian ideas of two centuries, from Adam Smith to the defenders of unfettered economic mobility. Hume provides a base for those anxious to press the claims of the individual against the state and against the theories of society buttressed by natural law. At the same time, Hume builds a near-perfect battering ram for those eager, for other reasons, to put asunder the authority of traditional institutions, temporal and spiritual. Authoritarian claims to legitimacy have commonly been lodged with some conception of moral injunction, some appeal to a higher law. Hume's denial of this nonexperiential judgment is an ideal weapon for those waging ideological warfare against the Establishment in its various forms. The fact that many reforming ideologies would impose collectivism as a replacement would no doubt have troubled Hume. But what the radicals did was to borrow Hume's sharp philosophical tool and reject his ideas for rehabilitation. Radicalism was perfectly willing to employ his arguments without accepting, necessarily, what Hume believed to be their implications.

No one has rested easy since David Hume. Moralists, clerics, philosophers, and politicians have spent many sleepless nights. The absolutists have lain awake planning their refutations. Even the relativists and latter-day radical empiricists have had anxious moments when musing on where their colleague might be taking them. Conservatives have muttered deep warnings, and subsequent radicals have asked themselves whether their own optimistic doctrines would summon up the Scottish sage's shriveling analysis. Perhaps Hume must be our philosophical alter ego, our wry companion who crooks a skeptical eyebrow when we are blithely flirting with folly.

. . . for further discussion:

1. Is causality necessary for the existence of science? for the existence of political science?
2. What advice do you think Hume might give to a politician seeking to win an election?
3. To what extent are Hume's ethics a good description of political relationships in the real world?
4. Since Hume's day, much has been written regarding the role of symbols. Scholars in various branches of knowledge have vigorously pursued symbols, ancient and modern, among widely scattered cultural groups. Mythology and literature have been examined. Psychologists have em-

ployed the analysis of symbols as a means both of explaining psychic phenomena and of treating the mentally disturbed. Some have gone so far as to argue that symbols contain perpetual values and universal aspects of understanding. It does appear that certain symbols occur in completely unconnected societies, and certain symbolic patterns seem to recur in all cultures. Assuming the validity, for the moment, of this symbolic universality, how does it affect Hume's basic ideas about human knowledge and behavior? Of what importance, if any, to political philosophy is the argument regarding the recurrence of symbolism and the widespread similarity of mythologies?

. . . for further investigation:

Aiken, Henry D., ed., ° *Hume's Moral and Political Philosophy.* New York: Hafner Publishing Co., Inc., 1948.

Broad, C. D., ° *Five Types of Ethical Theory.* Paterson, N. J.: Littlefield, Adams & Co., 1959.

Church, R. W., *Hume's Theory of the Understanding.* Ithaca, N. Y.: Cornell University Press, 1935.

Hendel, Charles W., *Studies in the Philosophy of David Hume.* Indianapolis, Ind.: Liberal Arts Press, 1962.

Hume, David, ° *An Inquiry Concerning Human Understanding.* Indianapolis, Ind.: Liberal Arts Press, 1955.

———, ° *An Inquiry Concerning the Principles of Morals.* Indianapolis, Ind.: Liberal Arts Press, 1957.

———, *A Treatise of Human Nature,* L. A. Selby-Bigge, ed. New York: Oxford University Press, Inc., 1941.

Windelband, Wilhelm, ° *A History of Philosophy,* J. E. Tufts, trans. Vol. II. New York: Torchbooks, 1958.

12

IN THE REALM OF
THE ABSOLUTE

Immanuel Kant (1724-1804), trudging his precisely routined way to his office at the University of Königsberg, stopped. "Hume," he muttered, "has awakened me from my dogmatic slumbers." And so began the prodigious task of refuting David Hume. It still goes on; we still live under the shadow of Hume's shattering implication that human knowledge is a subjective ruse. No wonder that thought troubled the intense German mind of Kant. It would be intolerable to proceed with the business of philosophy still plagued by Humean doubt.

Kant's "critical philosophy," aroused into being by the radical empiricism of Hume, was not originally or even very substantially concerned with the problems of politics.[1] Yet Kantian philosophy ushered in an entire era of political ideas—Kant raised the standard of German idealism.

[1] Rather late in the exposition of his system, Kant wrote some political essays. *The Principles of Political Right* appeared in 1793, followed by *Perpetual Peace* in 1795 and *The Philosophy of Law* in 1796.

It is neither necessary nor even possible to offer a thumbnail sketch of Kantian thought. There are a number of excellent essays available for those intrigued with the philosophic ideas of Kant, but it is not particularly recommended that the beginner launch himself into Kant's writing without the assistance of a capable guide. It is vital, for our purposes, that we relate in the most general terms the case that Kant makes for idealism, an idealism directly built upon by Hegel, the major target of this chapter.

Kant's refutation of Hume is anchored in a searching critique of experience.[2] But for Kant experience is considerably more intricate and perplexing than it is for Hume. In order to account for the diversity and complexity of experience, Kant argues that what the mind perceives is not really reality, but merely phenomena. Behind this phenomenal curtain is ultimate reality, unknowable yet ever-present. Kant dubs it the *Ding-an-Sich*—the thing-in-itself. Thus Kant divides up the realms of being between *noumena* and *phenomena*. The noumenous realm is beyond human comprehension, yet is the ultimate and seminal reality. Phenomena is but a veil, which is sensually perceived by mind.

If reality is the unknowable noumenon beyond direct experience, as Kant maintains it is, and if what we perceive is a sort of phantasmagoria masking the thing-in-itself from our knowledge, how is it that what we perceive appears orderly, understandable, regular, and, above all, consistent with the sense perceptions of others? That is the point, Kant rejoins; it is *minds* that are real, not the phenomenal images that they perceive. How can this be true? Kant argues that ideas exist a priori[3] in minds in the form of categories by which order and intelligibility are imposed upon phenomena. The mind comes with the "built-in" means, if you will, of sorting out the welter of sense impressions. Minds thus create the intelligible world of experience since they alone come equipped with the decoding devices needed to make sense out of nature.[4]

Is this esoteric proposition expounding the reality of "pure concepts of understanding" of any importance to students of political ideas?

---

[2] The first sentence of Kant's most famous work, *The Critique of Pure Reason*, is unequivocal: "There can be no doubt that all our knowledge begins with experience." But special note might be taken of the word "begins."

[3] Although the word has been previously used in this text and doubtless the reader is generally aware of its meaning, it is important to understand that in the Kantian context, a priori refers not only to logical "givens," but also to existence prior to consciousness or experience.

[4] Kant's theory of mind is presented under the imposing label: "Transcendental Unity of Apperception."

It is, because it constitutes the foundation for idealism, or that broad persuasion that holds that ideas, minds, or logical relationships are those categories of being possessing true reality. To the idealist, reality is not found in rocks, trees, horses, or bottles of beer, but in conceptual categories. There are numerous types of idealism, and Kant is indeed rather atypical of the school in some respects. But he laid the groundwork for a century of idealistic philosophy in Germany that produced some of the most striking and influential political ideas in recent times. Consider for a moment the implications of the assertion that what makes up the world are not physical objects or animate beings, but ideas in one form or another. Kant's view of experience, for example, supposes that a priori categories of mind impose order on a phenomenal confusion that is a perceptual manifestation of the noumenon, the thing-in-itself. Plato, you may remember, also advanced a theory that Ideas are real and appearances mere facsimiles. Both Plato and the German idealists are fundamentally agreed that since what is real is universal ideas, then political and moral questions can be approached in terms of absolute dicta. One can think in terms of moral and political laws. Indeed, Kant puts forth the idea of an inflexible moral law, describing it as the "moral imperative." [5] But the German idealists then went way beyond any Platonic theory of Ideas: If what is real is ideas or logical relationships, then reality is manifested in historical patterns, in institutions, in religions, in social structures. Thus the state can be thought of as an absolute Idea and is consequently not a human-contrived edifice, but an embodiment of ultimate reality. Idealism in this sense denies the significance of experience per se, save as unveiling the ideas or the Idea; idealism emphasizes discovery of universal truth via rationality or intuition. In taking this attitude, idealism also tends to deëmphasize the importance of individual decision-making, and its approach to social and political questions is rigorously moralistic, austere, and systematic. Whether highly logical (as it is with Hegel) or mystic (as it is with Schlegel or Schilling), German idealism of the nineteenth century displays a singular disinterest in or even contempt for what we might now call human affairs. Rather, idealism, conceiving as it does of the universe as divided between a realm of pure and absolute truth and a pale and spurious

---

[5] Kant's ethics rest upon a rather simple proposition, which he termed the "moral imperative": Act always in such a manner that your conduct could be framed as a universal moral law. Lying is always wrong, for example, regardless of how commendable the motives might be or how justifiable the consequences. The validity of moral acts, asserts Kant, rests not on their consequences, but on their obedience to moral absolutes.

stratum of human experience, is essentially preoccupied with the exposure of metaphysical truth. Yet in the case of Kant and Hegel, these
transcendental speculations lead with almost ponderous deliberation to
theories of politics.

Georg Wilhelm Friedrich Hegel (1770-1831) could never be accused
of shying away from ambitious undertakings. He set himself the task
of amassing and interpreting the entirety of human knowledge. But
even this was not his ultimate aim—his prime objective was to discover
the principle or principles upon which the universe rested. Whether
Hegel succeeded is quite another matter, and even his most enthusiastic advocates would admit that he fell somewhat short of his announced goal. But it is a massive and awe-inspiring project, perhaps
the most challenging synthesis since Aristotle. His thought has given
rise to violent criticisms and encomiums; his influence is to be found
in the most diversified quarters. Bertrand Russell has gone so far as to
suggest that Hegel was a fraud—or at least a purveyor of vast mischief.
Karl Marx publicly acknowledge his debt to Hegel and after certain
"corrections" incorporated Hegelian philosophy into his dialectical
materialism. The influence of Hegel, argue some, can be seen in virtually all totalitarian political systems since his time. He has been
called the philosopher of both the Left and the Right. He has been
accused of being a quasiofficial apologist for Prussian autocracy and
militarism, and his philosophy has been dismissed by some critics for
such farfetched reasons as that it was an attempt to ingratiate himself
with the House of Hohenzollern or that his passion for political order
is explainable by the fact that he was forced to flee Jena and abandon
his private library in 1806, one step ahead of Napoleon's troops. He
has been dubbed the arch-reactionary, but he was an unabashed admirer of the French Revolution. Paradoxes abound in Hegel, but perhaps the most striking of them all is that his philosophy has left its
stamp on the totalitarian ideologies of the twentieth century as well
as on its most radical theories.

Hegel was reared in middle-class surroundings in Stuttgart and
proved an abject failure as a theological student. As a scholar his
tastes ran to classical literature and, briefly, to poetry; his devotion to
Christianity never wavered, although it took him an excessive number
of years to attain a theological diploma. Personally, Hegel was shy,
intense, and gave little promise of the versatility that he later displayed. His early career was frankly unspectacular. He served for a

time as a private tutor, a minor professor at Jena, and a *Gymnasium* principal. By 1817 his work had attracted sufficient attention to merit a professorship at Heidelberg, and after a year he moved to the premier philosophy chair at the University of Berlin. His *Phenomenology of Mind* (1807) was his first important publication, and his political thought, while scattered through other works, is principally set out in *The Philosophy of Right* (1821). One feature of Hegel's life might be worthy of special notice: He was one of those rare instances of a philosopher who enjoys fame and even official blessing and modest wealth while still numbered among the living.

The starting point for Hegel was the Kantian philosophy. But a number of things about Kant's explanations disturbed the precise Teutonic mind of Hegel. How can you have a rational philosophy, mused Hegel, which features a thing-in-itself, a known unknowable? Surely one cannot be satisfied until the thing-in-itself is properly identified. And, too, there were Kant's famous categories, twelve of them that Kant believed to have exhausted the list of "original pure concepts of synthesis." Hegel was not satisfied with this either. And so he began to reform Kant. This reconstruction led Hegel to a formula that he was convinced could unlock the secrets of the universal order. Armed with the formula, Hegel argued, you could tour the cosmos.

From Kant's twelve categories, Hegel distills only one: Being. This is the single most fundamental category he can imagine. But is it not true, he reflects, that all things imply their opposite? If this is so, then this is true also of the primary category, Being. What is the opposite of Being? Clearly, Not-Being. Here, then, is the beginning of Hegel's famous formula, which he calls the dialectic.[6] The dialectic is built on the setting forth of opposites and their consolidation into a new term. It works like this: The first proposition is termed the *thesis*. It implies its opposite or contradiction, and this is the *antithesis*. When thesis and antithesis are set off against each other, they merge to produce a new proposition, the *synthesis*—Being = Not-Being = Becoming, for example. However, this synthesis itself immediately becomes a thesis (with its corresponding antithesis) and becomes part of a new syn-

---

[6] The term "dialectic" was not coined by Hegel. The word is used by Plato, and Kant makes much use of it. Separated from its expressly Hegelian connotations, dialectic is the process of reasoning, arriving at conclusions, by argument and counterargument, question and answer, challenge and response. The placing of two lines of argument in juxtaposition and evaluating the cross-implications is also sometimes called dialectic.

thesis. These triads [7] then form uninterrupted chains of interlinking logical progressions, becoming at once a comprehensive deductive system and an account of creation.

From the most abstract and general propositions, like Being–Not-Being–Becoming, the dialectic moves into propositions of a more specific nature.[8] Indeed, Hegel sought to account for *everything* as being within the scope of the dialectic. The universe could then be explored by the unfolding of the dialectical formula and progressive refinements of the dialectical categories. He was convinced that the structure of all that is known is the result of the dialectical process and that to assimiliate his logic was to understand the nature of reality.[9] This assumes of course that reality consists of some categories of ideation. But on this score Hegel leaves us in no doubt:

> Logic considers the province of thought in general. The thinking activity is its peculiar sphere. It is a whole (complete sphere) for and by itself. Logic has for its content the determinations peculiar to the thinking activity itself—which have no other ground than the Thinking. The "heteronomical" to it, is what is given to it through representation (a mere notion or mental picture which is devoid of universality and necessity—translator). Logic is, therefore, true science. A distinction must, of course, be made between pure thought and reality; but thought has reality insofar as *true actuality* is understood by this term. Insofar, however, as sensuous external existence is meant by "the Real," Thought has a far higher reality. The thinking activity has therefore a content (namely, itself) through its autonomy.[10]

---

[7] The triadic method is not wholly original with Hegel, either. It can be found in both Fichte and Kant. There are instances, but very few, in the Hegelian dialectic when the triads prove unwieldly and Hegel uses four terms.

[8] This additional explanation might prove helpful: "And this principle not only decides for us that the first category is being, but also determines the order of the subsequent categories. The more abstract concept will always be prior in thought, in the objective reason, to the less abstract. Therefore, the Logic will proceed from the *summum genus*, being, through further and further specifications, to the least abstract category of all, whatever that may be. Our method will be to proceed from the genus to the species, and then, treating the species as a new genus, to pass from it to a further and lower species, and so on. But we can only proceed from genus to species by adding a differentia to the genus. Therefore the order of progress will be through genus, differentia, species. Then treating the species as a genus we must find a new differentia to convert it into a new species. And with this triple rhythm of genus, differentia, species, our method will proceed throughout." [W. T. Stace, *The Philosophy of Hegel* (New York: Dover Publications, Inc., 1955), pp. 88-89.] Stace's account of the dialectic is by far the most lucid, and for those interested in pursuing the matter further, attention is called to pp. 88-114.

[9] This view is frequently called *panlogism*.

[10] G. W. F. Hegel, "Outlines of Hegel's Logic" (*Philosophical Propadeutics*), trans. by William Harris in *Selections*, J. Loewenberg, ed. (New York: Charles Scribner's Sons), p. 98.

What about the thing-in-itself? Hegel thinks he knows what this is, too. He calls it by a number of names, but he is profoundly convinced that the ultimate noumenous reality is Absolute Mind, the Absolute Idea, The Idea, or occasionally, God.[11] Whatever the terminology, the thing-in-itself, says Hegel, is perfect reason. What is behind experience is an Absolute Mind, which contains all reality and whose nature is disclosed only through the dialectic. The Idea, to use Hegelian language, is portrayed by a division into three aspects (this is a triad itself, of course): Logic, Philosophy of Nature, and Philosophy of Spirit. The Logic deals with the Idea "as it is in itself." The Philosophy of Nature is concerned with the opposite of the Idea, the realm of Not-Being, nature. The Philosophy of Spirit, as you might guess, deals with the synthesis, the unity of Idea and nature, the fulfillment of reason. There are three aspects (a triad again) of Spirit: Subjective Spirit, Objective Spirit, and Absolute Spirit. Of these, Objective Spirit is concerned with political thought.

Before we get lost in the Hegelian woods, it is advisable to summarize the important concepts we need to keep in mind before proceeding. To do so, we must face opposites and paradoxes. The Absolute Spirit is at once the beginning and the culmination of the dialectic. The dialectic is unwinding itself toward the final and complete exposition of truth, the disclosure of the full knowledge of the Absolute Spirit. This is the final act in the chain of triads. But at the same time, it is the Absolute Spirit that provides the foundation and logical rhythm of the dialectic. The Absolute Spirit is the Absolute Ideas, since the system of categories (logic) and the final phase of Spirit prove to be identical.

The dialectic can be described as the march of Absolute Spirit toward its final synthesis. History, says Hegel, is a record of the Absolute Spirit at work. He identifies certain phases of it in relation to historical process (coining the now familiar terms, *Zeitgeist* (Time-Spirit), *Weltgeist* (World-Spirit), and *Volksgeist* (Nation-Spirit). But since the dialectic itself is a continuing process of logical necessity, Hegel's historicism is far more than a mere synthetic look at historical events. The dialectic is history; history is the dialectic. In the *Introduction to the Philosophy of History* Hegel states:

> The History of the World begins with its general aim—the realization of the Idea of Spirit—only in an *implicit* form (*an sich*), that is, as Nature; a hidden, most profoundly hidden, unconscious instinct;

---

[11] Not God in the sense of a personal deity.

and the whole process of history (as already observed), is directed to rendering this unconscious impulse a conscious one. Thus appearing in the form of merely natural existence, natural will—that which has been called the subjective side—physical craving, instinct, passion, private interest, as also opinion and subjective conception—spontaneously present themselves at the very commencement. This vast congeries of volitions, interests, and activities, constitutes the instruments and means of the World-Spirit for attaining its object, bringing it to consciousness, and realizing it. And this aim is none other than finding itself—coming to itself—and contemplating itself in concrete actuality. But that those manifestations of vitality on the part of individuals and peoples, in which they seek and satisfy their own purposes, are, at the same time, the means and instruments of a higher and broader purpose of which they know nothing—which they realize unconsciously—might be made a matter of question, rather has been questioned, and in every variety of form negated, decried, and condemned as mere dreaming and "Philosophy." But on this point I announced my view at the very outset, and asserted our hypothesis—which, however, will appear in the sequel, in the form of a legitimate inference—and our belief, that Reason governs the world, and has consequently governed its history.[12]

Hegel's conception of the historical process is quite succinctly put in the paragraph above (his rather overwordy style notwithstanding). History is a narrative of reason seeking to complete itself. There are perhaps four implications in this historicism that need to be kept within easy recall prior to any analysis of his political views. First, history is not accidental, but purposeful, and the course of history is affected only by broad, general factors, cultural and ethnic movements of major proportion, not by the vagaries of individuals or small groups. Second, history provides its own remedies. Hegel is not a determinist, but is convinced that the apparent irrationalities and chaos are but temporary oppositions that will be reconciled by the inescapable process of historical necessity. The malfunctions of history are but brief and perhaps required configurations of the dialectical chain. Third, individuals and even states are instruments within the historical process, aiding the progress of the World-Spirit. True, individual men exercising choice can in petty ways change history or temporarily alter its course, but no amount of isolated human action can deter the mainstream of historical rationality. Fourth, history is primarily bound up with the destinies of states. The state, as we shall shortly see, occupies a thoroughly unique position in the dialectical scheme. For Hegel,

---

[12] G. W. F. Hegel, *The Philosophy of History*, trans. by J. Sibree (New York: Dover Publications, Inc., 1956), Introduction.

the state represents in the historical flow an embodiment of a single national mind, a corporate soul, and the state is therefore involved in a process of growth within the broader context of history itself. Put another way, states have their own private histories within the framework of the world, and within the World-Spirit there throbs the Nation-Spirit.

Hegel's political philosophy is available in most concentrated form in *The Philosophy of Right*. The title may be confusing, since those brought up in the West in the twentieth century tend to think of "right" in terms of "rights"—the *right* to vote or civil *rights,* broadly, the irrevocable franchise granted the citizen of a democratic state. Hegel uses the word in quite a different way (and part of the difficulty arises in translating *Rechts* into English). The Hegelian "right" is used most synonomously with law, but here a distinction must be made between positive law (statutes, ordinances, etc.) and law as rational order. It is in the latter sense that Hegel uses the word "right." He subdivides right into *abstract right, morality,* and *social ethics* and then divides the last of these into *Family, Civil Society,* and the *State.* In the precise sense that Hegel employs the word "right," he makes reference to the freedom of the individual will. Abstract right rests on self-consciousness, the self-awareness of the individual personality. Stace defines it this way:

> The self-conscious I-I is a self-enclosed unit. It refers only to itself, *and is therefore infinite.* As infinite it is an absolute end, and cannot be used as a means. Hence one person cannot treat another person merely as a means to his own ends, but is bound to treat that other person as, equally with himself, an end. This gives me, as a person, my rights, and also my duties to other persons.[13]

Hegel insists that "personality essentially involves the capacity for rights and constitutes the concept and the basis (itself abstract) of the system of abstract and therefore formal rights. Hence the imperative of right is: 'Be a person and respect others as persons.' " Under "abstract rights," Hegel lists property, contract, and punishment. It might be kept in mind, however, that the concept of abstract rights considers the person solely on the ground of personality, distinguished from animals and slaves only by virtue of the consciousness of the personal ego, the freedom of the will, and *not* as members of a political

---

[13] Stace, *op. cit.,* pp. 381-382.

society. Abstract right is a state of awareness well beneath moral sensibility.

It would be a lengthy chore to follow Hegel's dialectical development from abstract right through morality into all the aspects of social ethics. It would be superfluous to do so, as we can more directly tackle the problem of political theory, remembering as we do that right is the rational order within the sphere of Objective Spirit. At the most primitive level, this Objective Spirit is an awareness of self (abstract right); it then becomes a refinement of conscience (morality); and, finally, it is manifest in the participation of the individual in the objective moral order (social ethics), the identification of the individual will with the universal will or reason. It is this dialectical emergence that is the theme of *The Philosophy of Right*.

Having considered the meaning of right, we can now separate Hegel's political thought into four additional areas for analysis: (1) the state and the Nation-Spirit, (2) freedom and order, (3) the individual, and (4) the expressly "civil" society. This arrangement, however, while convenient, does some violence to the dialectical pattern, since civil society is a phase of social ethics that precedes the theory of the state.

The state is the apex of the dialectical process. It is a complete fulfillment of Objective Spirit; it is the total fusion of freedom and morality. In the following celebrated passage, Hegel defines the state:

> The state is the realized ethical idea or ethical spirit. It is the will which manifests itself, makes itself clear and visible, substantiates itself. It is the will which thinks and knows itself and carries out what it knows.
>
> The state, which is the realized substantive will, having its reality in the particular self-consciousness raised to the plane of the universal, is absolutely rational. This substantive unity is its own motive and absolute end. In this end freedom attains its highest right. This end has the highest right over the individual, whose highest duty in turn is to be a member of the state.
>
> The state as a completed reality is the ethical whole and the actualization of freedom. The state is the spirit, which abides in the world and there realizes itself consciously; while in nature it is realized only as the other of itself or the sleeping spirit. Let man be aware of it or not, this essence realizes itself as an independent power, in which particular persons are only phases. The state is the march of God in the world.[14]

---

[14] G. W. F. Hegel, *The Philosophy of Right*, trans. by T. M. Knox (New York: Oxford University Press, Inc., 1942), Sections 257-258.

To the extent that the dialectic is divine, Hegel's state is a creation of divinity. It is the crowning and perfect achievement of reason. It is an evolutionary product, born of the wisdom of history and the necessity of logic. It is not in any sense a purely political instrument or a device for coping with social problems. The state, to Hegel, is the highest integration of rationality and hence is the moral and spiritual summit of human aspiration. The state represents the total possibility for both human goodness and satisfaction. The state is the Idea in institutional form and as such transcends the lesser claim of persons, private interests, or subordinate institutions. These are conceived by syntheses of lower, more rudimentary stages.

The state is not only the highest manifestation of the Absolute, maintains Hegel, but it is an autonomous and self-sufficient idea. This has frequently been referred to as the "organic" theory of the state. If higher reality is to be found in the realm of absolute ideas, the state as a complete, self-contained Idea enjoys a status superior to the material beings that form a part of it. But the state's life within the World-Spirit is unconnected with the fortunes of its citizens; it transcends these and is reflective only of a Nation-Spirit, a single cultural voice that arises from the wellsprings of the nation. The state is *not* a fictitious person, Hegel makes clear (some commentators to the contrary); it is a discrete soul possessing a higher level of rationality than do mere human beings. It is an organic self, and its only counterpart is another state.

Each state is unique, argues Hegel. Each state is a national unity that exhibits Objective Spirit according to the cultural origins of the nation and the present stage of its historical development. Yet however dissimilar the characteristics of states may appear to be (Germany differs from France, let us say), they are in fact alike in regard to the universality of the Idea of the state and in that they participate actively in the emergence of the World-Spirit.

Total authority rests with the state. Barring the arrangements of governmental power (which we shall examine shortly), the state as a political entity has no limitation on its prerogatives and can demand unstinting obedience at all times. While this may be true in theory for any sovereign state, Hegel's state is omnipotent and omnicompetent, not only in a legal sense, but in a dynamic moral and political sense. Any curb on the state would be morally wrong; it would be abjectly irrational. No citizen, Hegel would contend, could question the state, since to do so would be to question reason and good morals.

Worse, it would be to deny freedom—for freedom, as we shall soon see, is not, as Hegel sees it, private liberty, but the mutual discharge of duties. The state is infallible; it is always right. Governments make mistakes, men are guilty of shocking follies and even gross crimes, but never the state. The state is perfect even if its agents may occasionally err. It is an "actual God," says Hegel, and "one easily falls into the mistake," he goes on, "of dwelling so much upon the special aspects of the state as to overlook its inner organic being."

Of the state and freedom Hegel has this to say:

> The state is the embodiment of concrete freedom. In this concrete freedom, personal individuality and its particular interests, as found in the family and civic community, have their complete development. In this concrete freedom, too, the rights of personal individuality receive adequate recognition. These interests and rights pass partly of their own accord into the interest of the universal. Partly, also, do the individuals recognize by their own knowledge and will the universal as their own substantive spirit, and work for it as their own end. Hence, neither is the universal completed without the assistance of the particular interest, knowledge, and will, nor, on the other hand, do individuals, as private persons, live merely for their own special concern.[15]

Hegel's argument is predicated on the assumption that freedom, individual freedom as well as universal freedom, consists not in unlimited choice (if choice implies the opportunity for the adoption of the irrational, the rejection of the logic of the Absolute), but in obedience to reason (reason being the rational progressive unfolding of the Idea). Can one be free if one is enslaved by the irrational? If I have duties to perform, Hegel reflects, either moral or legal ones, freedom lies in the discharge of these obligations. The argument can be put in very homely terms: Jones has an obligation to pay his tailor. Jones fails to do so. What results? Jones is plagued by pangs of conscience, or anxieties lest he be sued, or perhaps both. Or again, Jones' creditor may choose to coerce him into fulfilling his obligation, which he has a right to do. This state of affairs does not render a man free, Hegel would observe, but rather encroaches upon or vitiates freedom.

What agencies can claim the obligation of the individual? Those institutions, Hegel replies, that are the direct creation of the Idea, the Objective Spirit. The family is one, so is civil society, but, as we have already understood, Objective Spirit realizes itself in the ultimate

---

[15] Hegel, op. cit., Philosophy of Right, Section 260.

institution, the state, the highest integration of reason. The state is the source of freedom because it is also the fountainhead of rational obligation. Individual freedom is therefore impossible to realize on a purely private basis, since such realization would be logically incomplete. As a result, only in obedience and reverence to the state can true freedom be found. Abstract right, morality, and social ethics fuse in this synthesis, so without the state there can be no full embracing of right, morality, or social order.[16]

If "the state is the embodiment of concrete freedom," it is also, for much the same deductive necessity, the ultimate repository of moral judgment and self-realization. No man can be "good," Hegel asserts, without the state. He cannot be so for the straightforward reason that only the state can tell him what the good is, since only the state represents a logical composition of the completed Spirit. Abstract right, says Hegel, is objective, but incomplete. The phase of morality is subjective and not universal, but the objective rights of nature and the subjective intuitions of moral judgment combine to form the moral absolute of the state. Individuals, Hegel submits, can frequently be morally inadequate or ethically blind, but the state can never be anything but moral perfection.

Hegel's views on the relation of one state to another in no way detract from his argument that the state represents the highest plane of the dialectic. Yet the dialectic applies in the relations beween states; history obviously traces the rise and fall of states, of empires.[17] In the competition between states the Absolute may assert its will, but not in any sense of formalized authority; the Absolute works through the historical imposition of a stronger sovereignty upon a weaker one. "History," comments Hegel, "is the world's court of judgment," and states vary in their capacities and are subject to chance and risk, among which may be the loss of their independence. "The destinies and deeds of states," Hegel writes, "are the visible dialectic of the finite nature of these spirits." But states are independent, bound by none of the moral restraints or obligations appropriate to private individuals. The trial of the state is *war*, which is not only inevitable among states, but is a

---

[16] Hegel writes: "When the State of our country constitutes a community of existence; when the subjective will of man submits to laws—the contradictions between Liberty and Necessity vanish." (*Philosophy of History*, as abridged in *Selections, op. cit.*, p. 389.)

[17] Hegel believed that history revealed four great empires: the Oriental, the Greek, the Roman, and the Germanic (the nomenclature is Hegel's).

laudable means of restoring the vitality and temper of a state.[18] But ideally war is temporary, limited in scope, and in no way aimed at the total destruction of a defeated enemy. Hegel takes a view of war not unlike the cosmopolitan military theory of the eighteenth century. He looks at Europe as a political community:

> The nations of Europe form a family by virtue of the universal principle of their legislation, their ethical observances, and their civilization. Amongst them international behavior is ameliorated, while there prevails elsewhere a mutual infliction of evils. The relation of one state to another fluctuates; no judge is present to compose differences; the higher judge is simply the universal and absolute spirit, the spirit of the world.[19]

Hegel develops at length the contention that while any state is universal in logical principle, it is unique in its own make-up. Each state represents a "single principle, comprised under its geographical and anthropological existence." This view of national uniqueness goes a long way toward explaining the nationalistic cast of Hegelian writing and in particular his very evident pride in the German nation. While any state is an organic being and a culminating synthesis independent of its parts, it also incorporates and embodies the Nation-Spirit, a singular expression of ethnic and cultural determinations. Hegel makes it plain that this Nation-Spirit is qualitative—some nations are better than others. Nations are strong and virile or weak and decadent.[20] International life, history, is the acid bath of national wills. Hegel, like Herder and Fichte, was convinced of the fact that the Germanic peoples—the Prussian state in particular—possessed a superior Nation-Spirit, what Hegel sometimes refers to as "National Genius." [21] What he found attractive in the French Revolution was not the "rights of man," but a people "engaged in realizing its grand objects, and defending its work against external violence during the process of giving

---

[18] Hegel evidences considerable admiration for war. For example: ". . . war protects the people from a corruption which an everlasting peace would bring upon it." "War indeed causes insecurity in property, but the real insecurity is only a necessary commotion. . . . Let the insecurity finally come, in the form of Hussars with glistening sabres. . . ." "The military class is the class of universality."

[19] Hegel, op. cit., Philosophy of Right, Section 340.

[20] "The Nation," Hegel explains, "lived the same kind of life as the individual when passing from maturity to old age—in the enjoyment of itself—in the satisfaction of being exactly what it desired and was able to attain." (Op. cit., Philosophy of History, p. 436.)

[21] One might wish to compare Fichte's Reden an die deutschen Nation ("Addresses to the German Nation").

to its purposes an objective existence." Nation-Spirit must be constantly advancing to new aspirations and new destinies, counsels Hegel. The decline and even demise of Nation-Spirit can come about through sinking into the "senile life of mere custom." Activity and aspiration are the keys to the perpetuation of a vigorous and restless Nation-Spirit, a healthy concept of the national self.

Hegel's nationalism has frequently been misinterpreted in two main ways. First, too much stress can be laid on his "pan-Germanism." Admirer as he was of the Prussian state (and, one might add, the Greek city-states), much of his eulogizing of German virtues belong to his earlier and less reflective writing [22] and in tone indicates a greater influence upon him of Herder and Fichte than do his later works. It would be erroneous to deny to Hegel's nationalism a distinctly universal emphasis.

Secondly, the question might be asked if Hegel meant that the national state was the be-all and end-all of the dialectical process? Is the state the *final* embodiment of the World-Spirit? It is difficult to answer this with any certainty, although a substantial bloc of Hegelian commentators have arrived at the conclusion that Hegel never envisioned a synthesis beyond the state. While this may be true and while Hegel did not specifically discuss a higher integration of the Idea, there are some suggestions in his writings, in both *The Philosophy of Right* and *The Philosophy of History*, that the World-Spirit might enter a stage of development that would supplant the state by an even loftier political form. It is fair, perhaps, to leave the door open on this matter. Hegel appears to have done so. Consider this passage:

> Justice and virtue, wrong, force and crime, talents and their results, small and great passions, innocence and guilt, the splendour of individuals, national life, independence, the fortune or misfortune of states and individuals, have in their sphere of conscious reality their definite meaning and value, and find in that sphere judgment and their due. This due is, however, as yet incomplete. In world history, which lies beyond this range of vision, the idea of World-Spirit, in that neces-

---

[22] Hegel's German nationalistic fervor is most readily observable in his *Constitution of Germany*, written in 1802. It should be pointed out that this work was not only the product of his early years, but is more reminiscent of a political pamphlet than a philosophic treatise. Some critics have argued that it shows Hegel's basic political concepts uncluttered by the esoteric language that marks his later work. This may well be a hasty judgment. While it is certainly true that the *Constitution of Germany* shares many views in common with *The Philosophy of Right*, let us say, the latter work is both rooted in a different deductive base and largely immune from chauvinistic panegyrics.

sary phase of it which constitutes at any time its actual stage, is given its absolute right.[23]

Hegel warmly approves of "strong men." He has nothing but praise for Machiavelli; he cites Richelieu and Frederick Wilhelm as models. He views what he terms a "constitutional monarch" as an absolute ruler, the final arbiter of the universal character of the state. "The element which implies absolute decision," he remarks, "is not individuality in general, but one individual, the monarch." He even denies that a number of states (including Great Britain) are a sovereign people for the somewhat surprising reason that their monarchs are no longer fully independent. The most pernicious doctrine of the modern age, Hegel thinks, is putting the people and the monarch in opposition or even dividing the royal function. The "people" are a "formless mass." Yet the monarch in the Hegelian view is *not* a decision-maker; Hegel observes in one reflection that "he has often nothing to do but sign his name." The will of the monarch, expressed as "I will," is but the will of the state. The monarch individualizes in his person the monopoly of authority exercised by the state; he is in theory absolute and limited only by what particular constitutional arrangements a given state may adopt. Hegel calls him the "apex" and says that his is the "power of ultimate decision." The remainder of government is divided by Hegel between a legislature (which has only an interpretative legal authority and deals with "universal internal affairs") and an executive (which is in fact a sort of super-civil service). (His ideas about this branch of government merit a closer look a bit later.)

When all is said and done, what justification can Hegel offer for this evident political autocracy? Why does he curb individual choice, liberal opportunity, with such ruthless determination? Hegel's monolithic state is a necessity, in terms of his assumptions, for two principal reasons. One, Hegel's notions about freedom, which we have examined earlier, demand the curtailment of individual licentiousness and its replacement by communal and national duty and loyalty. Private interest is moral bankruptcy; personal egotism is contrary to reason.

But beyond this theory of freedom as unquestioning obedience to the higher will of the state, Hegel is apparently haunted by the specter of anarchy, of civil disorganization. Order, an inflexible order, becomes the critical precondition of societal life. Hegel is virtually obsessed with the need for so arranging the powers of government that uninterrupted tranquillity is assured. He is keenly aware of forces at

---

[23] Hegel, *op. cit.*, *Philosophy of Right*, Section 345.

work in Europe in his time; he is sensitive to elements within Germany
that might menace this continuity of order. The growth of atheism and
egalitarianism stirs him to countermeasures of obvious severity. In
France he could witness the Jacobin excesses, and in England he
thought he detected a social decay brought on by political democracy.
In Germany, liberal and individualistic rumblings raised the threat
of a fragmenting of the German nation, a situation that Hegel decries
so vehemently in his historical commentary.

Is order for order's sake the stimulus for Hegel's absolutism? The
terrible threat inherent in disorder, he concludes, is the destruction
of national unity. The state is a whole, but it is a whole in two senses:
It is a complete, autonomous Idea, a logical being, but it is also a
nation, a creation in nature expressing Spirit, a geographical and anthropological fact. Hegel as a German patriot had been dismayed by
the slow and irregular progress toward the unification of what he
considered the Germanic peoples. This feeling, added to the logical
imperatives of the dialectic, made national unity of transcendent importance. Order must be imposed by whatever stringent means were
required in order to insure the preservation of the unity of the state.

The need for order certainly restricts, for Hegel, the free play of
individual choice, but he is quite emphatic that collective opinion
(public opinion, if you will) is a necessary and legitimate political
phenomenon. "Public opinion contains the eternal substantial principles of justice, the true content, and the result of the whole constitution, legislation, and the universal condition in general." His
justification for this view reads not unlike Rousseau on the general
will, and the similarity is doubtless not accidental. He speaks of common sense and refers rather vaguely but repeatedly to a kind of wisdom latent in the *Volk*. He is, however, not deluded into conceiving
of public opinion as free of serious error, and his conception of it is
that it is an organic voice, not a collection of individual judgments. It
is a mélange of the false and the true. The primary worth of public
opinion, it would seem in Hegel's exposition of it, is that it may serve
as an expression of the Time-Spirit, and great leaders are those who
understand and act under the aegis of this "meaning of the age." But
by public opinion Hegel means the spontaneous collective spirit of a
people, not a calculated expression of political views. He denies to
the press, for example, the freedom to say and write what it pleases
on the same grounds that he rejects individual freedom of choice.
(His estimation of the worth of the journalistic profession in society
would cause an apoplectic reaction in any dedicated newspaperman.)

Hegel differentiates the state from what he terms "civil society" by classifying the latter as a part of the former. In itself it is incomplete and requires the state to give it meaning. Civil society is broken up by Hegel into the familiar three aspects: (1) the system of wants, (2) administration of justice, and (3) police and corporation. In more general terms, civil society is described in the context of the inter-dependence of persons. The most important feature of Hegel's discussion of this mutual dependence is his argument in defense of a sharply delineated class system, which he claims springs logically from the system of wants (i.e., mutual dependence, labor, and wealth). In essence, Hegel's classes rest upon a division-of-labor concept reinforced by a grouping of wants or desires. Like Plato, he has three major classifications: an agricultural class, a commercial class, and, lastly, what he labels the "universal" class. It is this last social stratum that is the most novel and important.

The universal class is so named because it is concerned solely with those matters that are of universal importance to the state. This of course makes it apparent that the universal class is a ruling oligarchy built around the ideal of state service and merit. What may be surprising is that Hegel neither views this class as a closed shop nor even as granting its present members the right to select new additions. Membership is ostensibly a matter of individual choice, limited only by the individual's ability and successful exercise of his responsibilities. Hegel criticizes the notion of a Platonic ruling élite founded on careful selectivity or a hereditary aristocracy. What Hegel proposes is an oversized, profoundly dedicated "meritocracy" along civil service lines. Moreover, its character is rather more middle-class than aristocratic.[24] He stresses the need for absolute devotion, efficiency, impartiality, incorruptibility, and, by no means of least importance, appropriate and exacting training and preparation. In fact, Hegel's recommendations regarding the universal class had a marked influence on the development of a professional civil service in Germany during the

---

[24] Hegel was a believer in the necessity of a large and stable middle class. He states: "The members of the executive and the state officials constitute the main part of the middle class, in which are found the educated intelligence and the consciousness of right of the mass of the people. The institutions of sovereignty operating from above and the rights of corporations from below prevent this class from occupying the position of an exclusive aristocracy and using their education and skill wilfully or despotically.

"The state, if it has no middle class, is still at a low stage of development. In Russia, for example, there is a multitude of serfs and a host of rulers." (*Op. cit.*, *Philosophy of Right*, Section 296).

nineteenth century, a service that went generally unequalled in either efficiency or probity until the advent of Herr Hitler's notorious regime. But the universal class is concerned with that phase of government which is generally termed "executive." These members of the universal class are not to be policy-makers; they are to be highly skilled administrators and agents of the state.

Other dependencies and wants are acknowledged by the administration of justice based upon a universal code of law. (Corporations, for example, are the formal recognition of particular interests of groups of individuals concerned with necessary commercial undertakings.) This law Hegel rests on reason, either through the universality of custom or self-evident propositions. He lays marked emphasis on the need for universal law to be universally known and publicized. "It is my right," Hegel comments, "to know and recognize the law as my own. Only to accept as binding what my reason recognizes as rational is part of the right of the subject."

There are basically two ways of offering criticism of the political philosophy of Hegel. One can take the political recommendations as they stand and decide whether or not they are valid, attractive, or justifiable and be done with it. The other avenue of approach is to assume that Hegel's political thought follows by logical inference, if not necessity, from his propositions of greater generality. This form of criticism entails questioning the basic assumptions of Hegelian philosophy or demonstrating that regardless of whether or not Absolute Idealism is a tenable position, Hegel's deductions from it into the realm of the political are fallacious. The first mode of analysis has the merit of greater simplicity; numerous critics, perhaps subjectively offended by Hegelian authoritarianism, have chosen this way out. Some have merely dismissed Hegel on the ground that he is a dismally vague and imprecise writer and that language as pedantically obscure as that of Hegel could not contain substantial understanding. This seems to be making short shrift of a figure whose influence appears to have the resilience of a rubber ball.

It is beyond the scope of this book to offer any comprehensive critique of Hegelian philosophy. Whether or not Hegel's contention that "the rational is real, the real is rational" contains a profound truth, we will let go unanswered; but it is tempting to suggest briefly a number of the problems that Hegelian idealism creates. Is it, in fact, possible to argue that reality is constituted not even by ideas or forms, but by logic itself? Is it possible that Hegel is confusing the "rules of thought" as a means of making the world of experience intelligible, with logic as a self-contained order of reality? However valid logic is, can it create anything? It is one thing to say that minds create the world, but quite another to assert that logical necessity creates the order of nature. If Hegel had been satisfied to take his stand on the ground that his logic—the dialectic—was a unique key to the mysteries of the universe, it would be one thing. But he did not stop there. He boldly attributed to his logic the essence of ultimate truth.

Also, Hegel's Spirit is a difficult morsel to swallow. Is the Absolute Spirit an absolute principle or some sort of pervading force in the cosmos? If it is the latter, in any sense, we are left with an inadequate account of it. The reconciliation of logical necessity and Spirit is nebulous and incomplete. The entire idea of necessity in Hegel raises problems of meaning. If he means by it the consequences of orderly deduction, then it is comprehensible, but one feels that Hegel's own concept of it ranges far beyond this and that the necessity of the dialectic is an imperative singularly present in the contradictions of the dialectical method. His entire argument regarding omnipresent logical contradiction has received rather intense criticism since his day.

The emphasis upon necessity frequently seems at odds with Hegel's stress upon Will—and Will, like Spirit, is a rather murky and imprecise category. If necessity implies some predetermined course of events or inescapable consequences, then how can this notion be successfully and fully harmonized with the conception of Will as an expression of selection, discrimination, dynamic activity? This is really the paradox of freedom in Hegel. His philosophy of history is described as the process of the realization of complete freedom; the entire dialectic is a process whose aim is the attainment of a perfect freedom. Yet the process seems predetermined and inexorable, and the very originating principle, the Absolute Idea, seeks only to realize itself and hence attain a freedom—which, it would appear, it must logically possess in the first place. Freedom is a term in the Hegelian lexicon that is divorced from any conventional meaning. Is it freedom to attain the inevitable? Is it freedom eventually to arrive at a *stasis*, an elimination of all potentialities for change? Put in another way: How far can contradictions be reasonably extended? Can that which is the whole be incomplete? Can God be omnipotent and yet seeking to fulfill Himself? Can freedom consist in obeying the dictates of an absolute principle?

Perhaps it would seem that we are getting enmeshed in considerations both rather rarefied and removed from the problems of political theory. But the heart of Hegel's thoughts on politics lie in these abstruse matters. Only on metaphysical grounds can Hegel's view of the political function be fully understood. In justice to Hegel, his absolute state must be examined against the background of his system. This is particularly true in the case of the dialectic. And here, too, nagging perplexities trouble the serious interpreter. Perhaps the most obvious and trenchant question—and one which it would be fascinating to hear Hegel answer—is this: If all things contain their contradictions and thus become amalgamated into a synthesis of higher objectivity and greater proximity to the ultimate realization of the Absolute Spirit, then is this true also of the dialectic itself or, indeed, of Hegelian philosophy in general? Could it not be argued with substantial cogency that the dialectic *must* itself form a part of a triad leading to a more significant synthesis? What evidence is there to suppose that Hegel's entire philosophic system is not merely one of the steppingstones to something else?

The most common ground of criticism of the dialectic is that it presents a temptation—which Hegel did not resist—to cut the facts to fit the formula. In order to incorporate the data into the rigidities and formalisms of the dialectic, does Hegel do violence to the data? On the other hand, it is not unreasonable to point out that when one has devised an explanatory pattern and then examines phenomena, it is never difficult to find a multitude of examples to prove the rightness of the pattern. Such is an inherent danger in a priori systems—and Hegel's dialectic is not exempt. In the act of compressing all human activity into the confines of the dialectic, Hegel is often forced to employ terms and expressions whose generality and even comprehensibility throw doubt on the real rigor of the method. Occasionally one suspects that he becomes a player with words, and George Santayana once described him as a "solemn sophist; he made discourse the key to reality." This "logic-chopping" in Hegel frequently makes the irrational a recalcitrant classification, and Hegel's devotion to logical symmetry perhaps has the tendency to deny covertly the true nature of the irrational.

The dialectical method need not lead to the type of political arrangement that Hegel envisages. It can be argued that Hegelianism in its broad implications need not specify the authoritarian state. Numerous neo-Hegelians, T. H. Green and Karl Marx, for illustration, followed major aspects of his system to political solutions either liberal or radical—idealism or the dialectic do not of themselves stipulate a closed political order. Could it have been that Hegel neglected to heed Hume's counsel that it was fallacious to frame the "Ought" from the "Is"? What Hegel observed in the arena of Europe in the first half of the nineteenth century might well have encouraged a view of politics similar to the one he announced as the result of transcendental logic. The advantages of the Prussian state might well have served to trigger his mind in the normative direction. It is curious that while Hegel takes such a deprecating view of empirical evidence, presumably standing aloof from the exigencies of experience, this very rejection of experience may in some fashion have been the result of his overemphasis on the significance of contemporary history.

There is ample room to reject Hegel's political philosophy on the broad categories on the grounds of the inadequacy of his basic propositions. One can merely throw out the system as spurious. But assuming the relative tenability of his system, how reasonable are his specific political judgments? Hegel most certainly was mesmerized by the need for order; it colored his evaluative balance. The state was far more austere and forceful than this conception of politics demanded. His repeated admonitions regarding the health of the Nation-Spirit and the vibrant pulsing of the national will do not seem suitably reconciled with the frankly oppressive character of his omnipresent order. The mysticism and rationalism of Hegel combine in this instance to form a most uneasy partnership.

For all Hegel's talk about law, he never comes to grips in any careful fashion with the problem of constitution-making or legislative process. He makes broad and indefinite references to constitutions as the basis for political organization, but he never discusses their actual formation or character. He speaks of national laws as a sort of *fait accompli*. He appears to have misunderstood the role of legislation and the need for law to be in some manner responsive, if not responsible, to social conditions and shifting needs. While it might be understandable, given his opinions, that Hegel would advocate a legislature to which he tosses a few inoffensive and innocuous constitutional bones, he nonetheless neglects to give attention to the positive character of representative bodies and their highly significant role in preserving the very conservative equilibrium that Hegel says he is seeking. Hegel did not apparently foresee that legislatures in the West would be, in the main, bulwarks of political caution and checks on the radical or at least experimental proclivities of executives and popular leaders.

The simple fact is that Hegel was naïve about power, even though he devoted much discussion to it. In assuming the inevitability of the dialectic, he also assumed that individual men in competing for power and exercising it could not significantly alter the course of history. Such a view rendered Hegel insensitive to the possibilities of tyranny, of political rule by unscrupulous and cunning usurpers. True, he thought great men would arise and personify the Time-Spirit, but he gave far too little attention to the possibility that perceptive demagogues, employing the trappings of Nation-Spirit, could seize and use power to both the detriment of the state and the general well-being. Such rule could scarcely be described as rational. And Hegel's argument that in time the forces of historical necessity would eliminate these selfish opportunists is somehow not very assuring. A vast amount of damage and suffering, some of it permanent, could be done before history or the dialectic unraveled its inscrutable skein. Hegel was acutely alive to the consequences of radical individualism, but he was oblivious to the dangers of despotism and failed to incorporate into his theory, however moralistic and pious in tone, adequate safeguards to protect not merely individuals, but his precious state from the ravages of political adventurers.

Finally, Hegel's doctrine of freedom as obedience, quite aside from argument regarding its moral implications *vis-à-vis* the individual, has consequences that affect the state. The Hegelian idea of freedom inevitably would create some measure of paralysis of the creative energies of the nation. The curtailment of choice and election also implies an absence of individual enterprise and of personal excitement. The closed state means a limitation on variety and ambition. This result might not necessarily be undesirable, except that Hegel continually emphasizes the need for these very same qualities within the state, albeit on a collective basis. The question becomes: Can the state enjoy a dynamic and creative collective existence while at the same time denying such an existence on an individual basis? The state, asserts Hegel, has the need and right of self-development, and this is predicated insofar as the state is concerned on a different definition of freedom. The state is free to choose, to experiment, to compete, and to risk. All these experiences are important in the maturation of the state. Is it, then, inconsistent to argue that these are unnecessary for the individual? Hegel apparently saw no circularity in this state of affairs.

Hegel left the world a different place from what he found it. He had stirred the waters; perhaps he muddied them, but few currents remained unmoved by his grandiose and irritating pronouncements. His impact on the nineteenth century was immense, and his thought is still being refuted in the twentieth. In his own Germany, Hegel's philosophy found a reconstruction in Karl Marx, as we shall see in Chapter 14, and to a lesser degree in Engels and Feuerbach. Even in America neo-Hegelianism was an important movement, primarily associated with Josiah Royce. But it was in England that his teaching found a sympathetic audience. His influence liberated English thought from the complete dominance of the associationalism of Locke and Hume and revived interest in social theory. Green, Bosanquet, Bradley, and McTaggart are the most celebrated names in British neo-Hegelianism. Of these, Green and Bosanquet are the most provocative from the standpoint of political ideas.

Hegel's followers in Britain struck off in two directions—Left and Right, liberal or absolutist. Idealism was conceived in liberal terms by *Thomas Hill Green* (1836-1882). Green, also deeply under the influence of Kant, differs from Hegel in one important respect. Green vigorously asserts the free moral participation of the individual as indispensable for the self-development of the state. At the same time, Green conceives of the individual as a "social self," possessing social bonds and attaining his highest satisfaction in social participation. This means, for Green, both moral equality among men and the recognition of freedom within the society for individualized moral opportunity. This societal state of freedom for social and moral involvement on the basis of equality means that the state (Green was the first to use the term in England) must rest upon collective will and general acquiescence, not upon force or coercion.

While rejecting the individualist notion of freedom as the absence of restriction, Green speaks of "positive freedom" and defines liberty as "a positive power or capacity of doing or enjoying something worth doing or enjoying." Freedom becomes self-development in a social milieu and a recognition of interdependence. Thus, asserts Green, freedom is both an individual and social condition, and its aim is not to permit unrestricted choice or unlimited prerogative, but to create a state of general good shared equally by individuals. This clearly does not mean that the ideal role of government is to abrogate the governing function. Quite the contrary. Like Aristotle, Green maintains that the object of politics and the aim of governments is to promote the moral development of society. But governments cannot *make* men be moral, condends Green; they can only provide the *opportunity* for the growth of moral judgment. The state becomes—unlike Hegel's equivalent—more an agent for the realization of the general moral welfare than a coercive force for the maintenance of moral proprieties. The state is not, for Green, a mere contrived instrument for meeting human needs, as it was for Locke, let us say; it is an Idea, but as an Idea, Green's state is an expression of a social striving after the good. On this basis, Green denies any validity for natural rights, as did Hegel, arguing that as long as the state remains a moral expression the individual can have no recourse against it and resistance to it would be tantamount to resisting the moral weight of society. This would involve, as well, an individual's denying his own moral nature, since that nature is social and not exclusively private.

Bernard Bosanquet (1848-1923) was both a more orthodox Hegelian and more inclined to elect the path of authoritarianism. His *Philosophical Theory of the State* (1899) sought to bring Hegel up-to-date, as it were, and to fuse more of Rousseau into the concept of the state. Like Green, Bosanquet accepted the idea of a general will and the role of the state as guarantor of moral freedom, but he rejected Green's emphasis on individual moral free will and replaced it with a conception of the state as a subconscious moral element in individual minds. Most striking are his remarks on the relationship between the state and society, between which he differentiates. Society, he explains, is cooperation for the realization of moral opportunity; the state approves and insures by force this social process. Yet society is but part of the state, which is supreme as a mediating agent over society and provides the necessary stimulation and control. Bosanquet's statist theories are virtually pure Hegelianism. The state is the whole of life, the manifestation of Objective Mind, and all other institutions, while themselves Ideas, are incomplete ethical expressions without the integrating majesty of the state. The state is also the collective or universal mind of all the citizens (here Rousseau reappears), and, in truth, Bosanquet's state, perhaps even more than Hegel's, is the Idea.

This state is a no-nonsense proposition. One of its first duties is to prevent moral laxity, and the law and police action are tools to deal with backsliding among the populace. And while the individual is sternly bound to a set of moral precepts and laws, the state is not. It can do as it chooses, provided that it never veers from its purpose, the advancement of the ethical growth of society. Nor can the individual legitimately question the moral goals of the state, argues Bosanquet. The good is what the state declares it is, and the only area of public criticism allowed is that of how the state proceeds with the business of embracing its self-declared moral purposes. The only implied limitation upon state power in Bosanquet is the mysterious general will.

Hegelianism can be a heady dose. It has repelled many by its sheer dogmatism and egotistical tenor of presentation. Santayana has written:

> This reign of official passion is not, let me repeat, egotism in natural man who is subject to it; it is the sacrifice of the natural man and of all men to an abstract obsession, called an ideal. The vice of absoluteness and egotism is transferred to that visionary agent. The man may be docile and gentle enough, but the demon he listens to is ruthless and deaf. It forbids him to ask, "At what price do I pursue this ideal? How much harm must I do to attain this good?" No; this imperative is categorical. The die is cast, the war against human nature and happiness is declared, and an idol that feeds on blood, the Absolute State, is set up in the heart and over the city.[25]

When the emotions cool and intellectual dispassion is for the moment sovereign, what big questions does Hegel leave with us? They are these: Is the sole concern with man's political arrangements a matter of his ethical nature? Is it essential to consider the material, the emotional, even the operational aspects of human nature and human requirements? Is political theory made in heaven, to coin a phrase? Do we exhaust human behavior by analysis of the *reasoning* mind alone? And if we do, what leads us to believe that the power to reason is the faculty to be either wise or humane?

. . . for further discussion:

1. How can Hegel's view of the state and the Nation-Spirit be reconciled with the mounting multiplicity of new sovereignties being created in Africa and Asia?

2. What might Hegel have thought about the possibilities and desirabilities of world government? regional federations? Could the dialectic envision a "superstate"?

3. Do you think Hegel would have adjusted his dialectic to take into account the possibilities presented by nuclear warfare? After the unleashing of nuclear power, what changes might be needed and what implications exist for his conception of Absolute Spirit and philosophy of history?

4. Even assuming Hegel's own depiction of the logical order, how far may we push his dialectical scheme? Is it really a *total* explanation or are some aspects of human existence mere accidents or habits or conventions that do not represent the workings of Absolute Spirit? Is it possible that Hegel would have argued that all social issues are resolvable in terms of the transcendental Logic?

---

[25] George Santayana, *Egotism in German Philosophy* (New York: Charles Scribner's Sons, 1916), p. 112.

. . . for further investigation:

Bosanquet, Bernard, *The Philosophical Theory of the State.* New York: St. Martin's Press, Inc., 1899.

Bradley, Francis H., * *Ethical Studies.* Indianapolis, Ind.: Liberal Arts Press, 1951.

Green, Thomas H., *Lectures on the Principles of Political Obligation.* New York: Longmans, Green & Co., Inc., 1931.

Hegel, Georg W. F., *The Philosophy of History,* J. Sibree, trans. New York: Dover Publications, Inc., 1956.

———, *The Phenomenology of Mind,* J. B. Baille, trans. New York: The Macmillan Company, 1910.

———, *The Philosophy of Right,* T. M. Knox, trans. New York: Oxford University Press, Inc., 1942.

———, * *Selections,* Jacob Loewenberg, ed. New York: Charles Scribner's Sons, n.d.

Kant, Immanuel, *The Critique of Pure Reason,* N. Kemp Smith, trans. New York: Modern Library, Inc., 1958.

Santayana, George, *Egotism in German Philosophy.* New York: Charles Scribner's Sons, 1916.

Stace, Walter T., * *The Philosophy of Hegel.* New York: Dover Publications, Inc., 1955.

13

THE GOAL OF THE

GENERAL

WELFARE

The nineteenth century could be called the "Century of Reform."
Reform was in the air; progress and optimism were the bywords. No
amount of Burkean pessimism or Hegelian dialectic could dampen
the reformist spirits. Things would get better and better if only human
beings managed things a trifle more successfully. Opinion was confident, even smug. One of the greatest of the reformers, Jeremy Bentham,
looking at his career in retrospect, commented that all that was left
to do was to conquer poverty and disease. It was true that war, the
scourge of the twentieth century, appeared to have been locked out
by the Congress of Vienna and British naval supremacy, except for
Hegel's little skirmishes of national revitalization and unification. Only
the Americans were apparently getting ready to shoot each other in
truly large numbers. Bentham could not have foreseen the shadow of
Bismarck and the ominous growth of Germany as a military power.

Some historians have argued with convincing logic that the nine-

teenth century ought to be dated from 1815 to 1914. Surely the in-
carceration of Bonaparte on his lonely island in the Atlantic marked
the final act of the eighteenth century. It had its *Dämmerung* on the
broken terrain of Waterloo. And when the Duke of Wellington, the
victor on that momentous field, capitulated under pressure from the
Parliamentary reformers, the new age was indeed born. The old guard
was passing; a combination of reforming Whigs and Radicals in England finally forced the Reform Bill of 1832. The Poor Laws followed,
then more electoral reforms, prison reforms, child labor and industrial
reforms, public health measures, and aid to the destitute. The brave
and visionary world of the nineteenth century was at hand, fathered
strangely by both reform and the Industrial Revolution.

The nineteenth century witnessed the emergence of a number of
influences that shaped the political life of Great Britain. Though Burke
had checked the spread of French Jacobinism, other French ideas
found wide acceptance, primarily those relating to social and economic
matters. In addition, Britain was the first major state to experience the
process of industrialization, aided by a happy conjunction of coal, iron
ore, capital, and a reasonably serene political development. Introduced
with breathtaking speed into the British scene were utilitarianism, social radicalism, and the revelations of Charles Darwin.

The reformist impulse in the early nineteenth century in Britain was
essentially an ethical one. The problem of reform was one of the moral
regeneration of the individual. Later this same reforming impetus
would grow utopian, collectivist, and scientific. The intellectual ferment
was accelerated by a religious revival in England of a Nonconformist
character. This was the period of the rapid growth of Methodism and
Presbyterianism. Calvinist elements in this Nonconformity (unwilling-
ness, as you recall, to accept the Church of England) squared ad-
mirably with both the moral evangelism of the time and the economic
opportunism and growth of the middle class during the Industrial
Revolution. Much of the urge toward the moral reformation of society came from the image of a revitalized and victorious popular
Protestantism. In effect, this channeled reform along rather definite
lines for a time; reform meant leadership, reform from above, and this
implied reform by example, the need for Christian stewardship of
social progress. It also frequently confused reform with charity, the
latter being a pet rallying cry of the increasingly prosperous industrial middle class. But however Nonconformist the religiously oriented
reformers chose to be regarding denominational autonomy, they never
questioned the assumption that any reform undertaken would be

undertaken within the existing social and political system. They were reformers, not revolutionaries—either in morals or politics.

This was not always to be true. Reform was to take quite radical forms of expression. Essential moral precepts were to be questioned and overturned. But whether or not the spirit of reform was identified with Nonconformists, utilitarians, utopians, or radicals, it had one constant element: The belief that man was basically good, could be taught, improved, and was capable of infinite progress because he was capable of cooperating with his fellow beings. What really needed alteration was man's environment, the reformers began to say. Progress through cooperation springing from fundamental human goodness and altruism —that was the ubiquitous thought of the social reformers.

No man bent on reform shook English complacency as much as *Jeremy Bentham* (1748-1832). Bentham himself credited his departure into radicalism to a reading of Hume, particularly the *Treatise of Human Nature,* and it is most evident that at least in spirit the Benthamite creed is Humean. The young Bentham was initially an unquestioning Tory and was the product of a family of some material well-being. Since Bentham was a lawyer by profession, the impact of Hume's radical empiricism took the form of an early zeal to reform British jurisprudence. Bentham's chief objections to the law as it stood were that it rested on imprecise moral mechanisms and that it was a haphazard collection of customs and personal opinions rather than a scientific code of principles. For much of his life Bentham was engaged on this project, expanding it to include political reflections. Juristic reform, he soon found, also required a statement of ethics, and Bentham turned his attention to the task of framing a body of moral ideas. His ethical thought in the long run proved more significant than his strictures against the common law, although he did influence a number of penal and procedural reforms.

Due to his association with James Mill (the father of John Stuart Mill), Bentham became more directly concerned with political action; he became a leading force among the growing radical faction (led in the House of Commons by Bright and Cobden). These radicals, primarily by needling and cajoling the Whigs, succeeded in influencing social legislation to a degree not commensurate to their numbers. Consequently, Bentham's reputation grew; he became a sort of radical seer. He wrote on virtually every topic of general concern, producing a constant stream of pamphlets and essays. Basically, the Benthamite doctrine (there were those who described themselves as "Benthamites") is contained in three works: *A Fragment on Government* (1776), *Principles of Morals and Legislation* (1789), and *Theory of Legislation* (1802). The bulk of Bentham's important writing falls within what could be called his "middle years."

Bentham was the founder of a movement called *utilitarianism*. This was primarily a school of thought concerned with ethics, but it had a direct political application, too. The very nature of utilitarianism as an ethical doctrine made that political credo inevitable. What Bentham did was to revive hedonism in a sweeping fashion and extend its essential meaning into the social sphere. Hedonism, as you may recall, suggests that the moral equation consists of the pursuit of pleasure and the avoidance of pain. Bentham was convinced that this was the inescapable nature of all moral judgment. He welded to this fundamental hedonistic conception three other ideas: (1) The process of maximizing pleasure and minimizing pain is no unsystematic affair. It requires the existence of a definite scale or continuum of consequences—in short, it requires *quantification* of the pleasure-pain axis. (2) Happiness or pleasure, whatever it is, is wholly a matter of subjective judgment. The individual alone can decide, and his judgment alone has validity. Bentham once remarked that "the quantity of pleasure being equal, pushpin is as good as poetry." [1] (3) Although the decision as to what provides happiness—and hence the good—is a matter of sheer individual selection, groups of people within a society do and must make up their minds on political questions in the same way. Once again, it becomes a matter of quantification, of summing up the total possibilities for the attainment of pleasure and the reduction of pain. This can be done among large numbers of people as it is done by the individual. Hence, the fundamental proposition of the utilitarians becomes: "the greatest good for the greatest number."

Bentham worked out this "calculus of pleasure" with a humorless deliberation that is one of his characteristics. It is, argues Bentham, a simple matter of ethical arithmetic. Considering the individual by

---

[1] Pushpin appears to have been a popular parlor-game of the time, somewhat similar to tiddlywinks. The point Bentham seeks to underscore by the quaint illustration is that no objective standard of value exists. Value can be defined only in terms of quantitative pleasure. Thus if one gets more of a "kick" out of pushpin or playing pinball machines than reading Milton, then there is more good in the former. Bentham is willing to accept the social implications of this, too. If TV *Sturm und Drang* (loosely, in this context, "blood and thunder") gives pleasure to more people than symphony concerts and serious drama, then on with Naked City and Bronco Lane!

himself, the value of a pleasure or a pain must be judged in terms of *intensity, duration, certainty* or *uncertainty, propinquity* or *remoteness*. Consider, then, Bentham's recommendation in a hypothetical situation: Jones is faced with a moral dilemma. If he sneaks out of the house for a game of golf, his wife will make life distinctly uncomfortable upon his return, since he has promised—tentatively—to paint the lawn furniture. But Jones is a keen golfer, weather conditions are favorable, and his friends await him at the first tee. What is Jones to do? Jones must, according to Bentham, tally up quantitatively and accurately the total pleasure presented by both courses of action. The same procedure must be done for all possible pain. When the two are compared, Jones will know which course of action will constitute the good for him.

This mechanism for moral decision is Bentham's "principle of utility." In the opening of his *Introduction to the Principles of Morals and Legislation* he writes:

> Nature has placed mankind under the governance of two sovereign masters, *pain* and *pleasure*. It is for them alone to point out what we ought to do, as well as to determine what we shall do. On the one hand the standard of right and wrong, on the other the chain of causes and effects, are fastened to their throne. They govern us in all we do, in all we say, in all we think: every effort we make to throw off our subjugation will serve but to demonstrate and confirm it. In words a man may pretend to abjure their empire; but in reality he will remain subject to it all the while. The *principle of utility* recognizes this subjugation, and assumes it for the foundation of that system, the object of which is to rear the fabric of felicity by the hands of reason and law. Systems which attempt to question it, deal in sounds instead of senses, in caprice instead of reason, in darkness instead of light.[2]

Two consequences logically follow from Bentham's ethic: (1) He reduces all moral questions to a sensationalist psychology—human behavior is restricted to stimuli presented by the senses. (2) What is good is always relative. Good can be thought of only in shifting terms, dependent upon changing human desires and definable only in terms of self-interest. The good can only be what someone thinks it is. If Jones, our former golfing associate, things he gets pleasure out of counting blades of grass, the only criterion for judgment must be his. The good is both relative to subjective appraisal and quantitative. If, for example, a majority of the citizens wish to ban the practice of medicine, no standard of good could be appealed to other than their

---

[2] Jeremy Bentham, *An Introduction to the Principles of Morals and Legislation*, Chapter 1, Section I.

self-conscious desires. True, they might make an error while applying
the calculus of pleasure to the situation, but there exists no a priori
means of judgment. The evaluation of whether the decision does in
fact offer the greatest good for the greatest number must be left to
experience.

What prevents Bentham's theory from advocating or at least tacitly
condoning unlimited individual egotism? Is Bentham's concept likely
to create a madhouse of conflicting individual desires with no means
of reconciliation, save perhaps brute force? Bentham would answer
along these lines: It is true that ethics should be defined as duty to
oneself. But "insofar as his happiness, and that of any other person or
persons whose interests are considered, depend upon such parts of
his behavior as may affect the interests of those about him," the individual has a duty to others. This, Bentham would argue, is the
secondary aspect of ethics. But what would cause an individual to
acknowledge this secondary duty, to moderate his own desires in the
face of those of his neighbor? Prudence, Bentham would reply, since
if the individual seeks to gain pleasure, it is rational to suppose he
must do so within the range of social involvement. Self-interest would
dictate a cooperative attitude. Beyond this, Bentham asserts, *sympathy,
love of amity and reputation,* and *reasoning faculties* mitigate a rapacious individualism and provide motives for social harmony.

Political utilitarianism is an extension of this doctrine. Bentham
describes the process this way:

> Take an account of the *number* of persons whose interests appear to
> be concerned, and repeat the above process with respect to each.
> *Sum up* the numbers expressive of the degrees of *good* tendency, which
> the act has, with respect to each individual, in regard to whom the
> tendency of it is *good* upon the whole; do this again with respect to
> each individual, in regard to whom the tendency is *bad* upon the
> whole. Take the *balance,* which if on the side of *pleasure,* will give
> the personal *good tendency* of the act, with respect to the total
> number or community of individuals concerned; if on the side of pain,
> the general *evil tendency,* with respect to the same community.[3]

This is a characteristically phrased, recipe-like Benthamite description of "the greatest good for the greatest number." In effect, it is a
thundering endorsement of absolute majority rule. It defines the entirety of political right in terms of the will of the greatest number,
since the only concept of rightness lies in the largest possible realization
of happiness. Only Rousseau offers a comparable justification for

---

[3] *Ibid.,* Chapter 4, Section VI.

political decision resting upon the expression of majority opinion. But where Rousseau is mystic, Bentham is mundane in the extreme. But this deification of the majority raises a number of issues for Bentham. How is majority rule to be reconciled with individual rights? And what is the role of law and government once the omnipotence of the majority is accepted?

Three propositions shape Bentham's ideas concerning the individual in his political relationships. First, he rejects completely the assumption of natural rights. These he denies on logical grounds; what rights a man possesses, he contends, are positive rights that can only be legally granted him. The source of law, positive law, is the utilitarian principle. What legal rights a man has depends on what effect the possession of these rights will have upon the general welfare. Rights, for Bentham, are not born of metaphysical verities, but of social usefulness. He dismisses, as well, the idea of the social contract as a simplistic fairy tale.

Secondly, equality can be dismissed on the same grounds. Equality is not a natural or metaphysical state; equality or the lack of it depends on communal usefuless. What is to be avoided, argues Bentham, is abitrary, and hence useless, differences in status. The effect of utilitarianism was distinctly in the direction of egalitarian change, but such a leveling influence was not rooted in any abstract principle of human equality.

Thirdly, individual liberty is subject to reasonable restraints. It is clear that if "the greatest good for the greatest number" is the paramount axiom, then the liberty of the individual is subject to considerable limitation. For Bentham, these limits are imposed by legal protection against encroachment of one individual upon the other in a manner that would be detrimental to the general welfare if the individuals were permitted unrestricted action. A case in point is the matter of private property. Bentham retains the institution of private property on the ground that it creates a stabilizing influence within society. But ownership is not an absolute right; the law can adjust inequities and even redistribute. In short, individual liberty is permissible to the degree that it serves the principle of utility.

It is convenient to deal with Bentham's ideas of government under three main headings: legislation, reform of governmental structure, and jurisprudence. The aim of legislation is perhaps already clear: It is to further the public welfare by enactments based on the principle of utility. For Bentham, this means that legislation is principally negative, regulatory, and limited in scope. Government in general is

to act more as a means of enforcing legal obligation than as a creative social innovator. People ought to be left to their own devices,
except when their selfishness infringes on the general good. The governing function, thinks Bentham, is somewhat akin to that of refereeing.
The omnipotent majority does not, however, imply the omnicompetent
legislator. The Benthamite ideal of a legislative system is one of leadership by exhortation rather than coercion, although Bentham advocates
strict law enforcement.

His proposal for governmental reform is interesting in light of subsequent events. His adherence is to full representative government,
and this is to exist on a base of universal manhood suffrage. How else,
he reasons, can the majority actually speak? He also proposes that the
length of a legislature be only one year to insure against political
entrenchment and to make legislators more responsive to the public
will. Voting, in Bentham's governmental plan, is to be entirely by
ballot. The blueprint is a rather complete exposition of now familiar
popular democratic practices. Bentham especially heralds the coming
age in one important regard. He conceives government as an informa-
tion-gathering agency, a fact-finding research organization that serves
the populace as a source of factual data, technical advice, and supplementary services to commerce and welfare. His notion vaguely resembles the operation of a Department of Agriculture extended across
the range of all governmental concerns. He also expresses views
favorable to unicameralism and republicanism.

Bentham begins his consideration of political affairs with a blistering
attack on the state of British jurisprudence, particularly on the revered
Blackstone.[4] The main tenet of his critique is the confusion and irrationality of the common law. It is far too loose and unsystematic to
suit Bentham. In its place should come a law far more explicit and
positive in character. One major step in the right direction would be
the development of a code—Bentham is reputed to have coined the
word "codification." To do this, of course, would drastically alter the
whole nature of the common law. He ruthlessly castigates the mythology and obscurity of legal proceedings; law should be simply
stated and universally understood. He lashes out with particular vio-

---

[4] Sir William Blackstone (1723-1780) was the author of the most influential
commentary on the common law since Coke's. His *Commentaries on the Laws of
England* (1765-1769) both markedly affected the subsequent development of
common law and served as a text for generations of lawyers coming after. His
influence in colonial America was particularly strong. It has been said that there
were as many copies of Blackstone's *Commentaries* in the Colonies just before
the American Revolution as there were in England at the same time.

lence at juristic administration in general and judges in particular. He urges comprehensive penal reforms, as well. The details of Bentham's voluminous criticisms are not of any importance here, but suffice to say that they dominated thought about legal reform for virtually a century.[5]

Bentham's economic opinions are largely those he acquired by reading Adam Smith's *Wealth of Nations*. He endorses free trade, free and vigorous economic competition, and *laissez-faire*.[6] He incorporates into his early utilitarianism the so-called "classical" theories of Smith, Ricardo, and, to some extent, the demographer, Malthus.[7] He shows great faith in the possibility of reducing political economy to laws. In economics as well as other areas of human behavior, Bentham sought and believed he could find principles as elegant and apparently incontestable as the physics of Newton.

Bentham's proposals for reform were radical in the true sense. They dealt with the roots of the matter. While it is undeniable that many of the recommendations he made in the political and legal area did in fact materialize, it is equally just to point out that even by the close of the nineteenth century Bentham's philosophy appeared both naïve and antique. His psychology is hopelessly oversimplified; his political argument has a distinctly ivory-tower hue; his ethics are candidly untenable. Why, then, did Bentham cause such a stir; why does he receive such a favorable retrospective estimation; and why does his name, as well as the term associated with him, "utilitarianism," continue to be invoked?

In the first place, Jeremy Bentham gave a voice to an age. True, he

---

[5] Bentham's main legal disciple was John Austin, who systematized the Benthamite analytical theory. [See his *Lectures on Jurisprudence* (1832).] Austin's theory is noteworthy because it contains a view of sovereignty which endows it with profound legal significance (law is defined as the "command of the sovereign"). Austin's ideas prompted vigorous rebuttal, especially from Sir Henry Maine and the "historical jurists" who rejected Austin's positivism in favor of an evolutionary and customary explanation for the genesis of law. See Maine's *Ancient Law*.

[6] *Laissez-faire*: literally, "let (it) do" (leave it alone) imperative mood. The belief that government should interfere as little as possible in the economic processes of society.

[7] Thomas Robert Malthus (1766-1834) startled his time with an essay entitled *Essay on Population* (1798). The main theme of his treatise was that while population increased geometrically, means of human subsistence increased only arithmetically, so that eventually the planet would have more people than it could support. However, argued Malthus, poverty, disease, famine, and war provide natural checks on population growth.

urged a thesis considerably more radical than the spirit of the times
would accept, but the major aspects of his thought put flesh on the
bones of liberalism. Prior to him, liberalism was a nebulous collection
of sentiments and rationalizations. After him, it became a far more
cogent body of ideas. Classical liberalism, in its full flowering in the
first half of the nineteenth century, had a political creed at one with
Bentham. Liberalism meant freedom from restraint or arbitrary curtailment of individual opportunity, the development of administrative
government, and, lastly, the recognition of the value of self-help, individual initiative, and private resourcefulness. Moreover, liberalism
was a political creed of the new rich, the middle classes seeking status
and anxious to alter a social system in which an aristocratic class enjoyed the greater privilege.[8] No one spoke more disparagingly of the
upper classes than did Bentham (unless it is the nineteenth-century
American economist Thorstein Veblen [9]), and the father of utilitarianism was vehement against the virtual control of politics in England by
a single, entrenched class. This was something the emerging middle
class could take to heart.

Secondly, Bentham was the first man in England to assemble (sometimes in a rather incoherent fashion) those influences, from Locke on-
ward, that when fitted together spelled democracy. This was not the
gentleman's democracy of Locke, the folk mysteries of Rousseau, the
traditional libertarianism of Burke, not even the republican sentiments
of the Whig Liberals, but popular, representative democracy, complete with universal suffrage and education, economic opportunity, and
an elimination of the élitist ritualism of the past. Whether or not
Bentham's society is attractive or admirable may be contested, but
that it was in fact a giant step toward the democratic societies of our
century is beyond question.

Some of the impetus for social and political reform in Britain was
provided by French inspiration, becoming a zeal for a scientific treatment of social problems. Paramount among these Gallic innovators was
the mathematician-philosopher *Auguste Comte* (1798-1857). Among
his claims to fame, Comte was responsible for the invention of the
word "sociology"—and one can still argue whether this has proved

---

[8] For an interesting and entertaining account of this, perhaps the best source
is H. G. Wells' novel *Tono Bungay.*

[9] See Veblen's *Theory of the Leisure Class* for a provocative and perhaps irritating discussion of this point.

in the long run to be a boon to the language. Comte's eccentricities must be immediately noted, if not accorded significance. In the late stages of his life, he devoted himself to what he labeled "cerebral hygiene"—this consisted of limiting his reading to his own works exclusively.

But these curiosities should not detract from Comte's not inconsiderable importance as a social thinker. He was convinced that what he called a *positive* philosophy could be developed. By "positive" [10] Comte meant that the history of science reveals that it is possible to introduce precision and exactitude into this field of knowledge. Why not, then, into philosophy in general and the study of human behavior in particular? Comte was persuaded that one of the real barriers to creating a "science of society" in the past had been the myths of religion and metaphysics. Indeed, the history of science—and the history of the human race, for that matter—shows that progress occurs according to the "Law of the Three Stages." Human knowledge, according to Comte, first goes through a *theological* stage. Man makes the world intelligible by conjuring up gods and supernatural forces. The second stage is the *metaphysical*. This is the phase of abstract ideas, eternal principles, and absolute forms. Finally, the last and most elevated stage is reached, the *positive*. Here man is concerned only with the agreement between knowledge and observable fact. All knowledge becomes akin to the "immutability of natural laws." [11]

Comte's sociology is an attempt to posit a positivistic theory of society, to frame "laws of phenomena." His approach is initially mathematical; he contends that the study of society means statics, the constants and dynamics, the laws of progression. The specifics of Comte's

---

[10] It is from this use of the word "positive" that the term "Positivism" is derived in order to classify a broad school of philosophy. Charles Frankel, a prominent contemporary positivist, has offered this informal definition: "It stands for a certain temper of mind as well as a particular system of philosophy. As a temper of mind, positivism has a matter-of-fact orientation, and in general, subordinates questions about what ought to be or what must necessarily be to questions of what in fact is. Positivistically inclined thinkers have usually been suspicious of theological and metaphysical doctrines as covert attempts to vindicate things as they are, and they have felt that human inquiry should be restricted to those questions to which fairly definite answers can be given. The positivistic temper of mind is primarily interested in the solution of particular problems, one by one, rather than in the construction of elaborate world-views," from "Positivism," in *A History of Philosophical Systems*, V. Ferm, ed. (New York: Philosophical Library, 1950), p. 329.

[11] The most lucid account of the "Law of the Three Stages" (and Comte's thought in general in brief treatment) can be found in Harald Hoffding, *A History of Modern Philosophy* (New York: Dover Publications, Inc., 1955), Volume II, pp. 320-360.

theory need not be dealt with here; the feature of it that is most
intriguing in our context is his concept of progress. In his elaboration
of the inevitability of progress he links the positive stage with industrialization. The forces of production are the significant facts of social
life; one of the by-products of industrialization, Comte asserts, is the
union of the proletariat and the positive philosophy. The remaking
of society in terms of political institutions will come about from the
mounting demand of the workers for fuller development of their minds
(Comte works out a system of positive education for this) and from
the need for useful work. Comte even advances ideas on the riddle of
full employment.

It is unfortunate that Comte's deep-seated belief in the fact that
intelligence and altruism would continually enlarge as men became
more socially interdependent led him in later life into bizarre mys-
ticisms. He created a "religion of humanity," personified humanity as
a deity, and ordained an order of positivist priests. He had in fact
constructed an elaborate utopia, not only visionary, but ludicrous.

Comte's influence in Britain centered principally on *John Stuart
Mill* (1806-1873). John Stuart was the son of Bentham's close colleague,
James Mill, and that dedicated gentleman imposed on his offspring an
educational preparation so strenuous that it is a wonder that the boy
survived. John Stuart learned Greek at three; arithmetic and Latin
soon followed. By early manhood, the younger Mill had, for all practical purposes, digested human knowledge under his father's watchful
eye. Here was a prodigy to rank with Alexander and Mozart. While
still a boy, he had become a participant in the Benthamite movement.
But this frenzied erudition was bound to take its toll, and Mill suffered
a collapse at twenty-one—although he stanchly refused in his *Auto-
biography* (1873) to attribute this physical and emotional disturbance
to his father's educational ambitions. Mill spent most of his adult life,
from 1822 to 1857, as an employee of the East India Company, where
his duties apparently gave him ample opportunity to write. His first
major effort was his *System of Logic* (1843), and his most renowned
piece, *On Liberty*, was published in 1859. The complete list of Mill's
works is as impressive as his personal life was singularly ordinary, save
for a three-year stint in the House of Commons after his retirement at
India House. In Commons, Mill was admired for his learning and
intellectual courage, but he was too radical on religious matters to

suit his constituents. The great Liberal stateman, Gladstone, called him the "Saint of Rationalism." [12]

Mill began his intellectual life a convinced Benthamite; utilitarianism was his creed, empiricism his orientation. He remained dedicated to the principles of utilitarianism and never ceased to be a thorough empiricist, but he developed misgivings about Bentham's ethics. It was not that he doubted Bentham's main thesis regarding the greatest good for the greatest number, but both on an individual and collective basis, Mill began to entertain doubts as to whether pleasure or happiness were to be determined only quantitatively. Was there not another factor to be considered? Was not happiness to be judged *qualitatively* as well? Surely, Mill reflects, some pleasures are more laudable than others, loftier, and morally more significant. Should not this factor be taken into account?

Mill decides that qualitative value is involved in the utilitarian principle. But when Mill advances this argument, the consequences ought immediately to be noted. If one can classify pleasures qualitatively, then an appeal must be made to some preconceived standard of quality. It was this very situation that Bentham sought to deny. It is indisputable that Mill reintroduces the notion of moral standards. To many students of Mill, this shifting of ethical ground from Benthamism is the result of Mill's own more sensitive moral nature, his uneasiness in the face of Bentham's radical dismissal of objective morality.[13] Some, too, have suggested that Wordsworth or Coleridge influenced him in this connection. It is not unlikely that some such subjective feeling is the origin of Mill's ethical attitude. On logical grounds, however, this argument is highly suspect. How can you appeal to a standard and still deny the objective existence of that standard? Mill attempts to get around this problem by arguing that happiness cannot be pursued directly and that only by *disinterestedness*—the emergence from concern for self to the concern for the welfare of one's fellow humans—can it be attained. This transformation, posits Mill, provides a qualitative base for the appraisal of happiness. He asserts that the Christian golden rule was "the complete spirit of the ethics of utility." But again logical consistency may be questioned. Many critics of Mill have pointed out that he cannot account adequately for why an in-

---

[12] Charles Evart Gladstone, celebrated as he was as a great Parliamentarian, the leader of the Liberals, Disraeli's stout opponent in debate, was also at times given to inaccurate statements. To classify Mill as a rationalist certainly throws some doubt on Gladstone's philosophical insights.

[13] Mill was quite aware of this rejection of Bentham. He once remarked, "And I am Peter, who denied his master."

dividual should desire to promote the general welfare if the basis of moral value is individual realization of happiness. Mill would answer this objection by insisting that the individual is so completely immersed in the social fabric that it is impossible to conceive of happiness as anything but a shared experience. Mill argues moreover that if "A's happiness is a good, B's a good, C's a good, etc., the sum of all these goods must be a good." Nonetheless, Mill's ethical view contains a yawning perplexity, and its appeal is more to ethical sensitivity than to logical fastidiousness.

On Liberty is the most striking of Mill's efforts. It has considerable literary merit; it has been compared as a statement of the ideal of freedom with Milton's *Areopagitica* (perhaps a bit uncritically). It has the ring of intense sincerity; it is frankly emotional. But its fascination arises from Mill's attempt to bring the freedom of the individual into harmony with the aim of promoting the general welfare. Need individual freedom and the general welfare be at variance? No, answers Mill. Freedom is a good in its own right, but certain adjustments are required. The general welfare implies authority, and authority and liberty have long contested. The very first sentence of *On Liberty* sets out this problem:

> The subject of this Essay is not the so-called Liberty of the Will, so unfortunately opposed to the misnamed doctrine of Philosophical Necessity; but Civil, or Social Liberty: the nature and limits of power which can be legitimately exercised by society over the individual.[14]

Mill's response is an eloquent plea for the individual, for an open society, for freedom of opinion, for variety and flexibility, and all of these aim at one goal: the opportunity to develop the human personality. In his libertarian conviction, Mill disowns Bentham's mechanistic state, and he spells out the dangers as well as the virtues of majority rule. Mill sees in absolute majority rule, as Bentham conceived it, threats to individual freedom of thought and to minorities espousing unpopular causes. The goal of an open society cannot be attained if nonconformity is crushed by an unchecked majority.

The following passage deserves quotation in full:

> Like other tyrannies, the tyranny of the majority was at first, and still is vulgarly, held in dread, chiefly as operating through the acts of the public authorities. But reflecting persons perceived that when society is itself the tyrant—society collectively over the separate individuals who compose it—its means of tyrannising are not restricted to

---

[14] John Stuart Mill, *On Liberty*, Chapter 1, Introduction.

the acts which it may do by the hands of its political functionaries. Society can and does execute its own mandates: and if it issues wrong mandates instead of right, or any mandates at all in things with which it ought not to meddle, it practices a social tyranny more formidable than many kinds of political oppression, since, though not usually upheld by such extreme penalties, it leaves fewer means of escape, penetrating much more deeply into the details of life, and enslaving the soul itself. Protection, therefore, against the tyranny of the magistrate is not enough; there needs protection also against the tyranny of the prevailing opinion and feeling; against the tendency of society to impose, by other means than civil penalties, its own ideas and practices as rules of conduct on those who dissent from them; to fetter the development, and, if possible, prevent the formation, of any individuality not in harmony with its ways, and compels all characters to fashion themselves upon the model of its own. There is a limit to the legitimate interference of collective opinion with individual independence; and to find that limit, and maintain it against encroachment, is as indispensable to a good condition of human affairs as protection against political despotism.[15]

In pressing for a "wide open" freedom of thought, the encouragement of dissent, and the toleration of minority views, Mill is not merely expressing a distaste for social conformity. Truth, he suggests, is most likely to be arrived at by the sharing of points of view; no one opinion holds a monopoly of truth, and by supressing opinion truth may be stifled. Truth is *not*, for Mill, what the largest number of people say it is. Truth is experience intelligently reflected on.

The justification for the free society rests not only in the greater possibility of arriving at truth. The free society, comments Mill, is vital for the creation of those conditions whereby the human personality can develop to its greatest extent and acquire subsequent moral and intellectual scope. Mill refers to this as *individuality*. The repressive society, the conformist community, throttles human development. Mill cites Calvinism as an example of this. He contrasts the Greek ideal of self-development.[16] Counsels Mill:

> It is not by wearing down to uniformity all that is individual in ourselves, but by cultivating it, and calling it forth, within the limits imposed by the rights and interests of others, that human beings become a noble and beautiful object of contemplation; and as the works partake the character of those who do them, by the same process

---

[15] *Ibid.*, Chapter 1.

[16] In a rather witty passage, Mill comments: "It may be better to be a John Knox than an Alcibiades, but it is better to be a Pericles than either; nor would a Pericles, if we had one in these days, be without anything good which belonged to John Knox." (*Ibid.*, Chapter 3.)

human life also becomes rich, diversified, and animating, furnishing more abundant aliment to high thoughts and elevated feelings, and strengthening the tie which binds each individual to the race, by making the race infinitely better worth belonging to.[17]

What about the original question? What are the limits of individualism? When can society legitimately curtail individual liberty? To begin with, Mill explains that freedom of opinion and freedom of action are not the same thing. Complete freedom of opinion can be extended without detriment to the society, but the same cannot be said for complete freedom of action. Opinion and thought are, after all, only ideationally offensive, but action can constitute a threat or a nuisance. Individual action, so long as its effect is confined solely to the individual and contributes to the individual's development, is beyond social censure, but such action often does touch upon the private rights and interests of others and in so doing restricts their own freedom for personal development. When action so impinges, society can legitimately restrain. But Mill sturdily urges "original experiments in living" and defends these on an individual basis. Of course drunkenness or other vices, however limited in effect to the individual, can be repressed by society, since they can hardly be "original" experiments—or as Mill puts it: "It is merely desired to prevent generation after generation from falling over the same precipice which has been fatal to their predecessors." But beyond these twin limits—action detrimental to others and the established vices—Mill insists upon individual liberty of action. In *On Liberty*, Mill draws ever tighter a cordon of limitations on societal interference with the individual.

Mill realizes that when he speaks of society as doing anything of a regulatory character, what is really being discussed is political institutions. His *Considerations on Representative Government* seeks to clarify the role of these institutions. Mill's view of the state is both utilitarian and unswervingly popular. His defense of popular democracy (as against the ideally enlightened despot) is twofold: (1) The rights of citizens are only secure when the citizens are in a position to stand up for them. (2) Prosperity is increased in proportion to the "amount and variety of the personal energies enlisted in promoting it." In substance, this means a government built upon universal participation and the principle of legislative supremacy. The crucial issues of political arrangement are, in this case, legislative ones. And it is with the legislative aspect of government that Mill encounters two broad problems: how to cope with the majority as a threat to individual rights and how

---

[17] *Ibid.*, Chapter 3.

to secure intelligent political leadership. Mill concludes that he has found a way out of the first difficulty by proposing a system of *proportional* representation. The second objective is to be realized by the introduction of a plural vote—the granting of additional votes on the basis of education, training, and even moral qualities. Both proportional representation and the plural vote would insure, Mill confidently assures us, that individualistic popular democracy would be able to withstand its most insidious threat: repression of freedom of thought and the leveling of society without regard to intellectual and moral worth. If equal and universal suffrage must be, Mill argues that proportional representation alone might be a sufficient check. However, in a revealing passage Mill defends the need for the plural vote:

> But if the best hopes which can be found on this subject were certainties, I should still contend for the principle of plural voting. I do not propose the plurality as a thing in itself undesirable, which, like the exclusion of a part of the community from the suffrage, may be temporarily tolerated while necessary to prevent greater evils. It is not useful, but hurtful, that the constitution of the country should declare ignorance to be entitled to as much political power as knowledge. The American institutions have imprinted strongly on the American mind that any one man (with white skin) is as good as any other; and it is felt that this false creed is nearly connected with some of the more unfavourable points in American character.[18]

Mill's additional thoughts on government are varied and occasionally surprising. He shows little interest in Bentham's advocacy of administrative efficiency and procedural refinement. He opposes the use of the ballot (again contrary to Bentham) on the supposition that it creates the impression that voting is a right, while in reality, Mill states, it is a trust. Secrecy in connection with voting, argues Mill, is pernicious. He is against paying legislators a salary, and he recommends what is for the time a rather unusual set of conditions for the franchise (exclusive of the plural vote). He favors universal adult suffrage (women included), but the voter must be able to read, write, do sums, and be a taxpayer. Mill also urges a thorough reform of the House of Lords.

Three tendencies arise in the political thought of Mill that set him apart from the orthodox Benthamites and render him a bridge between the early radicals and the "eminent" Victorians. In the first place, Mill

---

[18] John Stuart Mill, *Considerations on Representative Government*, Part II, Chapter 8.

considerably elevates the moral tone of utilitarianism, even if at the sacrifice of logical cogency. Secondly, he injects a spirit of more comprehensive humanitarianism, more "humaneness," if one dare use that seemingly redundant qualification. Mill recognizes far more fully than did Bentham the variety and range of human nature. Thirdly, Mill is far more cautious about exclaiming sanguine hopes for inevitable progress. He is more keenly aware of the difficulties inherent in political reform and more analytical in dealing with political processes.

Conversely, Mill, for all his attention to logic, is careless and overly facile in the presentation of his positions.[19] He is frequently vague and inexplicit in pivotal places; he almost invariably fails to provide sound justifications for his insights, some perceptive and some spontaneously superficial. He is untroubled by glaring circularities and paradoxes, and he can be accused with some justice of declining to deal with issues that suggest unpalatable consequences. Mill lacks any substantial originality and, regrettably, his synthesizing of other points of view is often chaotic and fragmentary. Oddly, considering his fondness for systematic exposition, he rarely organizes the body of his thoughts in orderly progression.

Taken together, Bentham and Mill both failed to create a cogent philosophy of liberalism. Significant and influential as many of their ideas were, they were taken piecemeal and absorbed into new ideologies that arose as classical liberalism began to disintegrate with the turn of the century. Neither Bentham nor Mill could prevent the liberal demise, since their thought rested on a number of tenets which contributed toward that fall. In the last analysis, liberalism succumbed from lack of popular appeal; it was too patly a philosophy of restricted attraction. It was a loose creed, in the end too individualistic for the economic and social pressures that came into being. Its preoccupation with the material, an inheritance from positivism, further confined its drawing power. The ideas of Bentham and Mill appeared, in consequence, in new and startling dress.

One new direction was utopianism (an imprecise label for a baffling assortment of theories contained in anything from literary romances to ideological tracts). Individualism, in a novel and extreme form, was presented by Spencer. Finally, the full circle was reached by the

---

[19] In his *Logic,* Mill sought to prove that mathematics was an empirical science.

appearance of a formal collectivist theory, socialism. How odd, indeed, to discover the name of Jeremy Bentham invoked on behalf of the militant antithesis of individualism.

Saving Karl Marx for the following chapter, early utopian socialism can be illustrated by the person of *Robert Owen* (1771-1858) and extreme individualism by *Herbert Spencer* (1820-1903). In the case of Spencer, this prodigiously active personality poured forth an unending stream of writing, ranging over the spectrum of human knowledge, combining with almost dazzling confusion a myriad of ideological penchants. He was a bombastic, self-taught rebel; Carlyle referred to him as an "immeasurable ass." His *Social Statics* (1850) contained the significant summary of his ideas, and it might be noted that since Darwin's *Origin of Species* did not appear until 1859, Spencer can lay claim to being a pre-Darwinian evolutionist.

Spencer's fundamental thesis is: "Every man has freedom to do all he wills, provided he infringes not the equal freedom of any other man." [20] And he means just that. In political terms, this is in Spencerian outlook the denial of any "ethical authority" for government; political order exists only to protect the "equal freedom." [21] Protection is the only function of a government, internal and external. Spencer denies to the state the right to administer charity and education, arguing that governmental passivity or inaction may be regrettable, but they do not infringe upon freedom, while governmental action, however commendable, would do so. In the broader sense, Spencer's rejection of an activist role for the state rests on his belief in the evolutionary character of life, a sort of trial-and-error *laissez-faire*, individuals left to their own devices, ignorance and wisdom grappling unimpeded. Cannot the state be wise? Can it not gently lead toward the better life? Cannot government act as a remedial force? No, replies Spencer, and he adds:

> Inconvenience, suffering, and death—the penalties attached by nature to ignorance, as well as to incompetence—are also the means of remedying these. It is impossible in any degree to suspend this discipline by stepping in between ignorance and its consequences, without, to a corresponding degree, suspending the process. If to be ignorant were as safe as to be wise, no one would become wise. And all measures which tend to put ignorance upon a par with wisdom, inevitably check the growth of wisdom.[22]

---

[20] Herbert Spencer, *Social Statics,* Chapter 6, Section I.

[21] It is revealing that Spencer entitled a series of political essays *Man Versus the State.*

[22] Spencer, *op. cit., Social Statics,* Chapter 28, Section III.

The excesses of rampant industrialization and the dissatisfactions with liberalism brought cries of protest that insisted upon wholesale change and radical reconstruction. Primarily, these demands for comprehensive reform were concerned with economic and social inequalities and the lamentable conditions of existence that industrialization had brought about for the new working class. Also, whatever form these proposed reforms took, the underlying sentiment was collectivist rather than individualist. The society, the state, these reformers argued, had to take whatever steps were required to insure not only political rights, but economic and social standards. Man became viewed as a creature of essentially material wants.

The proposals for sweeping economic reform fell broadly into two categories: (1) A utopian hope for a new society based upon a growing public conscience and human altruism. (2) The early beginnings of socialism. The utopian and humanitarian approach took root in England, and it was typified by Robert Owen. The socialist conception, far more doctrinaire and systematic in ideology, found receptive soil on the continent, where it became identified with Saint-Simon and Fourier.

Robert Owen was a man with a conscience and a plan. The plan was the establishment of small cooperative communities designed to produce economic justice. He called it the "New Institution." Failing to get much support in Britain for the practical effectuation of his scheme and after a discouraging experiment in Scotland, Owen founded a model community at New Harmony, Indiana. It proved a debacle and for Owen a financial disaster. He then devoted himself to the propagation of cooperative societies in Britain and, for a time, supported the rise of trade unions. Owen was never a political thinker; his writings are largely devoid of thoretical content. Specific proposal and detailed suggestions for practical employment and ameliorization were Owen's forte. He was, however, convinced that large-scale governmental action was the most efficacious means of economic reform. In his *Report for the Relief of the Manufacturing Poor*, Owen advises:

> Until the preventive principles shall become the basis of legislative proceedings, it will be in vain to look for any measures beyond partial temporary expedients, which will leave society unimproved, or involve it in a much worse state.
>
> If such should be the conviction of Government, the change proposed in the management of the poor and unemployed working classes will be much better directed nationally than privately.

In fact, many of the benefits to be derived to society at large will not be realized until the plan becomes national.[23]

Utopian experimentation had its day. The model villages came and went—from New Lanark to Brook Farm. The industrial managers scoffed, and the more hard-bitten radicals smiled patronizingly. It was all too fanciful, too "scientific," and to some, too "undialectical." Yet even Marxism, with its methodical bulk and pseudoscientism, did not discard the utopian incentive. Perhaps the perfectibility of man and society was attainable, provided you found the right system, the correct dialectic, the eternal formula. Surely, declaimed the nineteenth century, all the needed instruments are within our grasp. And it became increasingly apparent that government, in a profusion of forms, offered the nineteenth century the most appropriate tool. Government, bigger government, was necessary even if the best thing that could happen would be the "withering away of the state." Whatever angle of examination one selected, the nineteenth century, with a few colorful exceptions, assumed that the main chore of society was to make itself over and thereby to reach new heights of individual or collective satisfaction. All these notions were predicated, of course, on what is really a psychological premise: All men want things (whatever they may be), possibly the same things, and they recognize their wants as a general rule and are better off to the extent that they acquire what they yearn for. Also, the late nineteenth century began to be convinced that the only way wants could be fulfilled was on a collective or cooperative basis. This widespread conviction about human nature was to be made blindingly explicit. A massive synthesis of psychological, economic, and political factors was to shake the Victorian Age, to reverberate from the Crystal Palace to the Chicago stockyards. It was the Marxian revolution.

. . . for further discussion:

1. Most governments subsidize the fine arts (theatre, ballet, opera, symphony orchestras, art galleries, and even poets and scholars of art) in some form or other. These are invariably enjoyed by minorities of the total population. How would Bentham view this governmental function? Is it justifiable as far as you are concerned?

[23] Robert Owen, *Report to the Committee for the Relief of the Manufacturing Poor*, Section III.

2. Mill warns of the tyranny of the majority in ways other than direct political repression. Is social conformity in the United States today a good illustration of Mill's argument? Speculate on what Mill might think of contemporary life in the United States or Great Britain.

3. Mill advocates limitation of freedom of action, but no limits on freedom of thought and expression. Would you agree with unlimited freedom of thought and expression? When, if ever, does "expression" become dangerous to the general welfare?

4. How might Mill view the development in the United States of a gigantic effort to accelerate the growth of scientific and technological progress— of what has been termed the "Science Machine"? What might Mill's reaction be to this scientific effort being jointly undertaken by private organization and government? Much of this enterprise is conducted in considerable secrecy from the general public. Assuming progress to be desirable, in the nineteenth-century sense, how much concentration of governmental power and freedom from public scrutiny is technological advancement worth, even considering the factor of military security?

. . . for further investigation:

Barker, Ernest, *Political Thought in England, 1848-1914.* New York: Oxford University Press, Inc., 1947.

Baumgardt, David, *Bentham and the Ethics of Today.* Princeton, N. J.: Princeton University Press, 1952.

Bentham, Jeremy, *A Fragment on Government,* F. C. Montague, ed. New York: Oxford University Press, Inc., n.d.

Brinton, Crane, * *English Political Thought in the Nineteenth Century.* New York: Torchbooks, 1962.

Brown, W. J., *The Austinian Theory of Law.* London: John Murray, Publishers, Ltd., 1906.

Comte, Auguste, *A General View of Positivism.* London: Routledge & Kegan Paul, Ltd., 1908.

Davidson, W. L., *Political Thought in England: The Utilitarians from Bentham to Mill.* New York: Oxford University Press, Inc., 1915.

Halévy, Elie, * *The Growth of Philosophical Radicalism.* Boston, Mass.: Beacon Press, Inc., 1955.

Hearnshaw, F. J. C., ed., *The Social and Political Ideas of Some Representative Thinkers of the Victorian Age.* London: George G. Harrap & Co., Ltd., 1930.

Laski, Harold J., * *The Rise of European Liberalism: An Essay in Interpretation.* New York: Barnes & Noble, Inc., 1962.

Maine, Henry, *Ancient Law.* New York: E. P. Dutton & Co., Inc., 1931.

Mill, John Stuart, * *John Stuart Mill's Philosophy of Scientific Method.* New York: Hafner Publishing Co., Inc., 1950.

———, *Utilitarianism, Liberty,* and *Representative Government.* New York: E. P. Dutton & Co., Inc., 1910.

Mises, Ludwig von, *Socialism: An Economic and Social Analysis,* J. Kahane, trans. New Haven, Conn.: Yale University Press, 1959.

Morris, William, *News from Nowhere*. New York: Longmans, Green & Co., Inc., 1935.

Owen, Robert, *A New View of Society and Other Writing*, G. D. H. Cole, ed. New York: E. P. Dutton & Co., Inc., 1927.

Soltau, Roger H., *French Political Thought in the Nineteenth Century*. New York: Russell & Russell, Inc., n.d.

Spencer, Herbert, *Social Statics*. New York: Robert Schalkenbach Foundation, 1954.

14

REVOLUTION AND
REVOLUTIONARIES

There is observable a certain unsophisticated mystique about Karl Marx. He is the father of revolutions and revolutionaries. He must appear as a fiery-eyed zealot, at the very least, preferably depicted with bombs under each arm and a manuscript of a diabolical book, *Das Kapital*, in his rucksack. This image is hard to reconcile with that of a quiet, bearded little man who used to take his lunch in a brown paper bag into the library of the British Museum. Perhaps the final irony is that the best extant photograph of Marx shows him immaculately clad in a dinner jacket.

But let there be no mistake—Karl Marx *was* the fountainhead of revolutions, although his contributions were purely intellectual. He meant to shake his world, and he succeeded eminently. But he began in a much less truculent frame of mind regarding the established institutions of Europe. Early in his life he became a fervent admirer and student of Hegel. He once wrote his father exuberantly that "Hegel has made me see God in the streets!" Throughout his intellectual development, Marx preserved his dedication to Hegel, although he soon disowned Hegel the theist [1] and, to use his own phrase, "turned Hegel right side up."

Karl Marx (1818-1883) first saw the light of day at Treves, Germany, the son of a Christianized Jewish lawyer. He was given a first-class education by his father at Bonn and then at Berlin. Two influences immediately affected him as a student. The first was Hegel, and the second was the writings of the coterie of French socialists and anarchists, especially Proudhon. In 1843, Marx made a pilgrimage to Paris to encounter these gentlemen and also to pursue a journalistic career. His efforts as a member of the Fourth Estate were restricted to the press of the extreme Left and were, consequently, not very rewarding—in material terms at least. Fortunately for him, his closest friend, *Friedrich Engels* (1820-1895), was better fixed financially, being, somewhat incongruously perhaps, the son of a wealthy industrialist. Together Marx and Engels penned the *Communist Manifesto* in 1848, and Marx, forced to flee Germany to avoid arrest for his journalistic exhortations in the abortive uprising of that year, settled in as Engel's house guest in Britain, where the Engels family had connections. Marx's visit lasted some thirty-four years. [2]

Marx's exile in England was a most active one. His major effort was the uncompleted *Capital*, [3] certainly his most expansive work. Besides writing a procession of tracts, Marx played a significant role in the founding of an international political organization to foster the spread of socialism. This organizational work was frequently tempestuous and fraught with internecine strife. Marx personally figured in the organizing of the First Internationale in 1864. Setbacks in France and Germany and the attempts of an anarchist faction to capture the organization led to its eventual end. International communism was, it is needless to point out, subsequently revived.

Marx thought of himself as an economist, not as a political philosopher. He was certainly both and possibly could be described as a

---

[1] *Theism:* the concept that the universe was formed and is controlled by a supernatural entity or personality who exists outside the natural order. The opposite doctrine is *naturalism*.

[2] The first volume of the *Communist Manifesto* was published in 1867, and after Marx's death Engels brought out the two remaining volumes in 1885 and 1895.

[3] For about a decade Marx had seemingly unlikely employment as a correspondent for the *New York Tribune*.

"sociologist." Indeed, Marx could be classified as a psychologist, historian, literary critic, and with other designations that come to mind without contradicting Marx's own labeling of himself. This is so because Marx was entirely convinced that all human activity was the result, not of Hegel's Absolute Spirit (however sound Hegel's methods of historical analysis), but of *economic* motives. Everything could be explained by economic determinants. All of man's preoccupations were reducible to economic causes; human psychology was a complex of material wants; history was the record of the conflict resulting from clashing economic forces.

One need not draw back out of a spirit of scholarly caution. Marx's system stands on the *complete* economic reductionism—morals, art, politics, and even human emotions can be explained by recourse to a dialectical analysis of economic factors. This analytical paradigm of Marx's was Hegel's dialectic with the metaphysics removed (if that is really possible without making the Hegelian dialectic a mere exercise) and one categorical proposition: Man is an economic animal. This proposition replaces the idealistic assumption. This was the process of turning Hegel right side up. But it meant more than that, because it meant a total rejection of Hegelianism.[4] Hegel's theories—regarding knowledge, morals, religion, etc.—must logically be discarded; the only things Hegelian left are the triadic schema and a vague historical determinism to which Marx denies absolute inevitability.

To the extrapolated dialectic, Marx, quite consistently, weds a materialism as complete as his economic reductionism. The universe is matter; man is a biological organism with material wants and needs. That is all. Anything else is worse than fantasy, complains Marx; it is an attempt to keep the working classes in subjugation by means of fear, authority, myth, and superstition. He therefore can dismiss traditional philosophy and religion in one fell swoop. In the place of these conspiratorial doctrines, he proposes the merging of the dialectic with a materialist view of the world. Thus the name that is used to describe Marx's general philosophic position: *dialectical materialism*.

Marxian dialectic is far less encompassing than Hegel's. It does not purport to explain the whole history of man, only a part of it. It deals

---

[4] Marx himself appreciated this. In the preface to *Capital,* he reflects: "My dialectical method is not only different from the Hegelian, but its direct opposite. To Hegel, the life-process of the human brain, i.e., the process of thinking, which under the name of 'the Idea,' he even transforms into an independent subject, is the *demiurge* of the real world, and the real world is only the external, phenomenal form of the 'Idea.' With me, on the contrary, the ideal is nothing else than the material world reflected by the human mind, and translated into forms of thought."

with history only as far back as the origins of private property. The fundamental triad in Marxian dialectic then becomes:

THESIS: The period of "classless individualism," without the exploitation of the class system.

ANTITHESIS: Economic exploitation through capitalism, either feudal or bourgeois.

SYNTHESIS: Communism.

"The history of all hitherto existing society," Marx states, "is the history of class struggle." It is not difficult to see why Marx held this view if the fundamental dialectical set is kept in mind. Classes in society are the result of the exploitive temptations of private property. Marx is never very clear as to just what a "class" in fact is. A strict or consistent definition is not forthcoming; it is better to conceive a class in Marxian terms as a broad social division that merely designates the divisions of power and interest in the interclass conflict. Basically, all history since the innovation of private property, contends Marx, has evidenced two classes: the exploiters and the exploited. In feudal times, this meant "freeman and slave, patrician and plebeian, baron and serf, guildmaster and journeyman." During the capitalistic period, which was an outgrowth of the oppressions of feudalism, the class division was between the bourgeoisie and the proletariat. The former were the capitalists (employers, owners of means of production, managerial groups), the latter were wage earners, the laboring force, having in common no production ownership and thereby compelled to labor as a means of existence.

Marx summarizes his view of the bourgeois class in this stern paragraph:

> The bourgeoisie, wherever it has got the upper hand, has put an end to all feudal, patriarchal, idyllic relations. It has pitilessly torn asunder the motley feudal ties that bound man to his "natural superiors," and has left remaining no other nexus between man and man than naked self-interest, than callous "cash payments." It has drowned the most heavenly ecstasies of religious fervor, of chivalrous enthusiasm, of philistine sentimentalism, in the icy water of egotistical calculation. It has resolved personal worth into exchange value, and in place of the numberless indefeasible chartered freedoms, has set up that single, unconscionable freedom—Free Trade. In one word, for exploitation, veiled by religious and political illusions, it has substituted naked, shameless, direct, brutal exploitation.[5]

---

[5] Karl Marx and Friedrich Engels, *Communist Manifesto,* Section II.

So the struggle is joined, and with the same dialectical movement, the exploited class, the proletariat, must turn upon the bourgeoisie as the capitalist class destroyed the privileged class of feudalism. Marx holds that the victory of the working class is inevitable. This, Marx thinks, is clearly shown by the dialectical process, but also the triumph of the proletariat will be the result of the fatal defects of the capitalist class and the virtues of the working class. Capitalism will destroy itself in the long run by its inherent weaknesses, among which are overproduction and the saturation of markets. The strength of the working class lies in the fact that it possesses the only economic value: labor. In his presentation of the "labor theory of value," Marx means that profit from ownership or financial exchange is unnatural, artificial, and parasitic and that only human labor is actually productive, creating material goods and services. Capitalism is thus resting upon a house of cards, economically speaking.

Marx despises moral judgments. The Marxian ethic is a simple one: The good consists in conforming to the dialectic. Applied this might mean that if the dialectic reveals the triumph of the proletariat, then good moral behavior consists in aiding and abetting the cause of the workers. But Marx is not thoroughly consistent in the matter of moral relativism. He repeatedly mocks the validity of virtue, and yet with equal repetition he implies a multitude of moral judgments. Clearly, exploitation is bad and exploiters wicked; laziness, greed, and selfishness are moral defects, while loyalty, cooperation, and steadfastness of purpose are commendable. Marx's conception of the class war contains an intriguing postulate: It is morally good to support the war of the proletariat against the bourgeoisie because the victory of the former represents a higher phase of the dialectic, *but* all this is true because the dialectic represents the attainment of ends clearly and initially designated as moral and because the proletariat enjoys moral superiority. Put another way, Marx is arguing that it is good to support the good. If he turns Hegel right side up, he turns moral relativism wrong way round. However scientific Marx lays claim to being, his theory is predicated on a submerged moral judgment.

What weapons are to be used in the struggle between the classes? How will the battle be waged? The matter of technique is of great importance in Marxism. Much thought and discussion are devoted to it in Marx and in communist theorists after him. If this appears curious in the light of the inexorable dialectic, it must be kept in mind that Marx announces that the victory of the proletariat is *eventually* certain. Just how soon is another matter. This depends on the vigor and skill of revolutionary programing. While capitalism would topple of its own sins, a good push would hasten the glorious day. History is made by men, he reflects, and only by "the ever expanding union of the workers" can materialistic salvation be attained. But it will come, promises Marx. He predicts:

> The development of modern industry, therefore, cuts from under its feet the very foundation on which the bourgeoisie produces and appropriates products. What the bourgeoisie therefore produces, above all, are its own grave-diggers. Its fall and the victory of the proletariat are equally inevitable.[6]

The revolutionary struggle, as Marx sees it, calls for extreme measures. The technique is one of mounting pressure. This growth of socialist strength has a twofold aspect. First, the movement itself must mature; it must develop from individual workers, then small groups, national unions, and finally international parties. Secondly, the techniques must enlarge from strikes and indoctrination programs into mass movements and, if necessary, civil war. Nothing must be shunned that will facilitate the triumph of the proletariat. Marx assumes that the class war must be conducted along three general principles: (1) Moral and legal restraints must be abandoned, as they are devices of capitalist oppression. (2) Members of the socialist movement must not be recruited solely from the ranks of the workers. All groups within the society must be incorporated into the revolutionary front. Marx mentions particularly the amalgamation of the lower middle class into the proletariat. Eventually socialism must be completely international, entirely cosmopolitan. (3) All class struggle is political struggle. The reform of society cannot be gained, according to Marx, by alteration within the existing political system. Therefore any significant change can be effected only by political means and by overthrowing the political arrangements of society. This thesis is in marked contrast to much of socialist thought both in Marx's time and since; many have argued that economic change alone is all that is required and that this can be done within the existing social order. Socialism, in this view, can coexist with the liberal democratic systems of Europe and America. This evolutionary and constitutional approach Marx emphatically rejects. It was Robert Owen who once said that socialism could come "like a thief in the night." Not so, says Marx, it must come in the maelstrom of political action and revolutionary upheaval.

Assuming, then, that Marx's dialectical speculations are accurate

---

[6] *Ibid.*, Section III.

and his view of the class war valid, what in fact does he propose for the new social order? The answer to this question can be placed into four subdivisions: (1) Marx's view of ideology and his critique of capitalism, (2) the political formulation following the proletarian victory—the vision of the communist utopia, (3) Marxist sociology, and (4) Marx's guesses on the actualization of his theories.

The word "ideology" has become commonplace. Its meaning has been obscured by diverse connotations; it has become a handy catchword for referring to any political or social doctrine. In Marxian language, the word is far more explicit. Ideas, for Marx, are merely the adumbrated outcroppings of the economic facts of life. As such, ideas are rationalizations and half-understood statements about economic realities that lie close to the core of human behavior. An ideology, then, is a body of ideas joined together by a confluence of economic motives. Thus classes, as Marx conceives them, have their own particular ideologies. From Marx's point of view, ideologies are tricky things, objects of suspicion, and careful vigilance and scrutiny are required when dealing with them. They are formidable and dangerous as they are expressions of the only real human concern. The study of ideology, so frequently mentioned in Marx and other communist writers, is important for two reasons, one theoretical, the other practical. First, it can be of great significance if the relationship between ideas and their economic causations can be understood. Marx fails to do this to any substantial degree. Second, ideologies are weapons of undeniable power. The class war is in large measure a contest of rival ideologies, competing aggregations of economically derived ideas. Marx devotes huge sections of his works to the analysis of ideologies, frequently with rather dubious results.

Marx insists that the dialectic reveals that society must be constituted by two classes, that these classes must be in a state of constant hostility, and that one or the other must finally be dominant. This means that a double-barreled chore faces him. He must analyze the ideology of the currently dominant class; he must offer a telling critique of capitalism. Then he must frame a counterideology, the communist creed, as the superior and triumphant alternative. This is the general theme of *Capital*.

The tremendous impact of Marx on European thought is traceable in the main to the ideas contained in this volume. It is a book to be reckoned with, since in it Marx sees, more vividly than any of his contemporaries, the principal currents in the economic and social evolution of the mid-nineteenth century. Marx shows profound appreciation of the consequence of trends just beginning to reveal themselves. Foremost among these is the effect of science. While Marxism contains much pseudoscience, the author of *Capital* could see that the acceleration of scientific progress was bound to create permanent social dislocations and to disrupt economic balances. The technological revolution had just begun, but Marx foresaw with clarity the alterations it would make upon a *laissez-faire* economy. These factors made inevitable a far more interdependent economic life, an infinitely more complex set of economic relationships. In combination, science, as it opened new fields of progress and swept away old dogmas, and technology, as it rendered obsolete many of the existing economic techniques, and the diversification of economic relationships, as it piled up novel problems, lit the fires of social unrest. The ideological pattern shifted quickly; new ideas, confused and inarticulated, mirrored the substantial economic dislocations. In this sense, the Marxian ideological conception could be compared with Freud's view of the ideas of the conscious mind as censored and incomplete fragments or symbols arising out of subconscious knowledge preceding the ideas in time.

The thesis that capitalism is self-destructive is defended by Marx through the introduction of his theory of surplus value. It is this tendency, that of the creation of surplus value, that will in time bring about the overthrow of the bourgeoisie. All the changes brought about by technology hasten this, Marx observes. The new machines bring unemployment, overproduction, and the "boom and bust" cycles of capitalist economics. By "surplus value," Marx means essentially that all goods are produced by human labor. The value of goods depends on the labor that goes into their production.[7] Thus labor is itself goods, or a commodity. But an exchange is necessary; that is, labor is exchanged for the commodities needed to sustain the labor force. But this is never equal; the labor force never receives as much value as it creates. Therefore a surplus of value is created. The employers of labor perpetuate this inequality; surplus value equals profits.

Beyond any ethical reservations about the profit motive as the basis for competitive economics, Marx believes that this continual accumulation of surplus value via the exploitation of the workers, who alone make any concrete or productive contribution to the economic process, must result in an increasingly rapacious capitalism. The end product

---

[7] This is Marx's way of stating what the classical economists of the eighteenth century referred to as the "labor theory of value."

of this ever-mounting avarice will be overproduction, the exhaustion of markets, and the growth of concentrated industrial holdings that will in turn produce monopolistic combines and ever narrowing ownership. The control of wealth will fall to a diminishing number of major entrepreneurs. The accompanying result will be a reduction in the numbers of the loyal bourgeoisie, and these disenchanted middle-class elements will turn to the proletariat as a new locus. But beyond this shift of power, the inescapable result of surplus value will be so appalling to the oppressed classes, the labor force so ruthlessly used, that they will rise up and topple capitalism in a stroke of righteous wrath.

So Marx summarizes the critical defect of capitalism and predicts its downfall. What will replace it once the proletariat has successfully conducted its war of liberation? Certain distinct political consequences will follow, all directed toward the realization of future political objectives. These should be considered first. But the political arrangements recommended by Marx are, after all, means to an end, the propagation of the communist program, both economic and social. The bulk of non-Marxian socialism is content with one goal: to replace the capitalistic system with public control of the means of production and distribution. Communism means far more than that. It differs from garden-variety socialism in five main particulars: (1) It seeks to gain power by revolutionary means. (2) It insists upon a complete political change, not reform within existing political systems. (3) It requires the abolishment of virtually all private property. (4) It calls for blanket economic regulation. (5) It proposes to accompany the imposition of economic change with radical alteration of social relationships.

Following the successful revolution Marx envisions a series of political stages, phases of development. These stages are steppingstones to an ultimate end, and the process through the stages is dependent upon the ideological maturity of the populace. The ultimate end is the classless society and the "withering away of the state" (the phrase is Engels'). This is the great dream, the transcendental side of Marxism. What Marx means by the "classless society" is the complete absence of coercion and its replacement by perfect economic harmony and cooperation, an ideal society of economically sublimated and hence perfectly happy souls. Since the state exists as a coercive force, it can be joyfully dispensed with. The Marxian Eden will have then arrived.

But Marx will not predict when this state of affairs might come about, and he is careful not to underestimate the ponderous strides required in human relationships and the maintenance of plenty before the dream can become a reality. The interim stages are more immediately to be faced. How does one proceed after a rising of ideologically stirred proletarians have destroyed in a surge of violence the existing political order? What comes next?

Marx describes the ensuing period as the "dictatorship of the proletariat." This is rule by the victorious working classes, imposing, with uncompromising resolve, the new order of affairs. But this phase, while existing in theory as the transition to the classless society, does in fact give way to the also temporary expedient of what Engels labels "rule of the élite." The proletariat needs direction; it needs ideological guidance; and it requires political education. This is to be supplied by an élite made up of Marxian intellectuals and ideologically sophisticated revolutionary leaders. During this period, the major face lifting of the society is scheduled to be undertaken.

The primary economic objective of Marx's program is the abolishment of private property. It is the cardinal principle. In the *Communist Manifesto*, he states this unequivocally:

> The distinguishing feature of Communism is not the abolition of property generally, but the abolition of bourgeois property. But modern bourgeois private property is the final and most complete expression of the system of producing and appropriating products, that is based on class antagonism, on the exploitation of the many by the few.
>
> In this sense, the theory of the Communist may be summed up in the single sentence: Abolition of private property.[8]

Since capital is not a personal possession, it is, in Marx's phrase, a "social power"; capital, the means of production, is to become a state monopoly, a completely collectivized and regulated public enterprise. Only the "property of the petty artisan and of the small peasant" are to be immune from collectivization. All are required to work, to contribute, and initially to share on an equal basis, although eventually Marx advocates contribution according to one's abilities and receiving according to one's needs. All the impedimenta of the competitive system are to be replaced by a cooperative production of goods and services. The aim of production is accordingly geared to the collective need.

The social goals of the communist program, as articulated by Marx, are particularly startling to those steeped in the conventions of the nineteenth century, but even today they remain grotesque and repugnant to readers conditioned by the ethical and cultural practices of free societies. Among other things, Marx singles out religion, marriage,

---

[8] Karl Marx and Friedrich Engels, *Communist Manifesto*, Section IV.

and the family as "bourgeois claptrap." Communism, as Marx conceives it and as it remains today, is antithetical to religion. This would obviously be true on philosophic grounds; Marxism is an unwavering materialism. But Marx is not merely concerned with excluding theism from his theory. For him, religion is part of the class war. Since belief in God is an instrument forged by the exploiting classes, religion is a means of subjugation and intimidation—in his famous phrase, "religion is the opiate of the people." Consequently, the Marxian dogma requires a militant atheism, an active program designed to wipe the human mind clean of the religious perversion. The atheistic crusade is both ideological and anticlerical. To the objection that religion contains eternal truths or historical insights, Marx scoffs: "Communism abolishes eternal truths, it abolishes all religion, and all morality, instead of constituting them on a new basis; it therefore acts in contradiction to all past historical experience."

Marx supposes that the shining new society will be improved by the addition of free love—what he rather drolly calls the "community of women." The principal advantage, so he claims, to this system of free and unfettered coupling of the sexes is that it eliminates marriage, which is a Christian and capitalist holdover from medieval darkness. Marx accuses the bourgeoisie, somewhat paradoxically perhaps, of encouraging sexual promiscuity. Prostitution and the practice of adultery Marx lays at the door of the capitalist system. The corrective measure indicated, thinks Marx, is the abolition of private marital partners. Likewise, the family is to be eliminated as a counterrevolutionary force. The family is merely another form of capitalist exploitation, charges Marx, and children must be liberated from the tyrannies of bourgeois home life.

The communist blueprint for the new world just around the corner, as drawn up by Karl Marx, must, the architect advises, become a virtual secular religion, for only fervent and wholly devoted service to its principles will hasten the day that must surely come. The closing lines of the *Manifesto* sound a call for the communist crusade. They have often been quoted:

> The Communists disdain to conceal their views and aims. They openly declare that their ends can be attained only by the forcible overthrow of all existing social conditions. Let the ruling classes tremble at the Communist revolution. The proletarians have nothing to lose but their chains. They have a world to win.
> Working men of all countries, unite! [9]

----

[9] *Ibid.*, Section VI.

It is extremely difficult, perhaps impossible, to approach an evaluation of Marx with dispassion. The history of Marxian criticism itself
mirrors the shifts in popular ideology and the fluctuating tensions of
political warfare. Views of Marx have progressed from a satanic image
to a sincre theoretician to an evil genius to a sort of latter-day Anti-
Christ and a vegetative god of a new and terrible religion. Where do
sense and justice lie? Perhaps two initial observations may help to
clear the atmosphere: First, Marx was not a cynical prophet of a new
despotism. Nor was he a neurotic would-be secular saint. He was
half-scholar and half-propagandist, but he was himself convinced that
in dialectical materialism lay the best hope for an improved lot for
mankind. But, secondly, he was not a benign reformer nor a radical
humanitarian. What he preached was revolution, not a mere scuffling
in the streets over political fleshpots, but the sweeping away of all that
Western society and culture had presumably held precious. Perhaps
the biggest failure in Marx's sheaf of predictions was that Western
Europe would welcome this frightening demolition. It has been pointed
out innumerable times that Marx would have been astonished to learn
that his doctrine would find its first application in Russia, backward
and agricultural. This is likely true, but what transpired was not accidental, and Marx's probable surprise would reveal his huge misassump-
tion. Not understanding and contemptuous of traditions and moral
sentiments, Marx hopelessly underestimated them. Put a bit differently,
Britain, Germany, or France had too much to lose by the adoption of
Marx's recommendations. Even the frenzied barbarous experiments in
social upheaval that gripped Germany and Italy in the twentieth century did not represent a total rejection of the historical and national
continuity of those states, only vicious corruptions of them. Russia, on
the other hand, not only lying in abject poverty, but without the level
societal achievement of Western Europe and, indeed, still partially
but significantly Asiatic, could willingly take the risk, the gamble, so
to speak, for the communist millenium.[10]
   The crippling fallacy in Marxian reasoning is its premature dismissal
of all factors not compatible with its originating assumption. In this
sense, Marxism is neither objective nor scientific (as it claims to be),
because it doggedly refuses to take into account all the data, to treat

---

[10] It is hard to understand how so many were amazed by the communist revolution having its first experiment in Russia. One can only conclude that they were
not very well-read in Russian literature.

seriously the full range of the variables. Such is a logical defect of any reductionism, and in Marxism the reduction of all human behavior to economic motives is particularly rash and specious. Contrary to Marx's sympathetic commentators, this economic reductionism does not appear to be the result of prolonged and diligent analysis. It does not appear to merit the label of a careful inductive conclusion. Quite the contrary, the Marxian economic explanation seems more likely to be a proposition (possibly intuited or ethically suggested) from which deductive inferences are drawn and imposed on the interpretation of events. The dialectical method itself strongly intimates this. And if the interpretation of events, the sheer facts, prove reluctant to accede to the Marxian deductive categories, so much the worse for the facts.

All the difficulty springs from Marx's attempt to establish that dialectical materialism is a value-free and scientifically objective explanation of human affairs. What in fact is the case is that Marx is involved very deeply on a moral level. Indeed, he proceeds from a set of hidden but uncompromisable ethical beliefs. In order to protect and promulgate these, a philosophic justification must be found, and it must be a unique one if it is both to accomplish its moral ends and to take into account the rapid changes in modern society that Marx so lucidly observes. Thus the Marxian philosophy becomes an instrument designed to attack the evils of exploitation, nationalism, greed, inequality of opportunity, poverty, and so on. Marx has the impossible task of being at once Marx, the social scholar, the amoralist, and Marx, the crusader filled with righteous indignation.

Assuming, for the sake of argument, that Marxian theory in fact proceeds from moral assumptions that it publicly and intellectually denies, it must be pointed out that the philosophic position it chooses to adopt is not without serious defects. Regardless of how Marxism begs the ethical question or how simplistic is the economic reductionism, the dialectic and the materialism that it is wedded to have noticeable cracks. The marriage is not the most harmonious. Marx's materialism, as he takes pains to illustrate, is neither mechanical nor deterministic. Yet within this *Weltanschauung* of materiality, the dialectic exists. The dialectic of Marx, no less than that of Hegel, presupposes movement, dynamic process. Hegel accounts for this aspect of his dialectic with considerable cogency, assuming one accepts his premises: Absolute Spirit powers the dialectic on its way. What drives the Marxian dialectic? Some accounting must be made. Spirit, will, ego, necessity, psyche, *élan vital*, biological evolution? There must be some concept of reality that underlies the dialectical process. Marx's possible reply

that man is an economic animal and that the dialectic proceeds from
tensions created by competing economic ideologies and forces is not
very satisfying to the philosophically fastidious. Man may be a biological creature, and this may account for some or all of his acts, but
the leap from biology to economics is a very considerable one. If one
takes materialism seriously, then Marx offers very little basis to justify
the existence of the dialectical development of human affairs.

Moreover, Marxian materialism is candidly rather childish. It is
dated, as it were. The very science Marx professes to admire has done
away with any concept of naïve materialism just as Messrs. Freud and
company have buried such things as associational psychology and
phrenology. What we call the universe is just not that simple, the
scientific brethren tell us; what we call human nature is not that simple
either.

One of Marx's pervasive premises is that peremptory authority is the
indispensable prior step to a society free from coercion. The "dictatorship of the proletariat" is to lead to the classless society; the communi-
zation of the economic and social structure is eventually to eliminate
the ills of managerial autocracy and the linking of function and privilege. In Marx, the transition is frankly mysterious, and the consequences of the imposition of the completely planned and regulated
economy would reasonably lead to industrial, if public, bureaucracy
no less oppressive than that of the replaced entrepreneurs. It would be
unfair to Marx to criticize his theory on the evidence presented by the
experiment in the Soviet Union, but nonetheless it is highly suggestive
that in the first and oldest major state to adopt, virtually in toto, the
Marxist program, there are no signs that the dictatorship of the proletariat in the form of élitist rule shows any signs of "withering away."
And certainly insofar as economic and social life in the Soviet Union
is concerned, there has arisen a managerial or bureaucratic class that
is powerful, apparently rather arrogant, and basking in most unegali-
tarian privilege.

The root difficulty in Marx is his tendency toward the oversimplification of the class struggle. While class antagonisms doubtless have
long existed, Marx's notion of total hostility, a battle to the death,
seems exaggerated, and even if it were the case, his insistence on a
two-class struggle seems too rudimentary. He also displays little
understanding of class mobility, which is the result of his fixed theory
of economic determinism. He anticipates wrongly that large segments
of the middle class will hastily desert their traditional affiliations and
join with the proletariat; he seems oblivious to the possibility that

portions of the proletariat might well move into the middle class. His prediction that capitalism will eventually reduce the size of the managerial class is completely unfounded, and the growing specialization and skill required in the industrialized economy produce rather an increase in those with nominally middle-class identifications.

Marx's economic opinions have already been discussed in part. For all the avowed cosmopolitanism contained in his ideas, the economic theories are derived and applicable to a limited set of circumstances. When Marx talks about economics, he is thinking about Germany and Britain. It may be possible to argue that he is also convinced that all economies will eventually progress to a state similar to those observed by him in Western Europe. In this event, his comment would perhaps be universally applicable. This seems a tenuous defense, however, and if it were granted, the Marxist economic theory still faces difficulties. Among them is Marx's misunderstanding of the role of agriculture in the economy and the social ramifications of agricultural work. For all his eulogizing of collective ownership, his theory pays little attention to the critical need for economic policy and industrial management. The problem of economic efficiency and growth is not, prima facie, solved by the transfer of title.

The social ideas of Marxism are such as can be quickly disposed of. In their unadulterated form, they fly in the face of anthropological knowledge, quite aside from their ethical and spiritual implications. They were briefly tried, it might be added, in the Soviet Union during the period of "war communism," the years of social experimentation in the early 1920's, and were almost totally abandoned as impractical. Marx's contempt for the tenacity of cultural influences—he dubs them mere "artifacts"—in the area of social analysis is fatal to his understanding of social forces.

Marx remains the object of vilification and rapturous praise. His most famous disciple, Lenin, has said that Marxism is "all-powerful because it is true." "It is," Lenin goes on to remark, "complete and harmonious, providing men with a consistent view of the universe." A present-day scholar, F. S. C. Northrop, offers a more balanced appraisal:

> Marx has made it forever impossible hereafter for anyone to pretend to have an adequate economic or political theory or moral philosophy which does not pay attention to man's bodily as well as his ideational nature; and to the physical universe as well as to purely cultural institutions. To political democracy with its freedom to choose one's

political leaders, there has been added economic democracy with its
vision of freedom from physical want.[11]

Vladimir I. Ulyanov (1870-1924) is best known to the world at large
as *Nicolai Lenin.* If Marx was the Deity, then Lenin was his prophet.
The religious metaphor is not out of place. Lenin made Marx's theories
a secular religion. Where Marx had been principally a theorist, Lenin
was an activist, the founder of a political party and the father of communism in Russia. Forced to flee his native Russia in 1899 for radical
agitation, Lenin bided his time in exile. The German Government, in
the business of conducting a two-front war against the Allied Powers
in the West and Russia in the East, saw in its erstwhile guest a chance
to accelerate Russia's capitulation. With the Tsar overthrown in 1917
by an essentially moderate *coup,* Lenin, with German assistance, returned and began at once to agitate, demanding Russia's immediate
withdrawal from the "imperialist" war and an end to the mild regime
of Kerensky. He was successful in both projects, as Russia sued for
peace and a Bolshevist uprising in November (October by Old Style
reckoning) brought the extreme revolutionaries to power.[12] Lenin
was the first premier.

Lenin claimed on many occasions that he advocated "pure" Marxism,
that he did not alter the doctrines of the master. This is substantially
true; Lenin made no significant philosophic contributions to dialectical
materialism. But he made of Marx's ideas a political creed and supported it with a highly effective corps of revolutionary shock troops.
What was to be done, concluded Lenin, was to make Marxism an
even more avowedly political program than Marx had conceived it.
This involved restoring the idea of the state and constructing a model
communist polity. "The state," Lenin wrote, "is the product and manifestation of the *irreconcilability* of class antagonisms." The all-powerful
centralized state must be created to insure the success of the revolution. Lenin had a much livelier sense of the dangers of counterrevo-

---

[11] F. S. C. Northrop, *The Meeting of East and West* (New York: The Macmillan
Company, 1946), p. 252.

[12] Some clarification of terms may be helpful. At the party congress of the
Social Democratic Party in London in 1903, a split occurred on the issue of gradual
constitutional change versus revolutionary activity. The revolutionaries, led by
Lenin, carried the day and ejected the gradualists. Lenin's faction, the majority
group, took the name *Bolsheviki* or "majority"; the repudiated minority segment
was designated the *Mensheviki* or "minority."

lutionary strokes; he had, after all, lived closer than Marx to the raw combat for political mastery.

Five main facets of Lenin's thought emerge as additions or extensions of Marx's original doctrine. First, Lenin is far more convinced than Marx that the *only* way of achieving the victory of socialism is by violence. He is intolerant of any alternative means on the grounds that they would imply some form of compromise with the existing system. This is impossible, claims Lenin. He rejects popular fronts with non-revolutionary radicals; he is hostile to trade unionism as being non-political and heretical to the Marxist doctrine.

Secondly, Lenin is an intellectual and refers to himself thus. The word appears with a certain redundant frequency in his writings. He chooses to surround himself with fellow intellectuals. The importance of all this is that Lenin envisions a political movement headed by a small and carefully selected phalanx of socialist intelligentsia. He lays great emphasis upon the indispensability of the direction of the élite.

It follows, thirdly, that Lenin has a well-developed notion of political action and leadership. Lenin's unique achievement was the Communist party. The party forms the rock upon which the unchallengeable state is to be built. The party is not a political organization constructed to dispute for power in any democratic sense. Liberal democracy is a hoax, Lenin advises. He offers this description of the elective democratic system:

> Democracy for an insignificant minority, democracy for the rich— that is the democracy of capitalist society. If we look more closely into the mechanism of capitalist democracy, everywhere, both in the "petty"—so-called petty—details of the suffrage (residential qualification, exclusion of women, etc.) and in the technique of the representative institutions, in the actual obstacles to the right of assembly (public buildings are not for "beggars"!), in the purely capitalistic organization of the daily press, etc., etc.—on all sides we see restriction after restriction on democracy. These restrictions, exceptions, exclusions, obstacles for the poor, seem slight, especially in the eyes of one who has himself never known want and has never been in close contact with the oppressed classes in their mass life (and nine-tenths, if not ninety-nine hundredths of the bourgeois publicists and politicians are of this class), but in their sum total these restrictions exclude and squeeze out the poor from politics and from an active share in democracy.[13]

He applauds Marx for contending that elections are occasions when "the oppressed are allowed, once every few years, to decide which

---

[13] V. I. Lenin, *State and Revolution*, Part IV, Chapter 5, Section 1.

particular representatives of the oppressing classes should be in parliament to represent and repress them!" [14] Yet Lenin's remedy for the ills of democracy is to eliminate political competition for power and to replace it with the domination of one party. Lenin's party is no gathering of the boys of the old Fourth Ward. It resembles a military organization—the discipline is at least as severe. It is selective—only those with certain substantial qualifications will be admitted to membership. It is an élite corps of society that is not in any way the result of free choice on the part of the workers and peasants, but only symbolizes their collective will. The party is the expression of the purpose and ideals of the working class, but it is not responsive to their opinions or wishes. The party is, in fact, an avant-garde cadre of instructors and leaders presided over by a tiny circle of the communist intelligentsia. Since the party is the personification of the proletariat's ideals, the vanguard of the new era, and the cream of the Marxist dialecticians, it is infallible. Although the party is never wrong as to the selection of ends, some divergence of opinion is permitted over the choice of means and even criticism of techniques might be allowed.

Fourthly. Lenin waves the bloody shirt of "imperialism." In a word: Marxism is applied to foreign affairs. Because Lenin found himself at the helm of a nation-state and one received with something less than cordial welcome by the world as a whole, it is not unexpected that he applies to the relations between states the same reasoning that Marx had employed in the case of social classes. Lenin speaks of nations as "capitalist" and "bourgeois" and argues that they behave with the same sordid motives, directed by their bourgeois leaders, that prompted the capitalist class to oppress and harry the proletariat. This capitalist technique of oppression transferred to world affairs Lenin labels "imperialism." The Soviet Union, as Lenin depicts it, is a lamb in a den of wolves; he speaks of an "imperialist" conspiracy to attack and conquer the new Communist state. His associate, Leon Trotsky, the War Minister, warned of an "imperial encirclement." The class struggle becomes a struggle between nations. The curious feature of this attitude is that Lenin never departs from Marx's intense cosmopolitanism —the Marxist revolution must be worldwide and must be brought about by an international union of the working class. Lenin never abandons (as later Soviet leaders will, in favor of Russian expansion) the idea of the World Revolution. But he thinks of it in terms of existing national states and the more traditional methods of international

---

[14] *Ibid.*

290 REVOLUTION AND REVOLUTIONARIES

intercourse. While Lenin is never a distinctly Russian politician in any chauvinistic sense, he nonetheless is aware of the crisis facing the Soviet Union and the strenuous pressures being brought to bear on the communist experiment.

Lastly, Lenin gives to Marxism its mystique. In general, there is no apocryphal quality in Marx, no burning of magic incense—Lenin supplies this. He translates the somewhat academic discourses of his mentor into the passionate, disputatious, and semimystical language that is invariably put to use when moving masses of people to action or to dedication. In Lenin's hands, Marx becomes a kind of temporal divinity. There has followed, in consequence, a dynastic succession that has always preserved this aura of the "sainted leader," the high priest somehow bigger than life. Lenin himself (his corporal remains, to be precise) to this day lies under glass in a marble temple, to which day after day the faithful throng, doubtless reflecting on the sources of his wisdom and power.[15]

Much more might be said, but perhaps as fitting a summary of the doctrine of Marx and Lenin as any is contained in these lines by the German poet. Hölderlin: "What has always made the state a hell on earth has been precisely that man has tried to make it his heaven."[16]

Not all socialists were communists; there were those who acknowledged their debt to Karl Marx, but who had no wish to endorse the policies of the Communist Internationale. Some described themselves as "philosophical Marxists"; others were content to bear the title "socialist" and let it go at that. The time may now be at hand for a classification of terms. Marx was a socialist and preached socialism. The word is still in general usage in the U.S.S.R. (Union of Soviet *Socialist* Republics) and Red China. Chairman Nikita S. Khrushchev would call himself a socialist, but so did George Bernard Shaw and Ramsay MacDonald.

Without essaying an erudite definition, we can say that socialism is a broad economic and social theory calling for public ownership of

---

[15] The succession of Soviet demigods has not always been without annoying afterthoughts. After considerable shuffling of coffins, the earthly fragments of one Joseph Stalin were finally deposited, quite unceremoniously, beneath the walls of the Kremlin.

[16] This quotation from Hölderlin appears as an introduction to Chapter II of Friedrich A. Hayek's *Road to Serfdom*. Hayek's works in general form an impressive defense of a contemporary free competitive economy.

the means of production. There are many and frequently incompatible forms of this, but all socialists would agree to the general principle. In this sense, Clement Atlee and Norman Thomas are socialists, as well as Marx or Lenin or Khrushchev. But beyond this most general premise, socialism diverges in a number of conflicting directions, although most of them have some measure of Marxist influence. Karl Marx also used the term "communism," designating by it the particular theories and recommendations that he derived from the basic premise of public ownership. Thus, for Marx, communism was a total rejection of existing institutions and practices and the replacement of these by his own socialism. The term was further enlarged by Lenin's doctrines and by the literature of Soviet theorists.

In current general usage, the term "socialism" usually refers to various economic theories relating to degrees of public ownership and applied to certain democratically conceived political groups working for various economic and social goals related to the abandonment or substantial curtailment of the competitive economic system. In various countries, Socialist parties bear different names. In Britain, for example, it is the Labour party, while on the Continent the most common title is Social Democratic party. There is also a Socialist party in the United States. Many states of the world now incorporate either a socialist economy or a partially socialist one—sometimes called the "welfare state." Sweden, Great Britain, Holland, Australia, and Israel, to render an incomplete but representative list, all have moved in varying degrees toward a socialistic system. Socialist movements in these and other countries have been aimed not at political revolution, but at socioeconomic reform, and they have sought to effectuate this by political action through the constitutional channels created by those societies. The difference between communism and democratic socialism is one of both ends and means. The communist seeks complete overthrow of the *status quo* by violent revolution; the socialist seeks to reform society via public ownership through constitutional means and the influencing of public opinion.

Representative of a socialist movement, derived in part from Marx, but disclaiming communism, was the Fabian socialism of the late nineteenth and early twentieth centuries in Britain. The Fabians were gradualists and democrats.[17] Their origins, far back, were in Bentham

---

[17] The Roman general Fabius saved Rome from seizure by Hannibal, not by rushing out and doing immediate battle, but by outwaiting and outstaying the Carthaginians.

and Mill, the Chartists,[18] and the Social Democratic Federation,[19] and prior to the formation of the Fabian Society in 1884, William Morris (1834-1896)[20] and of course Karl Marx. The names of Sidney and Beatrice Webb (1859-1947 and 1858-1943) and George Bernard Shaw (1856-1950) are prominently associated with the movement.

Unlike Marxism, Fabian socialism was not initially concerned with attacking capitalism *per se*, but "landlordism," rents, and the existence of huge private estates. Absorbed with this region of reform, the Fabians rejected the concept of the Marxist class war. Too, they infused into their socialist point of view the utilitarian principle rather than the dialectic rigidity of Marx. They conceded, also, that value is not wholly the result of labor. But their sharpest cleavage with Marxism was their belief in governmental decentralization, the avoidance of a powerful and remote bureaucracy, and the proposal to entrust major governmental functions to local organs. These departures from conventional Marxism gave to Fabian socialism an assortment of more limited and more concrete economic and social objectives. The Fabians would be satisfied to attain a socialization of rents; the Marxists would insist upon revolution. The Fabians had marked faith in the powers of education and persuasion and sought to bring public pressure to bear on policy-makers. They were generally overoptimistic, and their temper was distinctly and even remotely intellectual rather than popular. Yet they were willing to work in harmony with almost any other reformist group, and they eventually welcomed association with trade unionism and were absorbed into the Labour party. The Fabians never veered from a support of democratic processes and representative government, dismissing theories of direct popular control of governmental machinery as too extreme.

Fabian socialism failed to realize its aims. It fell short of stirring the populace of Britain to campaign for the dream it sketched out so earnestly in its tracts. Yet long after its passing, many monuments to its influence survive. The Fabians shaped the course of trade unionism in Britain and brought to that rising force both an intellectualist cast and a sense of restraint and political forbearance. Fabian socialism

---

[18] A reform movement led by Place and Lovett built around a "People's Charter" and triggered by the moderate nature of the Reform Bill of 1832. It did not survive past 1848.

[19] The Social Democratic Federation was founded in 1881 by Hyndman and William Morris (see below) to agitate for a wide range of reforms, of which land nationalization was the foremost.

[20] *William Morris,* a social reformer and writer, who, after leaving the Social Democratic Federation, established the Socialist League in 1884. His major work is a utopian romance, *News from Nowhere.*

trailblazed for the creation of the British Labour party, which twice, after two World Wars, has had the opportunity to shape national policy. Much of the content of nearly five decades of legislation in Britain shows the pervading impression wrought by the gradualist doctrines of the Fabians. But perhaps of greater importance, the movement had the effect of insulating the surge toward reform against extremist temptations and socialist ideologies that would have smashed with relish many of the most admirable characteristics of British life, of which the most worthy may be the habit of political tolerance.

. . . for further discussion:

1. Do you think Marx's view of the class struggle is applicable in all societies? What may be the problems facing Marxism in backward agrarian cultures?

2. What reasons, if any, are there to suppose that Marx's analysis of the defects of the capitalist system are valid? What evidence is there that Marx was wrong? Is overproduction a current problem? What would Marx be likely to think about automation?

3. Does motivation research developed by modern advertising lend support to or does it disprove Marxist theory regarding human motivation?

4. How does Marx's conception of ideology adapt to the emergence of intense nationalism in new states in Asia and Africa? How might Marx explain this phenomenon coupled with the development of socialist economic and social patterns?

. . . for further investigation:

Barzun, Jacques, * Darwin, Marx, Wagner: Critique of a Heritage. New York: Anchor Books, 1958.

Berlin, Isaiah, * Karl Marx: His Life and Environment. New York: Oxford University Press, Inc., 1948.

Burns, Emile, ed., A Handbook of Marxism. New York: Random House, Inc., 1935.

Carr, Edward H., Karl Marx. London: J. M. Dent & Sons, Ltd., 1934

Cole, George D. H., What Marx Really Meant. New York: Alfred A. Knopf, Inc., 1934.

Cole, Margaret, ed., The Webbs and Their Work. London: Frederick Muller, Ltd., 1949.

Crossman, Richard, ed., * The God that Failed. New York: Bantam Books, 1960.

Hayek, Friedrich A., * The Road to Serfdom. Chicago, Ill.: University of Chicago Press, 1955.

Hook, Sidney, * Marx and the Marxists. Princeton, N. J.: Anvil Books, 1955.

———, Towards the Understanding of Karl Marx. New York: The John Day Company, Inc., 1933.

Kautsky, Karl, Terrorism and Communism, W. H. Kerridge, trans. London: George Allen & Unwin, Ltd., 1920.

Laski, Harold J., Karl Marx. London: Fabian Society, 1922.

Lawrence, John W., * A History of Russia. New York: Mentor Books, 1962.

Lenin, Vladimir I., * State and Revolution. New York: International Publishers Co., Inc., n.d.

Marx, Karl, Capital, Moore, Aveling, and Untermann, trans. 3 vols. Chicago, Ill.: Charles H. Kerr & Company, 1904.

——— and Friedrich Engels, * Basic Writings on Philosophy and Politics, Lewis S. Feuer, ed. New York: Anchor Books, 1959.

———, * The Communist Manifesto, New York: International Publishers Co. Inc., 1948.

Mayor, Henry B., * Introduction to Marxist Theory. New York: Oxford University Press, Inc., 1960.

Northrop, Filmer S. C., * The Meeting of East and West. New York: The Macmillan Company, 1946.

Shub, David, * Lenin. New York: Mentor Books, 1950.

Wetter, Gustavo A., Dialectical Materialism. New York: Frederick A. Praeger, Inc., 1959.

Wilson, Edmund, * To the Finland Station. New York: Anchor Books, 1953.

15

THE SUBTERRANEAN
MIND

The nineteenth century had been treated to a parade of glittering systems. One after another, erudite theories appeared, but they all had two elements in common: They all professed a belief in man as an essentially rational being, and they voiced a conviction that human events reflected some orderly process—whatever the pattern was reckoned to be—and that this symmetry was an outgrowth of some consistent characteristic in human nature. Whether or not that paradigm was in fact the pleasure calculus of Bentham, the dialectic of Hegel, the natural selection of Darwin, or the economic determinism of Marx, nature and human nature were thought to be constant, divinable, and even predictable. On one side of the fence (from Samuel Smiles and *Self-Help* to Graham Wallas and *Human Nature in Politics*) the underlying task was: Find the secret formula and solve the mysteries of human behavior, and, eschewing any notion of an organic society, this will do to explain the human community. On the other

side (from Kant to Bosanquet) the premise ran: Find the secret formula and solve the cosmic mysteries, and this will explain human
nature. But neither, empiricism or rationalism, the "Canons of Induction" of Mill or the *Wissenschaft der Logik* of Hegel, ever doubted for
a moment that *reason* in some form could provide answers and that
there was a continuity of meaning in human experience.

Arthur Schopenhauer (1788-1860) had his doubts. This curious figure supplied the counterweight to the reigning rationalism by announc-
ing that belief in the predictability of anything was nonsensical. The
world, Schopenhauer suggested, may not be orderly after all. Resting
his contentions on a subjectivity more embracing than Kant's plus a
revival of intuitionism and an estimation of the significance of feeling
and emotion unequalled since the mystic writings of Herder, Schopenhauer argued that he had indeed found that ultimate reality for which
the nineteenth century had been searching with such energy. What
lay behind it all was will. Oh, but not the rational will of the idealists.
This was a terrible, awesome, incomprehensible, primal, savage will
that coursed through the helpless universe, linking all living creatures
in a bond of common subjection to its unknown purpose and unrelent-
ing domination. Schopenhauer's will was irrational, compounded of
desire and striving, passion and impulse. It was not purposive in the
sense that the Hegelian will was; it was blind movement. If the will
had a purpose, Schopenhauer contended, only will knew what it was.
But the will was not an intelligence; it was a creature instinct, a cosmic
will-to-live, a subterranean movement of nature. Said Schopenhauer
of will:

> Will is the thing-in-itself, the inner content, the essence of the
> world. Life, the visible world, the phenomenon, is only the mirror
> of the will. Therefore life accompanies the will as inseparably as the
> shadow accompanies the body; and if will exists, so will life, the world,
> exist.[1]

He adds:

> The world, in all the multiplicity of its parts and forms, is the mani-
> festation, the objectivity, of the one will to love. Existence itself, and
> the kind of existence, both as the collective whole and in every part,
> proceeds from the will alone. The will is free, the will is mighty. The
> will appears in everything, just as it determines itself in itself and
> outside time. The world is only the mirror of this willing; and all

---

[1] Arthur Schopenhauer, *The World as Will and Idea*, Book IV, Section 54.

finitude, all suffering, all miseries, which it contains belong to the expression of that which the will wills, are as they are because the will so wills.[2]

And the will—the life-force—is beyond human reason to comprehend. Being completely free, it is bound to no rules, no patterns, no predestined course. Will cannot be understood; it can only be accepted and withstood. The incomprehensibility of will and its dominance over humanity gives rise to Schopenhauer's intense pessimism. The nature of the will creates a state of human futility; there is no permanent escape from its demands. Individual human wills are bound up in this ceaseless striving, instinctual and impulsive. From this conviction of the helplessness of the individual, "a fleeting phenomenon appearing in the form of time," Schopenhauer frames theories of ethics and art. Ethical behavior is simply sympathy, the refusal to increase the burdens of fellow creatures who are themselves tormented by the inexorable will. Art is a temporary, sensual surcease from the same torment.

Schopenhauer's philosophy does not fit any of the neat categories. Where does one assign a philosophy that argues that metaphysics is meaningless will, ethics brief pity, and aesthetics an anesthetic? In fact, Shopenhauer, iconoclastic and petulant, was for a long period dismissed as a stormy petrel, an eccentric dilettante, or possibly a madman. But gradually the implications of his irrationalism began to sink in. Schopenhauer had set off one of the backfires in the history of ideas —vitalism. In brief, "vitalism" is a term used to cover a wide belief that the essential nature of the universe is life, defined as a force. This life-force need not be mere biological energy, and, indeed, this reductionism is rejected. The life-force, rather, is conceived of as being a will, or a spirit, or a form of immaterial cosmic energy. From this hypothesis come two secondary concepts: (1) Change and flux are ever present and unpredictable. (2) Knowledge of reality, the life-force, is gained not through cold reason and logical analysis, but through feeling, emotion, intuition, instinctual ties with the life-force itself. These corollaries require a virtually total dismissal, in philosophy, morals, and politics, of the major currents of nineteenth-century thought.

On the heels of Schopenhauer's dark portents about the irrational will came a man whose niche in the history of ideas defies exact description—*Friedrich Wilhelm Nietzsche* (1844-1900). What *was*

---

[2] *Ibid.*, Section 63.

Nietzsche? A throwback to the age of the Golden Horde? A genius perhaps? An Anti-Christ? A poet to rank with Horace and Dante? A prophet of a new order? Or simply a maniac? Whatever classification one puts him in (and he has been placed in all of them), Nietzsche broods over the Western world, mocking and imperious; no sensible man, still professing the traditional beliefs of Christianity or humanitarianism, has since passed his grave without a nervous whistle.

Nietzsche, the most formidable antagonist the Christian dogma has had to contend with, was the son of a Lutheran clergyman, born in a village in Saxony in 1844. As a student his interests were in classical studies and philology, and his easily recognizable talents won him a chair at Basel at the tender age of twenty-four. His career as a university lecturer was interrupted by the Franco-Prussian War of 1870 in which he served as a male nurse and contracted diphtheria and dysentery. The effect of these diseases left Nietzsche a physically broken man; the remainder of his life was a mounting battle against complete incapacity. He weathered spells of profound depression and intense physical suffering; he moved frequently, trying to find locations where the climate and surroundings would ease his increasing pain. Yet the stream of writings never stopped: *Thus Spake Zarathustra, Beyond Good and Evil, The Genealogy of Morals, The Anti-Christ,* and *Ecce Homo* were the most important. Finally, by 1889, mental deterioration was evident, and he was hospitalized for some six years. Cared for by a devoted (if after his death not always ingenuous) sister, he died at Weimar in the last year of the old century.

Four major encounters shaped Nietzsche's thought: Greek paganism, Schopenhauer's philosophy, his association with the composer Richard Wagner, and Christianity. The first, Greek culture, he admired with but few qualifications. He looked with favor on some aspects of Schopenhauer's *Weltanschauung.* He first worshiped, then repulsed and abused Wagner. He loathed the Christian religion from the beginning—and with a fierce hatred.

From the Greeks, Nietzsche concluded that all civilizations could be divided into two types: the Apollonian and the Dionysian. The first type stressed tranquillity, harmony, restraint, and moral consciousness. The Dionysian was saturated with conflict, fevered longing, passion, and the exaltation of desire and strength.[3]

---

[3] His account of this theory (which he first applied to art) can be found in his first book *The Birth of Tragedy* (1872). The combination of both Apollonian and Dionysian elements is necessary for tragedy, he concluded. Later Nietzsche argued that a combination of these orientations is present in civilizations, but that a larger proportion of the Dionysian is to be preferred.

Schopenhauer provided him with the beginnings of his own vitalist conception of the world. He accepted in large part Schopenhauer's account of metaphysical matters, but rejected both the resigned pessimism and quietistic ethic of his predecessor. In tone, too, Nietzsche abounded in the zeal of fearless involvement, the joy of struggle, just as Schopehauer emphasized deliberate and cautious sensuality.

Initially, Wagner was thought to be the crowning genius of the age. Nietzsche applauded his sense of power, loftiness, passion, mythological splendor, and romantic verve. This was the Wagner of *Tristan und Isolde*. But Nietzsche had no use for the Wagner of *Parsifal*, with its pity and Christian allegory. The idol was discarded.

Christianity was the reason for the decline of the grandeur of Europe, alleged Nietzsche. The main line of excoriation was that Christianity was a "slave morality"; it was a conspiracy of the weak to cripple the strong. What happened, he argued, was that all the most petty and pallid characteristics of weakness were transfused into virtues by the Christians in order to compensate for their own weaknesses and to deny to the naturally strong the moral implication of their strength. Thus meekness, contrition, forbearance, humility, unselfishness, etc., which were held to be virtues by the Christians, were in fact merely defects of character and evidences of cowardice. Christianity, then, being afraid of the temporal world, chose to devise mythological justifications for belief in the rewards of some other existence. This was not only cowardice, roared Nietzsche, but bribery as well. Together, then, with an ethic of weakness and cowardice and a collection of dubious myths and fakir tricks, Christianity wormed its way into the foundations of European culture, sapped its strength and dignity, and reduced it to a state of whining and fearful decadence.

A lengthy quotation from *Beyond Good and Evil* should be examined here, not only for its insight into Nietzsche's views on Christianity, but also because it is a spritely illustration of his style, forceful and acid-etched:

> If one could observe the strangely painful, equally coarse and refined comedy of European Christianity with the derisive and impartial eye of an Epicurean god, I should think one would never cease marvelling and laughing; does it not seem that some single will has ruled over Europe for eighteen centuries in order to make a *sublime abortion* of man? He, however, who, with opposite requirements (no longer Epicurean) and with some divine hammer in his hand, could approach this almost voluntary degeneration and stunting of mankind, as exemplified in the European Christian (Pascal, for instance), would he not have to cry aloud with rage, pity, and horror: "Oh, you

bunglers, presumptuous pitiful bunglers, what have you done? Was
that a work for your hands? How you have hacked and botched my
finest stone! What have *you* presumed to do!"—I should say that
Christianity has hitherto been the most portentous of presumptions.
Men, not great enough, nor hard enough, to be entitled as artists to
take part in fashioning *man*, not sufficiently strong and far-sighted
to *allow*, with sublime self-constraint, the obvious law of the thousandfold failures and perishings to prevail; men, not sufficiently noble to
see the radically different grades of rank and intervals of rank that
separate man from man—*such* men, with their "equality before God,"
have hitherto swayed the destiny of Europe; until at last a dwarfed,
almost ludicrous species has been produced, a gregarious animal,
something obliging, sickly, mediocre, the European of the present
day.[4]

Such is Nietzsche's lifelong vendetta with Christianity, and such is
his pungent, vitriolic style. His literary talents are undeniable. The
history of letters has no counterpart for his long mystical prose poem,
Thus Spake Zarathustra (*Also Sprach Zarathustra*). It is impossible to
assign it to any orthodox classification, yet it is a philosophic work of
great power and suggestivity and at the same time a literary tour de
force of frequent beauty and luxuriance of expression. In it, through
the mouth of a shadowy, symbolic, Zoroaster-like prophet, Nietzsche
gives vent to the full range of his convictions: the nobility of Grecian
paganism, the life-force that is the "will to power," the concept of the
overman and the master class, the moral freedom of strength and
candor, the depravity of Christianity, and the passionate sublimity of
restless nature.

Nietzsche's vitalism comes to rest on one fundamental precept: The
life-force is the "will to power." If political philosophy in a vague sense
can be called speculation about the nature and use of power, then all
of Nietzschean thought is a commentary on politics, since all of his
ideas, from art to the treatment of women, trace back to the notion of
the commanding urge to covet power. Paradoxically, Nietzsche's not
inconsiderable influence has been felt very little in political theorizing
(those who argue, quite fallaciously, that Nietzsche was a proto-Nazi
notwithstanding) compared to what it has in other fields of thought.
The emergence of existentialism in the twentieth century, for instance,
derives impetus from him. Perhaps, as we shall later see, his most
noticeable legacy is contained in the depth psychology of Freud and
his followers. Cutting through the vast melange of ideas, then, those
directly confronting the political question can be reduced to three main

---

[4] Friedrich Nietzsche, *Beyond Good and Evil*, Section 62.

areas: (1) his drastically revisionist ethics, (2) the concept of the will to power, and (3) the idea of the overman—the superman—and the state.

Nietzsche's ethical views, for all their epigrammatic presentation, can be rephrased into fairly simple propositions. The entire moral orientation of Western society must be discarded, he contends, as not only unsound (because it is unnatural), but also as debilitating. The distinctions between good and evil are a conspiratorial artificiality, a deliberate, emasculating ruse. Morality is a code of the timid and un-talented mob, constructed to hamper the natural superiority of the stronger and more able. Nietzsche, holding to an uncompromising Darwinism, finds no justification for positive restraint. The struggle for survival is not only elemental and inescapable, it is ennobling. Thus a new and natural ethic must be evolved, and its cardinal prin-ciple must be the equation: power = value. All conduct must be judged by the standard of how it facilitates the acquisition of power. Hedonism, moral absolutism, moral intuitionism, and so on are all beside the point, argues Nietzsche. They are so much pompous non-sense. Moral codes and conscience are illusions of slaves, bred of de-meaning fear. Morality is a disease, an ulcer on the spirit.

In his transvaluation of ethics, Nietzsche substitutes for previous moral theory what is substantially a psychological morality. He speaks of morality as a "sickness"; the true concern of ethics, he advances, is the freeing of the human personality from the chains of guilt, pettiness, cowardice, and deception. He is not an immoralist in the sense that he advocates evil as an end. Quite the contrary, he disowns evil with the same certitude with which he rejects good. Love correctly understood, he comments, is a desire to conquer or seduce, *but* this is *not* wrong; it is right, since only the pursuit of power is a natural good. Nietzsche's ethics are designed to treat the human psyche and then to produce a state of egoistic sublimation in individuals. This will result, he tells us, in men's being strong, open, frank, gentle, secure, and creative. He writes:

> The beast of prey and the man of prey (for instance, Cesare Borgia) are fundamentally misunderstood, "nature" is misunderstood, so long as one seeks a "morbidnesss" in the constitution of these healthiest of all tropical monsters and growths, or even an innate "hell" in them— as almost all moralists have done hitherto. Does it seem that there is a hatred of the virgin forest and of the tropics among moralists? And that "tropical man" must be discredited at all costs, whether as disease or deterioration of mankind, or as his own hell and self-torture? And why? In favor of the "temperate zones"? In favor of the temperate

men? The "moral"? The mediocre?—This for the chapter: "Morals as Timidity." [5]

Cesare Borgia, it would seem, had both Nietzsche and Machiavelli as admirers. Indeed, Nietzsche was fond of an old medieval motto (reputed to be the creed of a guild of professional assassins): "Nothing is true; everything is allowed." But the Florentine courtier and the nineteenth-century German (who was actually a Swiss citizen) were without moral conviction. Both advocated the revision of ethics toward a new goal: power. For Machiavelli, moral restraints and codes could be discreetly abrogated by the prince in order to enhance the power and resulting glory of the state. Nietzsche was more radical. Chasing power was not a game indulged in by princes; it was a psychological fact and every normal man could and even must partake of it. Traditional society had chosen the wrong rules for the inevitable game. Moreover, immorality could without harm be indulged in for real gain, counseled Machiavelli; but Nietzsche's ethics were designed to be positive and beneficial. Throwing over the rules means the reconciliation between the natural instinctive drives of men and their social behavior. This would bring men back into essential psychological harmony with the rhythms of nature.

The will to power is both a metaphysical and a psychological category, although both are closely connected in Nietzschean thought. As a metaphysical fact, the will to power is the life-force, the *Geist*, coursing through all nature, a lust for and an exaltation of survival, an urge for combat and conquest, the underlying motive behind the "survival of the fittest." Psychologically, the will to power consists of the basic drive in the human personality; it is atavistic, aggressive, sexual, irrational. It craves sublimation.[6] This sublimation is not a pleasure principle, pain and suffering are not to be avoided, as they temper and harden both the desire for power and the means of getting it. Full sublimation is beyond attainment, but it produces a certain set of behavioral characteristics that includes generosity, candor, creativity, tolerance, self-confidence, and, perhaps curiously, gentleness.[7] The

[5] *Ibid.*, Section 197.

[6] The term "sublimation," well-known in Freudian writing, is repeatedly used by Nietzsche. Walter Kaufmann in his excellent study of Nietzsche illustrates the parallel between Freud and Nietzsche: "Speaking of sublimation, both tried to show how certain types of behavior could be explained, and how one striving might often be transformed into others. Least of all were they exhorting people to fulfill the desire in question in an unsublimated way. In one sentence: Nietzsche was not 'endorsing' the will to power any more than Freud 'endorsed' the sex impulse." [*Nietzsche* (New York: Meridian Books, 1956), p. 214.]

[7] Nietzsche listed four "virtues": courage, insight, sympathy, and solitude.

natural man is not just a beast of prey, Nietzsche explains; he is also an innocent child. But this is the state of true self-mastery, and it comes only *after* the sublimation of the will to power, not before. In *Zarathustra,* Nietzsche speaks of three "metamorphoses" of the personality. These are symbolized by the camel, the lion, and the child. Says Zarathustra:

> But tell me, my brethren, what the child can do, which even the lion could not do? Why hath the preying lion still to become a child?
>
> Innocence is the child, and forgetfulness, a new beginning, a game, a self-rolling wheel, a first movement, a holy Yea.[8]

The social and political significance of the will to power is that it is the creative force. For Nietzsche, the great man is always the artist. Power means creation, culture, and majesty of spirit. The noble creatures of the earth are set apart from their contemporaries, explains Nietzsche, by their constant creative striving. He writes:

> A man who strives after great things, looks upon every one whom he encounters on his way either as a means of advance or a delay and hindrance—or as a temporary resting-place. His peculiar lofty *bounty* to his fellow men is only possible when he attains his elevation and dominates.[9]

The will to power produces in some men the spark of nobility, of greatness. To Nietzsche, then, came the vision of the overman—the superman.[10] He uses the term with two connotations. First, he means the highest types of human beings, the best mankind has produced, the noble artists and warriors. Secondly, he alludes to the overman as a future type, a new man, a next higher step on the evolutionary ladder who will represent the ideal fulfillment of the Nietzschean dream. Again through Zarathustra, Nietzsche speaks to the "higher men":

> Oh my brethren, what I can love in man is that he is an over-going and a down-going. And also in you there is much that maketh me love and hope.
>
> In that ye have despised, ye higher men, that maketh me hope. For the despisers are the great reverers.
>
> In that ye have despaired, there is much to honour. For ye have not learned to submit yourselves, ye have not learned petty policy.[11]

---

[8] Friedrich Nietzsche, *Thus Spake Zarathustra,* Part I, Chapter 1.

[9] Nietzsche, *op. cit., Beyond Good and Evil,* Section 273.

[10] The word Nietzsche uses is *Ubermensch.* The more common translation, "superman," has many connotations in English that do violence to Nietzsche's meaning. For a more detailed discussion, see Kaufmann, *op. cit.,* pp. 266-267.

[11] Nietzsche, *op. cit., Zarathustra,* Part IV, Chapter 73.

The image of the overman is partially gained from the past, from the great captains of history. Borgia, Napoleon, and especially Julius Caesar are selected by Nietzsche. The real defect in these personalities, from Nietzsche's point of view, was their frequently limited cultural refinements. This reservation suggests that the overman really combines two images—the warrior and the artist. The warrior is fundamental; the evolutionary forces have produced this type as well as creative types, and will synthesize these elements into the future type, the true overman. While it is correct to attribute to Nietzsche's overman some of the features of the Prussian aristocracy, Nietzsche sensed a lack of aesthetic feeling in the *junker* type; he despaired of the Germans ever really understanding music, for example. Certainly the overman is not a sheer wielder of the sword; the contest of life is not wholly a bloodletting. The overman is not the Blonde Beast.

Rather is the overman a warrior who by virtue of his strength and domination, his sensitivity to beauty and the "purities" of nature, becomes a creator, a refined but not decadent aristocrat, cosmopolitan and open-minded, tolerant and perceptive by virtue of his unassailable status. Thereby is formed a new élite and a new political era—the rule of the overman, the new European. Nietzsche's concept is both anti-nationalistic and antistatist.

Espousing an iron-forged aristocracy and loathing the mediocrity of democratic sentimentalism, Nietzsche dismisses the national state as an artificiality. The state as a man-made edifice is oppressive to the degree that it thwarts the rise of the best, promotes mass values, and seeks to regulate society on doctrinaire principles. The national state and the overman are natural enemies in the Nietzschean view. The state is another device of the vulgar and weak. Again Zarathustra thunders:

> A state? What is that? Well! open your ears unto me, for now will I say unto you my word concerning the death of peoples.
>
> A state is called the coldest of all cold monsters. Coldly lieth it also; and lie seepeth from its mouth: "I, the state, am the people."
>
> It is a lie! Creators were they who created peoples, and hung a faith and a love over them; thus they served life.
>
> Destroyers are they who lay snares for many, and call it the state; they hang a sword and a hundred cravings over them.[12]

Does this make Nietzsche an anarchist? Far from it, since his objection to the state is that it promotes weakness and mediocrity, not that

---

[12] *Ibid.*, Part I, Chapter 11.

it enjoys excessive power. The state must make way for the unfettered rule of the overman. But does this not suggest a fatal circularity in Nietzsche? Surely the state has authority, which rests on the ability to coerce—to use power, in other words. Is not power good? Is not the state justifiable simply because it has acquired power? No, Nietzsche would reply, because power is not a collective matter in the first place and, secondly, the conniving of weaker individuals to pull down the strong as crows harry a hawk is not, Hobbes notwithstanding, true power. It is not true power because it does not spring from the life-force, it is a perversion of nature. Strength is measured in the iron of individual souls The state cannot pursue power, because the state is not a soul or an individual, it is an artifact of the mob; whether or not the state is democratic or autocratic does not matter in this sense. The authoritarian state is not the answer to the political ills of Europe; the remedy is to be found in an aristocracy of power, uninhibited by moral limitations or popular will. The state cannot represent races or peoples (as most totalitarians have insisted), because the state invariably rests on general ethnic traits which by definition must also be typical, average, mediocre. Thus the state represses what is exceptional or novel. The state cannot, Nietzsche insists, represent the best in a race without rendering itself useless and defunct. The state and the individual must be antagonists.

The charge, which some have made, that Nietzsche was the progenitor of the Nazi creed is too obvious a misinterpretation to need refutation here.[13] The same might be said of the allegation that he was a racist, a confirmed anti-Semite. There are some evident parallels between Nietzschean thought and the doctrines of *Mein Kampf*, for example, the deification of the leader, the detestation of bourgeois virtue, the praise of power, the countenancing of cruelty and violence, the romanticization of the primitive "heroic ages," and so on. But Nietzsche's view differs from Adolf Hitler's in two all-important respects: (1) He reveres the beautiful, praises cultural attainment, celebrates the excellent, and in so doing disowns vulgarity, barbarism, nationalism, regimentation, chicanery, and mass religiosity. (2) The will to power and the concept of the overman are the result of a con-

---

[13] Nietzsche was anything but a rabid admirer of Germans or German culture. If anything, he was pro-French. Following the Franco-Prussian War, Nietzsche announced to Germany that it had just defeated a nation infinitely its cultural superior.

sidered and reasonably detached analysis of the universe and human
nature, conducted with a high degree of philosophical sophistication.
Nietzsche's thought is neither a glorification of himself alone or a
rationalization for his personal appetites. Personally, he was quiet in
habit and was considered a warm and considerate person by his
intimates.

If the effect of Nietzsche on European Fascism, especially Nazism,
has been vastly exaggerated, it has had the result of obscuring the
influences of Nietzschean ideas elsewhere. No one could fairly put
forward the thesis that Nietzsche contributed one of the significant
theories of politics. His ideas were often fragmented, apocopated,
oblique. He was proudly unsystematic and often more heavily ironic
than didactic. He often sought more to disturb than to prescribe. No
school of political philosophy can be described as Nietzscheanism—
and how horrified Nietzsche doubtless would be if one were.

Yet he bore great weight in the history of political ideas. He was
the first to suggest that political behavior had its roots in the deep
subconscious layers of the human personality. He disclosed the presence of the irrational in political consciousness and exposed to view
the drives that move men toward aggression, combat, appetite for
power, and the urge to dominate. Nietzsche's invaluable contribution
was essentially psychological, and in framing political thought in this
fashion he offered new and exciting alternatives to theories that sought
to explain political life by either metaphysics or experience based on
fallacious psychologies, crude materialisms, or doctrinaire reduction-
isms. It has been argued with some justification that the most dramatic
revolution in ideas in the twentieth century was the emergence of the
teachings of Freud. To Nietzsche Freud owed a partial beginning. However easy it is to dismiss Nietzsche in more specific terms, perhaps the
most promising current of political theory in the present age stems
from his assumption that the key to understanding lies in an examination of the dark, irrational recesses of the human being.

He effectively smashed the smugness of the nineteenth century, and
that was no small order considering the entrenchment of excessive
sentimentality, vacant meliorism, and a palpable fondness for safety
and mediocrity. He would have taken pride in this, just as he might
have been dismayed to find that he had influenced both American
pragmatism and existentialism. The former borrowed to some extent
his mechanisms for the resolution of value choices on the basis of
self-interest and the latter his endorsement of the ascendency of the
self. That Nietzsche enjoyed some vogue among Christian existential-

ists is another of the ironies of philosophic genealogy. Nietzsche has been described as a "tonic," and it is not an inappropriate appellation —so long as one remembers that it is a heady tonic, indeed.

Henri Bergson (1859-1941) is more closely tied to Schopenhauer than to Nietzsche. His main importance stems from his vigorous assertion of intuitionism and his redefinition of the life-force as the *élan vital*—the vital impulse. Bergson need not be considered here apart from his vitalist connections, but his descriptions of the interaction of instinct and intelligence are a provocative application of the idea of irrational force shaping human personality and affairs. Intelligence, Bergson suggests, is not a device for knowing, but is really only a functional tool. Knowledge, on the other hand, is the result of a higher phase than either instinct or intelligence: intuition. This is defined principally as a feeling for life, an empathy with nature conjoined with the contemplational mood created by intelligence. This antirationalistic contention, coupled with the *élan vital* as a creative rather than mechanistic or logistic explanation of evolution, provided a view of both nature and personality stressing limitless freedom and possibility.

The foremost explorer of the subterranean mind was undoubtedly *Sigmund Freud* (1856-1939). His interests were therapeutic, and his orientations were those of a doctor of medicine and were only secondarily historical and theological.[14] His contribution to mankind was a new and portentous means of dealing with mental disorder: psychoanalysis. In formulating techniques to cope with the hitherto incurable maladies of the psyche, Freud made a number of assumptions regarding the personality he sought to repair. These hypotheses (and it is not slighting to Freud to call them this) proved even more pregnant with significance than the clinical procedures he outlined. Although it is clear that it was not Freud's intention, he in fact sketched out a new philosophy of human nature.

A flying survey of Freudian concepts of personality would be beyond the realm of this narrative, as well as very possibly being misleading and unjust to psychoanalytic theory. We are not here to discuss psychiatry. For the purposes of political theorizing, Freud's ideas can be summarized through four main premises: (1) The conscious mind is

---

[14] Some of Freud's later works deal with this area: *Moses and Monotheism, The Future of an Illusion, Civilization and Its Discontents.*

limited in scope and is a projection of the more significant content of
the subconscious. Human behavior, consequently, is more the result
of factors below the conscious level—the human personality is like an
iceberg, with only one-tenth visible on the surface. (2) The subconscious (id) contains drives, or deep-seated creature needs, and primitive repressed wishes. The subconscious expresses its nature in terms
of force or energy (libido). This libidinous outpouring is controlled,
shaped, and repressed by the partly socially influenced conscious mind
(ego). The content of the id is manifest in the ego in symbolic form.
(3) Morals are the result of primal taboos, the effect of conscience
(superego) and the rationalization of deep-rooted inhibition. (4) Studies of varying societies and institutions in primitive and civilized situations seem to suggest the universality of symbol and myth and hence
a universally consistent structuring of basic human nature.

The question can well be asked: What significance might these
theories hold for political philosophy? The tentative "might" is called
for, because the full implications of depth psychology (the psychology
of Freud, Jung and others in this broad tradition) for political thought
have not yet been clearly faced, let alone examined with adequate
vigor.[15] A number of general conclusions can be made, however.

Freud and his heirs have made impossible any concept of political
order that does not take carefully into account the nonrational component in human behavior. Further, depth psychology has vividly de-
limited the extent to which human reasonability and perfectibility
can be pushed. Freud has exposed the darker side of the human psyche,
not in moral terms, but in clinical ones. Nonetheless, psychoanalysis
has had the effect of a sort of inverted latter-day Calvinism, since it,
too, reveals a penchant in the human personality for the savage, the
atavistic, and the antisocial. Freud termed this "latent aggressiveness,"
and his studies throw considerable light on the subjects of human
conflict, the lust for power, and the intractability of the species. Man,
Freud pointed out, is not only civilized, rational, socially cooperative,
altruistic, carefully estimating with his conscious intelligence the attainment of his self-interests, but he is also a creature with imperious

---

[15] Some applications have been made directly to the area of political theory.
Prominent among those engaged in this enterprise might be listed: Erich Fromm,
H. D. Lasswell, and R. E. Money-Kyrle. The quality of such work is quite controversial—certainly it varies in quality. An unfortunate example might be *Authoritarian Personality* by T. W. Adorno, *et al.* (New York: Harper & Row, Publishers,
1950).

Freud's theories have found wider acceptance and often more careful adaptation
in anthropology and sociology, particularly by Róheim and Malinowski.

libido demands, unconscious strirrings, and primal urges that only his environmentally induced superego controls—part of the time. Freud showed the folly of being too sanguine about human rationality.

The psychoanalytic movement revealed the critical importance of symbol and myth as a means of interpreting both individual behavior and cultural phenomena. These insights and appraisals have fostered a flurry of symbolic analyses of political processes and institutions.[16] Freudianism has further suggested on this base of symbolic investigation the possibility of some common denominator in all societies and cultures, speculating that social institutions and political systems are outgrowths of psychological requirements. If there are constants in human personality and if the Freudians, Jungians, and neo-Freudians have isolated them and demonstrated their empirical consistency and universality, then the possibility presents itself that a similar analytical investigation might reveal constants or universal factors in social arrangements and institutions.

Freud (and more emphatically Jung [17]) has reëmphasized the momentous effects and even concrete psychic projections of social continuity and tradition upon the formation of the individual personality. Man may be psychologically something more than a combination of his biological organism, his immediate environment, and his formative experiences. In various ways, the depth psychologists suggest, human character may be shaped by the archetypal transmissions from the entirety of collective human experience.

Relatively little thought has been expended in attempting to ascertain whether the revelations of depth psychology will in the long run be more hospitable to political theories, radical or conservative, than they are now. Somewhat uncritically, perhaps, and possibly because Freud himself held left-of-center political opinions, it has been assumed that Freudian analysis is an added buttress to the citadel of radicalism. There is considerable ground for this belief. Certainly Freud's thorough moral relativism sounds a nonconservative note. Too, throughout Freud's writing there runs a plea for social elasticity and

---

[16] Some of these examinations are pro-Freud and others anti-Freud. An example of the former is Erich Fromm's *Escape from Freedom* (1941); an example of the latter is Ernst Cassirer's *Myth of the State* (1946).

[17] There are sharp and important differences between Freud and Jung. The latter develops a detailed theory of the "collective unconscious," "archetypes," and the "participation mystique" to account for what he calls the effect of "transpersonal" material in the formation of individual consciousness. For a sympathetic commentary on Jung, see Ira Progoff's *Jung's Psychology and Its Social Meaning* (1953), and for a critical summary see Edward Glover's *Freud or Jung?* (1956).

for a permissive atmosphere. On the other hand, Freudianism might well suggest conservative recommendations. His concept of the personality might imply a need for reëmphasized social control. Also, for all his relativistic attitudes, Freud's very root premises suggest the existence of nonmaterial universals, psychic "essences," if you will. This conviction is far oftener associated with authoritarian than with libertarian philosophies. Lastly, there is nothing in Freud to hint of admiration for collectivism or a depersonalized social order. The nature of psychoanalysis is almost exaggeratedly individualistic. In any case, the political applications of what Freud surmised about the human animal are yet to be fully seen.

From Schopenhauer to Freud, from vitalism to psychoanalysis, the problem of human behavior is the problem of understanding the irrational and dynamic dimensions of the world and the individual. From this often near-occult search came much that was to end a century of system and optimism and to usher in one of flux and pessimism. The twentieth century would leap out of the historical bottle like a frenzied genie pursuing some undisclosed end. It would soon reveal that it was to be a century of experiment and disillusion; a time of breathtaking expansion of knowledge and profound confusion. It was to be an era of political reckoning and the clash of systems of belief, an age of plenty and desolation. Not since the barbarian planted his footprints on the virgin turf of Europe would man have witnessed a comparable upheaval.

. . . for further discussion:

1. In what respects are Nietzsche's overman and Plato's philosopher-ruler alike and different?
2. Do you think Nietzsche would have approved or disapproved of the Rhodes Scholarships? Why?
3. Could an argument be made that psychoanalysis can provide norms for politics by creating standards of public emotional well-being against which to judge governmental policies? Should holders of public office be required to take tests of psychological fitness in order to assume their jobs? Should there be a lunacy examination for all legislators?
4. C. G. Jung comments in his *Essays on Contemporary Events:*
   Now the integration of unconscious contents is an individual act of realization, of understanding, and moral evaluation. It is a most difficult task, demanding a high degree of ethical responsibility.

Only relatively few individuals can be expected to be capable of such an accomplishment, and they are not the political but the moral rulers of mankind. The maintenance and further development of civilization depend upon such individuals.

Why does Jung say "not the political but the moral rulers of mankind"? Why is the distinction made? If there is a psychological and ethical élite, as Jung implies, might it be construed, if applied to political thought, as a sort of fulfillment of Platonism? How?

. . . for further investigation:

Bergson, Henri, * An Introduction to Metaphysics, T. E. Hulme, trans. Indianapolis, Ind.: Liberal Arts Press, Inc., 1949.

Bidney, David, Theoretical Anthropology. New York: Columbia University Press, 1953.

Cassirer, Ernst, * The Myth of the State. New Haven, Conn.: Yale University Press, 1946.

Freud, Sigmund, Basic Writings, A. A. Brill, ed. New York: Modern Library, Inc., 1938.

Fromm, Erich, Escape from Freedom. New York: Holt, Rinehart & Winston, Inc., 1941.

Glover, Edward, * Freud or Jung? New York: Meridian Books, 1956.

Hughes, H. Stuart, * Consciousness and Society. New York: Vintage Books, Inc., n.d.

Jung, Carl G., * Psyche and Symbol, Violet de Lazlo, ed. New York: Anchor Books, 1958.

Kaufmann, Walter, * Nietzsche. New York: Meridian Books, 1956.

Lasswell, Harold D., * Power and Personality. New York: Viking Press, 1962.

Marcuse, Herbert, * Eros and Civilization. New York: Vintage Books, Inc., 1962.

Neumann, Erich, * The Origins and History of Consciousness, R. F. C. Hull, trans., 2 vols. New York: Torchbooks, 1962.

Nietzsche, Friedrich, Philosophy. New York: Modern Library, Inc., 1927.

Progoff, Ira, * Jung's Psychology and Its Social Meaning. New York: Evergreen Books, 1955.

Schopenhauer, Arthur, Philosophy, Irwin Edman, ed. New York: Modern Library, Inc., 1928.

Stanton, Alfred H. and Stewart E. Perry, eds., Personality and Political Crisis. New York: Free Press of Glencoe, Inc., 1951.

16

DARK EMPIRES

The world has grown accustomed to savagery and despotism; it has seen enough of it. Yet in the twentieth century, the weary nonchalance of people well-used to witnessing or experiencing brutality and tyranny was shaken by a new and onerous political creed: *fascism*. What it wrought is familiar to virtually every human being involved in the general course of events. In Europe, Germany turned to a way out of its national dilemmas, and National Socialism and Adolph Hitler were the menacing alternatives. Under this political system the entirety of Europe and much of the world were led into a war unequalled in destructiveness. The Nazi rule resulted in the outright massacre of over six million helpless noncombatants. Italy, the first major state to turn to the fascist course, launched a career of wanton conquest against such harmless states as Ethiopia and Albania. Japan chose an orientalized fascism, a blend of the modern and the medieval, that brought on the terrible excesses of its pillage of China and Southeast

Asia and precipitated a conflict that prompted the employment of the bomb whose explosion still echoes everywhere—the atomic bomb.

What was this fascism that entrapped these great powers and ancient peoples and attracted others the world over? In what way was it different from an unbroken chain of autocratic political philosophies and systems? Why did it promote an orgy of violence unmatched since the hordes of Genghis Khan or the scorched earth of the Thirty Years' War? Fascism—and we will suspend the definition for a moment—introduced two novel features into the history of political ideas: (1) The concept of the total state (the police state, if you will) that controlled the complete range of human activity and encroached with a monopoly of authority into every facet of existence, including the hitherto private thoughts of individuals. (2) The creation of a secular religion based on mass identification. Rousseau and the French Revolution gave birth to the mass movement and mass consciousness, the mystique of the herd, and this was joined with an elaborate quasi-religious mythology of national and racial superiority and indomitable destiny.

More specifically, fascism is a word having two general meanings, one broadly political, the other more narrowly economic. In the stricter, economic sense, fascism is a theory of the "corporate state." This means the creation of government-subsidized and -regulated private monopolies and the parallel regimentation of the labor force. It provides for small and concentrated industrial control, under state auspices, in the midst of emotionalized mass identification. This accounts for the seeming incongruity between the collectivist, "workers' paradise" character of fascism (National Socialism, for example) and the presence of private monopolies and industrial cartels. In the last analysis, under this system the state merely uses economic arrangements for its purposes without any effort to reconcile them with theory.

But fascism came to mean more than this. It is the "total" solution, its advocates claimed. Never a philosophically coherent theory, fascism is a disorganized and variable collection of ideas and myths. It also changes its visage with the situation and with whoever personally epitomizes it. Thus the applied fascist program of Hitler differed from that of Mussolini or Franco. Much stress, as a matter of fact, is laid by the fascists upon "national character," and fascism is consequently adapted to suit these differences in national habit and attitude. Nazism was antagonistic to the church, to cite one illustration, although it arranged an expedient truce; but the Falangists in Spain took Roman Catholicism as a part of their party doctrine. And the Japanese leaders of the military revival encouraged the resurgence of a quasireligion, Shinto. But however fascism is adopted to the idiom of the culture, there are certain major precepts that can be isolated and examined. Fascism as a comprehensive belief contains the following main facets: (1) hypernationalism and the myth of the People, (2) élitism and racism, (3) the leader principle, (4) irrationalism and anti-intellectualism, (5) geographic determinism, (6) terror and ubiquitous control, and (7) antipathy for aristocratic values.

Fascism arose with and furthered the growth of hypernationalism, which reached at times an almost pathological intensity. Nationalism per se is usually thought to have its origins in the French Revolution, since that epochal turmoil gave rise to feelings of mass identification with the nation-state. Patriotism was a normal product of this identification and exhibited a switch from dynastic loyalty and regional pride to a full-blown sense of national oneness and admiration. People have long felt that there exists an innate superiority in the group to which they belong; this may well be an extension of their own egos. The anthropologists have called this "ethnocentrism"—loosely, a sense of racial or cultural superiority. Most primitive peoples have this attitude strongly ingrained; many tribes and clans merely refer to themselves as "the People."

Fascism rode in on a mounting ethnocentrism, unleashed by two main factors: Hegelianism and the insecurity that followed the dislocations caused by World War I. Representative of the neo-Hegelian school of supernationalists was *Heinrich von Treitschke* (1834-1896). He deified the state far beyond even Hegel's notions, and to his doctrine of its almost mystic origin Treitschke added the ideas of the necessity of war as a reconstitution of the nation, a sweeping definition of sovereignty (he applauded Gustavus Adolphus' remark: "I recognize no power over me but God and the conqueror's sword"), a glorification of strength, and a truculent concept of national honor.

Obviously influential on the fascist conception of nationalism as the ideas of Treitschke are, his theories, contained in *Politics* (1897), subtly reveal the beginnings of less apparent contributions. He often talks of "culture," but there is evident the notion that the state is to be more interested in power than refinement and that "blood and iron" (to use Bismarck's phrase) are more important than the softer accomplishments. "The State," Treitschke observes, "is not an Academy of Arts." As well, he speaks with adulatory language not just about the state, but about the *German* state. It is not a huge leap to move from the idea of the omnipotent state to a worship of a given nation-state. Treitschke specifically begins to call out against the allegedly unjust way in which Germany had been dealt with by circumstance. She had not received her due, if one takes into account her superiorities. Why? Treitschke answers with complete simplicity: She has not been strong enough to take what she wants. Germany is losing the race for colonies, he moans: [1]

> But any political community not in a position to assert its native strength as against any given group of neighbors will always be on the verge of losing its characteristics as a state. This has always been the case. Great changes in the art of war have destroyed numberless states. It is because an army of twenty thousand men can only be reckoned today as a weak army corps that the small states of Central Europe cannot maintain themselves in the long run. [2]

But Treitschke's nationalism is by fascist standards incomplete. It does not lay sufficient emphasis upon the creation myth of the People. Nationalism in the fascist sense leans heavily on the idea of a superior historical origination of the national character. This is at once racial, mythological, and historical. In essence, the concept runs like this: In some past age, a time of heroes and primal struggle, one tribe or horde or folk was dominant as a result of its natural endowments. This superior group fell upon bad times, principally because it relied on means other than its strength for survival and advancement. This was disastrous for two reasons. First, it was undesirable because it placed the people in a subservient position *vis-à-vis* their natural inferiors. But even this was not as serious as the fact that this state of weakness and lethargy prevented the folk from realizing its preshaped and ultimate destiny. It had a great goal, a quest, and it had a sacred mission to reach it.

In all fascist literature this myth appears in one form or another. Hitler speaks of it in terms of Germanic superiority: "We, as guardians of the highest humanity on this earth, are bound by the highest obligations." The element of destiny, a place in the sun, is ever-present.

---

[1] Writes Treitschke: "Up to the present Germany has always had too small a share of the spoils in the partition of non-European territories among the powers of Europe, and yet our existence as a State of the first rank is vitally affected by the question whether we can become a power beyond the seas. If not, there remains the appalling prospect of England and Russia dividing the world between them, and in such a case, it is hard to say whether the Russian knout or the English money bags would be the worst alternative" (*Politics*, Chapter 1).

[2] *Ibid.*

It has the flavor of Hegel's dialectic, but all the logical necessity is removed and replaced by primitivism and the ethnocentricity of the barbarian.

Closely bound up with the national myth is the fascist formulation of élitism and racialism. In its absolute rejection of the idea of human equality, fascism argues along two lines. First, political power must be exercised by an élite since that arrangement is not only superior but inevitable. Second, there are superior and inferior races, those meant to rule and those meant to be ruled. The argument, as we shall see, is a combination of biology, history, and occult metaphysics. The origins of the strictly élitist fascist doctrine can be best illustrated by reference to the ideas of *Vilfredo Pareto* (1848-1923). Although Pareto was himself not a fascist (even though he accepted a post under Mussolini) but rather a fervent supporter of individual freedom, it was nonetheless his sociology, which made élitism inescapable, that strongly stirred fascism in general (and Mussolini's version in particular). In substance, Pareto's theory, found in his *Mind and Society*, is an elaborate and frequently ponderous syllogism. The major premise is that a thoroughly scientific analysis of human behavior reveals that irrational contents (*residues*) are critical in the formation of attitudes. These residual motivations, minor premise, divide between traits identifiable as orderly, disciplined, and habitual and those adventurous, experimental, and restless. These differing nonrational components in behavior are expressed in social values, and the two blocs of sentiment are battling to dominate one another. Conclusion: a natural social balance.

Pareto's syllogism causes him to draw two main inferences. The first is that this balance can be drastically impinged upon to the disruption of healthy society by planning, social tampering, and, most important, by moralistic reform. The second inference is that the natural equilibrium does not in any case remain indefinitely fixed. A cyclic pattern is discernible; one or the other of the two competing sentiments will prevail—either a fondness for stability and discipline or the eagerness for experiment and dynamism. This is a power stuggle, contends Pareto, and with no holds barred, but each socially felt irrational disposition culminates in the creation of a small oligarchy, an élite. If the pendulum swings in a given direction, the appropriate élite gains power. But the possession of power is itself debilitating, and eventually the ruling élite gives way to an élite representing the new sentiment. But power is *always* surrendered by one élite to another. This is inescapable, argues Pareto, because only an élite can crystallize in itself the prevailing social spirit. Popular government or democracy is not really an alternative, he concludes, for even the state most responsive to the popular will (based on universal suffrage, let us say) is merely an outward façade concealing oligarchic leadership.

Robert Michels (1876-1936) rested his argument for the indispensability of the élite on an organizational imperative, the "iron law of oligarchy." Michel's line of reasoning differs materially from Pareto's, but it takes him to the same place. The élite, the small decision-making minority, always controls the instruments of powers, Michels claims, because in the actual organization of any group a small segment arises to direct and control. This is even more true for states, he contends, than it is for less complicated forms of organization. It follows, then, that while the power struggle goes on, it is warfare between élites, one gaining ascendancy over the other. Even if in theory the whole social structure were laid aside and the organizational process begun again, it would be inherent in that process that oligarchies would be formed and that these would exercise authority. Organization equals oligarchy; this is Michel's renowned "iron law."

The sociology of Pareto and the organizational analysis of Michels helped in varying degrees to shape fascist élitism, but it was racism that both widened the appeal of the movement and intensified it.[3] The argument that races are of unequal capacities due to their innately different natures was not an innovation of fascism. In the nineteenth century, *Count Joseph Arthur de Gobineau* (1816-1882) had written fully on the subject in his *Inequality of 'he Races* (1855). Gobineau reduced all social questions to matters of racial inheritance. He drew from his historical studies a theory of a great race that existed on the Eurasian steppes before historical record. These were the Aryans; their disappearance was accounted for by the fact that they dissipated their racial purity by interbreeding with inferior stock. The best of what remained, Gobineau rather disheartedly observed, was the European Caucasian.

Houston Stewart Chamberlain (1855-1927) forged a much closer connection with contemporary fascism. An English-born émigré to Germany, Chamberlain enjoyed the dubious honor of Hitler's esteem. Rephrasing Gobineau's basic theme, Chamberlain more specifically located the descendants of the "great race"—they were the Germans. Moreover, he made yet another discovery beyond the alleged findings

---

[3] While Pareto and Michels are suitable and adequate representatives of the élitist argument, mention should also be made of Gaetano Mosca. See his *Ruling Class* (1895) for an additional defense of élitism.

of his French predecessor. Not only were some races inferior, but in particular the Jewish "race" epitomized the results of allowing inferior bloodlines not only to contaminate Aryan biological purity, but to undermine its culture. Chamberlain created a sort of intellectual madhouse in which biological, psychological, and cultural factors all frantically intermixed. However, his *Foundations of the Nineteenth Century* (1910) became a handbook for fascist racial ideas, specifically in the case of the Nazi movement and more generally in that of fascism elsewhere. Wherever applied, the racial superiority doctrine in fascism was present. In Germany, it was the Aryan or Teutonic ascendency, tracing its origins to the stock of some Heroic Age. In Italy, the *fascisti* were lineal descendents, or so they announced, of the legions of the Caesars. The Japanese could unabashedly delve back into their past as far as their descent from the Sun God.

Fascism is a cry for the omnicompetent leader. He is an infallible man-god. This is the result, not of his wisdom or personal attributes particularly, but rather of his representing the "soul" or "spirit" of the people. His origins are mysterious, clouded in Wagnerian obscurity; he is initially humble and persecuted. He has visions; he has undeterrable resolve, because he is motivated by the instincts of the people whom he leads. He is the savior, the messianic manifestation, and as such he is at once one of the horde and above the horde. He will make any sacrifice. His actions are beyond question, because they are beyond the understanding of those not privy to the revelations of the ultimate destiny of the nation.

In practice, this type of leadership is both a "cult of personality" (to use a phrase popularized by Mr. Khrushchev) and an organizational device. In the first case, the leadership motif is a part of the mystic idealization of ethnocentrism. In the second instance, it is a blueprint for the disposition of power. Hitler's phraseology in this connection is applicable to fascism over-all: What makes the state work is the "leader principle" (*Führerprinzip*), which Hitler succinctly defined as "authority of every leader downward and responsibility upward." Of course, in point of fact, Hitler did not conceive of a hierarchical structure with actual delegations of authority on various levels. All authority culminated in a single leader, and only he actually possessed any; his subordinate "leaders" were mere agents of his personal will. The fascist supreme leader, then, enjoys both ultimate authority and complete freedom from responsibility, as he has no person or institution to whom he is responsible. Fascism, while ostensibly élitist, is in practice virtually controlled by a single "divinity," a single will.

Considerable comment has already been made about the irrational base of fascism. This worship of the irrational has a number of by-products. The fascist code is at once anti-intellectual, vociferously antimoral, and vigorously primitive. The characteristic features of fascism in practice are bonfires consuming prohibited books, fleeing professors, and artists banned for ideological incompatibility with the system. While it might be obvious that in any regime built on total control, no deviations, intellectual or otherwise, would be permitted, the underlying reason for the fascist hatred of intellectualism is deeper than that. The real fear is that in some fashion intellectualism saps the strength and softens the character. While it is true that free intellectual activity was suppressed in Germany and Italy on grounds of political nonconformity, the fascist mind feels threatened by learning and art, looking at them as a sort of enchantress, à la Delilah, who will rob it of its primitive virility and wolf-like passion. Fascism is an intestinal faith, not a cerebral theory; what is admired is the warrior of Nietzsche—without the essential Nietzschean component of artistic sensitivity. Hermann Göring, the late Reichsmarshal who took his own life at Nürnberg, is reputed to have quipped: "When I hear the word 'culture' mentioned, I reach for my pistol."

Fascism is a rejection of the general moral consensus of Western civilization. In form, this repudiation either takes on Nietzsche's ethic, by and large, or accepts Machiavelli's; here is the distinction between fascism as conceived by National Socialism in Germany and by the Italian Fascist Party. But whichever version of ethical nihilism is selected, fascism is a self-conscious regression. It avowedly yearns to return to the barbaric ages—dignifying this era by the term "heroic." Imperial splendors are recalled, but those invariably associated with fleshly indulgence and violence rather than stable magnificence. This primitivism, coupled with moral nihilism, suggests in some versions of fascism a dream of carnal fantasies and the abandonment of restraints, sexual and gustatory. However, this is not invariably the case, and some fascist programs have emphasized either Spartan-like self-restraint or the encouragement of bourgeois respectability.

The notion of the "great destiny" is linked with a carefully manufactured concept of geographical determinism—the special *Geopolitik*. Geopolitics was neither a German nor an Italian invention. Most credit must go to an English geographer, Sir Halford Mackinder,[4] with an assist from an American strategic theorist, Admiral Alfred T. Mahan.[5] Moreover, in specifics, geopolitics was ruthlessly fashioned in the hands of fascist writers to fit the requirements of given states. In Germany, for illustration, Professor Karl Haushofer established a uniquely nationalistic school of geopolitics. In Japan, the effects of geopolitical ideas were to be seen in the Tanaka Memorial, a working plan for Asiatic conquest. Simply put, geopolitics is a specialized study of international affairs, stressing the effect of geographical factors on the behavior of states. In fascist use, geopolitics became a theory of territorial expansion, usually by intimidation or conquest. In the main, it is an elaborate justification for national aggrandizement. In Hitlerian language, one of the erstwhile geopolitical principles was *Lebensraum* —"living space." Population pressures made territorial expansion not merely desirable, according to this principle, but obedient to deterministic geographical theory. The same held true for the gaining of needed foodstuffs and raw material. Mussolini, in setting about to subdue Ethiopia, could not even make these claims and justified the Italian action as a need for colonial empire of grander dimensions to befit Italy's image.

Fascism not only endorsed and improved the use of terror, but it also institutionalized it. Terror for political purposes is an old technique. The Romans used it; so did the Inquisition and Cromwell. The Committee of Public Safety in Revolutionary France applied it on a scale unknown except, perhaps, in remote civilizations of Asia. There is no need to digress with descriptions of the assorted technological and psychological refinements ushered in by fascist regimes. The arresting observation is that it was only fascism that had built-in terror as a regular and consistent feature of its governmental structure. While the device of mass intimidation by cruelty was known before, and while the Jacobins partially regularized it, not until the rise of fascism could one see permanent "departments of terror" as a normal component in government organization. Moreover, under fascism, terror was not necessarily directed at specific or limited goals, but was employed as a continuing coercive factor in maintaining political solidarity. The importance of the one-party political system was that it provided a dual structure in government reserving the terror function for the

---

[4] See Sir Halford Mackinder, "The Geographical Pivot of History," *Proceedings of the Royal Geographic Society* (1904), and *Democratic Ideals and Reality* (New York: W. W. Norton & Co., Inc., 1962).

[5] See Alfred T. Mahan, *The Influence of Sea Power on History* (New York: Hill & Wang, Inc., 1957).

élite party. This made it possible to use terror even against the political mechanism if that proved expedient.

This predilection for terror and violence was given some impetus by the writings of *Georges Sorel* (1847-1922). Sorel, a French radical and leader of syndicalism,[6] promoted the idea of the necessity of violence to attain political ends. In his *Reflections on Violence* (1908), he laid down an extensive program of pro-Marxist action that included the development of militant *syndicats* or trade unions, which would wage war on the bourgeois by means of the technique of the general strike. But Sorel's "general strike" was no ordinary work stoppage; it was a war, and he compared its operation to traditional military undertakings:

> The proletariat organises itself for battle, separating itself distinctly from the other parts of the nation, and regarding itself as the great motive power of history, all other social considerations being subordinated to that combat; it is very clearly conscious of the glory which will be attached to its historical role and of the heroism of its militant attitude; it longs for the final contest in which it will give proof of the whole measure of its valour.[7]

While fascism had no use for Sorel's political and economic objectives, the measures he sketched out were noticeably attractive. In the broader sense, fascism was influenced by Sorel's general endorsement of violence for social control—the use of ruthless intimidation after power has been secured. It accepted Sorel's dictum that "a social policy founded on middle-class cowardice, which insists on always surrendering before the threat of violence, cannot fail to engender the idea that the middle class is condemned to death, and that its disappearance is only a matter of time." [8]

For all its reverence for élitism, fascism is profoundly hostile toward traditional aristocracy and its values. It is, in the first place, a movement of the dispossessed, and its entire orientation, moral, social, and political, runs counter to the aristocratic spirit. Aristocrats are hated quite as much by the fascists as they are by the communists, only the former are willing to coerce, bribe, or use them to serve their own ends. In some instances, the fascists have reached a modus vivendi with the old aristocratic interests (in Spain, for example). In Germany, on the other hand, the Nazis remained unreconciled with the rigidly conserva-

---

[6] Sorel's syndicalism, a blending of Marxist and anarchist ideas, had a rather significant influence on fascism in Italy. Mussolini incorporated some of the syndicalist program and employed many of Sorel's agitational devices.

[7] Georges Sorel, *Reflections on Violence*, Chapter 5, Section III.

[8] *Ibid.*, Chapter 1, Section II.

tive elements. Indeed, a circle of *Junker* conspirators very nearly ended Hitler's life with a bomb during World War II. To the majority of aristocrats, the Nazis were loathed as barbarians and upstarts, and with like vehemence the Nazis held the German aristocracy to be the symbol of Germany's previous state of ignominy and defeat. The point to be made is that fascism is not a continuance of the modern aristocratic theory that began with Burke any more than Marxism is a continuance of the liberalism of Bentham. Fascism means total change—and the destruction of most of the hallowed traditions held in regard by conservatives in the spirit of Burke or Maistre or Metternich. Fascism is not even in the same stream of ideology with Bismarck, that pragmatic political realist and unsentimental conniver. Fascism means rule by the politically hungry, by "hypnotized hypnotists" or transient adventurers. How Moltke would have scorned; how Cavour would have been appalled.

Fascism is a bit short on "official" philosophers. That title among the National Socialists belongs to Albert Rosenberg, who was, by any standards, more "official" than "philosopher." [9] Somewhat more respectable are those associated with fascism in Italy. Foremost among these are *Alfredo Rocco* (1875-1935) and *Giovanni Gentile* (1875-1944). Rocco's defense stresses the ramifications of the organic state and the desirability of fascist "corporatism" in establishing a harmonious economy. A lawyer and Minister of Justice, Rocco offers this opinion:

> The time has now come when class self-defense also must be replaced by state justice. To facilitate the change fascism has created its own syndicalism. Fascism has transformed the syndicate, that old revolutionary instrument of syndicalist socialists, into an instrument of legal defense of the classes both within and without the law courts.[10]

Gentile is more subtle and, being a professional philosopher, more aware of his tasks. He, too, summons up as other fascists had done the glories of the past and the crisis of the present. The depressed state of Italy is, he announces, the result of ideas of the Left in general, although he singles out "crude positivism" as the major culprit. Idealism is in decline, Gentile observes, and he contrasts this deterioration with the patriotic spirit of Mazzini, the nationalist hero. The reaction has set in, he writes, combing "syndicalists, nationalists, idealists" against

---

[9] One important philosopher did express some approval of the National Socialists in their early days—Martin Heidegger, the well-known existentialist.

[10] Alberto Rocco, *The Political Doctrine of Fascism*.

"parliamentary socialism." Gentile candidly endorses the need for violence in order to break the grip of "official, legal, parliamentary Italy." He couples with extremism, an emotional irrationalism: "From the first, the Fascist party was not one of believers, but of action. What it needed was not a platform of principles, but an idea which would indicate a goal and a road by which the goal could be reached." [11]

What is unique about fascism, argues Gentile, is that it "concerns itself not only with political organization and political tendency, but with the whole will and thought and feeling of a nation." He reiterates the antirationalism of the movement by an intense admiration for action and a detestation of intellectualism—which he defines as "the divorce of thought from action, of knowledge from life, of brain from heart, of theory from practice." The reverence for action becomes a belief in expediency and improvisation. Interestingly enough, Gentile maintains that fascism is not a political system at all, but that circumstances compel it to present itself "as a political method." The heart of fascism, he proclaims with rather obscure reasoning, is moral and spiritual. A "deeper concept of life" underlies fascism's political methodology. Just what in fact this philosophic heartbeat is, Gentile does not specifically confide.

In dealing with the concept of the state, Gentile claims to have abandoned both the Hegelian organic theory and the liberal view. He explains:

> The State is a wholly spiritual creation. It is a national State, because, from the fascist point of view, the nation itself is a creation of the mind and is not a material presupposition, is not a datum of nature. The nation, says the fascist, is never really made; neither, therefore, can the State attain an absolute form, since it is merely the nation in the latter's concrete, political manifestation. For the fascist, the State is always *in fieri*. It is in our hands, wholly; whence our very serious responsibility towards it.[12]

From this somewhat tangled line of thought, Gentile makes the assertion that the fascist state is the manifestation of the popular will. Just how the state can be this as well as being infallible and totalitarian, to say nothing of being a fountainhead of revelation, is not explained. But the confusion is evident in this singular passage:

> The fascist State, on the contrary, is a people's state, and, as such, the democratic state *par excellence*. The relationship between the State

---

[11] Giovanni Gentile, "The Philosophical Basis of Fascism," *Foreign Affairs*, Vol. VI (January, 1928), 290-304.
[12] *Ibid.*

and citizen (not this or that citizen, but all citizens) is accordingly
so intimate that the State exists only as, and insofar as, the citizen
causes it to exist. Its formation therefore is the formation of a consciousness of it in individuals, in masses. Hence the need of the party,
and of all instruments of propaganda and education which fascism
uses to make the thought and the will of the Duce the thought and
the will of the masses. Hence the enormous task which fascism sets
itself in trying to bring the whole mass of the people, beginning with
the little children, inside the fold of the party.[13]

The blatant circularity appears not to disturb Gentile, who later
argues that "the authority of the State is absolute. It does not compromise, it does not bargain, it does not surrender any portion of its
field to other moral or religious principles which may interfere with
the individual conscience." [14] What Gentile puts forward is the thesis
that fascism is a mysterious synthesization of the state and the individual, but with a certain philosophic bravado he makes no attempt
to frame an explanation of this elusive merger. Fascism in general,
and despite whether or not all forms of it accept Gentile's quasihumanis-
tic tone, assumes this state-individual coalition both as self-evident and
as a unique truth of fascism. The problem of the One and the Many
is at least as old as Plato, but fascism clearly disavows the problem,
however sententiously it chooses to allude to it.

This ducking of the issue of the source and essence of the state is
not the only problem to plague fascist thought. One of the most prominent is the persistent insecurity created by the system. This is an
ironic situation considering the totalitarian dedication of the fascist
mind. This undeniable flux is felt both on the level of political control
and among the rank-and-file. In the first instance, the reification of
power, the idea of the élite as a cult of the revealed mysteries, and
the principle of the leaders as a personification of the spirit of the
folk all contribute to creating a situation in which power is tenuously
held and in which the protective instincts of both the élite and the
leader soon begin to overshadow other more critical considerations.
This brings into being a state of constant suspicion and for those in
power a bad case of nerves. Power, resting on no base of legitimacy
and the acquisition of it imposing no restraints as to technique, becomes
a prize open to anyone with the ambition to reach out for it. And what
insurance is there that a new and more potent mystery may not come

---

[13] *Ibid.*
[14] *Ibid.*

to life? Who can predict that a new prophet may not arise to embody the national spirit? What results is a balance of fear.

The totalitarian state limits participation in the national life to a very significant degree. It rejects prima facie the employment of the full resources of talent available to the state. In placing such a high price on allegiance it sharply depreciates talent and in the long run stimulates mediocrity. In this sense, fascism is self-consuming. It arises with the cry for the need for excellence, an end to cautious and inept mediocrity, but once installed its necessary regimentation invariably creates within itself an even more ubiquitous mediocrity, a suspicion of the excellent as overly discriminating, critical, and independent. In practice, this need not be a universal fact. There are isolated instances in fascist regimes of individuals of marked talent being permitted to operate. But almost without exception this takes place within restricted fields of endeavor and in areas usually removed from political sensitivity. On the other hand, there are many more illustrations of the deterioration of state operation, both in policy and function, through this preference for ideological safety and sycophantic enthusiasm. The steady decline in the quality of German military leadership in World War II as a result of standards unrelated to excellence may serve as a case in point.

When applied to the act of governing, fascist theory inevitably means rule by excess. Moderation is impossible, and measures of extreme character become both a pattern and a requirement. Excess frequently is the progenitor of excessive reaction. Severity breeds equally stringent countermeasures. Rigidity of control makes ameliorization dependent upon the unleashing of force. Put another way: There are limits to terror. The effects of extremism are twofold. First, it imposes upon policy-making an habitual attitude that is often destructive of governmental soundness and prudence. Secondly, it makes change and adaptation a matter of harsh upheaval rather than adjustment. The pattern of the rise and fall of dictators need not be recounted as it is a part of the common fund of knowledge; Mussolini began his career by marching on Rome at the head of his Blackshirt "legions," but he ended it hanging upside down from a gasoline pump. Fascist leaders do not retire to the quiet of country retreats when they leave the political forum. Some appear to be able to exile themselves in no mean splendor, but even here the long reach of terror may snatch at them. The political maturation of societies is rendered difficult if not impossible by cycles of purges and dislocations. Civilization creeps; it does not often leap.

Fascism as a political phenomenon tends to divert attention from problems rather than to solve them. This is a significant self-destructive feature of the ideology. Frequently, it dares not even acknowledge the existence of the vital difficulty. Like all "total solutions," fascism is forced to fit circumstances into hypotheses. In application, this causes fascism as a program of action to utilize diversion and adventure as a sort of palliative. When Gibbon talked of "bread and circuses" in connection with the decline of Roman political vitality, he might just as well have referred to a fascist state. Quite aside from the need for vulgar displays and childish symbolisms in the form of flags, uniforms, parades, festivals, and rallies, the ever-mounting need for diversion causes the selection of policy alternatives often against the best interests of the state itself. It is not only neighboring states that suffer from the necessity of fascist regimes to wage wars and engage in international freebooting; the state itself is damaged. However effectively fascism may control internal affairs, it cannot change the international verities. Consequently, undertakings designed to divert attention from pressing internal troubles may maximize the total difficulties. The pressure to fulfill the mystic destiny becomes too great to sustain effective political development in the face of it.

Benito Mussolini gives voice to both the militancy of fascism and to its sense of destiny:

> War alone brings up to their highest tension all human energies and puts the stamp of nobility upon the peoples who have the courage to meet it. All other trials are substitutes, which never really put a man in front of himself in the alternative of life and death. . . . Thus the fascist accepts and loves life; he knows nothing of suicide and despises it; he looks on life as duty, ascent, conquest; life, which must be noble and full, lived for oneself, but above all for those others near and far away, present and future.[15]

But Mussolini was a biased historian and an unreliable prophet, at least regarding his own outcome. Perhaps the real shortcoming, not only of fascist leaders, but of fascism itself, is its lack of introspection, its inability to look intelligently at itself. This frequently pathological self-deception makes propitious adjustment and canny compromise impossible, assuming for the sake of argument that we are evaluating fascism on utilitarian grounds. Self-delusion is the most damning de-

---

[15] Benito Mussolini, *The Doctrine of Fascism*, Michael Oakeshott, trans., quoted in his *Social and Political Doctrines of Contemporary Europe* (New York: Cambridge University Press, 1942), Section II.

fect of politicians and political theories. The degree to which this is involved in current Communist policy is intriguing to speculate on.

But the grievous flaw in fascism, the terrible bar sinister on its heraldry, is its reduction of the human being to the status of a predator. Those who would argue (and many have in the history of political ideas) that existence involves *only* the preying of one human being on another in the lust of savagery are blind to what human activity has already attained. These primitives have never been alone with Goethe or communed with Bach. They have never, to use Nietzsche's splendid phrase, "listened with the third ear."

. . . for further discussion:

1. Did fascism die with the fall of Hitler, Mussolini, *et al.*, following World War II? Is it still a going concern anywhere in the world? From what you know about it, could you make any predictions regarding where fascism might be applied in the future and the specific forms it might adopt in these instances?

2. What similarities and differences can you find between fascism as a general theory of society and Marxism? Is it accurate to describe both fascist and communist states as "totalitarian"?

3. If you were going to introduce fascism into the United States, how would you go about it? What kind of ideological appeals would you make? What sort of a political program would you offer?

4. In his *Genesis and Structure of Society*, Giovanni Gentile writes: "Hence even the esentially critical activity of philosophy involves an essential and indispensable recognition of the positive element or content of every regime or specific organization of the State in its historical actuality." Is this an exclusively fascist view? To what extent is political philosophy tempered or should it be tempered by any loyalties to political or cultural establishments?

. . . for further investigation:

Arendt, Hannah, * The Origins of Totalitarianism. New York: Meridian Books, 1958.

Ebenstein, William, * Today's Isms. Englewood Cliffs, N. J.: Prentice-Hall, Inc., 1961.

Fichte, Johann G., * Addresses to the German Nation. LaSalle, Ill.: Open Court Publishing Co., in preparation.

Friedrich, Carl J. and Z. K. Brzezinski, * Totalitarian Dictatorship and Autocracy. New York: Frederick A. Praeger, Inc., n.d.

Gentile, Giovanni, Genesis and Structure of Society, H. S. Harris, trans. Urbana, Ill.: University of Illinois Press, 1960.

Gentile, Giovanni, "The Philosophic Basis of Fascism," *Foreign Affairs,* Vol. VI, January, 1928.

Gobineau, Arthur de, *The Inequality of Human Races,* A. Collins, trans. New York: G. P. Putnam's Sons, 1915.

Henderson, L. J., *Pareto's General Sociology.* Cambridge, Mass.: Harvard University Press, 1935.

Hitler, Adolf, ° *Mein Kampf,* Ralph Manheim, trans. Boston, Mass.: Houghton Mifflin Co., 1962.

Hoffer, Eric, ° *The True Believer.* New York: Mentor Books, 1958.

Homans, George C. and Charles P. Curtis, Jr., *An Introduction to Pareto.* New York: Alfred A. Knopf, Inc., 1934.

Mosca, Gaetano, ° *The Ruling Class.* New York: McGraw-Hill Book Co., Inc., n.d.

Rocco, Alberto, ° *The Political Doctrine of Fascism,* D. Bigongiari, trans. New York: International Conciliation Pamphlet No. 223, Carnegie Endowment for International Peace, 1926.

Shirer, William L., ° *The Rise and Fall of the Third Reich.* Greenwich, Conn.: Crest Books, 1962.

Sorel, Georges, ° *Reflections on Violence,* T. E. Hulme and J. Roth, trans. New York: Collier Books, n.d.

Treitschke, Heinrich von, *Politics,* B. Dugdale and T. de Bille, trans. London: Constable & Co. Ltd., 1916.

17

DEMOCRACY AT THE
BAR OF REASON—
AND UNREASON

Democracy is a tricky word to cope with. It means different things to different people. To a party worker in Peiping it means one thing, to a Chicago business man quite another—and to a Bushman in the Kalahari Desert it is completely incomprehensible. To clothe the word with some precise meaning is no small undertaking. The fashion in which the term is used in the communist context may be easily dismissed, not out of any chauvinistic disdain, but for the reason that the communist usage represents no historical continuity. The roots of democracy are, whatever else one may choose to say, irrefutably in the European Enlightenment. What vague democratic suggestions are to be found in Marx are the result of his own affinity to the Enlightenment.

But within the range of the use of the term in Western society, difficulties of definition are still to be encountered. The first major obstacle is historical, the second philosophic. The historical problem is simply that democracy in the twentieth century is not what it was in the nineteenth. While this may not be surprising perhaps, it is nonetheless frequently confusing since the changes are often the result of significant alterations of value and principle. Moreover, the shift of values did not neatly parallel the turning of the century; the modifications took place at different times in different places. The growth of democracy in America or Britain might be said to have undergone three rather distinct phases: (1) constitutional democracy, (2) liberal democracy, and (3) popular or social democracy. A prolonged recourse to history is unnecessary, and the principal theoretic development of the first two has already been discussed. Constitutional democracy was the period of the legal enforcement of individual rights, the growth of legislative institutions, and the preservation of an essentially aristocratic or republican social outlook. In America, it was the Federalist period, the time of Adams and Hamilton. In Britain, it was the age before the Reform Bill of 1832, the era of Burke and Pitt.

Liberal democracy was the child of liberalism. It was the period of *laissez-faire*, individual prerogative, the extension of suffrage, the rise of the middle class, reform and industrialization, the slow beginnings of bureaucratic centralization. It was the age of expansion in America, marked by the presidency of Andrew Jackson and the receding of Whig ideas. In Britain, liberal democracy was identified with Mill and Gladstone.

Popular or social democracy is mainly identifiable with the twentieth century. Its most striking feature is the harmonization of the rugged individualism of the nineteenth century with the cooperative interdependencies of the twentieth, verging at times on a sort of uneasy amalgamation of individualism and collectivism. The individual welfare and the general welfare are merged. Too, popular democracy represents a spreading egalitarian feeling and the application of ideas about equality and economic and social justice to wider and hitherto private sectors of national life. The state, a limited instrument of equilibrium and regulation under *laissez-faire* democracy, broadens its scope of action and grows both in statutory powers and in social responsibilities. The full implications of popular democracy will be treated shortly.

But historical change alone does not make defining democracy troublesome. There is a philosophic divergence of view, too. Virtually all definitions of democracy (and there are as many as there are writers on the subject) fall into two categories: Democracy is defined (1) as a body of moral principles or (2) as attitudes toward procedure. The first definition wishes to consider democracy as a way of life, the second as a functional concept. Implicit in the first approach is the conviction that democracy has in fact a number of broad philosophic premises, and the second approach patently denies this. There is something to be said for both schools of thought. For our purposes, democracy will be approached first as popular democracy and then from the standpoint of its moral base, but we shall endeavor to include the procedural orientations when possible. But it can be said without much scholarly risk that democracy is *not* a political philosophy. If it is a collection of moral truths, then it is *more* than a political philosophy; if it is a set of attitudes about procedural matters, then it is *less* than a political philosophy.

John Dewey (1859-1952), perhaps popular democracy's sturdiest defender—for all his pragmatism—looked upon democracy in the broader and more comprehensive sense. Writes Dewey:

> The political and governmental phase of democracy is a means, the best means so far found, for realizing ends that lie in the wide domain of human relationships and the development of human personality. It is, as we often say, though perhaps without appreciating all that is involved in the saying, a way of life, social and individual. The keynote of democracy as a way of life may be expressed, it seems to me, as the necessity for the participation of every mature human being in formation of values that regulate the living of men together: which is necessary from the standpoint of both the general social welfare and the full development of human beings as individuals.[1]

In any effort to characterize popular democracy in some orderly manner, the following are suggested as principles and attributes of substantial generality that there would be agreement among supporters of democratic theory at least on a majority of them: (1) A belief in decision by majority rule. (2) A belief that there is a need for some type of popular representation. (3) A belief that the state was created to meet social needs and that sovereignty rests with the people. (4) A belief in human equality (differing as to specific application). (5) A legalistic temper and a belief in the indispensability of the "rule of

---

[1] John Dewey, "Democracy and Educational Administration," an address before the National Education Association, February 22, 1937, published in *School and Society* (April 3, 1937). Included in *Intelligence in the Modern World; John Dewey's Philosophy,* Joseph Ratner, ed. (New York: Modern Library, Inc., 1939), p. 400.

law." (6) An endorsement of individual liberty, reflecting a cognizance of the sanctity of the person and of private property (in varying degrees). (7) An endorsement of value relativism as opposed to value absolutism and a belief in tolerance and the desirability of a plural society. (8) An optimistic orientation, including the supposition that human nature is basically good and improvable. (9) An altruistic component, assuming man to be gregarious, cooperative, and disposed toward rejection of total selfishness. (10) A belief that freedom to express ideas and to experiment without unnecessary limitation is a catalytic agent that maximizes social well-being. (11) A belief that truth wins out over error (assuming all other conditions are equal). (12) A pragmatic inclination that defines truth as that which solves problems.

Democratic theory defends the concept of *majority rule* on two fronts: (1) Since there are no absolute rights or wrongs, the only criterion of the good is what the majority wants. It is not even a question of wisdom or folly, since those are themselves arbitrary and artificial terms. The only standard of judgment is the majority will. This is essentially Bentham's argument. (2) Democracy as a theory of politics faces a considerable problem in majority rule as a principle once any normative precept is introduced. How can intelligent decisions be made by counting heads? Is not the quality of the decisions affected by the quality of the heads counted? What rational decision could be reached via majority rule if, say, out of twenty men, nineteen were idiots? This difficulty is brought home even more trenchantly by the fact (which even the most enthusiastic democrats admit) that a large portion of citizens in a democratic society are in ignorance of the issues over which they exercise their influence and choice.

Granted, then, that there are wise and foolish decisions, how can majority rule be justified? The answer put forth goes like this: Admitted that the quality of individual heads to be counted leaves something to be desired, when they are placed in concert, in a collective whole, a wisdom asserts itself that transcends the limitations of individual intelligence and understanding. This argument takes a number of forms: "The people are always right in the long run," or some notion of "folk wisdom," or a faith in collective, if unsophisticated, common sense. The superiority of common sense over intellect is often pressed in democratic justification. However shy some democrats are about this question, the general will seems to be alluded to in a veiled fashion. And, too, some theorists make a distinction between the broad fundamental issues about which the judgment of the whole population can be appealed to and the growing body of more technical decisions which ought to be left to experts. The problem of majority rule versus the expert remains to be ironed out in applied democracy. The extremely rapid growth of administrative discretionary powers in government, decision by nonelected bureaucratic specialists, underscores this tendency

Disputes in large number have centered around the specifics of *popular representation*. The United States Constitution represents the classic compromise. There are good and sufficient reasons why the *idea* of representation is universally applauded in democratic thought, but much acrimony exists over its *form*. In 1962, the United States Supreme Court finally made up its mind on the matter of legal enforcement of provisions in state constitutions relating to periodic redistricting of state legislatures in order to reflect changes in population pattern. The decision by the Court to approve legal means of compelling such redistricting is a harbinger of rather drastic change, since the shift of population to urban areas has not, in many instances, been fully mirrored in the representation enjoyed by city residents. Strict proportional representation, in this instance, means virtual rule by the larger cities in many states. Is this wise, some ask, even if it is an accurate reflection of *numbers?* But the larger issue is this: Granted that representative government is desirable, what should be represented? Bodies only? Regions or localities? Interest groups? What about minority interests? Does property have any claim to representation (as once it did)? There are numerous unresolved questions lurking about. And, as well, do representatives themselves represent their constituents and their express wishes and opinions, or do these legislators have a larger obligation to national interest or their own views? Opinion remains divided.

Democracy certainly developed its idea of the state from the contract theory. *The state*—and hence government, which tends to be equitable in democratic thinking—*was created to serve the requirements of society.* It is a man-made construction, an instrument to protect the fundamental rights of individuals. The state is a desirable institution to the extent that it fulfills its mission of service; it is the servant, not the master. Explains John Dewey:

> The lasting, extensive, and serious consequences of associated activity bring into existence a public. In itself it is unorganized and formless. By means of officials and their special powers it becomes a state. A public articulated and operating through representative officers

is the state; there is no state without a government, but also there is
none without a public.[2]

There are. however, two complications to this general position. First,
and perhaps of small importance, the contract theory has dubious merit
and has in fact been retired in most current thought and replaced with
other, nonorganic explanations. Secondly, however a state came into
being, a state is a state; that is to say, it is sovereign. A democratic state,
in consequence, is not any less powerful in theory than a totalitarian
state. One can be deprived of life in a democracy just as readily as one
can in a police state—one is just as dead. The difference lies in how it
is done. The police state accomplishes it by sheer caprice or revenge;
the democratic state employs publicly acceptable procedures. The
democratic state is thus bound to procedural restraints (constitutions,
for example), but as a sovereign state it is *actually* not so bound and
is capable of changing at will the instrument that inhibits it. This means
that the question of both procedural arrangement and less apparent
political equilibrium are far more significant than any theory of the
popular origins of government.

Again in Dewey's words, the idea of *equality* is defended:

> The democratic faith in equality is the faith that each individual
> shall have the chance and opportunity to contribute whatever he is
> capable of contributing and that the value of his contribution be
> decided by its place and function in the organized total of similar
> contributions, not on the basis of prior status of any kind whatever.[3]

Democracy believes in the basic and fundamental equality of all
human beings This is an ethical or religious concept rather difficult to
deal with precisely. No serious theorist has argued the case for absolute
equality; that is, that all human individuals are of equal strength,
intelligence talent, endurance, or whatever category one chooses to
select. Individual differences exist, if one is to accept empirical evidence
at all. The democrat, however, insists that beneath the surface variations the human being shares an equality that springs either from
his possession of an immortal soul (if the theistic tradition is appealed
to) or has equal status as a creature or as a moral entity (taking the
naturalistic tack). The application of this broad belief to the realm
of political and social theory is more complex.

Originally, democracy's concept of equality was principally legalistic

---

[2] John Dewey, *The Public and Its Problems,* contained in *op. cit., Intelligence in
the Modern World,* p. 379.

[3] Dewey, *op. cit.,* "Democracy and Educational Administration" in *Intelligence
in the Modern World,* pp. 403-404.

—all men are equal before the bar of justice. This expanded to include equal political participation.[4] In most democratic thought, the egalitarian ideal has been extended to include equal economic opportunity, frequently by direct governmental guarantee. Still an issue is the question of *social* equality, the egalitarian principle advanced into the social sphere. This raises a number of subsidiary problems, such as the rights of private property, private association, and the morals of social discrimination. It does, however, underscore the fact that liberty and equality are not necessarily sisters, as some have blithely assumed. It was the eccentric John Randolph of Roanoke who in the early nineteenth century said, "I love liberty, but I hate equality." Discounting Randolph's aristocratic predispositions, it is evident that a rationally oriented society must establish some balance between the right of the individual to do just what he chooses and the enforcement of absolute equality in all things. The history of democracy suggests a continuing reëxamination of this balance.

Rule of law is another way of saying that democratic political society rests on a moral consensus as to the equity and suitability of procedures and the public and impartial administration of those procedures. It also includes a deep-rooted belief in the efficacy of jurisprudence, the sanctity of legal institutions, and the availability of them to any citizen in conflict with the machinery of the state. Democracy does not necessarily demand a "separation of powers," but it does strongly imply an independent judiciary and the operation of judicial review on various levels. The rule of law does mean at its very base that every man is entitled to his "day in court." In a democratic theory, opportunity for appeal from the actions of government must always be present and the appeal is to a body of procedures, personified by the courts, that themselves represent both the sovereignty and the moral conscience of the total population.

Individual liberty is thought to be socially beneficial, but its prime value is that it is in accordance with the concept of natural rights. Democratic political thought has never strayed very far from natural rights language; there has been a change of phraseology attributable to the pragmatists, but the doctrine has been unaffected. The "life, liberty, and property" of Locke still hold, although there has been a good deal of refinement of these categories. What justification is there

---

[4] This extension does not belong to the remote past. Women were permitted to vote everywhere in the United States only in 1920 with the adoption of the Twentieth Amendment to the United States Constitution. There are still those who favor, *sub rosa*, the disfranchisement of certain minority groups.

in democratic thought for any abridgment of these? First, either the common law or the Roman law doctrine prevails with only slight modification. The limitations of individual liberty have always been acknowledged in terms of the general welfare and the protection of other individuals' rights. In some areas, the curtailment of personal prerogative has been justified by new conditions. Thus freedom of speech, at one time limited by acts constituting a "clear and present danger," is now further restrained by the test of "clear and *probable* danger." On the other hand, the liberalization of censorship laws and the striking down of restrictive blue laws suggest an opposite trend.

But it is in the case of private property that the question of limitation arises with most prominence. Traditionally, private property and its use were limited by a common law precept of noninterference unless the safety, health, or morals of the community were in some way jeopardized. This was clearly a negative prohibition—"thou shalt not." There is some evidence to support the conclusion that some contemporary democratic theory would advocate further limitations of a positive sort, the regulation of property rights on the basis of contribution to the general welfare. Put another way: Private ownership means public responsibilities other than merely refraining from creating a dangerous or repulsive nuisance. The use of property, this point of view contends, must make a contribution toward the general benefit of society to justify the privilege of private ownership. This is not an insignificant shift of outlook. The extent of regulation of personal liberty and property is another continuing democratic debate.

Moral absolutism is generally shunned by most democratic advocates, even though this is surely the position of Christianity, from which democracy lays claim to garnering many of its principles. Undeniably, the tone of democratic theory is *relativistic,* denying the existence of moral universals, perhaps out of the suspicion, frequently justified, that a moral certitude often implies political autocracy. The issue is clearly an ethical one, and the merits of this aspect of democracy must be evaluated in terms of the claims and counterclaims of relativism and absolutism. It is fair to point out, however, that some democratic writers seem to employ the value-laden language of moral universals, while accepting the relativist theory of value. Dewey, at least, is never guilty of confusion on this point. His moral relativism is proudly proclaimed:

> In fact, the most significant change that would issue from carrying over the experimental method of physics to man concerns the status and import of standards, principles, rules. With the transfer, these,

and all tenets and creeds about good and goods, would be recognized to be hypotheses. Instead of being rigidly fixed, they would be treated as intellectual instruments to be tested and confirmed—and altered—through consequence effected by acting upon them. They would lose all pretence of finality—the ulterior source of dogmatism. It is both astonishing and depressing that so much of the energy of mankind has gone into fighting for (with weapons of the flesh as well as of the spirit) the truth of creeds, religious, moral, and political, as distinct from what has gone into effort to try creeds by putting them to the test of acting upon them. The change would do away with the intolerance and fanaticism that attend the notion that beliefs and judgments are capable of inherent truth and authority; inherent in the sense of being independent of what they lead to when used as directive principles.[5]

This moral relativism—whether explicit, as in the case of Dewey, or merely a latent attitude—provides democracy with a "live and let live" point of view. Toleration of ideological and doctrinal diversities is a consequence, and popular democracy endorses the concept of the pluralistic society, a social order comprising the spectrum of social groups and opinions.

Democracy is persistently optimistic. This *optimism* reflects a firm confidence in the notion of progress, which, in turn, is based on the belief that human nature is disposed toward intelligent and humane behavior if environmental conditions are suitable. This predisposition supposes, as well, that human nature is capable of improvement. The effect of pragmatism [6] on democratic thought has been to define both the individual and social predicament in terms of problems and their solutions. This problem-orientation has induced the idea that most social problems can be dealt with by increased amounts of education. Only democratic ideology lays so much stress on popular education and, in fact, subscribes to the ideal of universal education. This influence often gives rise in democratic societies to the paradoxical situation of strenuous approval of education paralleling frequently anti-intellectual attitudes. The paradox is not so strange when one realizes that the distrust of professional intellectualism is the product of pragmatic skepticism, egalitarian feelings, and the memories of class discrimination. Democratic education tends to stress the universal, the

---

[5] John Dewey, *The Quest for Certainty* in *op. cit., Intelligence in the Modern World*, pp. 791-792.

[6] *Pragmatism:* A philosophic point of view identified with *Charles Peirce* (1839-1914), *William James* (1842-1910), and Dewey (although he preferred to call himself an "instrumentalist"). Pragmatism argues that truth can be defined only in terms of the workability of the consequences of a hypothesis. Dewey wished to define intelligence as responses to problematic situations.

practical, the technological, and even the vocational and is hostile, in the main, to dilettantism and what has recently been labeled "egg-headism." Contends Dewey: "The foundation of democracy is faith in the capacities of human nature; faith in human intelligence and in the power of pooled and cooperative experience." [7]

This faith not only revolves around the "capacities of (individual) human nature(s)," but also around the *altruistic congeniality* of men. Human association, for Dewey, is a natural fact. "Associated activity," he comments, "needs no explanation; things are made that way." Aside from this associational impulse, communal living is the result of human intelligence realizing the benefits of "participation in activities and sharing in results." Dewey's ethics of ends and means, whereby intelligence is invoked to reconcile these two factors, is presumably rescued from egoistic self-interest by human intelligence realizing the satisfactions of communal intercourse.

Freedom is not only a good in itself for individual members of society, democracy maintains, but it also produces a situation in which the *free exchange of ideas and views* produces a catalytic result. The clash of ideas, with a framework of legality, is a creative process. Dewey puts it this way:

> Without freedom of expression, not even methods of social inquiry can be developed. For tools can be evolved and perfected only in operation; in application to observing, reporting, and organizing actual subject matter; and this application cannot occur save through free and systematic communication. [8]

At a deeper level, there is the assumption that if the prevailing conditions are neutral, *truth will emerge victorious* from its encounter with error. This notion is more rhetorical than logical, however. There is the obvious temptation to identify as truth that which emerges dominant. Even the contentions of pragmatism regarding truth as utility cannot wholly escape this tendency. The power to sway, to influence, or to persuade is not a reliable criterion of truth even from the pragmatic angle. Moreover, it is simplistic to assume that the clash of ideas is a sort of philosophic horse opera in which truth and error meet for some cataclysmic showdown. The vagaries of thought are a bit more complex than that.

The pragmatic view of truth, however, is well ingrained in demo-

---

[7] Dewey, *op. cit.*, "Democracy and Educational Administration" in *Intelligence in the Modern World*, p. 402.

[8] John Dewey, *Experience and Nature* in *op. cit.*, *Intelligence in the Modern World*, pp. 391-392.

cratic thinking. One can suspect that this is more the result of democracy's defensive feelings about various old absolutisms than it is the
cogency of the pragmatic definition. Indeed, long after the pragmatic
concept had been rather battered about by philosophic criticism, the
spirit of it remained fixed in the democratic mind.

These democratic assumptions have been vigorously challenged in
the twentieth century. A portion of this criticism has been aimed at
the destruction of these assumptions as barriers to the expansion of
new competing totalitarian ideologies. We have already examined
Marxism and fascism and we will briefly glance at the present import
of communism. But not all the demurrers to democratic ideas have
sprung from totalitarianism. A large and literate body of theory has
rejected popular democracy, not in favor of fascism or communism,
but for either a significantly reformed democratic ideal or an authoritarian substitute. This antidemocratic argument is founded on one of
two main objections: (1) Democracy is not possible. It is a delusion.
All political power is exercised by small élites. It makes no difference
at all if democracy is morally or theoretically desirable since it is not
attainable. The "iron law of oligarchy" applies. This argument is essentially that of Pareto-Michels-Mosca. (2) Democracy is either morally
reprehensible or patently illogical.

There is no need to consider again the line of reasoning advanced
to support the contention that democracy is not feasible; the contemporary democratic critics employ the basic arguments of Pareto and
Michels. But the second line of attack—that democracy is morally or
logically untenable—is worthy of serious reflection, as it is a probing
and formidable critique. In adopting this basis of criticism, the antidemocrats either reject the root assumptions of democracy or, in
some cases, accept them but disagree as to their consequences or
implementation.

The principle of majority rule is either jettisoned outright or reinter-
preted. The main line of argument is that if truth is not merely relative to what people think it is, but enjoys an objective status (is an
eternal universal), then polling the populace will not discover it. Nor
will the will of the majority necessarily reflect what is truthful. The
same situation applies to moral universals. Majority acceptance does
not make a course of action right or good. One morally conscious man
may exercise better ethical judgment than fifty men who do not have
the same insight. Truth and morality, the antimajoritarians argue, are

to be discovered, and therefore decisions regarding political and social questions should be made not on the basis of majority rule, but on the basis of the guidance of those best equipped and most likely to have uncovered truth and justice. To say that the judgments of a hod-carrier and a philosopher are to receive equal political recognition is to the critics of democracy an obvious folly and a degrading of moral significance.

It is not a question of the intrinsic worth of the person, the antidemocrats explain. A can be conceived as the equal of B in the sense that he shares membership in humanity, possesses a soul, or is entitled to rights respecting the sanctity of the person. But this does not imply that a political system must include an equality of political participation or opportunity for leadership or that the whims of the most numerous take precedence over the considered opinions of the most qualified. In short, democracy is wrong, the critics protest, if it argues that people invariably know what is best for them and that their self-conceived desires must be arbitrarily accepted as the base of social policy. This is the exact reverse of Bentham's position. The fact that more people might prefer Chubby Checkers to Bach, or Mickey Spillane to Baudelaire, does not alter the value status of the objects in question. The value is *in* the objects perceived, not *created by* the reactions of the perceivers. You cannot, the antidemocrats reason, take a random poll to decide whether Painting A is a great piece of art. You might, on the other hand, take a poll among a group of art critics. This would not give you *certainty* about the aesthetic merits of A, but you would be far closer to the truth, since the pursuit of truth is the province either of reason (which implies discipline and refinement) or of intuition (which implies a varying range of sensitivity). Likewise a moral decision cannot be made by an appeal to the majority; a moral decision, like an aesthetic one, must be made by an attempt to determine the moral imperative, the moral absolute. To rest the decision-making process of a society on the will of the largest numbers is, the critics of democracy argue, inherently irrational and immoral. This is the refutation offered by many who choose to repudiate democracy.

This general position prompts the following rejoinders to other democratic assumptions: (1) Representationalism may be desirable, but it should be balanced; it should reflect not sheer numbers, but status based on education, merit, interests, and possessions. (2) The state and society are not artificial constructs, but natural institutions, and institutions are not only indispensable to civilized society, but have legitimate rights and demands that are both distinct from and frequently more imperative than those of individuals. (3) Human beings are inherently unequal and this inequality ought to be reflected in political and social arrangements. Artificial enforcement of equality is injurious to the extent that it makes impossible the rule of the "best" or the "most able." (4) The rule of law is essential, but law as popular democracy frequently conceives it is not a means of social coercion, a doctrinaire instrument of change. (5) Individual liberty and the recognition of the rights of people and property are generally desirable, but they ought to be interpreted in light of the fact that (a) rights and duties are inseparable (rights must follow from the recognition of obligations) and (b) that freedom can never in itself be an absolute value, since freedom can never consist of defying reason or endorsing wickedness. (6) The relativism of values is untenable, and the objectivity of ethical standards can be adequately demonstrated. (7) Facile optimism is unjustified, as human nature is not invariably or even predominantly good. It contains irrational, animalistic, and antisocial predilections that must be controlled either by self-discipline or by the extrinsic disciplines of social control. (8) Man may be a social creature, but he is not so from any conscious feelings of altruism or any urge for cooperation. (9) Freedom of expression is good to the extent that it promotes the search for truth, but it is not in itself a catalyst (though it may be a catharsis) and it should not imply the equal validity of all opinions. The free clash of opinions does not alter the fact that some opinions enjoy a stronger claim and require universal response. (10) Truth wins out over error only when truth is recognized and acted upon. (11) The pragmatic definition of truth is a fallacy for a number of reasons, among which are: (a) Defining truth as solutions to problems hinges upon a conception of what a problem is. The definition of "truth" itself imposes an unwarranted definition of the term "problem," which induces a fatal circularity. (b) What is a "solution"? How does one know when something "works"? What may appear presumably efficacious may prove quite the reverse; the logical evaluations of the "instrumental" are hopelessly imprecise for so fundamental a conception as truth.

Of the thinkers sharing this general view, one of the most representative and provocative is *Irving Babbitt* (1865-1933).[9] Babbitt, a

---

[9] Among Babbitt's contemporaries highly critical of democracy might be mentioned *George Santayana* [see *Domination and Powers* (1951)], Paul Elmer More [see *Shelburne Essays*, IX, "Aristocracy and Justice" (1921)], and H. L. Mencken [see *Notes on Democracy* (1926)].

Harvard University professor of literature, was an avowed enemy of romanticism and an admirer of classicism. Rousseau was his arch-foe; [10] the "new humanism" was his battle standard. Witty, learned, and imbued with the high style of classicism, he viewed democracy as a romantic egoistic debauch, the remedy for which was his own concept of austere aristocracy.

Babbitt's dissatisfaction with popular democracy arises from its pandering to the baser elements in human nature. Democracy, as he sees it, is a sort of carnival of mass egoism. He sympathetically quotes an English observer who commented that "America is not a country; it is a picnic." In his curt style, Babbitt muses:

> Demos, as we pointed out long ago, craves flattery like any other monarch, and in his theory of popular sovereignty Rousseau has, it must be admitted, laid this flattery on with a trowel. In general, his notion that evil is not in man himself, but in his institutions, has enjoyed immense popularity, not because it is true, but because it is flattering.[11]

Rather than following the optimism of Rousseau or Dewey, Babbitt's reading of human nature stresses the less attractive elements, especially vulgarity and crude sentimentality. The human creature is a mixture, a combination of elevating and degrading inclinations; Babbitt accepts the Platonic concept of a higher and lower self. The higher arises from human will, the freedom to choose that, when controlled and disciplined, is the motive power for both creativity and ethical enlightenment. The temptations are to abuse the freedom of the will either by coarse indulgence or by lethargic inactivity. Human nature in order to be properly developed, counsels Babbitt, requires discipline and work (which he conceives of as self-reform and creative refinement). Mingling classicism, a neo-Puritanism, and elements of Buddhism, Babbitt argues that only by the introduction of discipline, both individually and socially, can man suppress his egoistic cravings and at the same time realize the true human dimension. The attainment of the full dimensions of human potential—the aim of humanism—is not through impulse and the emotionally voracious self-expression and libertarianism that the romantics had adored. It is a twofold process, involving, first, the discipline of the will—the "vital control"—in order to free the will for higher callings. It is more human,

---

[10] Babbitt's *Rousseau and Romanticism* (1919) has already been cited in Chapter 9. His vehement indictment of Rousseau is noticeable in virtually all his works.

[11] Irving Babbitt, *Democracy and Leadership* (Boston, Mass.: Houghton Mifflin Co., 1924), p. 276.

Babbitt contends, to be a civilized and ethically responsible being than to be a mass of unreflective emotions, to be a "noble savage." At the same time, discipline must be wedded to a constant and energetic effort toward self-cultivation and the creation of rational standards.[12] This is the "work" side of the control-work axis.

Babbitt's analysis is not essentially psychological; it is ethical. The ethic is spiritualistic (although not Christian) and absolutist. The human problem, for Babbitt, is always the problem of ethical choice, of the recognition of moral standards. The base choice is between appetite, materialistic greed, and sloth, on the one hand, and moral dedication on the other. It is here that democracy fails, he asserts, because it is built to accommodate the lower self, the selfish and avaricious. It denies the immutable standards.

Babbitt's remedy is *leadership*, the aristocratic principle. An élite of intellect? Of property? Of talent? No, answers Babbitt, the aristocracy must be made up of the ethically enlightened, those who have best utilized the precious possibilities of the will, those who have risen above the sordid passions to true human understanding (he uses the word "humility" to describe this state of ethical consciousness, although in quite an unconventional way). He writes:

> We are assured, indeed, that the highly heterogeneous elements that enter into our population will, like various instruments in an orchestra, merely result in a richer harmony; they will, one may reply, provided that, like an orchestra, they be properly led. Otherwise the outcome may be an unexampled cacophony. This question of leadership is not primarily biological, but moral. Leaders may vary in quality from the man who is so loyal to sound standards that he inspires right conduct in others by the sheer rightness of his example, to the man who stands for nothing higher than the law of cunning and the law of force, and so is, in the sense I have sought to define, imperialistic. If democracy means simply the attempt to eliminate the qualitative and selective principle in favor of some general will, based in turn on a theory of natural rights, it may prove to be only a form of the vertigo of the abyss. As I have tried to show in dealing with the influence of Rousseau on the French Revolution, it will result practically, not in equality, but in a sort of inverted aristocracy. One's choice may be, not between a democracy that is properly led and a democracy that hopes to find the equivalent of standards and leadership in the appeal to a numerical majority, that indulges in other words in a sort of quantitative impressionism, but between a democracy that is prop-

---

[12] In Babbitt's language: "To have standards means practically to select and reject; and this again means that one must discipline one's feelings or affections, to use the older word, to some ethical center" (*Ibid.*, p. 299).

erly led and a decadent imperialism. One should, therefore, in the interests of democracy itself seek to substitute the doctrine of the right man for the doctrine of the rights of man.[13]

The creation of an aristocracy of the morally superior requires a searching social introspection. It demands a turn to traditional ethical concepts. The "new ethics," charges Babbitt, makes the tragic error of assuming that "the significant struggle between good and evil is not in the individual but in society." This reëxamination of moral attitudes can either take place within the existing political structure or it can create some new political order. If the aristocratic principle is imposed upon the existing institutions, it would be imperative, in Babbitt's view, to disavow many of the accepted democratic tenets. But it may be too late for this, speculates Babbitt, and with disturbing prescience he suggests the possibility of the disappearance of moderate, representative political institutions. Their death, if that comes to be, will result from the debauchery of democratic excess and the vanity with which democracy rejects the claims of moral leadership. He warns:

> The hope of cooperation with a State that has an unethical leadership is chimerical. The value of political thinking is therefore in direct ratio to its adequacy in dealing with the problem of leadership. The unit to which all things must finally be referred is not the State or humanity or any other abstraction, but the man of character. Compared with this ultimate human reality, every other reality is only a shadow in the mist.[14]

Communism in the twentieth century has undergone many alterations since the days of Lenin. The most apparent of these changes is the emergence of what Milovan Djilas [15] calls "national communism." By this is meant the fusion of Marxism with both nationalism and national individuality. The most celebrated case is Russia herself. In the scramble for power after the death of Lenin, two distinct points of view were manifested in connection with two prominent personalities and Lenin lieutenants, *Leon Trotsky* (1877-1940) and *Joseph Stalin* (1879-1953). Trotsky, probably Lenin's choice as heir apparent,

---

[13] *Ibid.*, pp. 245-246.
[14] *Ibid.*, pp. 309-310.
[15] See Milovan Djilas, *The New Class* (New York: Frederick A. Praeger, Inc., 1959).

was the conventional Marxist in the sense that his view of the revolutionary movement was cosmopolitan; the struggle was not to be conducted along national lines, but on the basis of international unions of the proletariat. Stalin, on the other hand, was a Slavophile, a man of Eastern orientations and un-European habits of mind, and an announced nationalist. He conceived Marxist doctrine in terms of world expansion with the nation-state as the principal instrument. The Stalin period, which followed his successful expulsion of Trotsky, made expedient revisions of the Marxist-Leninist dogma. These modifications were almost invariably designed to strengthen the central authority of the state and to prepare the Soviet Union for a policy of "imperialistic" foreign affairs, the nature of which would doubtless have shocked both Marx and Lenin. This revisionism, plus Stalin's ready adoption of despotic methods of political control, gave to communism a physical militancy that it did not before have to this degree and that it has not since lost—despite Khrushchev's condemnations of the Stalin era. The ideological shifts, however, were sufficient to prompt Khrushchev in his now famous attack on Stalin in 1956 to say that the U.S.S.R. must "return to and actually practice in all our ideological work the most important theses of Marxist-Leninist science."

The rise of nationalized communism and the corresponding fragmentization of the world communist movement have not had the general effect of dampening the revolutionary zeal. Save, perhaps, in the case of Yugoslavia, the Marxist-Leninist doctrine of world revolution is at least as prominent a part of the ideology as it was in previous times. In fact, the rise of such states as Communist China has added an additionally sinister threat to the security of the democratic moderate states of Western Europe and America as well as to that of the neutralist states of Asia. Communist ideology in China tends to be even more rigorously doctrinaire regarding the inevitability of conflict between Communist and bourgeois states. The argument has also been advanced that China takes too literally the Marxian estimates of capitalist incapacity to remain vigorous and to be able to act with appropriate decision.[16] In any case, the adaptation of Marxism that has already taken place does not mitigate Marx's call for the destruction of democ-

---

[16] This argument is well put in William McGovern's *Strategic Intelligence and the Shape of Tomorrow* (Chicago, Ill.: Henry Regnery Co., 1961). McGovern contends: "There are many of the younger leaders in Communist China who tend to think of the United States as a 'paper dragon,' fearsome in outward appearance but weak and powerless in reality. For this reason they are more willing to face the United States in a head-on collision" (p. 140).

racy, but rather has intensified this antagonism. The very proliferation places democracy under heavier attack, ideologically and militarily. As Mao Tse-tung reiterates: "Marxism can only develop through struggle—this is true not only in the past and present, it is necessarily true in the future also."

Crane Brinton (1898-   ), certainly numbered among the defenders of democratic ideas, has summed up the present problems facing democracy in concise, but stimulating, language:

> An *idealistic* democracy, a *believing* democracy (in the old transcendental sense of religious belief) is perhaps possible, though such a democracy would find it hard to accommodate its this-worldly and scientific heritage to an other-worldly faith. Its God would at the very least need to make some difficult compromises with the psychiatrist. A *realistic,* pessimistic democracy—a democracy in which ordinary citizens approach morals and politics with the willingness to cope with imperfection that characterizes the good farmer, the good physician, the good holder of the cure of souls, be he priest, clergyman, counselor, or psychiatrist—such a democracy would demand more of its citizens than any human culture has ever demanded. Were its demands met, it might well be the most successful of cultures. Finally, a *cynical* democracy, a democracy whose citizens profess in this world one set of ideas and live another, is wholly impossible. No such society can long endure anywhere. The tension between the ideal and the real may be resolved in many ways in a healthy society; but it can never be taken as nonexistent.[17]

Popular democracy stands—defended by its John Deweys and Crane Brintons, criticized by its Irving Babbitts—under the arbitration of history. Beyond polite discourse, there is an appeal not to reason, but to a new rebellion, a new scourging of the human spirit. The upheaval may be a terrible convolution of the ideological engagement of this century. The fate of democracy and the fate of the reign of human reason are not the same, but they are inextricably linked. If reason survives, then democracy can be either maintained or discarded—but a choice is possible. The rule of reason permits the rational appraisal, Under the irrationalism of the Barbarian, whoever he may be, there is no choice, no appeal to the considered discriminations of intelligence or perception, only the primal anarchy of dehumanized power. Is democracy equal to the task of keeping these dark eventualities at bay?

---

[17] Crane Brinton, *Ideas and Men* (Englewood Cliffs, N. J.: Prentice-Hall, Inc., 1950), p. 550.

. . . *for further discussion:*

1. Should government enforce racial desegregation of private country clubs or labor unions or professional societies in order to be consistent with democratic theory?
2. Is John Stuart Mill's idea of a plural vote antidemocratic? Why?
3. Irving Babbitt argues for leadership of "men of character." What do you think is good moral character? What evidence is there to suppose that the possession of moral character improves political leadership? Are there any or have there ever been superb political leaders who have benefited their following and yet were morally deficient? Evaluate some political leaders. What of those who have been moral giants and yet offered only the weakest leadership? Take as samples: Napoleon, Andrew Jackson, Jefferson Davis, Herbert Hoover, Neville Chamberlain, Franklin Roosevelt, Winston Churchill, Joseph Stalin, Senator Joseph McCarthy, or Fidel Castro.
4. Morton White has insightfully pointed out [see his *Social Thought in America* (Boston, Mass.: Beacon Press, Inc., n.d.)] that John Dewey seemed torn between a desire "to build a political technology" and a fear that "even the modest theorizing, generalizing, and fixing of ends which a technology involves would lead us into rigidity and dogmatism." Do you think this same dilemma troubles contemporary democratic political thinking?

. . . *for further investigation:*

Babbitt, Irving, *Democracy and Leadership*. Boston, Mass.: Houghton Mifflin Co., 1924.

———, * *Literature and the American College*. Chicago, Ill.: Henry Regnery Co., 1956.

Bell, Bernard I., * *Crowd Culture*. Chicago, Ill.: Henry Regnery Co., 1956.

Clark, Gerald, *Impatient Giant: Red China Today*. New York: David McKay Co., Inc., 1959.

Crankshaw, Edward, * *Khrushchev's Russia*. Baltimore, Md.: Penguin Books, Inc., 1960.

Dahl, Robert A., *A Preface to Democratic Theory*. Chicago, Ill.: University of Chicago Press, 1956.

Dewey, John, *Intelligence in the Modern World: John Dewey's Philosophy*, Joseph Ratner, ed. New York: Modern Library, Inc., 1939.

Djilas, Milovan, * *The New Class*. New York: Frederick A. Praeger, Inc., 1959.

Gabriel, Ralph H., *The Course of American Democratic Thought*. New York: The Ronald Press Company, 1956.

Goodman, Elliot R., *The Soviet Design for a World State*. New York: Columbia University Press, 1960.

Hook, Sidney, *Reason, Social Myths and Democracy*. New York: Humanities Press, Inc., 1940.

McGovern, William M., *Strategic Intelligence and the Shape of Tomorrow.* Chicago, Ill.: Henry Regnery Co., 1961.

Mao Tse-tung, * *An Anthology of His Writings,* Anne Fremantle, ed. New York: Mentor Books, 1962.

——, *On the Protracted War.* Peking: Foreign Languages Press, 1954.

Niebuhr, Reinhold, * *The Children of Light and the Children of Darkness.* New York: Charles Scribner's Sons, n.d.

——, * *Moral Man and Immoral Society.* New York: Charles Scribner's Sons, n.d.

Ortega y Gasset, José, *The Revolt of the Masses.* New York: W. W. Norton & Co., Inc., 1932.

Perkins, Dexter, * *The American Way.* Ithaca, N.Y.: Great Seal Books, 1959.

Perry, Ralph B., *Puritanism and Democracy.* New York: Vanguard Press, 1944.

Santayana, George, *Dominations and Powers.* New York: Charles Scribner's Sons, 1951.

Seton-Watson, Hugh, * *From Lenin to Khrushchev.* New York: Frederick A. Praeger, Inc., 1960.

Smith, Thomas V. and Eduard Lindeman, * *The Democratic Way of Life.* New York: Mentor Books, 1951.

Talmon, J. L., * *Origins of Totalitarian Democracy.* New York: Frederick A. Praeger, Inc., 1960.

18

UNDER THE
MUSHROOM
CLOUD

The Bomb was a gigantic exclamation point full-stopping the first half of the twentieth century. But its appearance, awesome and dramatic as it was, did not usher in a new era in political ideas or even cast a pall of urgency over political speculation. This may seem a curious fact. The scientific reality of a "Doomsday Machine" might certainly suggest that the world sorely needs political reform in some particulars in order to avoid mass destruction. Such notions of reform have been forthcoming from time to time since the advent of nuclear armament; they have been largely frenetic and even bizarre, ranging from Moral Re-Armament to Vegetarianism. Billy Graham has enlightened all with the dual prediction of the end of the world and the Second Coming. The point of interest is that these post-Bomb recommendations for reform are essentially antipolitical, nonpolitical or, if political, procedural rather than normative.

It need not be surprising, then, that the Bomb has not stimulated a revival of political philosophy. It has merely underscored what had already taken place in the first fifty years of the century: the retreat from political philosophy (in the traditional and prescriptive sense of that term). Perhaps it would be clearer to put this another way: At most stages in the history of political ideas, political conditions in the real world have borne a close relationship and often motivated what we have been calling political philosophy. Examples are legion—Plato, Cicero, Machiavelli, Hobbes, Locke, Burke, and so on. Political philosophy, historically, has either consisted of recommendations for the general benefit of existing political conditions or, at the very least, cogent observations of contemporary events implying certain values to be realized.

The twentieth century, on the other hand, has seen the virtually complete divorce of political philosophizing and political realities. No such schism had previously existed. This predicament can be illustrated by the briefest analysis of contemporary philosophic or ideological trends *vis-à-vis* political phenomena. In general, there are two such trends: (1) philosophic attitudes that deny the significance or validity of political questions or hold that all political speculation is useless or pernicious, and (2) another philosophic cast of mind which declares that political phenomena are a necessary area of investigation, but that no values can be apprehended or attached there and that political analysis is essentially similar to the methods of science. It follows from this line of thinking that normative recommendations are mere unscientific, and therefore lamentable, exercises of personal bias.

If, then, the two philosophic moods presently dominant in the West—existentialism and positivism—are both hostile in different ways to what we have come to know as political philosophy, it is not a matter of sudden amazement that the twentieth century has produced such a relatively meager crop of political thinkers.

But these are admittedly quickly stated judgments, and the matter is deserving of more careful attention. Let us examine these two theses: (1) Politics is not worth thinking about, and (2) politics can be reduced to scientific, or at least psychological, observation and system-building.

The thesis that politics is not worth thinking about arises from a distaste for German idealism, particularly Hegelianism. The twentieth century has witnessed the reintroduction of the individual as the primary center for philosophic speculation. This is not just a new variety of individualism; it is rather a supposition that individual existence, consciousness, experience, sensation, feeling are the only useful objects of either philosophic attention or personal concern. Its quite familiar classificatory word is *existentialism*. It is not required that we attempt to plumb the depths of this term—a term that the existentialists themselves specifically disown, incidentally.[1] For our purposes it is enough to point out that existentialism is a revolt against two of the major currents of nineteenth-century thought: scientism and logism. In making this repudiation existentialism turns its back on both idealism and the philosophies resting their cases on scientific methodology, namely positivism and pragmatism. Replacing, then, a philosophic orientation either scientific or logistic, existentialism turns to a radical subjectivism—a concern with the consciousness, the "existential situation," the *Existenz* of individual human beings as isolated islands of meaning in essentially meaningless impersonal existence. The tone of this almost morbid sense of individual detachment from social roots is found in the progenitor of existentialism, Søren Kierkegaard (1813-1855). This Danish theologian-philosopher contributed a mystical reinterpretation of the self, splitting, he thought, the nature of man away from its reliance on "artificial," external values.

Existentialism's rejection of the idea of the community by its subjective denial of value exterior to the self, takes on two slightly incongruous directions—one toward a code of personal nihilism and pessimism (Jean-Paul Sartre is representative), which owes some debt to Nietzsche, and the other a Christian existentialism (Gabriel Marcel is illustrative), which identifies the quasimystic existential self with "soul" and replaces the conventional notion of community with an assertion that human relatedness is spiritual, an indirect but positive communion of souls. Both the existentialism of Sartre and that of the Christian wing rail against the destruction of the individual by the mechanization of his nature, a result of science (and its offspring, technology) and systematic philosophy.

A denial of the significance of community (at least in a more literal sense), reduces the importance of political theorizing, and, in the main, the existentialists are little concerned with it. What political writing exists is the product of *Jean-Paul Sartre* (1905-   ), a militant atheist, and *Karl Jaspers* (1883-   ), a Protestant. Sartre's notions are seemingly not intimately related to his general philosophy, and in essence they are a declaration of virtually unlimited freedom, equating

---

[1] For perhaps the clearest explanation of existentialism, see Marjorie Grene, *Introduction to Existentialism* (Chicago, Ill.: University of Chicago Press, 1948).

freedom with the concept of both personal and social revolution. Sartre speaks of a "revolutionary philosophy" as being a "philosophy of transcendence." By this he means that the only political value is the unrestricted opportunity to transcend or to discard existing political arrangements. Since, for Sartre, neither man nor society can lay claim to origins other than its own immediate being, all is temporary, all is capable of being transcended. The concept of revolution is introduced because any social order, however artificial and ephemeral, develops values and seeks to perpetuate them. However, within that society there are individuals who perceive a new political system, one that will transcend the present. These individuals, Sartre contends, must lead a new revolutionary emergence. In effect this places Sartre on the political Left, but his affection for Marxism is distinctly curbed by his disapproval of materialism.[2]

Jasper's existentialism takes him in a diverse political direction. His individualistic convictions prompt him to a more conservative point of view. Deeply affected by what he feels is the degradation of the individual by the conception of society in machine-like terms, which, in turn, tends to produce the mass man, the mediocre substitute for true individuality, Jaspers revives the argument for social differentiation based on individual characteristics and capacities. He speaks of a "true aristocracy" of those who have undergone the process of self-understanding and have gleaned meaning and promise from their own existential situations.[3] Although emanating from a very different philosophic assumption, Jasper's aristocracy is not unlike that envisioned by Irving Babbitt. His political orientations, however, are not antidemocratic, but are distinctly reformist. Jasper's mood is not unlike that of Reinhold Niebuhr, whom we shall mention shortly. Both Jaspers and Niebuhr decry the tendency in popular democracy toward moral mediocrity, although their ethical conceptions are far from being the same.

The thesis that politics can be reduced to scientific observation and system-building evidences no such philosophic disdain for grappling with the immediate and worldly problems of politics. Quite the contrary, it suggests a strong preoccupation with them. It does, however,

---

[2] For a further account of Sartre's political ideas, a good source is his essay, "Materialisme et revolution" in Les Temps modernes, Vol. I, Nos. 9-10, (June-July, 1946).

[3] For a fuller account, see Karl Jaspers, Man in the Modern Age (New York: Anchor Books, 1957).

seek to remove the question of value from the continuing dialogue about political remedies. This thesis, espoused by a movement in philosophy that is generally described as positivism, justifies its rejection of value in two general ways.

1. Values do not exist of and by themselves. They are not facts, and science must deal only with facts. And since science is the only rational means of inquiry, such inquiry must be concerned only with what is directly observable and provable. If values can be said to exist in some sense, what they are is clear; they are attitudes, prejudices, opinions held by people, and thus they are significant only to the extent that they form part of the social data to be examined. The true function of political investigation is to determine the factual nature of political behavior and process, not to offer prescriptions about what *ought* to be done, for this is unscientific. One would not expect a biologist to offer advice on what his rats ought to do; his job is to attempt to discover what the cause of their behavior *is*. Some positivistic political theorists argue a complete value relativism; others acknowledge the possibility of valid value judgments, but assert that rendering them is not the responsibility of a political scientist.

2. Another segment of positivism—sometimes referred to as "logical positivism" or "language analysis"—takes the position that values are linguistic symbols that have no meaning apart from the symbols themselves. At base, this movement suggests that philosophy is equivalent to the logical analysis of language and that the "clarification of the language which we all speak in everyday life" (to quote Gustav Bergmann, a well-known contemporary positivist) is the chief activity of the philosopher. Thus with values, too, it is a question of refining terms; but objective study of value is impossible, simply because, by definition, metaphysics are rejected and nothing remains *behind* language except the psychological machinery of the individual.

What effects have been wrought by these positivistic convictions on political philosophy? The impact of pure positivism has been immense, and the influence of language analysis, while much slighter, is growing. The general result of the prominence of positivism in the realm of the political has been to split the study of politics into two areas: "political science" as an empirical investigation of political phenomena and "political philosophy" as an attempt to introduce normative or value concepts. This separation has been regrettable in many ways. First, it has discouraged the vital spirit of speculation within the area of political philosophizing, but as well—and of perhaps equal significance—it has cut off from political investigation the necessary component of philosophic discipline and concern for the adequacy of both method and range of data. Before we examine in more detail the position of political positivism, three rather omnibus questions might be kept in mind, although we shall not attempt to answer each one specifically:

1. Can the study of politics be made a science in the same way that the study of biology, let us say, is a science?
2. Can political phenomena be adequately explained only in terms of the direct analysis of experience?
3. To what extent is political theory socially useful if it is only descriptive?

To the positivistically oriented political student there are two major problems to be faced—assuming for the moment that the scientific method (at least as it is conceived by most positivists) can be made applicable in the area of political or social affairs. The first problem is: What is worth investigating? The second is: How is the investigation to be conducted? Both problems require recourse to judgment, and much literature has been devoted to the matter of selection and methodology. The latter term is often interchanged with the word "theory," and this is confusing to one not familiar with the terminology of the behaviorists.[4] "Theory" when used in this context does not mean speculative political thought, but rather the field of political methodology and analysis.

While this approach to political analysis has its roots in Comte and Mill, the attempt to introduce both the methods and attitudes of science into the study of politics is much more recent. It has a more concrete connection with Walter Bagehot, but certainly the publication in 1908 of both Graham Wallas' *Human Nature in Politics* and Arthur F. Bentley's *Process of Government* brought the movement into full gear. In the Twenties, John Dewey and Mary Follett encouraged it, but the principal stimulus to positivistic social research came from sociology and anti-Freudian psychology. This had the effect of channeling political research not only toward a scientific orientation, but one as already interpreted by others of the social sciences. An example of this tendency is Robert MacIver's *The Web of Government,* published

---

[4] The political positivists often refer to themselves as "behaviorists" and speak of the "behavioral sciences," meaning politics, psychology, sociology, etc. This may be a convenient word, and it does have a jusifiable connotation, but confusion might arise between this usage and "behaviorism" as a more limited school of psychological theory identified with the late John B. Watson.

in 1947. What, in fact, do these theorists wish to reject and what do they propose?

Richard C Snyder, who has long championed the cause of positivistically conceived political study, finds a number of traditional approaches unsatisfactory. Among these he lists: (1) "The Boundary Problem" or insufficient attention to discovering what is uniquely political and differentiating between political and nonpolitical phenomena. (2) "The Problem of Undergeneralization" or the failure to develop analysis of "common properties" in political phenomena that would permit the framing of general propositions. (3) "The Problem of an Adequate Vocabulary" or the failure to introduce theories of language analysis into politics. (4) "The Problem of 'Real' People, the 'Real' World, and 'Concrete Entities'" or the undesirability of being preoccupied with political affairs at the cost of "systematic and experimental analysis of the conditions correlated with the events initially described." [5]

Affirmatively, David Easton in his influential book, *The Political System* (1953), puts the goals of political positivism in these terms:

> Whatever form such a systematic theory should take, two aspects of it seemed exceedingly clear at this stage. In the first place, such a theory would be compelled to specify the varieties of data involved in the analysis of any political relations. At the broadest level we would wish to know what varieties of data contribute to an exhaustive description of the determinants and the functioning of social policy. Such knowledge would provide some sure clue to inform the investigator when his research had exploited all relevant types of data. And in the second place, as we saw, a general theory would be compelled to provide categories for examining the moral premises out of which the theory itself emerged. In this way, it could introduce a self-correcting mechanism to reduce error caused by the limitations imposed by the research worker's moral outlook. [6]

Without attempting to trace down the varying systems of investigation proposed by contemporary positivistic theorists, the essential position of the behaviorists rests on six premises: (1) The proper base for political investigation is human behavior, principally group behavior (as contrasted with study of institutions, ideas, historical influences, personalities, etc.). (2) Such investigation will reveal general theories

---

[5] Richard C. Snyder, "A Decision-Making Approach to the Study of Political Phenomena" in *Approaches to the Study of Politics*, Roland Young, ed. (Evanston, Ill.: Northwestern University Press, 1962), pp. 4-9, *et passim*.

[6] David Easton, *The Political System* (New York: Alfred A. Knopf, Inc., 1953), p. 319.

or laws of human political behavior having approximately the same rigor as biological or physical laws. Presumably, the discovery of these behavioral principles will permit prediction. (3) There exists a causal order both in nature and in human behavior, and, assuming the identification of all relevant variables, this is constant. (4) These constants being similar to physical laws can be arrived at fundamentally by the same means—by empirical research and inductive analysis. (5) Values are relative cultural artifacts whose importance lies in the fact that as human attitudes they affect human behavior. (6) The function of political study is the description of political behavior and the construction of explanatory systems. This implies no prescriptive function other than that an accurate description of existing factors might conceivably serve as a criterion, at least for purposes of expediency. Some theorists would argue, however, that given such systematic knowledge, the framing of alternative policies should and would be forthcoming.

The general position assumed by positivism applied to political philosophy is by no means as pat a case as it might seem from reading the behaviorist literature. Knotty problems intrude. Some of the difficulties are rather technical ones, involving questions of logic and language, but, boiled down, the core difficulties are these: First, positivistic political theory is frequently philosophically naïve. While it tosses aside philosophic questions as "mere metaphysics," it nonetheless makes numerous philosophic assumptions. It usually assumes a "naïve realism," [7] for one thing, and its naturalistic cosmology is mechanistic and obsolete. It frequently refuses to accept the full implications of positivism *qua* positivism. Its *Weltanschauung* of causal simplicity and its curt denial of teleology, while only implicit, are nevertheless critical to the validity of its methodology.

Secondly, positivistic political theory's idea of science and scientific method is frequently old-fashioned. It has a Newtonian air about it. It has the ingenuousness of Mill's empiricism. It exists as if the revelations of quantum physics and the more recent puzzles in genetics were insignificant. Its reliance on induction flies in the face of much contemporary scientific theory, which increasingly begins to link science and logic and science and mathematics.[8]

---

[7] While this is true of most political behaviorists, the charge would be grossly unfair to level against the positivists in general. Most of them tend, indeed, toward the opposite pole of phenomenalism.

[8] Interesting discussions of these questions can be found by reading A. N. Whitehead or Sir Arthur Eddington.

Thirdly, its value theory—leaving aside the broader ethical issue— suggests both a confusion and a bias. The confusion arises from its veiled suggestion that somehow a theory of the good can be derived from empirical examination of the existing. Its bias is more subtly manifest. Suspicious of idealism and value absolutism and what they imported in a direct political way, the behaviorists have been led to a sometimes ill-considered value relativism out of their vague anxieties about value theory hinting at political authoritarianism.

Fourthly, the claim of objectivity is open to question. However an approach is conceived, certain standards must be appealed to. There is, after all, a criterion of relevance if nothing else. One must decide what is *worth* investigating and what data one chooses to select. And if one is approaching the investigation of phenomena with as doctrinaire a set of convictions as do the social positivists, the question may well be raised as to whether one's selection of objects of study and the data one deems relevant may not in some fashion be the result of predetermined attitudes. The range of the data can be limited by the conception of the real; no one would seriously argue that profitable research would result from pursuing the nonexistent—surely that would be a scientific non sequitur. The behaviorist might offer this rejoinder: One does not need to be convinced of the truth of religion, for example, in order to conduct research on the impact of religious belief on voting behavior. What is real or unreal is beside the point, the behaviorist goes on, but the *effect* on behavior is real, and that is what is being studied. Is this a fair escape? Doubtful, for the illustration makes it too simple. Suppose that the behavior of statesmen is being analyzed *vis-à-vis* policy decision-making. The behaviorist attempts to discover all the possible factors that affect the decision. Is he likely to include sheer intuition? Or the impact of deep-seated moral conviction? If the behaviorist answers "yes," he must do so with rather severe qualifications unless he wishes to deny the validity of his position. How can he evaluate the efficacy of the intuition or the intensity of the moral conviction? Even if he chooses to admit the pertinence of the intangible, the immeasurable, he cannot, then, argue that he can measure that which he has already denied on the ground of its nonexistence, its immeasurability. The chances are much better that he will select his data on the basis of what he believes to be relevant, and this constitutes a prior judgment of rather sweeping dimension in the case of behavioral research.

In the attempt to evolve a reasonable basis of justification for a criterion of relevance and validity, the behaviorists often engage in

frankly dubious circumlocution. An excellent example of this can be
found in the essay by Snyder previously cited:

> Any scheme of analysis ought to be evaluated according to two
> sets of criteria: first, its internal properties—assumptions, definitions,
> categories, logical consistency, operational qualities, and so on; second,
> its possible contribution to the critical problems of the particular in-
> tellectual enterprise to which it is dedicated—in this case political
> science.[9]

This statement clearly begs the question and implies, beyond refinement of language and logical coherence, an appeal to prior synthetic
judgments and unverified assumptions.

Fifthly, it is just, if not kind, to point out the paucity of significant
political theory to emerge from the welter of positivistic encouragement. The volume has been great, without doubt, but the disturbing
characteristic of this literature is the formidable amount of it devoted to lengthy and presumably erudite discussions on how to begin.
Somehow the act of political philosophizing, even by the behavioral
definition, is never reached. Humility is admirable, and the behaviorists
are almost frantically modest about their objectives, if not about their
convictions, but after a time one wonders whether this self-effacement
and commendable caution about starting off in the right manner are
not part of some elaborate rationalization for toying about with meth-
odological niceties instead of grappling with assorted unpleasantnesses.
Certainly it is true that many useful data have been accumulated, but
this solid, if unexciting, research is offset on the behavioral balance
sheet by some shockingly exotic excursions into such murky regions as
"small group models," "interstate simulation" games, "action theories,"
"game theories," and "group dynamics."

The insights of logical positivism or linguistic analysis have been
applied to politics in their most direct form by T. D. Weldon in his
much-discussed book, *The Vocabulary of Politics* (1953). Weldon's
chief point is that words do not stand for things. His thesis is this:

1. Questions put by traditional political philosophy are wrongly
posed.

2. The theoretical foundations of political thinking which are
claimed by Democracy, Hegelian Idealism, and Marxism are all equally
worthless.

3. [The difficuty is that since Plato we have assumed that words
(Justice, Truth, State, Right) have] intrinsic or essential meaning
which it is the aim of political philosophers to discover and explain.

---

[9] Snyder, *op. cit.*, p. 3.

Weldon goes on:

> There have always been widespread doubts as to the efficacy of this essentialist assumption even in the minds of many of those who have made use of it. Beginning with the Sophist Thrasymachus, whose views on politics are reported or parodied in the first book of the *Republic*, there has been a persistent positivist opposition which has maintained that the recommended procedure of searching for the essential meaning of "justice" and similar words is futile. It does nothing to help the solution of any practical political problem. For this we need an accurate description of what actually happens, or tends to happen, in human associations. There is no sense in asking what ought to happen, or what would happen under imaginary ideal conditions, and disputes on such points are purely verbal and a waste of time.[10]

This passage raises two terrible questions. Has all political philosophy (up to Weldon) been a waste of time and, perhaps of less moment, has reading this book been a waste of time, as well? How is one to justify the history of political ideas and the time spent reading this book? Weldon at least lays down an unequivocal challenge. There are several ways of attacking the main lines of Weldon's reasoning. One is to reaffirm the notion that since universals exist, assuming they can be adequately defended, then word symbols representing universal essences are useful. But this refutation would require a lengthy rejoinder and would be inconclusive anyway; it would merely redraw the lines of battle Of the remaining justifications for traditional political philosophy, three brief ones may do the job:

1. There can be no objections to reforming and refining the language of philosophic or political discourse. This is often necessary; it is also a very old occupation, which can at least be dated back to Aristotle and then up through Leibniz and Spinoza to Hegel and Bergson to Whitehead and Heidegger. It is constantly going on and, indeed, the living language itself forges new instruments of discourse to deal with new eventualities. But one cannot say the old language was worthless or futile, simply because no new language (collection of linguistic symbols) can be intelligible without some reference to the old. It makes no difference whatsoever if we arbitrarily decide to call a horse something else—"esroh" will do. But the new term becomes intelligible only when connected either to the object itself or to symbols in past use indicating the meaning of the newer symbol. Now Weldon himself wishes to make the point that there is no such thing as a "state" per se, so obviously it is impossible to refer to something that does not exist.

---

[10] Thomas D. Weldon, *The Vocabulary of Politics* (Baltimore, Md.: Penguin Books, Inc., 1953), p. 12.

Yet the word "state" is not a mere accident of sounds or letters; it must refer to *something*. Perhaps the difficulty with the word "state" is that it does not refer to that which it purports to refer to. This may well be, but in order for us now to isolate and examine that which in fact does exist, some applicable symbol must be invoked to designate it. This symbol gains intelligibility either when one connects it with the existing entity (as by shouting "That is an esroh!" over and over again to a primitive who has never seen a horse, while diligently pointing toward the appropriate ungulate) or by the use of a linguistic referent. The first method is hardly a feasible means of carrying on intellectual communication. Symbols must thus be referred to other symbols. If, then, our political language is inadequate, which it may be, it must nonetheless form a bridge of meaning to newer and more adequate linguistic conceptualizations. In this sense, it is untenable to argue that political philosophy has been futile, even assuming that it has been guilty of using imprecise and inaccurate language.

2. Weldon presumably thinks as other mortals do. And if this is the case, then his thought processes have been necessarily conditioned by language. It is not, then, solely a question of communication; it is also a matter of conceptualization. If Weldon thinks a thought, to put it a bit unromantically in the language of ordinary usage, it is not a pure cerebration; its intelligibility to Weldon rests on his ability to conceptualize it in linguistic symbols. Now let us suppose that Weldon has a new thought about politics that does not perhaps lend itself to definition by traditional terminology. Consequently, he makes new terms. But his initial conceptualization and his reclassification on a mental level proceed, at the beginning at least, by the manipulation of the symbols he has acquired from his experience. These symbols he has inherited, for good or ill, from the lexicon of political vocabulary. If for no other reason than that this possibly archaic language permits the formation of ideas, it is useful.

3. Weldon tells us that political theory ought to confine itself to what actually happens and that "there is no sense in asking what ought to happen." But what are the causative factors that prompt certain things to happen? It is not a matter of blind accident or the odd conjunctions of human beings or random thoughts. Unless one chooses to accept a complete determinism, one must say that human beings bring about events by *willing* them in some fashion, although the term "willing" perhaps introduces some conflicting connotations. In short, things do not just happen, and not even the most circumspect positivist is a completely detached observer in time-space. What people think *ought*

to happen affects very intensely what eventually does happen. The discussion of moral and political "oughts" cannot reasonably be said to be only an intellectual game, since the values espoused surely have a connection with the consequent participation of the individual in events.

The sum total of the effect of existentialism and positivism has been to depress the political imagination. Yet there are some indications that humanistically oriented political philosophy is still extant and even reviving on a modest scale. The problems facing a renaissance of political humanism are considerable, not the least among them being the amassed information regarding human behavior and the present inability to formulate a sufficiently acceptable concept of human nature upon which to base new and more adequate political theories. Positivistic attempts along these lines have the merit of occasional clarity and requisite abstractness, but they appear lacking in philosophic adequacy. It would be a bold man—perhaps a foolhardy one—who would present a full-blown theory of politics, akin to that of Hobbes or Hegel, in the 1960's. Man is at least more aware now of the immense difficulties confronting him. But these difficulties, indeed these perils, demand some return to reason, some application of human intellect to the job of prompting rational political judgment. While this is not a popular undertaking, there are those who are trying it. One might mention in this connection Bertrand de Jouvenel, Eric Voegelin, Reinhold Niebuhr, and John Courtney Murray as representative of differing approaches.

George Santayana, certainly one of the wise men of this century, entitled one of his books *The Winds of Doctrine*. The book itself is interesting, but it is the title that lingers in the mind (it is borrowed from a phrase of Burke's). It is an attractive figure of speech; British Prime Minister Harold Macmillan, when speaking of political unrest in Africa, spoke of the "winds of change." One could hardly be alive in the mid-twentieth century and not wonder how the winds, doctrinally and otherwise, might blow as the century grows older. While the future is imponderable—as poets and Oriental travelers keep reminding us—it is really its full shape that is obscured from mortal view. Whatever the future is, it does not fall upon us completely unannounced. One is tempted to read the signs, not trying in some occult aberration to divine future events, but to determine which way the wind is blowing.

How might the winds of doctrine blow as the world huddles, alternately fearful and reckless, under the shadow of the mushroom cloud? Predictable, perhaps, is the crisis of democratic society. Niebuhr has put this well:

> The preservation of a democratic civilization requires the wisdom of the serpent and the harmlessness of a dove. The children of light must be armed with the wisdom of the children of darkness but remain free from their malice. They must know the power of self-interest in human society without giving it moral justification. They must have this wisdom in order that they may beguile, deflect, harness, and restrain self-interest, individual and collective, for the sake of the community.[11]

At root, the basis of community, the democratic society is an awareness that self-interest and uninhibited passion must be gently but firmly checked by moral consensus and, more directly, by a recognition of the rule of law. There are signs of the deterioration of both this moral consensus and the rule of law. To survive, democracy must remain faithful to its legalistic foundations. Yet one of the disturbing indications of the drift of doctrine is the growing impatience with and antagonism toward legal restraint and procedure in the West. These indications are at present rather superficial, but they might be harbingers of more significant swings of attitude. If one casts an eye over a number of current "causes," many of which are admirable or at least understandable, one can detect the rejection of legalism and the belief that a moral end can justify not only direct action, but action at variance with the declared legal precepts of the society and the established constitutional avenues of redress. This tendency toward extralegal political action is not limited to any shade of political persuasion. Whether one selects the antinuclear groups in any of the Western countries, or the proponents of racial equality who adopt a variety of nonviolent disobediences, or the semisecret organizations devoted to anticommunist activity and the propagation of dubious nationalistic goals, or, for that matter, the violent legal nihilism of the leaders of the emerging nations of Africa and Asia, these diversified movements all share a common characteristic—a rejection of the processes of legal redress and traditional political procedures. They suggest the specter of the political solution found at the barricade or at the mass meeting. This dissatisfaction with democratic restraint may increase.

There is some evidence to suppose as well that the century-old reign

---

[11] Reinhold Niebuhr, *The Children of Light and the Children of Darkness* (New York: Charles Scribner's Sons, 1944), p. 41.

of the moderates as the most potent political force in the West may be passing. Into the vacuum created by the collapse of moderate political alignments in presumably democratic countries may surge extremes of Left and Right, both dissatisfied with the equilibrium of moderate democracy. The twentieth century may possibly see the final demise of liberal, nineteenth-century democracy, to be replaced by some yet unknown political ideology and system. As the West and the East square off in the war of ideas, it is not outside the realm of possibility that the threats to the present systems, in both West and East, may not come from their opponent across some iron or bamboo curtain, but from major political upheavals within.

The West waits by its guns, armed to keep at bay a philosophy that has taken on the adjunct of ICBM's. The great democracies send and receive volley after volley of ideological invective and blandishment. But they need to look behind as well as in front of their ramparts. Civilization is tediously slow to grow, but it is quick to die—and it is worth saving.

> And we are here as on a darkling plain
> Swept with confused alarms of struggle and flight,
> Where ignorant armies clash by night.
>
> —MATTHEW ARNOLD, "Dover Beach"

. . . for further discussion:

1. Is a science of politics possible? If possible, is it desirable?
2. What areas of intellectual investigation do you think are most likely to yield important insights for political philosophy in the future? Why?
3. To what extent do you think contemporary political action (party platforms, campaign oratory, legislative proposals, governmental policies) reflects clear-cut philosophies of politics? Regardless of your response, do you think the present situation desirable? Should we encourage more or less philosophic content in practical politics?
4. C. Wright Mills has offered this definition of a political idea: ". . . a definition of reality in terms of which decisions are formulated and acted upon by élites, accepted by masses, used in the reasoning of intellectuals." Is this an adequate summary? What are its rather sweeping implications?

. . . for further investigation:

Arendt, Hannah, * The Human Condition. New York: Anchor Books, 1959.

Ayer, Alfred J., ° *Language, Truth, and Logic*. New York: Dover Publications, Inc., n.d.

Bagehot, Walter, ° *Physics and Politics*. Boston, Mass.: Beacon Press, Inc., 1956.

Bentley, Arthur F., *The Process of Government*. San Antonio, Texas: Principia Press of Trinity University, 1949.

Black, Max, ed., *The Social Theories of Talcott Parsons*. Englewood Cliffs, N.J.: Prentice-Hall, Inc., 1961.

Easton, David, *The Political System*. New York: Alfred A. Knopf, Inc., 1953.

Grene, Marjorie, ° *Introduction to Existentialism*. Chicago, Ill.: University of Chicago Press, 1948.

Jaspers, Karl, ° *Man in the Modern Age*. New York: Anchor Books, 1957.

Jouvenel, Bertrand de, ° *On Power*, J. F. Huntington, trans. Boston, Mass.: Beacon Press, Inc., n.d.

Kelsen, Hans, *General Theory of Law and State*, A. Wedberg, trans. Cambridge, Mass.: Harvard University Press, 1945.

Kluckhohn, Clyde, ° *Mirror for Man*. New York: Premier Books, n.d.

Laslett, Peter, *Philosophy, Politics and Society*. New York: The Macmillan Company, 1956.

Laswell, Harold D. and Abraham Kaplan, *Power and Society*. New Haven, Conn.: Yale University Press, 1950.

MacIver, Robert M., *The Web of Government*. New York: The Macmillan Company, 1947.

Murray, John C., *We Hold These Truths*. New York: Sheed & Ward, Inc., 1961.

Pole, David, *Conditions of Rational Inquiry*. New York: Oxford University Press, Inc., 1961.

Santayana, George, *The Life of Reason*. New York: Charles Scribner's Sons, 1954.

Vivas, Eliseo, *The Moral Life and the Ethical Life*. Chicago, Ill.: University of Chicago Press, 1950.

Voegelin, Eric, *The New Science of Politics*. Chicago, Ill.: University of Chicago Press, 1952.

Wallas, Graham, ° *Human Nature in Politics*. Lincoln, Neb.: University of Nebraska Press, 1962.

Weldon, Thomas D., ° *The Vocabulary of Politics*. Baltimore, Md.: Penguin Books, Inc., 1953.

Wild, John, ed., *The Return to Reason*. Chicago, Ill.: Henry Regnery Co., 1953.

Young, Roland, ed., ° *Approaches to the Study of Politics*. Evanston, Ill.: Northwestern University Press, 1962.

INDEX

A

Absolute monarchy, 141-162, 206-207, 237, 238 (*see also* Monarchy)
Absolutism:
 Babbitt, 343
 Burke, 200-201, 202
 democracy, 332, 336-337
 Hegel, 225-247
 Hume, 216
 Kant, 222-225
 Nietzsche, 301
 Plato, 22, 24, 26
 positivists, 357
Albertus Magnus, 83, 88
Anarchism, 56, 154, 155, 237
Aquinas, St. Thomas, 67, 83, 86, 88-100, 136
Aristocracy:
 Aristotle, 40, 41-42
 Burke, 193-194, 196-198
 fascism, 321-322

Aristocracy (*Cont.*)
 Jaspers, 352
 Nietzsche, 304
 Plato, 11, 14, 23, 26
Aristotle:
 analysis, 30-46
 Burke impact, 193, 203, 204
 family life, 21
 Hobbes impact, 149
 human nature, 14
 Luther view, 126
 Middle Ages impact, 84, 85-86, 88, 93, 95
 moderation, 178
 popular rule, 8
 Roman impact, 47-48, 58
 society, 137
 writing purpose, 64
Augustine, St., 70, 72-78, 81, 85
Authoritarianism (*see also* Totalitarianism):
 Bosanquet, 246